Design by Sonja.
Photos by Allyssa,
Eleanor, and María
Fernanda.

Design by Sonja. Type/lettering by Cynthia. Photos by Alyssa, Shayes, Dana, and Amanda Leigh Smith.

ROOKIE
YEARBOOK
THREE

razor
bill

RAZORBILL
AN IMPRINT OF PENGUIN GROUP (USA)

Editor-in-Chief: Tavi Gevinson

Editorial Director: Anaheed Alani

Art Director: Tavi Gevinson

Art & Design: Sonja Ahlers

Designers: Kristin Smith, Vanessa Han, Maria Fazio & Maggie Olson

Managing Editor: Lauren Redding

Story Editors: Anaheed Alani, Danielle Henderson, Lena Singer & Amy Rose Spiegel

Razorbill Editor: Jessica Almon

Copy Editor: Jerome Ludwig

Design Assistant: Ellie Kibbe

Publisher: Ben Schrank

∘ ∘ ∘

Cover design: Sonja Ahlers
Cover art:
Petra Collins
Eleanor Hardwick
Sandy Honig
María Fernanda Molins
Lindsey Rome
Chrissie White

razor bill

A division of Penguin Young Readers Group
Published by the Penguin Group
Penguin Group (USA) LLC
345 Hudson Street
New York, New York 10014

USA / Canada / UK / Ireland / Australia / New Zealand / India / South Africa / China
Penguin.com
A Penguin Random House Company

ISBN: 9781595147943

Printed in the United States of America

1 3 5 7 9 10 8 6 4 2

CONTENTS

CONTRIBUTORS

Kelly Abeln
Sonja Ahlers
Leeay Aikawa
Ruby Aitken
Anaheed Alani
Olivia Bee
Tina Belcher and the folks at
   Bob's Burgers
Tova Benjamin
Esme Blegvad
Ruby Book
Dana Boulos
Krista Burton
Arvida Byström
Rachel Caires
Pixie Casey
Hazel Cills
Naomi Christina
Petra Collins
Joe Coscarelli
Emma Dajska
Molly Dektar
Katherine Denney
Kimberly Denson
Zaid Díaz

Caitlin Donohue
Maria Fazio
Anna Fitzpatrick
Tyler Ford
Britney Franco
Laia Garcia
Tavi Gevinson
Minna Gilligan
Emily V. Gordon
Grimes
María Inés Gul
Vanessa Han
Eleanor Hardwick
Caitlin Hazell
Danielle Henderson
Tahina Hill
Ana Hinojosa
Beth Hoeckel
Sandy Honig
Jessica Hopper
María Rangel Isas
Kelis
Ellie Kibbe
Nao Koyabu
Stephanie Kuehnert

Brodie Lancaster
Rose Lichter-Marck
Allegra Lockstadt
Lorde
Jerome Ludwig
Lisa Maione
Marah*
Anna McConnell
Katie McMahon
Cynthia Merhej
Grace Miceli
Mike and Claire
Michael Miranda
María Fernanda Molins
Brooke Nechvatel
Indigo Nelson
Gabby Noone
Maggie Olson
Chanel Parks
Lola Pellegrino
Verity Pemberton
Maria Pizzeria
Lauren Poor
Marlena Pope
Monica Ramos

Ragini Nag Rao
Lauren Redding
Lindsey Rome
Dylan Tupper Rupert
Maddy Ruvolo
Shriya Samavai
Anna Shechtman
Julianne Escobedo Shepherd
Sia
Arabelle Sicardi
Lena Singer
Amanda Leigh Smith
Kristin Smith
Brittany Spanos
Amy Rose Spiegel
Amandla Stenberg
Hattie Stewart
Estelle Tang
Maggie Thrash
Jamia Wilson
Leanna Wright
Suzy X.
Kendra Yee
Allyssa Yohana
Jenny Zhang

Kelly Abeln Margin artwork for Summer Camp. Sticker sheet design.
Sonja Ahlers Lettering for Star Crossings, Do Right by Me, Bombastic Anthems, and Hanging Out With the Belchers.
Leeay Aikawa Margin artwork for School's Out, Secrets of the Sisterhood, Summer Crush, and Cures for Love.
Ruby Aitken Backgrounds for Sporting Life.
Esme Blegvad Lettering for When All Other Lights Go Out, I Needed to See a Reflection of Myself: An Interview With Alison Bechdel, and Coloring Book. Margin artwork for the Welcome letter, Let's Be Friends; Between Two Beats; Sister, Sister; The Long Goodbye; and When All Other Lights Go Out.
Tavi Gevinson Lettering for School's Out, Summer Sads, Hanging Out With the Lisbon Sisters, Secrets of the Sisterhood, Summer Crush, Someday We'll Be Together, and Ghost Prom. Margin artwork for School's Out, Goodbye Googly Eyes, and This Is My Thing: An Interview With Kathleen Hanna.
Minna Gilligan Lettering for Remembering, Best Friends Forever, Life Skills 301, Ahead of Their Time, Kids Won't Listen, and Cosmic Love. Margin artwork for Goodbye Googly Eyes, Stand for Something, You Have the Answer: An Interview With Lara Setrakian, and The Gilded Age. Backgrounds for 24 Hour Party People, Who Will Survive in America: A Kanye Roundtable, and The Gilded Age.
María Inés Gul Lettering for In the Stacks, How to Be Alone, British Bummer Sounds, Neither/Both, Busy Being Free, and Seafaring Songs. Margin artwork for How to Deal When You're Caught Masturbating and Do Right by Me. Backgrounds for How to Be Alone and Neither/Both.
Vanessa Han Lettering for Hanging Out With Rory Gilmore; That's What Friends Do; Family Bands; Sister, Sister; and signatures page.
Caitlin Hazell Lettering for Just Wondering and Dear Diary. Margin artwork for Summer's Last Hurrah, Follow What's Alive: An Interview With Greta Gerwig, All in Good Time, Literally the Best Thing Ever: Aerosmith's "Crazy" Video,

Teen Angst Circus, The 27 Club, Use What You Have: An Interview With Kim Gordon, and Dear Diary. Backgrounds for Dear Diary.
Beth Hoeckel Margin artwork for Birds of Paradise, Unusual World, and Class Actresses.
Lisa Maione Lettering for Birds of Paradise, Unusual World, Let's Be Friends, DIY Finger-Knitted Scarf, After-School Snacks: A Taxonomy, Between Two Beats, DIY Pet Photo Shoot, The Long Goodbye, DIY BFF Earrings, Open Relationships, Follow Me, You Have the Answer: An Interview With Lara Setrakian, Fast Car, Just the Way You Are, Kick 'Em to the Curb, Out of (My) Body, The Gilded Age, Still Lives, Freewheeling, and You Can Be Free: An Interview With Janet Mock.
Cynthia Merhej Lettering for the book's cover, The Sex Crylebration, and Ouija Board, Ouija Board. Margin artwork for Class Actresses.
Grace Miceli Lettering for 24 Hour Party People and Who Will Survive in America: A Kanye Roundtable.
Brooke Nechvatel Lettering for The Wallow, Summer Camp, Cures for Love, Girl-on-Girl Crime, and The Safety Closet.
Monica Ramos Lettering for signatures page and crossword key.
Hattie Stewart Lettering for Goodbye Googly Eyes, Stand for Something, This Is My Thing: An Interview With Kathleen Hanna, and Dancing With the Q-Kidz. Margin artwork for This Is My Thing: An Interview With Kathleen Hanna, Ahead of Their Time, Kick 'Em to the Curb, and Out of (My) Body.
Suzy X. Lettering for More, More, More; Hanging Out With the Bling Ring; and High Life, Low Budget. Margin artwork for The Great Big Beyoncé Roundtable and Super Heroine: An Interview With Lorde.
Kendra Yee Margin artwork for Birds of Paradise, Poser Pride, Candy Crush, It's a New Wave: An Interview With Amandla Stenberg, and Unusual World.
Allyssa Yohana Background for Star Crossings.

ACKNOWLEDGMENTS

Thank you to…

Our incredible staff of editors, writers, photographers, and illustrators for how much you share of yourselves, for believing in this, and for the Facebook group therapy. On a profesh level: Rookie would not exist without you. On a personal level: I am more myself because I've been growing up in our coven of love, and going out into the world every day is less scary because we have one another's backs.

Sonja Ahlers, literal superhero, for collaging the entirety of this book, making it truly Rookie. Your ride-or-die devotion to this machine and to never settling for anything less than beautiful is inspiring beyond all words.

Lauren Redding for helping to orchestrate and organize this mess, for your killer sensibilities, and for your Wild Heart-style commitment to our powerhouse operation.

Anaheed Alani for making Rookie possible from the very beginning, for knowing what we need at every turn, and for your invaluable friendship.

Danielle Henderson, Lena Singer, and Amy Rose Spiegel for editing the writing in this book and on our site, making everything the best it can be.

Music editrix extraordinaire Jessica Hopper for making Rookie sound so damn good.

Ellie Kibbe for assisting Sonja and for designing a handful of stellar spreads.

Jessica Almon, Ben Schrank, Kristin Smith, Vanessa Han, Maria Fazio, and Maggie Olson at Razorbill for your loyalty to our vision and for helping us to make something wonderful.

David Kuhn, Nicole Tourtelot, Jessie Borkan, and everyone at Kuhn Projects for helping to bring Rookie and Razorbill together.

The illustrators who created new work just for this book: Kelly Abeln, Leeay Aikawa, Ruby Aitken, Esme Blegvad, Minna Gilligan, María Inés Gul, Caitlin Hazell, Ana Hinojosa, Beth Hoeckel, Allegra Lockstadt, Lisa Maione, Cynthia Merhej, Grace Miceli, Brooke Nechvatel, Monica Ramos, Hattie Stewart, Leanna Wright, Suzy X., and Kendra Yee. You are an absolute dream team, and made *Yearbook Three* feel like a secret diary as opposed to a MS Paint file.

Monica Ramos, María Inés Gul, Grimes, Sia, Lorde, Anna Shechtman, Loren Bouchard and the *Bob's Burgers* writing staff, and Kendra Yee, for creating incredible new stuff just for our extra-special print-exclusives. Thank you to Dakota Fanning, Elle Fanning, Shailene Woodley, Kelis, Haim, and Ilana Glazer and Abbi Jacobson of *Broad City* for agreeing to be interviewed for that section.

Cynthia Merhej for lettering our title and subtitle, making them just what they oughta be.

Minna Gilligan for scanning and sending us her thorough archive of antique goods to help us decorate these pages.

Petra Collins, Eleanor Hardwick, Sandy Honig, María Fernanda Molins, Lindsey Rome, and Chrissie White for taking the photos that make up our gorgeous cover.

Steve Gevinson for acting as Rookie's unofficial business advisor. Berit Engen for letting us use her childhood photos throughout this book. Both of you for birthing and raising me.

Grace Denise Madigan. You know what you did.

Our readers for giving Rookie a place in the world and for supporting us and each other. You know when singers get really depressed because they end up attracting an audience made up of the exact same kinds of people they hated in high school? THIS IS THE OPPOSITE OF THAT. I love you, Rookies, and can't thank you enough for the dream-high-school community you've created.

WELCOME

Dear Rookies,

Welcome to *Yearbook Three*, a comprehensive compilation of our favorite stuff from the site's junior year. I put off writing this letter until every other part of the book was done, maybe because I don't quite know how to introduce all of the incredible work that follows, nor how to thank everyone who contributes to the site, who helped put the site in book form, and who may be reading it right now. But you can be sure that should you ever find yourself deeply, heart-pangingly, head-bangingly vibing with anything in these pages, that's because our staffers and readers alike are so committed to cultivating a space where sharing yourself is not only OK, but also kind of the thing that keeps the world together, that makes us all feel less alone.

I just graduated from high school, making me a year ahead of Rookie, and while my feelings about going from teen to young adult are wildly mixed between nostalgia and relief, I feel so lucky that I get to continue to fixate on the most wondrous and weirdest parts of teenagedom here. With all the changes I'm facing, coming back to Rookie—deciding on the themes with Anaheed, designing the book with Sonja, planning world domination with Lauren, brainstorming with our staffers about this baffling time in a person's life—is what makes me feel most myself, and I'm happy that reading it can help others feel the same way. Whether you've been with us since we were wee freshmen or are just now picking up this colorful book because you saw the word *pizza* on the back cover, it's less scary to grow up knowing that we share this piece of home together.

love, Tavi*

SOLEIL

Queen Anne's lace

Design by Sonja.
Title lettering by Tavi.

MASON

JUNE 2013: *longing*

Hey Rookies!

SCHOOL'S OUT! I am so ready to sleep all day and party for like half an hour and then sleep some more all night. Love sleep. Sleep is great. Sleeeeep. I'm very sorry if you're still in school, but then at least this month's theme will resonate extra deeply: LONGING. Here's what I sent our staffers when it was time to come up with ideas:

Hot summer bedrooms (not hot like sexy, hot like stuffy and "I waited the whole school year for summer and now this feels miserable, and it's sunny but everything is not automatically fixed"). Summer homes and cottages, camp, secret neighborhood hangout spots like bridges, overpasses, rivers, and cemeteries. Feeling homesick. Taking sad baths. "Last Days of Disco" by Yo La Tengo/everything by Yo La Tengo. Miranda July's short stories. Gerhard Richter's paintings that look like old photographs. Overalls, white cotton dresses, chain-link fences, the beach, lighthouses, clotheslines, backyards, watercolors, butterflies and butterfly nets, seashells, the pool and all the gross pool chairs, homemade lemonade, sunflowers, dandelions, straw, fields, all those dirty-looking flowers, and those vaguely Scandinavian floral patterns that you find on dish towels and shit. The little things you only have time to notice in the summer and are like, "Oh, I haven't paid this much attention to the light hitting my glass since I was very little." The sun when it dances on water, the way old memories of summer are kind of overexposed and blown out from the sun, the way the sunshine cuts in and out of your vision when you walk under the shadows of scattered branches and leaves, the way sun persists against closed eyelids. The dimension between us and the material world, light, glares, records crackling, TV static, the sounds when fingers move up and down a guitar neck between chords, negative space, and waiting.

Longing for the future: wanting to change for the sake of change, wanting to change but not knowing how to become the person you want to be. The show *Enlightened* did such a good job of capturing the relationship everyone has with their smaller, darker self. Sometimes—and I would feel crazy sharing this if I didn't think it was how most people are—I feel like I'm constantly trying to keep down and tame and teach a part of myself that gets irritable and lazy and insecure and self-absorbed. Then when I slip up just a little bit I'm like, WELL, THAT'S IT, I'M DONE, CLEARLY I AM JUST INNATELY EVIL. *Enlightened* is so good at showing how you can continue to change regardless—not by reinventing yourself in extremes like Bob Dylan or whatever, but just by becoming more of who you are and making peace with yourself.

Longing for the past: missing something you never had, missing a glorified idea of something, missing ignorance, missing simplicity. The paradox of getting what you longed for, that nothing can ever be truly what you wanted.

The longing in *The Virgin Suicides* with all the girls wanting to leeeeaaave and trying to escape by reading travel brochures and books and listening to music, how that is all a form of escape, how it can create your own private reality and fulfill you in ways Real Experience can't.

Longing for something just because it's become your default, even if you don't want it anymore.

Learning to ask for what you want.

Getting what you longed for and finding that the act of longing itself had been sustaining you. Like with crushes. Or like when I used to go to Fashion Week, and I realized at some point that some people really are just meant to be fans, that it was more fulfilling for me to keep that distance than to get as close as possible.

Figuring out what you want in relation to what makes you happy. When I hear teachers at my school talk about college, they make it seem like the purpose of education is solely to one day get a job instead of to enrich your brain and inspire you and help you grow. I think many people expect that once they get into that college or get that romantic partner, they will automatically be happier and live in a state of eternal bliss. But I think we all like to never be satisfied, and will always look for little things to get irritated about no matter how good we have it. I think the goal is not utopia/paradise/everythinghappyallthetimealways, just general contentment and a healthy day-to-day mind, which will sometimes be disrupted by extreme happiness or extreme sadness, which you can decide how to deal with, since you can't control if it happens or not. There are people who are "successful" and extremely unhappy, and there are people who live alone on a farm in the middle of nowhere and are extremely happy, and who cares if their happiness is not recognized by the rest of the world, because one day they'll die and so will everybody else. (I am TIRED and have also lately been thinking about becoming a recluse.)

From a zine I made for myself recently-ish: "There are holes in the universe. Lost dreams, expectations, the pictures you see in your mind when you read a book (and all the pictures other people see when they read the same book and how different all these pictures can be). Where do these alternate realities go? Do they fit into alternate timelines? Or do the watercolors of memory just mix until old hope becomes a black hole?" DEEP AF/I KNOW/GOD.

I'm aware this whole email is super cheese, but whatever! I wish I could see a gallery of all the visuals every human has ever had in their mind of fantasies and daydreams, picturing themselves getting what they want.

love, tavi

school's out

A photo diary of Petra's little sister and her friends on their last day of high school. By Petra

we got no innocence

school's out for summer!
school's out forever!

the wallow

A healthy way to drown your sorrows.   By Emily

When I was in high school, my emotions overwhelmed me. Joy, misery, confusion, embarrassment—I was powerless against the undertow of every one, constantly grasping toward the shore. When my mother accidentally hit a raccoon on a road trip when I was 10, I cried for two hours. Outings to theme parks got me so excited that I usually threw up in the yard before we even pulled out of the driveway. In ninth grade a boy I barely liked broke up with me and I wandered around school like a zombie for weeks, my eyes red and swollen.

I think being emotional and giving yourself permission to be vulnerable are both great and brave things that are undervalued in our world, but this wasn't that—I was walking around so emotionally raw that it was interfering with my life. I once missed a term paper deadline because I was consumed with being angry with a boy, and when I was granted an audience with the teacher to explain myself, I gravely said that I was going through some "pretty serious stuff right now." The teacher must have hurt herself trying not to roll her eyes, but she granted me a very harsh extension, and I had to spend a sleepless night writing a paper. This just added more fuel to my fire. Had my life been a sitcom, it would have gone something like this:

INTERIOR. COFFEE SHOP. DAY.
A group of my friends are hanging out.

FRIEND Where is Emily? Is she still miserable over what's-his-name?
The camera pans to the corner, where we see ME, sitting on the floor, knees to my chest, crying softly.

Giving myself over to emotion so completely made me feel like I was on a roller coaster that kept speeding up—I never knew what would knock me around next, and I had no way to control it.

Part of growing up is learning to put a buffer between our emotions and our actions. That buffer is our thoughts. Let's say a friend does something that upsets you—maybe you saw that he friended your asshole ex on Facebook. But it's one o'clock in the morning on a school night. Your heart wants to call him RIGHT AWAY and unload. This is where your head steps in and says, "Hey, maybe this can wait until the morning." This is where you type out an angry email to him and DON'T SEND IT until you've had a chance to reread it after you've cooled down. On the other hand, you don't want to NEVER confront him about it and just stew for days or weeks or months and get all passive-aggressive and ugh. Your goal is to put your emotions in the passenger seat, where they're riding shotgun to your thoughts, like a constant companion and advisor, but never give them the steering wheel (they will just constantly get you into accidents). Ideally you'll find the sweet spot of rational, healthy communication somewhere between selfishly exploding and self-destructively bottling everything up. (And, believe me, this is something you will keep negotiating and renegotiating for the rest of your life, so you might as well start practicing now.)

So, how do you do this? I'll tell you how you *don't* do it. Ever the extremist, when I went to college I decided to counteract my teenage emotional tornado by intellectualizing all my feelings away. I thought I could control my emotions by ignoring them. I became a robot, basically. The first time a guy dumped me in this new regime, I exhaled noisily as he walked away and imagined I was exhaling *him*. I distracted myself from crying by telling myself, and my friends, all the reasons why he was never going to succeed as a person. I repeated over and over how little I needed him until I believed it. No breakup could hurt me, because when you think about it, all relationships end, and we die alone anyway. (Go ahead and roll your eyes now.) A friend was terribly rude to me in public, and I shrugged it right off—I just told everyone else that I'd suspected she'd felt insecure for a long time. A band I loved came to town and, rather than dance around and sing along, I stood stock-still in the audience. Why be excited about a good concert or a friend's engagement or anything, when all happiness is fleeting?

I was proud of this self-control. I would explain to friends how much more "liberated" I felt. I pitied people who couldn't hold back their tears. I felt evolved. In truth, though, I was terrified. I was afraid of the power of my feelings, of how easily they might take me down, and I was afraid of seeming like an emotional person because I'd internalized our culture's misogynistic view of women as "hysterical" and weak. Also, to be honest, after experiencing everything so intensely for most of my childhood, I think I needed a break from emoting. It was nice to finally feel in control of my heart.

But the thing about never expressing your feelings is that it doesn't just include pain and sorrow—you also never get to show happiness, bemusement, pure joy. I'd see kittens and silently acknowledge their cuteness and my wish to scoop them up and take them home, instead of just grabbing them and snorfing their tummies like I wanted to. About a year in, I realized that this was not a lifestyle I could sustain any longer—aside from being obviously unhealthy, it was just *boring*.

Right around the time I started getting sick of my Ice Queen routine, I experienced some major health problems that landed me in the hospital for a month (it's a long story involving a coma and an operation, but I'm totally fine now). I felt like an infant, both because my body was too weak to hold a cellphone or walk, and because I was scared and didn't know how to process it. This was not a situation that I could intellectualize away. My feelings were huge and confusing and they came crashing in like a tidal wave, knocking down the walls I'd built against them. I spent a few days crying, which was followed by a flood of relief (that I'd gotten through it) and gratitude (for everything around me).

When I got out of the hospital, I would take walks around my neighborhood to build up my strength. On one of those walks I remember hearing a lyric from Peter Bjorn and John's song "Objects of My Affection" that stopped me in my tracks. I have to paraphrase here for copyright reasons, but it goes something like: "I laugh more, cry more, am more me." Maybe it was cliché, but I did feel more me. I felt more alive, and it wasn't just because I had almost died. It was because I was feeling my damn *feelings* again. I had always thought of my emotions as being separate from me, as being these alien things that descended upon me, but now I finally saw them as part of me: my hormones, my brain chemistry, my heartstrings.

You know how a dog with a lot of energy needs to be walked or it'll find some other way to burn off that energy (usually by destroying something valuable in your home)? That dog = my emotions; those walks = what I call the Wallow. When something happens to me that brings on a flood of emotions, I give myself a set amount of time to feel those emotions fully, deeply, as dramatically as I want—but for 20 minutes max. (Obviously, I'm talking about everyday issues, not something traumatic like a death or the end of a long-term relationship, although the idea is the same: Don't become so attached to feeling one way that you spend longer with an emotion than you want/need to.)

In those 20 minutes, I devote all my energy to being furious, or embarrassed, or uncomfortable, or whatever. If I get bored with my emotions, too bad: I order myself to continue. I sit in them, alone, without distractions. *You wanted my attention,* I tell them, *and now you've got it.* I feel my feelings so intensely that I get physically tired. After that, it's easy to push them aside and move on to processing and thinking. I am no longer blinded by anger or guilt or a thirst for justice. I ask myself questions: Why did this event affect me so much? What do I actually want out of this situation? How can I get closer to what I want?

Once they've had their day in the sun, my feelings don't feel so powerful anymore. They no longer threaten to pull me under and drown me. Instead, they teach me a few things. If I'd really paid attention to what I was feeling with the dude in high school, for instance, I would have realized that my sadness over the breakup had nothing to do with him—I just needed attention and didn't know how else to get it. If I'd known that then, I might've shaken my funk quickly and let myself have fun at dance parties, which I now regret not having done. The Wallow lets me tune in to my emotional advisors and act in a way that appropriately honors them, whether that's sending an email, asking for a hug, accepting a job offer or quitting a job, or telling someone they're acting like a jackass.

Not everyone's emotions are turned all the way up to 11 like mine were. If yours aren't, be happy about that. But no matter what it feels like inside your head and heart, know that you can't control how you feel, but you can control what you do with your feelings. Figuring out how to work with them instead of being bullied by them takes some experimentation with different combinations of logic, feelings, intelligence, and gut instinct. The run-over raccoons of your life deserve your time and your sympathy, but they aren't getting anything from your self-imposed suffering. Neither are you. ❁

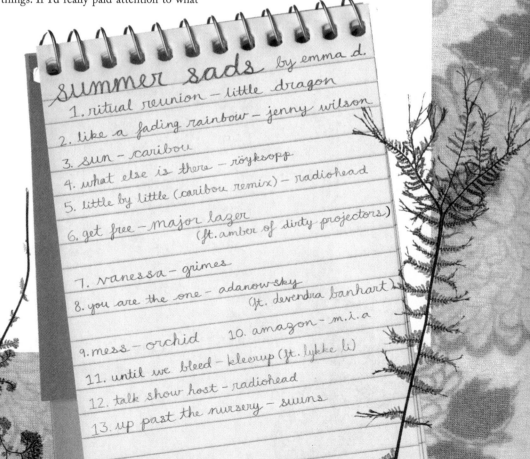

summer sads *by emma d.*

1. ritual reunion – little dragon
2. like a fading rainbow – jenny wilson
3. sun – caribou
4. what else is there – röyksopp
5. little by little (caribou remix) – radiohead
6. get free – major lazer (ft. amber of dirty projectors)
7. vanessa – grimes
8. you are the one – adanowsky (ft. devendra banhart)
9. mess – orchid
10. amazon – m.i.a
11. until we bleed – kleerup (ft. lykke li)
12. talk show host – radiohead
13. up past the nursery – swins

Girls With Power and Mystique:
An Interview With Sofia Coppola

The maker of our most cherished movies talks about longing, identity, and how Hollywood underestimates teenagers.
By Tavi. Illustration by Brooke Nechvatel.

Sofia Coppola has written and directed some of my favorite movies—*The Virgin Suicides, Lost in Translation, Marie Antoinette, Somewhere*—and has now blessed us with a fifth movie, *The Bling Ring*. Based on a *Vanity Fair* article about a pack of L.A. teens who burglarized celebrity homes a few years ago, it avoids feeling preachy in a WHAT'S THE MATTER WITH KIDS TODAY? way, instead getting its point across by leaving you with an unnerving sense of discomfort.

Sofia generously spoke to me about the film, her moodboards, and the new internet wave of *Virgin Suicides* love.

TAVI I've read some reviews of *The Bling Ring* that are like IT'S A CRITICISM OF OUR LIVES, but when I interviewed Emma Watson recently, she said she felt it was filmed in a nonjudgmental way. I kind of felt that way when I saw it, so I would just like to ask you: How did you want your audience to feel?

SOFIA COPPOLA I saw this culture growing and growing, so I wanted the audience to experience it for themselves, and by the end of [the movie] to think about what's important to them and how they feel about it—I didn't want to tell them what to think.

Did you find it hard to do that without glamorizing that culture?

Yeah. I wanted to see it through their point of view, to understand how they got so into it. I wanted, in the beginning, to shoot all of this stuff in a really seductive way and make it look fun—you want to be able to be part of it so you understand where they're coming from. But then by the end of it, you have a shift and take a step back and, you know, kind of look at it.

A lot of your movies can be kind of critical of these settings of privilege and glamour and fame, but you have to operate within that realm to make films. How do you reconcile that, and what makes it worth it?

It's important for me to promote my movies, so I do press that's about promoting my work—which is really different from promoting oneself. I wouldn't do press just about myself. The side of our tabloid culture that these kids are into, for a lot of them it's more about just being famous—which is so different from people who are being celebrated for what they've accomplished. This idea that anyone and everyone can be famous—it seems like it's from reality TV and social media. It's just such a big part of our life now. We didn't have that when I was growing up.

I read one interview where you said that you felt that there weren't many movies for teens like *The Bling Ring*—movies that carefully consider cinematography or have any visual ambitions. Did you feel that was missing when you were a teen?

You know, I loved John Hughes's movies, and I connected to those movies. But a lot of the movies that were made for teenagers were really, um, dorky and unsophisticated. And I feel like kids are more sophisticated and thoughtful than the [movie] studios give them credit for. I remember them worrying about *The Virgin Suicides*, like, girls are going to see it and they'll kill themselves. They didn't understand that [teenagehood] is a time when you're just focused on thinking about things, you're not distracted by your career, family, you know—it's a thoughtful time. There's a tradition that I love, movies like *Over the Edge*

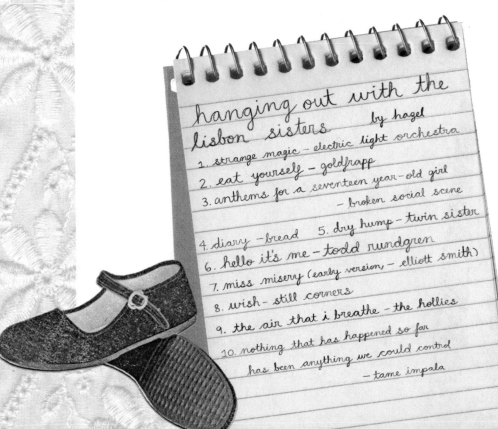

hanging out with the lisbon sisters   by hazel

1. strange magic - electric light orchestra
2. eat yourself - goldfrapp
3. anthems for a seventeen year-old girl
   - broken social scene
4. diary - bread   5. dry hump - twin sister
6. hello it's me - todd rundgren
7. miss misery (early version) - elliott smith
8. wish - still corners
9. the air that i breathe - the hollies
10. nothing that has happened so far
    has been anything we could control
    - tame impala

and *Foxes*—which I was thinking about when I made this movie—that had a real spirit and felt real and authentic to that age. Or *Rumble Fish*, my dad's movie that was like a teenage art film. I like that you can make a teen movie that has beautiful photography and try to approach it in an artful way. I feel like that's not that common.

So many of your movies are about teenagers. What continually draws you to us as subjects?

I always like characters who are in the midst of a transition and trying to find their place in the world. That is the most heightened when you're a teenager, but I definitely like it at the different stages of life. I like stories where the drama comes more as an internal part of the character as opposed to from outside forces that make you change.

Usually in your films there's an ingénue who's so immediately likable that you just want to watch her, but *The Bling Ring* is kind of different.

Yeah, I thought, *How am I going to make a movie where the characters are so unsympathetic?* Usually there's a girl or a character that I connect with and see part of myself in, and in this one I didn't. It was really a challenge to find a way to tell the story in a way that would engage you, 'cause if you don't care about the characters, how can you get into it? But then I met [Bling Ring member Nick Prugo], and I thought he was really the most sympathetic one—you could understand how he could have gotten caught up in this group and why he wanted to be a part of it. I remembered being that age and, you know, you do things you wouldn't do as an adult, because you want the excitement of feeling like you're part of something.

I know you make moodboards and little mood books when you're getting started on a film. Are there any images or influences that come up repeatedly?

Oh, usually they're pretty different. I think if you see them, you can see a connection, because it's my sensibility, but they always have a different feeling. But whenever I look at them after I finish a movie, I'm always surprised that they look like the feeling of the movie. There's a photographer called Bill Owens who did photos of '70s suburbia that were references for *The Virgin Suicides*. Do you have that book?

No.

It's called *Suburbia*. There's a picture of a girl and some kids at a high school dance with little tinfoil stars hanging over them, which was what I looked at for that [homecoming] scene. And then for *The Bling Ring*, Claire [Julien], the blond girl, she has these pictures on her Facebook of her in a pink bikini with, like, lots of attitude. So that [moodboard] was stuff like that and shots of the night sky with the twinkly lights in the distance.

Our theme on the site this month is Longing, and I think your films capture that feeling so well, and I have to ask a *Virgin Suicides* question because—

OK! I love that you brought that movie to a whole new audience! When I met Leslie Mann for this movie she said, "My daughter loves *The Virgin Suicides*," and I thought, *How does she even know about that? She wasn't even born then!* And it's through you, so—

Aaah!

That movie didn't have a big audience when it came out, so I'm happy that it lives on.

Oh my gosh—girls WORSHIP it. When you read [Jeffrey Eugenides's] book, what resonated with you? Because it's a lot about feeling kind of locked up at home in the suburbs—that's where [the main characters] the Lisbon sisters are. And I think your life must have been somewhat different. Were you just kind of fascinated by them? Or was there something that you related to about that feeling of being confined?

I loved Eugenides's writing, and I felt like I could be there with [the Lisbon sisters]. I really loved how the boys were looking at the girls and the girls had this kind of power and mystique over them. I think when you're that age you're kind of playing with that power and trying to understand it. I liked how the girls were playing with the boys' confusion about them, and I was interested in how girls could get stuck in lives that were too small for them.

Thank you so much for talking to me!

I'm happy to do something with you, and thanks for all your support.

Of course! Our readers will be so excited!

Have a good summer!

secrets of the sisterhood

Meet us in the woods at four. By Dana
Thanks to Carmela, Gabby, Kimia,
and Savannah for modeling.

summer camp

Noncampers just don't understand. Here, an attempt to explain.
By Tyler. Illustration by Monica Ramos.

When people ask, "What's your favorite place in the world?" I have two answers: Disney World and summer camp. I don't need to explain the first one—it's the Happiest Place on Earth!™ As for the second, the only people who need an explanation are the unlucky ones who've never been to camp. But I'm not sure I can even explain it—there's just something about camp that defies reason, that transcends geography and bends time. Camp isn't really a *place* at all—it's a feeling, a spirit. No matter where you went to summer camp or when, you know what I'm talking about. You feel it in your heart.

I know that all of you noncampers are rolling your eyes right now. When camp people talk about camp, we can sound like cult members. To tell you the truth, we kind of are. We're crazily devoted to this community that asks us to leave our family, friends, and cellphones behind to hang out in the woods and learn secret chants and rituals, do trust exercises, and become One of Them (Us). And, just like a cult, it only looks weird from the outside. Once you're a true camper, it's the rest of the year that feels wrong.

I won't attempt to explain the inexplicable, but I can, perhaps, give noncampers a window into the world of camp and show you a bit of what makes it so great. Though to be honest, it's a bit mysterious to us lifers as well.

I. CAMP FRIENDS

I've spent eight years of my life as a camper and six as a counselor, all at the same place, a Jewish camp in Florida that my mom picked out when I was seven years old. I was a quiet, cautious kid, scared to try new things or stick my neck out. Then, as now, it was hard for me to outwardly show emotion. But there was something liberating about camp. None of these people went to my school or knew anything of the social hierarchies there. There was no stress about looking good (there's really not much you can do about that when you're playing outside all day in 100-degree weather). The only thing you're concerned about at camp is "What fun things are on the

schedule today?" You're not getting graded for anything you do, so you feel free to experiment. In such a creative, stress-free environment, it's hard not to fall in love with everyone and everything around you.

On the first day of camp, everyone gets together and introduces themselves, and then we're off to our first activity. There's no time to split off into cliques or to cast judgment on anyone—you're still trying to commit everyone's names to memory when you suddenly find yourself in the middle of a game of freeze-dance with 20 other kids. At the end of the day you go to your cabin, where you're squeezed into a room with four to seven other kids—that becomes your friend group, your team, your family. And everyone supports one another, just like family.

The summer between my seventh and eighth grades, the camp took us on an overnight trip to Myrtle Beach. On the way, the bus broke down on the side of the highway for what felt like hours. We sat in the bus waiting, sweaty and miserable—I remember someone got off the bus to throw up. You know how when a bunch of girls live in close quarters for a while, all of their periods sync up? Well, it seemed like *everyone* on the bus that day had their period. We finally got the bus going again, and then, perhaps caused by a combination of that menstrual synchrony and some stress-induced hormonal surge, the one girl who hadn't started menstruating yet…started menstruating. Right there, right then, on this hot, miserable bus. We pulled over at the next rest stop, and a few campers and counselors took her into the bathroom and taught her how to use a tampon. That, to me, captures true camp spirit.

II. COLOR WAR

Color War, usually held during the last week of camp, is where the entire camp is split into two teams—red and blue at my camp—to compete in a weeklong battle of games, sports, songs, cheers, and other displays of "spirit." At home I was never really into sports or competition, but when that

week came around, I made it my personal mission to lose my voice cheering, "B-L-U-E, THAT SPELLS VICTORY!"

Suddenly, every single activity felt like it would make or break the entire contest. Did your side lose a game? Make sure you cheer, "Two, four, six, eight, who do we appreciate? RED! RED! *GOOOOOO*, RED!" to gain extra points for sportsmanship. Are you sitting in the corner while everyone else is playing soccer? You're getting precious participation points docked from your entire team's score. My favorite part of Color War was learning our team song and cheer (always in secret so the other team couldn't steal our lyrics), which we would perform in front of the entire camp at closing ceremonies. We'd sit on opposite sides of the gym, seas of red and blue, everyone completely exhausted but still energized and ready to give their all to the judges. You got points for being respectful, so the gym was usually silent but buzzing with nervous energy between performances. And the announcement of the winning team was high drama—there were always tears. Color War took all the emotions and energy of the whole summer, condensed them into a few days, and then amplified them to an insane degree. I lived for Color War.

III. FIRSTS

Every camper has at least one new experience during the summer. Mine came during a day trip to Busch Gardens, an amusement park in Tampa. I was 10, and too short for most of the more exciting rides at theme parks. My mom used to warn me that if I went on something I was too short for, I could fall out and die, so I was petrified of roller coasters and all other "grown-up" rides. But my camp self was so much braver than my home self, and so, at the suggestion of one of my counselors, I stuffed my sneakers with tissue and barely made the height requirement for the Python, a short roller coaster with two loop-the-loops. It was the most fun. I've loved roller coasters ever since.

IV. COUNSELORS

As a kid, I idolized my counselors. I wanted to be just like them. They weren't strict or formal like most of my teachers were, and they were all between 21 and 25 years old, so they were cool with hanging out with us, but responsible enough to take care of us. They would let us walk around theme parks in groups without a chaperone, but they wouldn't embarrass us if we came to them crying over a fight with a friend over something dumb like what ride to go on next (dumb fights always happen on overnight trips). They gave us the freedom to learn our own lessons. If we didn't feel like putting on sunscreen, they wouldn't force us to wear it; they'd just let us get sunburned so we'd see exactly why our parents had been so insistent.

When I was 12, my unit was involved in a *serious* game of Wiffle ball. Two minutes before the end of an inning, I was the last person up to bat. My team already had two outs, the bases were loaded, we were down by a couple runs, and the literal clock was ticking behind me. When one of my counselors pitched me the ball, I made contact—and I hit it out of the park. I helped score four runs with that swing. We won the game, and everyone ran up to hug me. The next thing I knew, my counselor, Marc, was holding me on his shoulders above the crowd, shouting "BABE RUTH," which he called me for the rest of the week. I had never been particularly athletic at school, and I certainly was never treated like the most valuable player of anything. But Marc made me feel like a hero, and I still feel awesome about myself any time I think of that moment. And if I'd struck out and lost us the game, I know he would have consoled me and congratulated me for trying. That's just what counselors do.

My last summer as a camper was the summer after eighth grade. The next year I returned to the same camp as a counselor-in-training. As amazing as it is to be a camper, I think counselors get the better end of the deal. We're paid to make summers unforgettable for young people, and even though it's exhausting and a lot of responsibility, who wouldn't want to make art, go swimming, and play music with 20 kids who love you day in and day out?

A few summers ago, on an overnight trip to Universal Studios, a bunch of my campers were in line for a roller coaster. One of them, a 13-year-old named Matthew, had never been on a roller coaster, and he was scared. I encouraged him to give it a try. He finally relented, but on one condition: He wanted to sit next to *me*. I'd figured he would want to look "cool" by sitting next to his "cool" friends, so I was touched that he chose the low-status seat next to mine on the ride. The roller coaster was awesome, and as we disembarked, Matt threw his arms around me and yelled, "Thank you!" I asked what he was thanking me for and he said, "For the best experience of my life!" He spent the rest of the day hopping from ride to ride with his friends. It's still hard for me to hold back tears when I tell this story.

V. CHANGE

Cramming so many new experiences into eight short weeks makes camp a pressure cooker for personal growth—the camper who arrives in June is different in so many ways from the one who goes back home in August. Most kids become more confident, with a wider range of abilities, a better understanding of themselves and others, and, of course, more friends.

Saying goodbye to camp friends is terribly hard, especially when they don't live near you. When I was 13, on the last night of my last summer as a camper, about 60 of us sat in a big circle outside, and one by one we listed our funniest/best moments of the summer and what we'd miss most when it came time to say goodbye. "My favorite part of the summer was the ghost tour," one kid said. "I'll miss the white-chocolate bread," said another. When my turn finally came to speak, I got up, inhaled—and then immediately collapsed onto the ground, sobbing. I was so sad about leaving camp, and so thankful for everything it had given me. My friends and counselors came running over to hug me, which was really nice, but I couldn't even formulate a sentence. I couldn't see, I couldn't breathe, I just had to sit there and let it happen. That still ranks as one of the most emotional moments of my life.

There's an expression that camp people use: "We live 10 for 2"—meaning we spend 10 months of the year counting down the days until those eight weeks at camp. We write frantic emails to one another: "Are you coming back this summer?! Jared, Benny, Barbara, and I are all going back! You have to come back!!!" We live for camp, we long for camp, we love camp. Camp will forever be a part of me in everything I do, because camp is more than a place—it's a way of life. 🕊

What Are You?

As a light-skinned biracial teenager growing up in Canada,
I didn't know how to answer that question.
By Anna F. Illustration by Kelly.

As with any of my Poppy's stories, I had to press him to learn the details behind his tattoos. They were easy to miss, a muddled s.d. on his left forearm and an even shakier s.p. on his right, in faded ink that barely stood out against his weathered skin.

"They are my initials" was his answer the first time I asked him about them, when I was about eight.

Oh, I thought. That seemed simple enough. But it brought on a whole new wave of questions. I knew my grandfather's "real" name was Satya Pal (though almost everybody I knew, including my grandmother, called him "Peter"). But that didn't explain how the *D* came in. I pressed further.

"Satya Dev was the name I was born with," he said. "When I was a boy—eight or nine—a man with a business on the side of the road asked if I wanted to get my initials tattooed, and I thought, *Why not?* Not long after, my father changed my name to Satya Pal." He went and got those letters tattooed as well.

With each explanation came more questions. How did his father change his name? Was there a ceremony? A ritual? Did he tell him why he changed it?

"No. He just started calling me Satya Pal one day."

How did he know his father was even addressing him?

"When my father spoke to you, you knew. When he learned about my tattoos, he walloped me upside the head."

My Poppy's stories made the India he grew up in seem like a fairy tale, a place where a boy wandering the streets could get a tattoo from a stranger and where first names can change without a moment's notice. I've always been obsessed with recording and archiving everything that happens to me (I have filled scores of diaries, scrapbooks, and blogs), and somewhere in the back of my mind I intended to collect and record all of Poppy's stories too.

Then, early last month, he died, leaving so many stories unrecorded, so many questions still unanswered (How much time passed between the two tattoos? Was it the same man who did it both times?). I had all these half-stories, none of them written down, and now I'd never be able to fill in the blanks.

My mother—Poppy's daughter—didn't even know the story behind his tattoos until I asked him in front of her. Unlike me, he didn't dwell in the past. He rarely kept photos or mementos, and he spoke about his life only when provoked. Most people who knew him knew only the most basic details of his life: He left India in his 20s to work in England as a marine engineer, and met my Nana in a small English town. They moved to Calcutta, where my mom and her brothers were born, then emigrated to Canada, where I was born and have lived my entire life, a few years later.

Compared with my Poppy's childhood, mine was pretty dull. I grew up in a fairly multicultural neighborhood where having parents from a different place wasn't a big deal. Sundays we would go to my grandparents' house and eat tandoori chicken and dal. There'd usually be an Indian movie playing on TV, but the only person watching would be my English grandmother. My mom took me to a Hindu temple once when I was very young, I suppose as a way to connect me to my culture. The priest gave us fruit blessed by the gods. I was trying to learn to juggle at the time, and I thought this would be a good opportunity to blow everybody's minds. Instead, I just dropped my oranges in front of a statue of Ganesh, the patron saint of arts and sciences. My mom was not impressed.

Physically, I don't look very Indian. My skin is light, with yellowish undertones. I have dark, bushy hair and eyebrows, and muddled blue eyes. From middle school on, curious classmates would ask, *"So, what are you?"*—the question that every mixed-race person is all too familiar with. I had a hard time answering. To call myself "brown" felt like a farce. I was born and raised in Canada. My dad is white, and my mother is from India but has completely assimilated into Western culture. Claiming brownness felt like inserting myself into a culture that wasn't my own—and this was long before I knew what the word *appropriation* meant. Calling myself "white" felt equally wrong, like dipping a paintbrush into a pot of white paint and streaking it over our family portrait until it erased my Poppy's stories, my mom's childhood, and the family members lost during the violent partition of India in 1947, creating a blank slate onto which could be projected a picture of quintessential Caucasian girlhood. So I usually answered "What are you?" with the simple, safe, monosyllabic "Mixed."

As I got older, I started to read more about identity politics and became protective of—and sometimes defensive about—my Indian background. With a name like Fitzpatrick, I never had to explain to anybody that I had Irish ancestors, despite the fact that the last one came three generations before me. It could be taken for granted that, as a light-skinned, English-speaking person living in Canada, I must have some European blood. But I felt like I had to almost *prove* my Indianness. "You don't *look* Indian," said one girl in my eighth grade social studies class when I was working on a family-tree project, as if I was trying to dupe the class. At other times it was treated like a novelty, a conversation starter at parties: "That's so cool that you have something *interesting* in your history."

I tried, in whatever ways I knew, to be "Indian." I took my cues from Western movies with Indian characters, like *Bend It Like Beckham*, which were way more accessible to my teen self than three-hour-long Bollywood movies. I would look to my Indian friends, whose parents had immigrated later in their lives, and who still had a grasp on their parents' language, or practiced Hinduism. When I became a vegetarian, I started to cook more curries. I listened to popular Indian music and started teaching myself Hindi with books from the library. While I developed a genuine love for all these things, it still felt hollow to distill an entire culture down to food, music, and language, and my superficial knowledge of all three. Reading texts on Hinduism, or the history of India's independence, I felt like I was coming to the subject as an outsider, like an academic studying the topic of India rather than someone trying to connect with her family.

My grandfather and I started talking all the time when I was in my late teens. I went through a depression in college, around the same time he and my grandmother moved into an assisted living home. While my Nana required full-time care, Poppy became restless within the new boundaries imposed on him. Soon we were talking on the phone several times a week, seeking escape from our respective boredoms through each other's voices. We had a ritual: I would call him and he would answer the phone, hang up immediately, and call me right back so I wouldn't have to pay long-distance fees. We'd each ask how the other was doing, but since most of our days consisted of sitting alone in

our respective rooms, there wasn't a lot to report. So I starting asking him about his life.

There was that summer he met Gandhi. There was the story of how he became "Peter" (when he was studying to become an engineer, one of his instructors got him confused with the only other non-white guy in the class, and it stuck). These stories became my cultural history. My understanding of India wasn't shaped by the Asha Bhosle songs on my iPod or the mutter paneer on my stove—though I still love those things very much—but by the relationship I forged with a family member when I needed somebody to talk to.

This past March, when Poppy became sick—like, really sick—I came home to be with my family. His sister, my great-aunt Shakuntala, was in from Chandigarh and was staying at our house. She came to visit every few years, but she usually stayed with my grandfather, who would act as her cultural host and Hindi translator. Now, she was staying at our house full-time, and without Poppy acting as a buffer, it became clear to me how different my mother was from the people she'd left in India, and how assimilated my immediate family had become.

One day during Shakuntala's visit, some of our family were in Nana's room at the retirement home, trying to organize plans to visit Poppy in the hospital. In the midst of our conversation my aunt started crying. She avoided eye contact with all of us, then she got up and moved to the washroom. A few minutes later she came back out, dabbing at her eyes.

"How are you doing?" I asked in broken Hindi, one of the beginner phrases.

She replied using words I couldn't recognize. My course had taught me to understand "I am well" and "I am not well," but hadn't bothered with colloquialisms. I responded with a look of confusion. "She says she is OK," a cousin translated. My aunt and I exchanged small smiles, which had become a default during that visit. It was my only way of communicating with someone with whom I shared a family connection but seemingly little else, not even a common language.

I reached out to my sister over a Skype chat late one recent night and asked how she answers the question "What are you?"

"I think of myself as white, I guess, but of Indian descent," she said. "I don't want to play up whatever the most 'exotic' part of our culture is supposed to be. I'm proud of all the parts of our background—British, Indian, Catholic, Protestant—and the way they mixed despite the circumstances. I just think of myself as a mutt." I showed her an earlier draft of this piece, and she cringed at one instance where I described the brownness of my grandpa's skin. "What are you trying to prove to the internet? Poppy is Poppy."

Four days after Poppy died, I celebrated my 23rd birthday. I had originally planned to go out with friends in Toronto, but due to the circumstances I found myself in my hometown of Ottawa. My aunt wanted to go to the Hindu temple, and my sister, mother, and I decided to accompany her. Shakuntala took us to each shrine, explaining the importance of every deity.

She stopped at Durga's shrine to pray. She dipped a finger into the bowl of red powder in front of the shrine and gently dotted all of our foreheads. I tried to make my face look solemn, which felt appropriate in the temple. I thought that by adopting a serious air I could appreciate the sacredness of what was happening, but in truth, I didn't know the significance of the red powder. I didn't know why she had stopped to pray at Durga and not the other shrines. I wanted to understand, to react the way my aunt does, to feel that sense of connection: *This is my history, this is my family, this is my identity.* But I couldn't feel it—not there in the temple.

Later that day, my brother drove my sister and me downtown and dropped us off in front of a tattoo parlor ("It's your birthday present," my siblings explained). I showed the man behind the counter the blurry cellphone picture I had taken of my Poppy's forearms last Thanksgiving, and within minutes I was sitting in a leather chair, gripping my sister's hand, as the ink-filled needle scratched an S.D. and an S.P. into my own skin. 🌷

summer crush

Dreaming the days away. By María Fernanda. Styling by María Rangel Isas and Zaid Díaz. Thanks to Fera, Liz, Mario, and Momo for modeling. Special thanks to Club Deportivo UDG for being so nice to us.

cures for love

Rituals to get you to the other side of heartbreak.   By Lola

It's 10 years ago and I've just been dumped. I'm feeling a combination of frenzied restlessness and total paralysis. I am projecting a breakup furor so nuclear that you'd need tinted glasses to even look at me. My friend Joe kindly suggests idea after idea—watch a movie, take a walk, sit still, be alone, be with people—and one by one I shoot them all down. Then he remembers a technique his therapist used on him when he was a child: "Cut a heart out of red construction paper, then tear it into pieces until it looks like your heart feels. As you heal, you can tape the pieces back together."

Fuck it. I have paper and scissors but no tape, which is OK, as I am never getting better. I cut out a really nice fat heart and stab a jagged diagonal through the middle. Then there's crying and ripping, and friends come over and we cut out more hearts and tear them in half and take these broken hearts out running all over campus and we paste them up on buildings and bulletin boards and there's more crying (me) and high-fiving (us), and check it: I have swapped inertia for action, emotional self-destruction for creation, and somehow several hours have been clocked toward a state of healing I don't even necessarily believe in! *Hell yes,* I thought. *IS THERE OTHER STUFF LIKE THIS I CAN DO?*

To answer that question, I embarked on a research project that consisted of dating people and then breaking up and getting my heart broken over and over and over again. The feeling has not gotten any less devastating—the shift from "girlfriend" to "ex-girlfriend" status always leaves me utterly paralyzed by the pit of shiny and well-meaning jellyfish I have come to understand as my heartplace. What has changed is that I now beast through the aching immobility of heartbreak by conducting specific rituals, exercises, and experiments, all designed to snap me out of paralysis and to channel my angry energy into making things instead

of destroying everything. These activities are like magic tricks that turn my rage into forward motion. And so now I'm presenting to you—or to those among you who are currently staring at your own broken hearts in helpless horror—my personal collection of cures for several common post-heartbreak problems. May we all blaze a warpath of vengeful healing.

1. PROBLEM: COMPULSIVE OBSESSIONS.

These typically occur right after your breakup is final, but they can really strike *at any time.* Possessed by the angry scorned spirit of your choosing, you feel compelled to cry, scream, write the most intense poetry, look at every picture of the two of you together, read every one of their texts starting from the day you met. These desires are often, at least for me, accompanied by feeling like total shit: My heart hurts so bad that I can't stop myself from doing these things, but my brain is still sharp enough to side-eye my heart's desires as excessive, dramatic, and, most of all, embarrassing.

Here's how I cure myself of these destructive urges: I flood them with exactly what they're asking for until they're sorry they asked for it in the first place. Whatever it is that you want to do, do it. Then do it and do it and do it again and again and again, and eventually you will be dying to do literally anything else.

Got the cries? Set a timer for three hours. (YES, THREE HOURS.) Now, cry for three hours. (NOT A MINUTE LESS.) As you cry, observe your feelings. Take notes, even. In hour two, is your reason for crying the same one you had when you started, or has it shifted? Have you cried for every reason you can think of and now you're struggling to come up with new ones? Entertain the possibility, then, that you *won't* spend eternity crying over the person who stomped on your heart.

Are you wasting precious time obsessively cyberstalking your ex every day? Reset your timer: three hours of straight cyberstalking. Go to their Facebook timeline and read *everything* from the very beginning. Note the moment you get sick of learning that they "liked" Twizzlers and which Linkin Park lyrics they found "totally inspiring." This feeling of apathy might last only a second or two, but it's important: If you're capable of not caring what your heart's enemy is up to now, while you're deep in the cycle of compulsively obsessing about them, that's a small indication that shit will actually be OK at some point. It's a taste of how you will soon feel *all the time.*

Generally, the more dramatic the gesture, the more satisfying the payoff (and—not unrelated—the higher your chance of cracking up laughing at some point). By the time you're done force-feeding your addiction, you will hopefully have exhausted the part of your heart that kept asking for more, more, more. You might even feel a little peace. The only way to find out if it's going to work is to try it. If you do and it doesn't work, at least you're three hours farther from that bullshit thing you just went through.

2. PROBLEM: STUFF, OLD.

A weird thing about human beings is that even when they're not around anymore, their stuff still is: a pen doodle, a neglected scarf. Giving their things all the way away can be hard to fathom, especially at first: These objects are your last tangible connections to someone you may never see again. I recommend handing them over to a trusted friend on a permanent-borrow basis. Write up a contract for you both to sign: "I, [your name here], give my trusted friend [friend's name here] the following items to keep out of my sight forever, for purposes of my emotional preservation, with the condition that one day if I need them back I can ask to have them back."

someday we'll be together by pixie

1. someday we'll be together- diana ross & the supremes
2. our day will come - amy winehouse   3. these arms of mine - otis redding   4. my prayer - roy orbison
5. let's stay together - al green   6. nothing can change this love - sam cooke   7. heart - stars
8. i don't want to get over you - the magnetic fields   9. still in love songs - the stills   10. don't i love you - islands
11. willing to wait - sebadoh   12. world spins madly on - the weepies   13. walking after you - foo fighters   14. amt form - eel
15. the blizzard of '96 - the walkmen   16. the ballad of love and hate - the avett brothers   17. true love will find you in the end - daniel johnston

Or maybe you're no longer attached to these things at all. Maybe, in fact, you never want to see them again. You could donate them: to charity, to a friend, or to art. If that's not dramatic enough for you, I recommend fire. Before you ask, "Um, can she recommend fire on Rookie?" let me tell you that my BFF/fellow Rookie Marie reports that disposing of the single Michael Jackson glove left behind by her ex by throwing it on a hot grill was both safe and "v. therapeutic."

3. PROBLEM: STUFF, NEW.

At the hand-on-the-car-door-handle last moment of a breakup years ago, I pulled a dollar out of my wallet, wrote "this ca$h-money is my proof" on it, and then tore it in two so each of us could keep one half. After he left my car (and me, for good), I couldn't stand to look at my piece of the dollar, but I didn't want it to go away forever. (I was also holding out hope for a future in which we might put the dollar back together as friends.) So I put it in an envelope, and a weird practice was born: the Emotional Envelope.

The Emotional Envelope is useful when your relationship to a person is in that kind of middle space: You need to take a hard break from them after the romantic relationship is over, but you still harbor genuine fondness for them as a person, and you can't wait until you get to hang out with them again as friends. (And I advise a hard break: There's almost never such a thing as a seamless transition from a romantic relationship to a platonic one. Your only hope of sustaining a real friendship in the future is to enforce at least a few weeks of ZERO CONTACT before you try hanging out on these new, un-smoochy terms.)

The problem is, even when you've ceased contact so hard their children will be born unfriended from your Facebook, they remain stubbornly in your daily life, in the form of the thoughts that enter your head when you see something they would find funny, or you want to tell them something really, really badly, like when you're struck (repeatedly, square in the face) by a memory of a shared time that was so moving or beautiful that you want to make sure they remember it too. Yikes. These compulsions used to fuck me all up: I'd email the person JUST BECAUSE THEY MIGHT LIKE THIS FUNNY PICTURE and, bam, my heartbreak clock was reset to zero. If this is you, too, may I suggest making an Emotional Envelope of your own? Here's how:

Take out an envelope and address it to "Future _____." (Fill in the name of your ex. I'm going with Dylan for this hypothetical, because in my case that was his name. Things were so good between us and then I don't know what happened!) Whenever you see something you want to tell Dylan or give to Dylan but can't/won't/shouldn't, into the Emotional Envelope it goes. I like to write memories down on little index cards as an exercise in perspective. E.g., "June 2013, Brooklyn: That time we made out in the rain."

The Emotional Envelope lets you take comfort in a hopeful future when you'll be able to give your ex all the stuff you've been collecting and say, "Here, I saved this for you while we weren't talking." The Emotional Envelope:

- eases the discomfort of disconnection without actual contact, which would make it waaaay worse.
- stashes the pain of the present in the more-forgiving future.
- brings the forgiving future into the painful present.
- is portable and easy to store.

4. PROBLEM: TORCH-BEARING.

Torch-bearing is the act of loving someone who is no longer there, and it has a terrible reputation as a way to spend your time. But I find it almost impossible to NOT carry a torch for at least a couple weeks, so I've figured out how to turn it into a positive experience: Let's call it being "true to the torch." (I'm ribbon-dancing right now, FYI.)

Your feelings, including love, are always your own. All the good ways your ex once made you feel—smart, strong, really funny—are still yours to have. Being true to the torch means using those posi feelings to keep pushing yourself forward. Maybe this week that means doing alone that thing that you were supposed to do together. Or doing that thing you were/are afraid of.

Or maybe being true to the torch is memorializing the time you shared. Make some breakup art! "But it's soooo bad," you say. Listen: Do you know who breakup art is bad to? People not going through breakups. Do you know who doesn't need it? Those dudes. Do you know who does? You. Get out those acrylics.

Which brings me to my final strategy for mending a broken heart: Maybe you're really good at this torch-bearing thing. Have you ever thought about making it one of your friendship services? Helping others is always healing, and chances are you have a friend who is suffering through a feelwave you've already conquered. Someone hit me with the Zen thought that you should see your broken heart as broken open to the world. It helps you empathize with others who might be in pain. The more people you talk to about heartbreak, the easier it is to realize that this is bullshit we *all* go through. Every new connection, especially to a community of similar cool brokenhearted people, speeds up the healing process. In fact, thinking of you reading this is, right now, this very second, helping me get over my most recent breakup. Thank you, Heartbreak Buddy. We'll get through this! ♥

JULY 2013: *IMITATION*

Greetings, Rooks!

This month's theme is IMITATION. Vibes-wise, we just wanted a happy fun neon month, but these are some other thoughts from the email I sent our staff when we got started, with notes from Anaheed in bold:

How when you don't know what you're doing it's actually good to imitate the work of those you admire (even though people are constantly telling you to "be original"—you usually can't be original right away). Yeah, like how musicians will start writing by taking a riff they like and changing it here and there. Or how in *Just Kids* so much of Patti Smith's early life was modeling herself after Bob Dylan and others; that was something I really related to in that book, how her obsessions with these people went beyond fandom—it was more like they were each giving her the secret on how to live and how to become who she was. Eventually, of course, she became this person who is so awesome that she has no equal, but that first phase was essential. I don't think being able to trace someone's influences makes them less authentic, because they still absorbed all that art in a way nobody else did. I am happiest as a set of eyes, and my goal whenever I go into a movie or album or book is to lose myself in the story and find myself on the way out.

There's a less positive side to this, too—I recently went through a thing in my journals where I realized I was trying so hard to sound all fancy and descriptive and be Nabokov, basically. Now I see that that has already been done, that sometimes less is more, and that the best thing is to just describe things as I see them. I don't care at all about sounding original, I just want to be sincere and be myself.

Doing something over and over and hoping for different results (isn't there some definition of insanity that's kind of like that?). On that note, just how powerful habits are—not even in something as extreme as addiction, but like every time you stop yourself from comparing yourself with other people, you become a little stronger and a little less likely to do that again in the future. Or looking at websites or people's FBs that you know will piss you off just so you can b a h8r. I think we all give in to little actions like that because smaller, tired-er parts of us get some kind of satisfaction out of it, even though we know our ultimate desire is to not have that energy in our lives. We think it's just something we do and that it doesn't matter, but these habits cloud your brain and take you out of what's important. There are just so many things in the world to be annoyed about or that make you feel bad that you can't avoid, so why would you seek out more of them? Ugh, sorry if I sound *Eat Pray Love*-y.

"Authenticity," camouflage, that stuff Baudrillard wrote about our world being a simulation of reality and all that. Covers and remakes; the phenomenon of realizing you don't want to date your romantic partner, you just want to BE THEM; imitating older siblings; the fear of becoming like your parents. The way people imitate feeling high or drunk or sexy, and how teenagers fall into that because we're just grasping for how to act in those new situations. It doesn't do any good for anyone—it's just a lot of people pretending to be having a good time and not getting what they really want. I guess that happens with all sorts of experiences; in some ways it's good (I am able to enjoy certain aspects of high school because I'm like, *It's like* Freaks and Geeks *IRL!*), and in some ways it's sad because you're always measuring your experiences against what you're told your life should look like.

And finally, this Jim Jarmusch quote (from a 2004 piece in *MovieMaker* magazine):

> Nothing is original. Steal from anywhere that resonates with inspiration or fuels your imagination. Devour old films, new films, music, books, paintings, photographs, poems, dreams, random conversations, architecture, bridges, street signs, trees, clouds, bodies of water, light and shadows. Select only things to steal from that speak directly to your soul. If you do this, your work (and theft) will be authentic. Authenticity is invaluable; originality is nonexistent. And don't bother concealing your thievery—celebrate it if you feel like it. In any case, always remember what Jean-Luc Godard said: "It's not where you take things from—it's where you take them to."

LOVE,
TAVI

Design by Sonja. Title lettering by Lisa Maione. Portrait of Grimes by Brooke Nechvatel.

BIRDS OF PARADISE

Running around Harajuku with one of its coolest girl gangs.
By Eleanor

The district of Harajuku in Tokyo is famous for its street style, particularly among its teenage girls. I recently spent an afternoon with some of the coolest young ladies in Harajuku—Coi, Elle, Hirari, Juria, Maya, and Momo—and photographed them as they showed me their favorite hangout spots and gave me a glimpse into their magical world.

POSER PRIDE

You know what's dumber than pretending to like something you don't? Caring if someone else does.

By Hazel

I've been a poser more than a few times in my life. In middle school, I pretended to like the same music as a boy I had a crush on just so we could have something in common, which is how I ended up with Coldplay on my iTunes even though we never got together. In high school, I tried to fake my knowledge of a cultural theorist just to impress a few seniors in my class. Posing was my way of feeling less awkward.

On the flipside, I've definitely called people out for being posers, like classmates who were suddenly into the same bands I had been listening to for YEARS or my friend who got really into fashion, a territory I had sort of claimed as mine. I've probably rolled my eyes at your Sex Pistols T-shirt, and even looked down my nose at girls who became feminists years after making fun of me for being one.

Being called a poser is an inevitable teenage rite of passage. Most of us try on different personalities in our teen years in an effort to find ourselves, but we're still quick to cry foul when others do the same. We are simultaneously protective of our own identities and unwilling to let other people find theirs. Whether it's a wardrobe switch (suddenly the preppy girl is goth) or a personality flip (pill-popper goes straight-edge), when someone changes their script others are quick to judge them for being insincere. But how are you supposed to learn what you like if you don't try different things? If

we're lucky, we will spend most of our lives evolving—who's to say which stage we go through is the "real" one and which ones are "just a pose"?

I mean, I get it: When we love something like a book or movie or video game or song or whatevs—truly *love* it, not just enjoy it sometimes—it's usually because it touches something within our core. We *identify* with it—our identity has a soulmates-y relationship with it. So when someone with whom you seemingly have nothing in common suddenly is *really into* that thing too, in a way you're just being loyal by protecting the thing you love from this obvious impostor. They couldn't possibly identify with the same thing you do; their identity and your identity do not even live in the same universe. You want to expose them as a liar. Questioning the longevity of their interest in X or Y thing is a classic whistle-blowing technique: "Wow, it's funny that you're at this reading, because weren't you talking in class last year about how much you hated poetry?" you might say, or "Do you actually like Nirvana, or did you just buy that Kurt Cobain T-shirt because it looks cool?" BOOM. You have proved your mastery of this cultural domain. (In this case I'm using "mastery" to mean "acting like a jerky baby.")

This behavior often starts in high school, a period when we are so fiercely protective of our identities that we instinctively dislike anyone who comes close to

mirroring them. Thankfully, as most of us get older and more sure of ourselves, we let go of our need to act like some kind of cultural gatekeeper, making value judgments about people before we know anything about them. Sadly, some people never outgrow it.

Earlier this year, the comedian and adult Scott Aukerman wrote this seriously sexist tweet:

Scott Aukerman @ScottAukerman — Following

In my research, I've found the hot girl wearing the Joy Division t-shirt never wants to actually talk about Joy Division.

Reply · Retweet · Favorite · More

By espousing that it's impossible to be a Joy Division fan *and* good-looking *and* a girl, he was basically calling any female in a Joy Division T-shirt who is attractive to *him*, personally, a *poser*. Women are posers by default, just by virtue of being women, and Aukerman automatically has the authority to judge who's "real" and who's "faking it" because I'm not sure why. (To be fair, these cases aren't very hard to adjudicate: "Is she a girl? Do I want to have sex with her?" VERDICT: POSER. CASE CLOSED.)

For some reason (OK it's sexism), girls are a popular target for this kind of authenticity trolling. The *TechLife* editor Rae Johnston posted this awesome tweet after a dude called her out her for wearing a BioShock Infinite T-shirt:

COVER SONGS

By the Rookie staff

1. Teenage Kicks—Thee Headcoatees
2. One Way or Another (Teenage Kicks)—One Direction
3. Since U Been Gone—Tokyo Police Club
4. Just Like Heaven—Dinosaur Jr.
5. Across the Universe—Fiona Apple
6. Thirteen—Elliott Smith
7. You Really Got a Hold on Me—Meshell Ndegeocello
8. (Sittin' on) the Dock of the Bay (live)—Sara Bareilles
9. Love is All Around—Joan Jett & the Blackhearts
10. Being for the Benefit of Mr. Kite—Eddie Izzard

Rae Johnston
@miss_raej

🔲▾ 🐦 Follow

Snarky guy in coffee queue eyes off my Bioshock Infinite t-shirt, suggests I "probably haven't even played it". So I told him the ending.

← Reply ⟲ Retweet ★ Favorite ••• More

The snarky coffee shop guy and self-appointed authenticity-police officer in question was obviously hoping to catch Johnston in the act of posing, but instead got his ass handed to him (and the game ruined, aw). This kind of thing happens a lot when female fans participate in comic-book conferences and gamer forums—we are accused of being Fake Geek Girls. Nerdery was never a purely male arena—girls have been made fun of for playing D&D, wearing glasses, and having braces for just as long as dudes have—so it's weird that guys still cannot handle the presence of women in these spaces. A lot of guys assume that girls only *pretend* to be geeks to get attention—and it's true that people often do things outside their comfort zone when they find someone attractive and want to be noticed by them (I repeat: Coldplay in my iTunes). Aside from the larger point of "who cares," attributing that attitude to a considerable segment of the nerd population based solely on gender is the very definition of prejudice. It's also pretty stupid for a notoriously shy, largely male subculture to actively discourage women who share their interests from *coming to them*. Not that we're there for them, of course, but you would think they would've thought this through a little.

Poser policing isn't restricted to the male-dominated worlds of comedy and gaming; in academic and professional settings women are constantly told we don't know what we're talking about, even when we know as much as or more than our male counterparts. Rebecca Solnit wrote a piece on The Huffington Post last year about a conversation she once had with a man who insisted she didn't know as much about the photographer Eadweard Muybridge as he did. He haughtily quoted a recent *New York Times* best-seller he had read about Muybridge, showing off his superior expertise. Little did he know, *Solnit wrote the fucking book he was talking about*, and—plot twist—he hadn't even read it! What a posing liar!

Having been on both sides of this divide—poser and poser-pointer-outer—I'm glad that none of the people I called out ever slapped me in the face with the business end of the truth like that, but I'm also a little sad that I wasn't clever enough to come back at my accusers with comparable badassery. Not that I ever got it *so* bad—pretending to love Coldplay for the attentions of a boy is about as far as I was willing to go, but it could have turned out much worse. Or it could have turned out great! What if my feigned love for Coldplay was an on-ramp to a lifelong, heartfelt passion for Coldplay? How this soul-stirring, unshakeable love started shouldn't matter, should it? Are we now disqualifying women for getting into something the "wrong way"? Do we essentially have to present some sort of long-form fandom birth certificate as proof of our authenticity?

Ironically, the worst I ever got it from the poser police was over an incident where I was actually not posing at all. They couldn't even see how *real* I was, man! Two years ago I wrote about my love of R.L. Stine on Rookie. A few months later, I found—I honestly can't remember how—an entire LiveJournal comment thread making fun of me. According to the commenters, I was too young to have even *heard* of R.L. Stine, and therefore I was adopting a nostalgia that I had no right to. Never mind that I grew up on the Goosebumps series and that R.L. Stine doesn't belong to any one generation and that it's not like you're only allowed to enjoy art that came out when you were a specific age. (I hope that none of the people in that forum ever reads Jane Austen. I hope that they have never seen *The Godfather*. If I ever catch one of them listening to David Bowie or Mozart, I will call out their poser shenanigans.)

I'm happy to report that my concern about what other people are into and the manner in which they enjoy it vanished when I got a little older and stopped caring so much what anyone else thought of *me*. I realized there is no cultural value in liking something first, and that I can't make judgment calls on people for coming to a shared interest in their own way. To the poser police, I say: You are not a toddler, so you can't expect to keep getting rewarded for doing something for the first time, and you sort of have to use the social skills you've developed since then to let other people play with your toys. Acting like there's a *right* way to like something is snobby, petty, and mean, and no one makes friends that way. It's OK to give a person some space while they figure out who they really want to be instead of policing every pleasure they manage to eke out of life. Save your energy for making fun of things that are actually important. ✿

CANDY CRUSH

Stomp, squish, repeat.
By Arvida. Styling by Maria Pizzeria.

Thanks to Jessica and Maria for modeling, and to Juju for providing all the sandals.

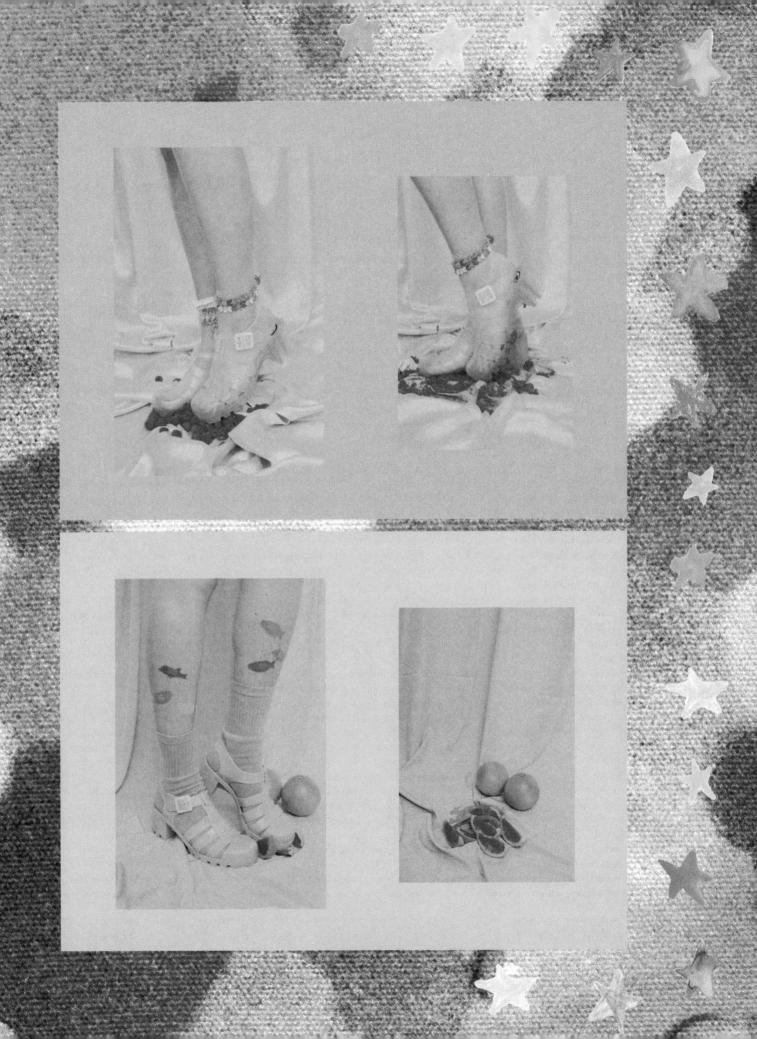

The Hunger Games *actor talks to us about role models, beauty standards, and her "psychedelic rebellious teenage years."*
By Jamia. Photo by Amandla.

Amandla Stenberg captured my heart as District 11's brave tribute Rue in *The Hunger Games*. It was a remarkable performance that showed her strength, vulnerability, and major action-movie skills. I started paying attention whenever she popped up in magazines or on websites (which happened a lot—you couldn't really escape *The Hunger Games* last year!) and became so impressed with her, not just as an actor, but as a *person*. First there was the way she reacted to the flurry of tweets by racist trolls who were upset that Rue was being played by a black girl (never mind that the character was described as having dark skin and hair in the book): She rose above the stupidity and stayed resolutely positive, saying in a statement to the press, "As a fan of the books, I feel fortunate to be part of the *Hunger Games* family […] I am proud of the film and my performance. I want to thank all of my fans […] for their support and loyalty." Then she and her mom were interviewed by in April 2012 *Essence* magazine, and she said, "My mom reminds me that all things are possible," and you could tell how much they love each other, and my heart melted. And then I started reading Amandla's blog, where I learned about her extensive charity work and her devotion to helping kids who are hungry and living in poverty around the world.

I was beyond excited to get a chance to chat with Amandla. I found her not just delightful but inspiring, and I can't wait to see what she does next.

JAMIA I saw on your blog that you're involved with Share Our Strength, an organization that's working to end child hunger in America. Can you tell us a little bit about that group, and how we can join you in supporting that cause?

AMANDLA STENBERG Share Our Strength is an incredible organization that works with school districts to provide meals for kids. It can be too easy to forget that there are hungry kids here in America—it's not something that's focused on very often. The best way to show support is to go to the No Kid Hungry website [nokidhungry.org] and make a pledge to help out, either by sending money or by volunteering somewhere in your area. Your help will be appreciated!

Another organization I work with is the Ubuntu Education Fund, which is located in Port Elizabeth, South Africa, and they cater to the needs of all the kids there. They provide food, medical supplies, and medical treatment. They offer classes like math and yoga and really try to nurture the kids. They reached out to me last summer and asked me to attend their gala and get to know their organization. So I flew to New York and spent a couple of days with a couple of the young women who had graduated from the program. They were so light and bubbly, and we had a great time. A few days later, at the gala, one of these women gave a speech. She spoke about her life and the things she had been through, then she recited a poem that she had written. The last line was something like "Because the father of my child is my father too." I must have looked emotional, because after the speech this young woman and her mentor came up to me and asked if I was OK. These women had been through so much, but were some of the most kind, lovely, brave, and effervescent women I'd ever met. From that moment on I have been so passionate about their cause.

I love learning stuff from you! Do you ever feel like people assume things about you because of your age? Do you think you're treated differently in show business because you're younger?

It definitely happens. I'm kind of in an awkward stage right now, just because there aren't many roles for girls my age or girls of my ethnicity. Also, I look like I'm 12 [*laughs*], so I think I can be kind of babied because of that. It is something that I have to overcome. I get cast as people younger than my age, too.

Have you ever wanted to audition for a role that your parents wouldn't let you try out for?

Yes! [*Laughs*] I think my parents can be a little protective when it comes to subject matter. There are roles that look very indie and cool and I think, *Maybe this could go to Cannes! It would be so cool!* And then my parents are like, "We don't know if that's a good idea." But I do really appreciate their judgment, because I wouldn't want to be in any inappropriate films.

What has been your favorite role to play so far?

I don't know if I can pick a favorite, because my experience has been so varied. But what I loved about *The Hunger Games* is that it had a fantastic cast. It was basically like summer camp—we were all in the woods together for three months. There were a lot of pranks pulled and sleepovers and that kind of thing. It is kind of a rare experience when all of the members of a cast like each other. There were no conflicts or anything!

Was it weird to have your *Hunger Games* character made into an action figure?

It was pretty bizarre. *The Hunger Games* was one of the very few films I've made, and I got an action figure! It's really cool. I love to play with it with my niece. I like the fact that it is an image of a young girl, not a weird sexualized action figure like you often see.

There's so much pressure for women and girls in Hollywood to fit a specific body and beauty ideal. How does it feel to be a young woman coming of age in an industry that is so focused on looks?

My opinion on how I should look would be completely different if it weren't for Rookie. Rookie completely changed my thoughts about what it means to be an individual and how I can show my individuality through my wardrobe. It doesn't have to be so perfect and Barbie-like, you know? I've found that one of my favorite ways to express myself is through my clothes, because I'm not conforming to some ideal. I do know some other young girls in the industry who are affected by those ideals. It is very sad to see. So, I feel very lucky to have come across Rookie!

Oh my goodness! Thank you so much. What else are you into right now? Books, music…

I'm into '60s and '70s music right now. I've been listening to the Turtles, Fleetwood Mac, Jimi Hendrix, those kinds of people. I'm watching *Dazed and Confused*. I'm in my teens and feeling all psychedelic and cool and rebellious!

As for books, I've always loved *A Tree Grows in Brooklyn*. I am rereading it now. The last time I read it was when I was 11. It is interesting to see how my opinions about what goes down in the book have changed. I'm also reading *The Doors of Perception* by Aldous Huxley—another part of my psychedelic rebellious teenage years!—and *Buddha in Your Backpack*, which I'm finding really fun and interesting. I'm exploring religion right now. And I just started reading *The Crying of Lot 49*.

Oprah recently interviewed Alfre Woodard, Viola Davis, Phylicia Rashād, and Gabrielle Union about the challenges black actresses face in Hollywood. They discussed the lack of quality roles for black women as well as

the criticism women of color sometimes receive in a hostile and competitive media landscape. At this point in your acting career, have you experienced anything like this? If so, what is your hope for the future?

With *The Hunger Games*, there was some drama over the fact that a lot of people didn't expect my character, Rue, to be African-American. So I received some negative feedback, especially on Twitter. I kind of distanced myself from it, because it seemed very silly to me. I didn't really think I needed to focus my energy on it.

I don't really check my personal mentions that much on Twitter. I think it is best to abstain from looking at them rather than come across one negative comment and have it stick in my mind. This happens to a lot of young people in the industry, and it kind of breaks them down. When [those tweets] happened, I really tried not to look at what was going on. It was pretty shocking to see some of the articles that compiled the [negative] tweets I received. I remember calling my friend Jackie Emerson and telling her I wouldn't understand all of the drama even if Rue *wasn't* supposed to be black, and she comforted me. She told me I had to realize it was nothing personal, but it was unfortunately how society was reacting to the "shocking" presence of an African-American actress. [*Laughs*] I tried not to let it get to me.

I've also been told, "We're going in another direction" when I've auditioned for roles, and the "other direction" turns out

to be a girl with blue eyes and blond hair. I agree that it may be more competitive when you're an African-American actress, but at the same time, I can almost use [my race] to demonstrate my ability: Since there are fewer roles for African-American women, perhaps I can make a deeper impression. I can feel more special about my roles because I know I've worked hard to get where I am, and I know that I'm one of the people who have made it.

In the future, I think there will be a lot more roles in this kind of new wave of African-American actresses, like Kerry Washington. Kerry Washington is really revolutionizing the industry. She's a great role model for me.

This is kind of a personal question, so feel free not to answer it if you don't feel comfortable. I read that your mom is African-American and your dad is Danish. I'm about to marry my fiancé, who has an Irish and French background, and I really want to make sure that I'm raising our future kids to feel proud of every part of who they are. I'm so glad they will have people like you and President Obama to look up to. Do you have any advice for me about how to teach my kids to celebrate being in a multiracial family?

When I was younger, I remember people not believing that my dad was my dad, because I was black and he was white. When they saw us together, some people thought he was my neighbor or someone like that. There are a lot of people who don't understand, because that is how they have been raised to think. Also, because we don't see multiracial families very often in the media, it has become something that some people think is radical or strange.

But there are a lot more multiracial families out there than there were when I was younger. In the past few years, I've met a lot more mixed kids and people like me, so I think the best way to raise a kid is to teach your child that there's nothing wrong with being multiracial, and even though it is so rare in the media, it is something that is growing. It is much bigger under the surface of what we see every day. Teach your kids that it is a new wave. ♥

UNUSUAL WORLD

Lone pleasures at the theme park.
By Eleanor. Styling by Nao Koyabu.

Thanks to Tenko for modeling
and for showing us her favorite
old amusement park in Tokyo.

SONGS FOR SNEAKING OUT

BY MINNA

1.) LUST FOR LIFE – GIRLS

2.) CHERRY BOMB – *THE RUNAWAYS*

3.) MASCARA – KILLING HEIDI

4.) IT'S MY LIFE – NO DOUBT

5.) ROCKING THE SUBURBS – BEN FOLDS FIVE

6.) ALL THE SMALL THINGS – BLINK-182

7.) DECEPTACON – LE TIGRE

8.) 4EVER – THE VERONICAS

9.) BAD GIRLS – M.I.A.

10.) ALRIGHT – SUPERGRASS

11.) YOU GET WHAT YOU GIVE – NEW RADICALS

Design by Sonja.
Title lettering by Esme. Playlist lettering by Ana.
Group photos by Allyssa. Single photos by María Fernanda.

AUGUST 2013: THRILLS & CHILLS

STEP RIGHT UP, ROOKIES.

This month's theme is THRILLS & CHILLS. Here's how I described it in the email I sent to our staff to start them brainstorming ideas:

Basically we want this to be a fun last-hurrah-of-summer month that's just about CRAZY SHIT THAT HAPPENS, MAN. I keep a list in one of my notebooks called WONDERS OF THE WORLD. It's all of this type of fascinating stuff: cults, the Brown Mountain Lights, Robert Johnson's crossroads, JT LeRoy, etc. This month is about that stuff, but also about REAL-LIFE STORIES: Anger! Fights with friends 'n' family! Taking risks—ones that don't necessarily involve PHYSI-CAL ACTION but that feel HUGE because they indicate change (like getting into a new style of dress or a band or something), all the *My So-Called Life/Perks of Being a Wallflower* first "bad kid" experiences, friends that are "bad influences." The feeling when you KNOW you're about to do something bad (suspense! thrills!) but go ahead anyways—or don't and regret it (or don't regret it!). Realizing that it's OK to not be WILD AND CRAZY, and to not force it by acting like you are on *Skins* or something. People clutching on to that kind of playacting as an identity because they're worried they're not actually interesting people or they feel like they HAVE to be "interesting" when, really, you just have to be nice!

Enjoy!

LOVE,
TAVI

SUMMER'S LAST HURRAH

Don't waste another moment getting ready for school!
By the Rookie staff

It's August, and the shadow of September looms large. Every magazine and website that you usually love is suddenly striking fear in your heart by warning you about all the things you have to do to PREPARE YOURSELF for the onset of another school year. There are back-to-school shopping lists, back-to-school style guides, back-to-school lunch planners, even back-to-school *workouts*. If you listened to all of them, you'd spend the entire month of August getting ready for September.

Well, we at Rookie say EFF THAT. There's only one month left of vacation! Don't waste a whole third of it preparing for it to be over. You don't have to "get ready" for school—school will start no matter how many checklists you have or haven't completed. You can buy a protractor anytime! Now is the time to squeeze every last drop of sweet summer nectar out of August!

Here are 31 ways, one for each day of the month, to savor these precious final days of summer. You're not gonna be ready to return to school, after all, if you feel like you barely even got a break.

1. Build a bonfire and invite your friends over to make voodoo s'mores: little marshmallow figures of people who are stressing you out. Forgive those people, then eat the s'mores.

2. Grab at least one friend, set an alarm for 5 AM, and ride your bikes until the sun comes up. This isn't about talking or making a scene—just enjoy a quiet moment at a time of day you rarely get to see.

3. Learn the choreography from Beyoncé's "Love on Top" video. You've been meaning to for at least a year, and it's the easiest Bey routine in absolutely ages. Stop putting it off, learn it today, and get closer to a state of true Beyvana.

4. Swim in as many pools as possible in a single day.

5. Make your own ice cream sandwiches. This is actually not as hard as it sounds—here's how you do it: Make (or buy) a batch of your favorite cookie dough, but instead of dividing it up into dozens of little globs, spread it evenly into two giant rectangular cookies. Bake those, and once they're cool, soften up some ice cream, spread it on one layer, and then cover it with the other giant cookie. Wrap the whole shebang in plastic wrap and stick it in the freezer. In a couple of hours, take it out and cut it into brick-shaped sandwiches. You are now a genius with a whole bunch of delicious ice cream sandwiches. If you want to get super fancy, melt some chocolate and dip the sandwiches in it as you eat.

6. Find some outdoor steps that don't get used much in the summer (like a school's) and make a DIY water slide. (Google "DIY water slide" for instructions.)

7. Ask out a guy/girl you fancy. Just do it. Even if they say no, it's a great feeling to know that you asked. *You asked.* And now you know.

8. Go berry picking. (Maybe even make some jam.)

9. Get all your friends together and hold a séance. Make a ghost-themed playlist and bake ghost-shaped cookies. Not creepy at all.

10. Plan an alone day. Clear your schedule, turn your phone off and stuff it in the deep recesses of your bag, get a blanket and some snacks and a giant drink and the book you have been meaning to read, and take them all to the park. Once you are too hot and out of snacks, go cool off at a matinee. Do not text or check your tweets or emails or tell Facebook what you are doing. Exist in your own little orbit.

11. Go to a nature preserve or a park at dusk and spend a couple of hours creeping around, pretending to be a mountain lion. Get really into it: No talking, just wander around with your eyes wide open and walk on your paws as softly as you can, hyperalert to everything.

12. Next time you hear a storm roll through, don't hibernate—run outside! Getting drenched in the fall, winter, or even spring sucks because it's cold and you could get sick. But summer rain is warm and smells delicious and is perfect for dancing and cavorting like a fairy goddess in. Do cartwheels, splash in puddles, and get completely soaked in Mother Nature's water park. (Avoid lightning and strong winds, obviously, but otherwise enjoy yourself!)

13. Be a tourist in your own town. Look up your city or village or neighborhood online and find all the tourist spots that you never go to because, duh, you live

there. Try to visit them all within 24 hours.

14. Trespass in an abandoned amusement park, if you live near one.

15. Read a book in a day, even (especially) if it takes all day. When you're swamped with homework in a couple of months and unable to take time out, you'll think fondly of this day. Optional: Stock up on candy first.

16. Have you been to the beach yet this summer? Grab a group of friends, some beach towels, snacks, and bottled water—maybe a kite?—and get going!

17. Set up a bird feeder and watch it.

18. Go out with your camera and ask at least eight interesting-looking people if you can take their picture. Tell 'em you're in a summer photography class and your assignment is to photograph strangers—that usually makes people a little more amenable and less suspicious. Do this during the day, when it's safer and the light is better, and try to vary it up in terms of age, gender, ethnicity, size, style, etc. You'll be amazed by the brilliant and vast life that exists in your little corner of the world.

19. Kool-Aid Krafternoon: Get a variety pack of Kool-Aid and use the drink mix to make slushies, tie-dye old T-shirts, and dye your hair.

20. Celebrate the full moon. A summer full moon is particularly special for the simple reason that you have *no school to wake up to in the morning.* You have total freedom to stay up late—or even all night—with the moon. You can do this by yourself, quietly observing any odd occurrences that might coincide with this lunar phase, or make a celebration with friends—you could make a full-moon dinner together and then go on a walk at nightfall (stick to well-lit, well-populated areas, and don't walk alone). Don't be disappointed if

it's cloudy or rainy. The full moon is still out there hiding and casting all kinds of *moooony* vibes.

21. Girls with naturally textured hair, especially of the type-four, or coil-y, variety: Learn how to flat-twist your hair. YouTube is full of tutorials, and with a dedicated few hours, you can master it. Your twist-outs will look BOMB, and your winter protective styling game will be fresh. Best of all, it's a skill that keeps improving the more you do it.

22. Go an entire day eating only ice cream: ice cream for breakfast, lunch, and dinner. Bonus points if you can get weird flavors of ice cream to match the traditional meals—like french toast and/or bacon at breakfast time and tomato and basil or avocado for lunch or dinner.

23. Write, cast, shoot, and edit a short film in a day. Or make a short audio or video documentary. Or style and shoot a fashion editorial, casting your friends as models.

24. Go on a nature ramble. A ramble isn't just for kids in old British children's books! Something between a walk in the park and a proper hike, a ramble is a long walk in the countryside (if you're a city slicker, take a day trip somewhere greener). Take off early in the morning with something to eat and plenty of water, a fully charged cellphone (preferably with GPS) in case you get lost, and a camera if you want to capture nature. (And definitely get back before sundown, because woods and meadows are hard to navigate at night, even in moonlight.) You'll rarely find solitude of this kind, and there's something so peaceful about wandering around in the wilderness on a late-summer's day.

25. Find a pool that has a restaurant attached (hotels are good for this). Order food to come to you at that pool—and try to include french fries in your order.

Eat that meal poolside and pat yourself on the back.

26. Collect wildflowers and put them in water in your room or press them and make your own stationery or cards.

27. Finally make a real effort to learn how to hula-hoop. In public.

28. Find one of those old-timey soda counters and order an egg cream, a Green River, or another relic-y sugar-beverage.

29. Get a knapsack, pack it with snacks, books, and a pair of binoculars à la *Moonrise Kingdom,* and run away! Escape to the woods, under the jungle gym, or wherever you please. Send letters to your friends beforehand explaining why you've dramatically decided to run away; include a map if you want them to find you. Or bring someone along and share your rations throughout the day. Just come back before dark (and tell an adult where you're going you leave if you don't want to get grounded!).

30. Climb a tree! Climb several!

31. Stay in bed all day. Sunshine can be wonderful, but so can blankets and pillows and Netflix. When your alarm goes off for school at the buttcrack of dawn every day for the rest of the year, all you'll want to do is hit snooze and cling to the sanctuary that is your bed. Do it while you still can! Read a not-as-signed-for-school book, plow through an entire season of television, or just take a bunch of naps interspersed with snack breaks. For added indulgence, go ahead and set your alarm on the slothy day of your choosing, just so you can experience the pleasure of turning it off and going back to sleep.

What, are you still here? Put this book down and close the season out right. Hurry up now, time's a-wasting. ☛

HOW TO DEAL when YOU'RE CAUGHT MASTURBATING

written by EMILY and drawn by ESME

Masturbation is a fantastic way to de-stress, figure out what you like sexually, and have fun... but that doesn't mean you want it to be PUBLIC KNOWLEDGE! Like most private things, it seems inevitable that at some point in your life, someone is going to catch you doing it. It won't be the end of the world - it might even be kinda funny - but getting caught is still embarrassing! So here are a few possible excuses you could use to explain what you were doing instead of masturbating.

THE CRAMP

WOAH!

WHAT a WEIRD MUSCLE SPASM! I should stop doing that WORKOUT.

THE BOOGIE

I was Practicing a new dance, but I got tired so I decided to practice lying down!

JAZZ HANDS

FOLLOW WHAT'S ALIVE:

AN INTERVIEW WITH GRETA GERWIG

The screenwriter and star of Frances Ha *talks to us about making movies, the joys of collaboration, and the perils of writing about your friends.*
By Tavi. Illustration by Allegra.

I'd been trying to avoid movies for a long time when I saw *Frances Ha*. I'd gone back to that safe, emotional-commitment-less space of watching *Bob's Burgers* all day, and I was in no mood to be moved and inspired and have the FIRE OF MY LIFE REIGNITED. Well, reignite it did! After this lovely movie, I walked outside and everything looked nicer than it had before, and I felt like I could move a little more confidently and that no matter what happened, it would be on some level hilarious, and on every level OK.

Greta Gerwig starred in and co-wrote the film with its director, and her real-life partner, Noah Baumbach (*The Squid and the Whale*, *Greenberg*). She's also worked with Whit Stillman and Woody Allen, but it was truly special to get to see her in something where her own voice could come through. (Plus you KNOW I am all over a pretty black-and-white comedy about female friendship.) She is so wonderful in it, perfectly cringe-inducing in Frances's many embarrassing moments, and utterly captivating the whole way through. When we spoke a few weeks ago for this interview, she was totally captivating and not at all cringe-inducing. Enjoy!

TAVI **My friend went to a screening [of** ***Frances Ha*] where there was a Q&A afterward, and she said people kept asking you how influenced you were by** *Girls*, **and you had to be like, "I wrote this first!" Which means that when you wrote it, there was probably less space for a female character like Frances to be so flawed.**

Why did you choose to write this kind of character?

GRETA GERWIG Well, this sounds incredibly douchey, but I don't feel like I ever *choose* to write something. I started writing, and this is the character that came out. I wrote a list of ideas and moments, and the thing that really seemed to lock into who the character was didn't even end up in the movie! It was a scene I wrote that, as soon as I showed it to Noah, we felt like, *Oh, that's who she is!* It was a scene where Frances runs into an old dance teacher/manager–type person, and helps [the teacher] carry her groceries home. But instead of leaving, Frances stays for hours and eats a portion of the groceries that she just helped carry, then she inadvertently insults her old mentor and is kind of sincere and sweet but also a complete wrecking ball. It didn't end up having a place in the movie, but it felt like we'd tapped into who she was. Then it's just about following what seems to be alive in your writing, as opposed to deciding something and then doing it. I feel like I have to let it come to me.

What did you learn about friendship by making *Frances Ha*?

It was kind of a complicated process for me. I love the movie, and I loved it as a piece of writing, and I love the acting in it. I think of it as this complete love letter to that time in life. But I didn't have a perfectly seamless experience with my own friends,

with their reaction to it. They've been very supportive and lovely about it, but it didn't start there. The thing with using auto-biographical [material] is that once you start writing it, it becomes absorbed into the world of fiction, so you no longer think about it as related to other people who are actually alive at all—you think of it as belonging to this character that you made up, and then there's other stuff that you make up, and it all gets thrown into one soup whose ingredients I couldn't even tell you. But the experience of someone [else] reading the script is that they read it and they're like, "You fucking bitch—it didn't happen that way!"

Ahhh!

And they're right, it *didn't* happen that way—because this is a *movie*, you know? Things are made up! But there's enough stuff in it from [real] life that isn't made up. I might use a phrase or a moment that really happened, but then it grows into something else. As a writer, you know, you never can really get permission from people. But I don't feel totally 100 percent like I'm allowed to [write about real people] just because I'm an artist and a writer and "fuck all y'all"—but that's what people do! I feel kind of bad about it. But I'm learning how to be better at it.

It was kind of an odd experience, because the shooting of it was so idyllic, and I loved making it, and it was, like, the ultimate fulfillment of what I want to do as a writer and an actress, and it felt so…

good; but the actual life that was going on alongside it was kind of a mess. So I think I learned about—and hopefully in the future I'll be better about—other people's feelings and sensitivities and the way they'll perceive something, and about letting people in earlier.

I mean, luckily I'll never write another movie about this particular subject again, but I'll probably write something else that I'll need to have some conversations about with people. The whole thing made me feel like I was an undercover reporter or something—like, it made people feel exposed, because they thought we were all just *living*, and then I took some of it and made it into something.

I think everyone who makes things probably has to deal with this in some form or another.

Yeah. It's interesting, too, because I'm a people-pleaser by nature—which is the actress part of me, I think, and the part of me that wants approval. And then there's another part of me that doesn't want approval—if you're a writer I think people know you're [gathering material] all the time, and that becomes part of how people experience you. They [see you as someone] who does this and who doesn't really care how they feel about it. In a way that would be easier; sometimes I wish I had a shell of certainty around me that would let me say, "I don't give a shit." But that's not who I am—I do! [*Laughs*]

My friend has a theory that writers wish they had actor personalities and actors wish they had writer personalities. Like, writers wish they could be performer-y and people-pleas-y, and actors wish they could be the underappreciated genius or something. But the nice thing about making this movie the way you did is that you were able to be both of those things.

I mean, I've always wanted to be a person who did just one thing. I'm jealous of actresses who knew that's what they wanted to do when they were five and pursued it doggedly and went to Juilliard

or another fancy, nice place and are totally dedicated to their craft. I always felt like I was somehow less than those people because they seem more artistically pure. I always did it in a more gray area where I was writing *and* acting *and* directing and making things.

I took ballet when I was growing up. I loved to dance and I really was very serious about it, but there was a point where I was also taking up tap and jazz and musical theater, and a teacher said to me, "You're gonna have to pick one at some point, because otherwise you're not going to be great at any of them. You'll just be a dabbler." I was like, *Oh my god*.

Yikes! What an awful thing to say to a child!

It's the worst way to talk! But I took it very seriously, and since then I've always worried that I'm *just a dabbler*, not a master at anything. But I can't change it. So.

I read an interview with Lena Dunham and Miranda July where they were like, you know, it's easier now to do more than one thing.

I do think it is easier. I also think, in some ways—this is a huge generalization and I might regret it instantly—but I feel that in a way women are kind of built to do lots of things. I know that might sound, I don't know, maybe anti-feminist, but when I look at women like my mother and her friends and my grandmother and professors I've had and women I've known who are artists, a lot of them have had lots of different chapters in their lives. That's a generalization, and I have nothing to back it up. It's just something I've observed in the world.

So many of my favorite creations of all kinds are, like, the creator just trying to be heard, and to establish an identity. When you collaborate—especially, I imagine, with someone who's also a part of your personal life—you have to put that aside. What was that like? Was it different from when your friends were

saying, "How could you use that thing that we had," or whatever?

You know, it's funny—sometimes people say [about a collaboration], "I don't remember who wrote what lines." I feel like that's a lie, whenever anyone says that. I remember. I know who wrote every single line. I can totally tell you which lines are mine and which lines are his. But they still all feel like mine! I think in any pure collaboration that's really great, it feels like both people entirely. The best metaphor for it is songwriting: There's something about songwriting where two people can work on the same song, but it's 100 percent both people. I'm not comparing myself to these people but, like, Paul McCartney and John Lennon—their songs are *both* of them, but each one is 100 percent each of them. It's almost like a paradox of collaboration. So I feel like *Frances Ha* is 100 percent mine and also 100 percent Noah's.

It definitely felt more like my struggle to find myself as a creator than [it was for] Noah, because this was something that I had been sitting on for years, while he has been in the

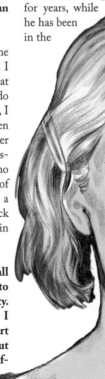

process of very productive filmmaking for years. It was much more cathartic for me to write it and get it into the world. For him, I think it was just part of what he was used to doing as a filmmaker. It felt like much more of a leap for me.

The personal part of our relationship is both separate and part of it. I think we communicate really well [as a creative team]. It's something we know we like to do together. And it's really fun! I think it would feel like a part of us in our relationship was missing if we ever wholesale stopped writing together or making something together. It's so fun to show Noah writing, because he's my favorite person and I respect him so much, and when I can make him laugh or he likes something that I've written it feels, like, *great*. But I have to keep myself from showing him everything, because I find that when I involve him, it's like a magnetic force field—everything gets pulled toward him. I don't want to create an artificial barrier, but I have to know what something *is* before I show it to him. Otherwise it starts belonging to both of us, because it's living in both of our heads.

I am by nature a collaborator. And in some ways, by nature, he's not. So, in a way, working together strengthens the weak parts of each of us—it strengthens his collaborative instinct, and I think it strengthens my individualist instinct.

I thought your interview with Terry Gross [on NPR's *Fresh Air*] was so great; I remember you said you felt a lot of pressure to look a certain way because you didn't think there were stories being told of women who were, like, heavier than a ballerina.

Yeah. I didn't think I was going to end up talking about that at all on that show. I was kind of embarrassed about it afterward.

Oh no!

I mean, it's something I feel complicated about. Certainly being an actor and working in film, you're working in a visual medium.

Yeah.

And there is such a history of photographing beautiful people. I don't think there's anything wrong with that. Recently I went to a screening at Film Forum of *L'Avventura*, and I was watching Monica Vitti, who is one of the most beautiful women who's ever lived, and I was thinking, you know, that's part of it! I think it's ridiculous to say, "Why don't they look like regular people?" because that's part of the thrill of those movies. So I don't want to say that movies that showcase traditionally gorgeous specimens of humanity are somehow less than.

But I wish I had a more consistent view of it. Because some days I think, like, *Why don't you just treat this like you're an athlete and you need to be this size to be an athlete, and wouldn't it be easier on you and you'd get more parts if you fit into sample sizes?* Then I put effort into it—I'm careful about what I eat or what I do. And then I'll swing in the other direction and say, *I don't give a fuck! I'm never going to look like these people anyway, so why am I trying?* For me, the pain has been feeling one way and then the other and then the first way again. I feel like if I could just pick a lane of either, like, self-acceptance or athleticism, I would be happier. But I think the pain is in feeling like no matter which lane you pick, part of you hates it.

That makes a lot of sense. I think Lena Dunham was very purposeful in being like, *I want visibility for my kind of body on TV*. But not everyone wants to put themselves out there like that, and not everyone feels that way consistently.

I also want to say—and I'm not saying this as a boast—but I've never been seriously overweight, and I don't know what that feels like. So I don't want to claim that I'm somehow representative of, or that I really understand, what it's like to deal with that in a bigger way. What's interesting to me is that I struggle with it anyway. That it occupies my mind in a way that's disproportionate to how much of an issue it actually should be for me. I think that's the culture.

Have you ever found yourself having a moment like Frances does in the movie, of just, like, "I'm not doing anything—oh, I know, I'll go to Paris"? Anything impulsive like that?

[*Laughs*] I mean, I've never actually taken a spur-of-the-moment trip with money I didn't have, but I've definitely had my moments of lostness and heartbreak that feel like they can only be dealt with by doing something drastic. I've allowed myself to be in a movie that maybe I shouldn't have been in, just because I so didn't want to be myself. Being on a movie set is GREAT if you hate yourself, because on a movie set, you're working 14 hours a day, and it's so much effort, and it takes so much out of you that you almost don't have room for your own problems or your own thoughts, be they self-loathing or confusion or you feel like your personal life is in shambles, or what have you. That can be incredibly addictive. I have had moments where I thought, like, *I just can't face up to anything, I have to escape, and I'm gonna escape into this movie*. I think that's a bad way to use movies, and sometimes I've regretted it.

How was *Frances Ha* different in that respect?

When you're an actor, you can act on your own, but you kind of need to get hired. You need to be chosen. And when you're chosen to act in something, the thing itself is already validated—it's already real in some way. But for the most part, people who are creators—writers and directors—are always starting from zero. Nobody is *asking* them to make what they make. Every time you set out to create something from nothing that nobody has asked for, you feel the void more than you do in any other art form. I do, anyway. I'd never experienced that with a film before *Frances Ha*, where at first there was nothing, and then there was something because we made it. *Frances Ha* felt like *I* gave birth to it. And then I realized that that's what you have to do on every single project for the rest of your life, if this is what you want to do.

ALL IN GOOD TIME

 I spent most of my time in high school thinking I was "doing youth wrong."
By Pixie

My favorite high-school-party memory involves the first boy I ever kissed throwing up on me. We were 18, he was drunk, and I was trying to comfort him as he stumbled around in our mutual friend's backyard. I was sitting on a bench; he came up and started telling me how happy he was that we were friends, because, in his words, I was "poetic, like Britney Spears." Then he threw up on my shoes. It was perfect in its absurdity, and the memory has always stayed with me.

The People Who Bring You High School in movies or on television would have you believe that everyone just sprints through all of life's standard checkpoints unimpeded. I believed them, and as a result I spent roughly 75 percent of my high school experience thinking I was "doing youth wrong," because I spent more time playing DreamPhone and laughing with my best friends on Saturday nights than I did drinking out of red Solo cups or breaking laws. This is not to say that I *never* went to a party or made out with anyone or broke a law (OK, I didn't break any laws, but I did wear silver lipstick for most of 1998, and that counts as far as I'm concerned), but my life was not a party scene from a John Hughes movie. For a long time I thought that meant I was terrible at being a high school student, when all it really meant was that I was just pretty good at being myself.

My friends and I were relatively tame, partially because it was just our nature, but mostly because we were obsessed with getting into good colleges and terrified of anything that might get in our way of doing so. We had SO MUCH FUN together on low-key weekend nights, just driving around, singing at the top of our lungs, making up stupid jokes, gossiping about people we had crushes on, and imagining what our lives would be like after high school. When we did go to parties, I was the designated driver—drinking has never really been my thing, and I was worried about everyone getting home safely—and so I wound up watching a lot of people get drunk. Unlike in the movies, my friends' drinking wasn't necessarily cute or fun or interesting, and it certainly didn't lead to any major romantic moments or life revelations; it was just a bunch of drunk nerds trying to act cool while throwing up in the bushes outside someone's suburban house. These parties were filled with people milling about, holding red cups filled with horrible high school liquor decisions (just because you like vanilla and cinnamon does not mean you should mix flavored vodka with flavored schnapps). But I usually had a ton of fun anyway, because I ate candy and laughed a lot instead of getting drunk and puking a lot.

People seem to think that they need to have a very specific set of experiences between their freshman and senior years that will turn them into interesting, well-adjusted adults—which is a *complete lie*. Sneaking out, getting drunk, having sex, skipping class—all of that stuff is optional, man. And all of it is easily accomplished post–high school, regardless of what the Teen Movie Industrial Complex tells you or what your cousin's friend's sister's boyfriend's best friend says about how many people you need to sleep with or how many parties you need to attend to be considered "normal" by the time you go to college. We buy into the idea that our teenage lives have to be produced by Baz Luhrmann in order to be fun. But no one told me that half of the "teenagers" on TV are actually in their 20s and actually millionaires, so of course their lives looked more fun than mine! It's hard to reproduce a party on the scale of *The O.C.* when you live in No One Cares Falls, Iowa.

Some people party a lot in high school, and that's totally fine. I didn't. I spent my downtime trying to figure myself out, just like people who experiment earlier than others are trying to figure themselves out in a different way. There's no set timetable for this complicated and messy process; some people just take a while to figure out what they like by trying a lot of things. My life may have seemed dull to some, but I had a good time on my own terms.

I worried about whether I'd done high school wrong well into my 20s. And when I got to college and met people who seemed to have a million experiences and stories to share about their wild high school times, like massive road trips or a party where someone fell from a roof into a pool, I felt like maybe I had missed out. But as I got older, I gained a little perspective— I realized that *no one* has the "perfect" high school experience. The only way I could have done it "wrong" would have been if I'd forced myself to do things I wasn't ready or willing to do. I had a good time in high school, and it shaped the person I am today. I read, I listened to records, I drew, I stared at the ceiling, I laughed so hard my stomach felt sick, and though sometimes I worried that I was missing out, I still found things to fill the holes that adolescence likes to punch into one's heart.

Life is better, and weirder, and more ridiculous than you could ever imagine, and filled with characters that stay with you long after the so-called "big moments" of your life (proms, parties, first kisses) have faded away. The surroundings don't matter as much as the person you are when you're in them. ♥

LITERALLY THE BEST THING EVER:
AEROSMITH'S "CRAZY" VIDEO

It turned my world upside down.
By Ragini

It was the summer of 1999. I was 13 years old and horny. I spent my afternoons reading alone in my bedroom, curtains drawn, while outside I could hear my parents fighting so violently that sometimes the neighbors had to intervene. I was the target of their violence often enough that it was a relief when they directed it against each other.

I was always disappointing them. I wasn't brilliant enough academically to satisfy their expectations, nor was I as docile and subdued as they felt a "good Indian girl" should be, and they heaped guilt on me for these shortcomings. I also had another, secret source of guilt—my shame about touching myself and liking it.

I remember the first time I felt horny. It happened early that summer, and it was a feeling I couldn't explain; I just waited till it went away. I had been brought up in such a repressed household and in such a repressed society that it didn't even occur to me to touch myself. Sex education was unknown in most Indian schools at the time, and the very idea of a teenage girl masturbating was too shocking for anyone to talk about publicly. I was hopelessly sheltered, and taught that someday I would grow up and marry a guy my parents found for me, have two and a half kids with him, and live happily ever after. I didn't question it.

My first and only moment of rebellion had occurred three summers earlier, when, in the absence of parental supervision and high on hormones, I had practically run wild. My mother had been away in Delhi, my father too drunk to care. I ran around in ragged clothes and played cricket with the neighborhood kids, coming home only for meals and to watch films on cable—films in which adults kissed passionately and

they showed boobs—late into the night. One day I broke my big toe while playing on the roof, and then proceeded to climb a half-built skyscraper with my broken toe. The next week my mother returned home, and my summer of abandon was over. But its flame still burned deep within me. It wasn't until halfway through the summer of 1999, when I was 13, that it exploded into an inferno. The trigger? My best friend.

I had known Shia (let's call her Shia) since I was 11, but we'd only recently become close. It started with music, as most things do when you are a teenager. I remember the battered tape she thrust into my hand one day, a copy of Pink Floyd's *The Division Bell*, and insisted I listen to. I wasn't particularly excited; I preferred boy bands. But one afternoon when I got home from school, after being shouted at by my mother, feeling absolutely miserable, I popped the tape into my boombox and hit play. And the world was changed forever.

Shia and I started hanging out all the time after that, talking about music, boys, parents, and books and giggling about the guys she was seeing, while I secretly wished that some boy, any boy, would fancy me for a change. That, however, was a pipe dream—I was taller than everyone in my year, boys included, and the fattest. Boys looked at me only to laugh, and when they actually talked to me, it was just to get to know Shia—pretty, frail, delicate Shia—better. While I was jealous, I didn't love her any less for it. And I loved her *a lot*. We spent all our free time at school together, arm in arm, and when we got back home, we would talk on the phone for hours.

Soon after Shia and I became friends, Maya (let's call her Maya) joined us. Maya was a skinny little thing with a crop of wild

hair, dirty shoes, and disheveled clothes from running around playing basketball all day. She was the one who introduced me and Shia to the concept of sharing physical affection. This is something I had briefly experienced the year before with my then best friend—let's call her Lina. She was a small, birdlike girl who would put her arms around me at the slightest provocation. When eighth grade came around and we no longer shared any classes, Lina began distancing herself from me, but I always remembered how soft she felt in my arms and the surge of warmth that would go through me whenever I held her.

Even now I remember the day of our group kiss. It was during our meager 15-minute lunch break; we were all happily sucking on ice lollies when Maya pulled Shia and me close and tried to kiss us both on the lips at the same time. Suddenly I had two orange-flavored mouths on mine, slick with saliva and melted ice. It ended too quickly for me to process anything, and afterward we all giggled nervously. But something shifted subtly after that—there was an added physicality to our friendship. I would casually caress Shia's back while talking to her, or cuddle into her while we sat side by side. We never did anything overtly sexual; it could all be placed firmly in the realm of "friendly affection." At that point I had no clue that the comfort I felt when touching my best friend would feel more or less the same as the pleasure I would derive from touching my first (and only) boyfriend 12 years later.

My family got satellite television in 1999, and I quickly became hooked on the music channels. One day I was watching one of them after school—probably MTV India—and I saw a video that spun my head around. It was for Aerosmith's song

"Crazy," and it was EPIC. A six-minute, 16-second narrative from 1994, it tells the story of two teenage best friends, played by Liv Tyler and Alicia Silverstone, who cut school to go on a road trip. They begin their journey by stripping off their button-downs and flinging them into the wind (don't worry—they have demure white camis on underneath), and singing along to the radio at the top of their lungs. They stop at a gas station, where they squeeze into a photo booth together, coming out a few seconds later wearing different clothes. They slip a photo strip into the cashier's hands on their way out; his expression is enough to confirm the nature of its contents.

From there the girls make a stop at a strip club on amateur night. This, unsurprisingly, is the scene that really captivated my 13-year-old imagination. Silverstone, dressed in a man's suit and hat, makes an entrance with Tyler, who is giggly and girly in a crop top and white flares. Tyler takes a turn onstage, and while there's a whole audience watching, it's obvious she's performing for just one person: her best friend.

They use their prize money from the strip club to rent a motel room, and we see them jumping on the bed together, then the video cuts to the next morning, as they sleepily emerge from their room, blinking in the sunlight. What exactly happened between the romp on the bed and the morning after is anyone's guess, and at 13 I didn't think about the sequence of events. What I noticed was the way Tyler and Silverstone looked at each other. It was the way Shia and I looked at each other—the same loving glances, the same smiles.

The video's last scene restores heteronormative safety to the proceedings in the form of a ripped, shirtless dude on a tractor, but after a quick skinny-dip the girls ditch him and drive off on their own. We don't know where they're going, but we can only guess that there are more adventures to come.

That video gave me a new thought: Girls could like girls the way girls liked boys. *I'm a lesbian*, I told myself. *I like girls.* I wasn't totally comfortable with this realization. Normal girls liked boys, so why did I like girls? The obvious answer was that I wasn't normal. I tried to rationalize my unwelcome desires, writing in my journal, "Some girls are born lesbian, they are naturally lesbian. Other girls are forced to turn to lesbianism because they are ignored by boys." I fell in the latter category, I told myself. If only a guy would pay attention to me, I wouldn't go for girls. I often told Shia that I wished she was a boy, and she would respond that she wished *I* was a boy instead.

My first proper kiss was with her, about a month later. It was the last day of school before vacation in October, and we were hugging goodbye, when suddenly I turned my face toward hers and kissed her. She kissed me back, and there we stood, in front of a classroom full of people, kissing each other like we never wanted to stop. It couldn't have lasted more than a few seconds, but it felt like hours. When we broke off, she smiled at me, and we became the talk of the entire school. I kissed her a few more times that year, but it never felt as special as the first time.

That January, my mother found the letters Shia and I had written to each other. Each one spanned several pages and included the pet names we called each other, as well as our innermost thoughts, wishes, and desires. That bundle of letters, wrapped in a plastic bag, was one of the most precious things I had ever owned, and I kept it hidden, lest my mother find it. But find it she did, and she read every single one of the letters as I watched. She declared them "lesbian filth" and made me tear them to pieces. "She is my friend, just my friend," I sobbed as I ripped the frail blue paper in two with trembling hands. I was forced to cut off contact with Shia after that.

Thankfully, the school year ended in June, and the long summer vacation arrived. When we went back, Shia and I were in different classes and hardly talked to each other. A few months later I had my first real crush on a boy, and I all but forgot about my year of "aberrant" love.

Since Shia, I have had intense friendships with many female "best friends" that have easily been as romantic as any of my heterosexual relationships. I've slept with three of my "best friends"—one of my them even became my girlfriend for a while. She remains the only person (besides myself) that I've ever had an orgasm with. But for some reason I can't bring myself to define these relationships with women the same way I define those with men. Somewhere in my head I still hear myself saying that the only reason I look at girls is that I can't get a guy. Objectively I know this isn't true, but that's how I act—I don't get together with girls if there's a boy around.

I stopped sleeping with women in 2010, the year I got my first boyfriend. There is one thing I got from him that I never got from girls: the comfort of knowing that I *fit in*, that I'm "normal" and not "too fat to get a guy." These days, I deal with my attraction to women by avoiding them altogether, except for very clearly stated platonic connections. My sexuality remains as confusing to me as ever, and thinking about it only makes it worse, so I don't. In a way, I am no different now than I was at 13, trying to manage desires I didn't understand but which seemed dangerous somehow.

I don't know what to call this tangled web that is my sexuality, but I know what it looks like. It looks like two girls running away together, rejecting society, rejecting even boys, and choosing each other for now and forever. I dream those dreams still: road trips and campfires and secret romps in shady motel rooms. In my head I am still back in 1999, heading off on adventures with my best friend, arm in arm, my head tucked into the crook of her neck, with nothing between us and the vast unknown except for our love. ☆

TEEN ANGST CIRCUS

DEDICATED TO THE SMALL CHALLENGES THAT CAN RUIN YOUR DAY.

BY ANA AND KENDRA

TEEN ANGST CIRCUS

BAD HAIR DAY

CAN IT BE TAMED ?!

WHAT WILL IT DO NEXT?

NO CHILDREN ALLOWED! TOO SCARY!

TEEN ANGST CIRCUS

THE MOST TERRIFYING THING YOU WILL EVER SEE.....

THE TEENAGE BEDROOM!

WHAT'S THAT NOISE? WHAT'S THAT SMELL? WHAT DID I STEP ON?

DO NOT ENTER

TEEN ANGST CIRCUS

THE AMAZING ACT OF PERFECTING WINGED EYELINER

YOU'LL BE AT THE EDGE OF YOUR SEAT!

☆ may cause attraction to performer ☆

THE 27 CLUB

A weirdly large number of musical geniuses died at the age of 27.
I thought I had to do the same if I was going to make anything great.
By Stephanie. Illustration by Esme.

When Kurt Cobain was found dead—from an apparently self-inflicted gunshot wound—on April 8, 1994, his mother, Wendy O'Connor, said something mysterious to their local paper, *The Daily World*: "Now he's gone and joined that stupid club. I told him not to join that stupid club."

The "stupid club" she was talking about doesn't hold meetings—all its members are dead (though one can only imagine the band they could form in heaven). Known as the 27 Club, it's a list of rock stars who died tragically at the age of 27. Among its most famous members are Brian Jones, the Rolling Stones guitarist who drowned in a swimming pool in 1969; Jimi Hendrix, who purportedly choked on his own vomit while under the influence of barbiturates in 1970; Janis Joplin, who died 16 days after Jimi, from a heroin overdose; Jim Morrison of the Doors, 1971, cause undetermined but seemingly drug related; Chris Bell, Big Star founder and songwriter, car crash, 1978; D. Boon of the Minutemen, van accident, 1985; Hole bassist Kristen Pfaff, heroin overdose, 1994; Richey Edwards of the Manic Street Preachers, who suffered from depression and disappeared without a trace in 1995; and Amy Winehouse, who was found dead on her bed, surrounded by empty vodka bottles, in 2011.

Ever a huge nerd, I did some research. I already knew how Jimi, Janis, and Jim had died because I'd gone through a '60s phase in seventh grade

(before I discovered grunge), but I hadn't realized that they'd all been the same age. Twenty-seven. Eerie. Messed-up. But *legendary*. I was (and still am) obsessed with myths, and here was one that was going on in the real world. The old myths I read about in books were invented to help humans explain things like why the seasons change, but that's just another way of saying they help us make sense of the bad in the world. The 27 Club did that for me—it gave me a way to understand the climate of my own life.

Like many of Kurt Cobain's fans, I was devastated when he died. I was a freshman in high school struggling with depression, self-injury, and being bullied, and Nirvana was my favorite band. Kurt had been an outsider like me, and if he was able to become insanely famous and adored, maybe the world was a more accepting and less cruel place than it seemed to me at the time. In the journal entry I wrote the day I learned the news of his death, I was straight-up pissed. I called him "dumb" and wondered if he'd considered his wife or their daughter. I questioned why people take their own lives, asked Kurt why he did it, and said I never thought he was "like that." Meaning suicidal. Meaning not "strong enough" to fight through his depression. But I knew why—not why he, specifically, chose suicide, but why *anyone* might feel like doing that. By that point in my high school career I'd been sent to the guidance counselor for writing poems that "sounded suicidal" ("I lie there, thinking, wondering / How would it be if I were gone?"—in retrospect, I understand my eighth grade English teacher's concern), and there had been a couple of incidents where my best friend had to wrestle a bottle of Tylenol from my hand. Though I couldn't explain it to her or even articulate

it in my tortured poetry, sometimes it felt like I was trying to contain a thunderstorm inside of me—I had flashes of anger that burned my stomach, I often wanted to cry so hard I couldn't breathe, and the world around me was tinged gray like I was living inside a dark cloud. Suicide would be a way of stopping those feelings. I think I was angry at Kurt for being "like that" because I was afraid that I might be "like that." I wanted him to be stronger to assure me that I could be too.

In the days following Kurt's death, I read every article about his life that I could get my hands on. His mother's quote about "that stupid club" made such an impact on me that I memorized it. I found it weirdly comforting, because if so many of these brilliant artists struggled with depression and/or addiction, that meant it might be possible to make something beautiful out of my own dark feelings. Even though they died young, they had managed to leave behind an incredible legacy, and that was inspiring.

The most fascinating story in all 27 Club lore is undoubtedly Robert Johnson's. Johnson was a master of blues guitar whom people like Eric Clapton, Keith Richards, and Jack White count among their biggest influences. But he wasn't a prodigy—the story goes that in the beginning, even though he loved the blues, he was terrible at playing it. Then one day he disappeared, and when he returned to his hometown of Robinson, Mississippi, a year or two later, he was *scary* good. Like, *supernaturally* good. A legend sprang up that he had had a midnight meeting with the Devil himself at a crossroads in Clarksdale, 50 miles away. Satan had offered Johnson musical genius in exchange for his immortal soul, and Johnson took the deal. Sadly, the Devil didn't have to wait long to collect on his end of the bargain: Johnson died, apparently of strychnine poisoning, seven or eight years later, at, yes, the age of 27.

Back when I first read that story, I decided that the Devil had written Kurt's, Janis's, Jimi's, Kristen's, and the rest of the club's deaths into the fine print of Johnson's contract, and that metaphorically, this meant an early death was the price that Satan had decided all mortals should pay for artistic brilliance. I didn't even believe in the Devil, but this made a good story, and even back then I thought of myself as a storyteller. I was also a depressed person looking to give her depression a purpose.

Around the same time I first heard Nirvana, I discovered another bastion of teen angst: Sylvia Plath. Her poetry spoke to me even more directly than the band's music, because she wasn't just a tormented artist, she was also a woman, and her writing seemed to capture with intimate precision the rage and sorrow I was battling. The first thing you learn when you start reading about Sylvia Plath is that she killed herself when she was 30 years old. I remember hearing this fact in English class, I had mixed feelings about it. I empathized with her depression and heartache, but I wondered what more there was to her life, and to her art. If she had lived longer, would she have written something completely different from *The Bell Jar*—something more optimistic? Or did being a creative woman mean you had to be tortured until it killed you? I noticed that people talked about Sylvia and Janis differently from how they talked about Jimi, Kurt, and Jim. The men were revered as gods, practically, while the women were more often seen as tragic figures who just couldn't handle life.

I went back and forth a lot about whether it was good or bad to die for your art. On one hand it looked noble somehow, and, more important, it seemed like a nice escape plan from pain. On the other, it seemed unnecessary—Courtney Love was a hero of mine, too, and she was a *survivor*, which I thought was even more powerful. Part of me wanted to be a survivor, too, but sometimes it felt like I would never escape the tumult of emotion inside of me, so I might as well embrace it and use it to make

stuff, and then when I didn't feel like I could cope with it anymore I could just let my illness consume me.

I had a lot of friends who lived by the maxim (from the 1949 movie *Knock on Any Door* and not, as it's often misattributed, uttered by James Dean) "Live fast, die young, leave a good-looking corpse." In practice this meant they engaged in a lot of wild and crazy behavior. I didn't necessarily care about the dying young part, but I naïvely believed that living fast was a necessity for making art. People like Courtney, Kurt, the Beats, Hunter S. Thompson, and everyone else I was reading and listening to at the time seemed to bear this out. I needed *experiences* to write about, and they had to be outrageous to be interesting. While I didn't necessarily take risks just to gather material, I gravitated toward and tolerated risky situations throughout my teenage years because I felt like they fueled my work. I stayed in bad relationships with addicts and abusive guys, I pushed my friends away so I could wallow in my anger and my sadness, I drank too much, I did drugs. I did these things because I was depressed, but I had also decided that being a writer justified my self-destructive behavior, and that if I got treatment for my depression I would lose my ability to write. Being healthy meant being "normal," and I'd bought into the myth that "normal" people couldn't be creative.

But drugs didn't work for me the way they did for Hunter S. Thompson. I'd get high or drunk and the words would just flow out of me, but when I looked at them later they were gibberish. The characters and stories, which at the time I thought were really promising, were flat and empty, because I was.

After a few years of this, my writing slowed down. I ran out of ideas. It became clear to me then that self-destruction was not actually a magical fountain of talent or inspiration. So I finally started going to therapy, stopped using drugs, moderated my drinking, and focused

on my writing. And instead of dying at 27, I sold my first book that year. And a year later I sold another one.

In 2009, *Demo*, my college's alumni publication, ran an interview with me when my second book, *Ballads of Suburbia*, came out. That novel was informed by my struggles with depression, addiction, and self-injury, and the interview was accompanied by a photo of me looking haunted in the park where I did drugs as a teen and a splashy pull quote: "I had to go to dark places." Staring at it, I felt like I'd arrived. All that pain had been worth it.

I always tell people that it's better to pour your dark feelings into creating something rather than into destroying yourself, and that is how I handle those emotions now. But after *Ballads* came out, I spent years worrying that I had used all my darkness up, and without that, what was there to write about? Well, a lot of things. First of all, you don't have to *live* something in order to be able to *imagine* it. And second (and more important for my mental health), I had to remind myself that one of the most incredible things that art can do is to bring beauty to the world. I had been obsessed with darkness because it seemed "honest" and "real," but I was ignoring other honest, real feelings— like love, happiness, and excitement. I still write about sad stuff, because I think it's important to acknowledge it, but I have a lot of fun writing about lighter things too these days. That's the part of life that's important for me to acknowledge. That's the part that made me live past 27. I wish it could have done the same for all of those artists whose work has meant so much to the world. I wish they'd never gone and joined that stupid club. ⚡

USE WHAT YOU HAVE:
AN INTERVIEW WITH KIM GORDON

On art, power, and the enduring appeal of Tim Riggins.
By Jessica. Illustration by Allegra.

Thirty-odd years ago Kim Gordon was an L.A. girl fresh out of art school and set loose on the New York City art scene. She co-founded the influential band Sonic Youth in 1981 and has since issued 15 studio albums with them, as well as several with her side band, Free Kitten. She is also a painter and a writer (a memoir is forthcoming); she has designed two clothing lines (X-Girl and Mirror/Dash); and she's inspired many other women to pick up instruments and start their own bands. Along the way, she ditched the Manhattan rock scene for the familial idyll of Northampton, Massachusetts, and scheduled Sonic Youth's tours around the school year while she raised her daughter, Coco, who's now in college.

Since Sonic Youth went on hiatus in 2011, on the heels of Kim's split with her husband and bandmate, Thurston Moore, Gordon's creative output has only increased: A survey of her artwork will be shown in New York this fall, and she's been busy performing with her new duo, Body/Head, a collaboration with the guitarist Bill Nace. Together the two make ragged, minimal experimental unrock that features Gordon howling, whispering, sounding alive and driven. After decades of hearing her as part of an ensemble, it's thrilling to hear her this new way, in the spotlight, but cool as ever.

JESSICA What was your first apartment in New York like?

KIM GORDON Other than sublets, my first one was a railroad apartment with the bathtub in the kitchen and these two beautiful arches—a very classic Lower East Side tenement apartment. A million coats of paint on the wall, but crackly. Cockroaches scurrying around. It was kind of scary when the lights were off. It had a really nice ceiling.

How did it feel to be in the city by yourself and starting out as an artist?

It was kind of lonely. It was exciting. Everything seemed to have so much significance. I remember I saw Andy Warhol once crossing the street. You'd kind of hear about things going on, and it sort of felt like, *How do I get into this world?* The nightclubs were fun around then. There was no sign outside—it was always kind of an illegal club. You were going there to see what was going to happen and what the fuss was all about who was playing. Everything I went to see was a new experience.

What made you think you could be a musician? Or did you just already have a sense of permission?

I fell into it, really. It was nothing I aspired to. It was almost like an art project that became something else—I started playing music when the artist Dan Graham asked me to start an all-girl band with these two other girls for a performance piece of his. I was writing [a lot] at the time. No-wave bands were playing downtown—it was anarchistic, free music. Being around those bands, I felt like, *I could do this.*

Musicians sometimes talk about performance as a way to be more real or to try on other identities. I am wondering how performance allows you to be your "real" self and how it allows you to be "fake."

Sometimes performing, if all the aspects are going well, allows you to be in the moment—you lose a certain self consciousness; you are not really aware of yourself or your body in a way that is separate from the music. It's a visceral experience and a physical experience—you feel in the moment, and it's a really great feeling. Whatever ambition you have, you don't really think about it much. Sometimes I am aware that certain moves are considered—like, people like it if you are very assertive onstage, if you lead the audience, so to speak. That is part of the whole rock-star posturing. [With Body/Head] I have shied away from that a little bit.

Do you feel less bound by expectation with this new band?

People might have incredible expectations and hopes of what they want the music to be. But you can never control any of that. Nothing is ever going to be Sonic Youth. Anyone who thinks they are going to get that, they are not going to get that.

Where do you get your power from?

That's a tough question. I don't think of myself as powerful. I somehow have this *drive*. I really don't try to overthink it too much, but I think I use my weaknesses and turn them into strengths. It's a weird way to think about things—in terms of strengths and weaknesses. Nothing is black-and-white, nothing is strong or weak, it's a combination of both. But you use what you have. I like working from a place of not having anything, working with limitations. The idea that you don't have limitations creates a whole other set of problems and pressure. I know women who are very Type A, who think of themselves as strong and confident—but I always overthink things. I am looking for, I guess, some recognition or approval. At my core, though, I feel confident. I don't question myself.

Was there a catalyst for your feminism or was it always part of your understanding of the world?

I don't think I consciously became a feminist—it was a pretty gradual awakening. I was a tomboy when I was young, and I had an older brother I was always competing against, so I knew there were double standards. I never really wanted to grow up and be a mother or a housewife; I really just wanted to be an artist. I wasn't really aware of how sexist the art world was, I guess, growing up. I was never politically active the way, say, Kathleen Hanna was—she really took action when she felt the need to, when she was aware of the issues and aware of her surroundings. I was older than the hardcore scene—we were never on the receiving end of the mosh pit. I grew up in a weird time. I was too young to be a hippie, but I was around it. You were supposed to have really relaxed sexual ideas and attitudes—everyone did the whole free-love thing. But it wasn't comfortable. And I also felt, when [Sonic Youth] started going to England, that there were more ageist and sexist attitudes in the press [there]. Guys would interview you who were too cowardly to actually confront you about something in a question, but they would write really snide things afterwards. But then when I was writing songs, I felt like there were so many experiences as a woman that you can write about that had not been written about—rather than conventional relationship songs.

I think a lot of people imagine you to be the coolest mom, but when you're a teenager, no matter how cool your mom is, she's like Stella Dallas—a source of endless embarrassment to you. Can you burst our bubble a little? Was there ever a time when Coco was younger when

you were like, "You are not leaving the house dressed like that!"?

It was never about what she wore. There was some R&B stuff that she liked—or the super-dirty rap that she likes now—and I am just like, *I don't get it.* Musically it's not that interesting to me, and as far as I can tell it's not ironic. [*Laughs*] I just can't.

So, can we talk about [the *Friday Night Lights* character] Tim Riggins? Are you still in the throes of your obsession? What is the locus of his appeal for you?

In the context of *Friday Night Lights*, his character is supposed to be the brooding running back with cute looks who is not really verbal, so every time he opens his mouth there is the drama of what's he going to say? Is it going to be incredibly stupid? Ultimately he would say something vulnerable or minimal but also smart. He showed himself to be a lover, not a fighter.

I feel like there is not a female cultural analogue to that character.

There's really not. I have had this conversation with people. Who do you think?

I am not super aware of TV, but I feel like Connie Britton could be it.

Oh yeah! That's true. Bill Nace, my partner in Body/Head, always brings her up. He thinks she's hot, and so do I. I am totally into *Nashville*. Her guitar player/love interest on the show is the new Tim Riggins to me.

TOTALLY. OK, so I have an important final question about a topic very close to Rookie's heart. What's your favorite, most crucial pizza topping?

Whoa. OK. My fave, most crucial pizza topping has to be red pepper flakes, if we are talking New York–style pizza by the slice. Red pepper flakes are *it*. 🍕

SEPTEMBER 2013: VICTORY

HAPPY BIRTHDAY, ROOKIES!

As of September 5t, Rookie is two years old! Crazy, right? I can't quite wrap my brain around it. What I CAN wrap my brain around is that I am a happier person because every month, a bunch of talented people make a bunch of exquisite stuff, and then a bunch of smart, funny, thoughtful people read and look at and comment on it. What lovelier cycle is there? The MENSTRUAL one? How CLOUDS get made? (Sorry, Mother Nature!) You guys are the best, and we get to do this only because you read it, and we get better when you tell us what you need or share your own work, so please continue to do all of the above, along with continuing to be your beautiful selves.

This month's theme is VICTORY, and I must credit Amy Rose for the terrific idea. Here's what Anaheed said about it when we asked our staffers for ideas:

It's important to talk about stuff like depression and sadness and the pain of being a teenager and the pain of being a girl in an anti-girl world. It is essential that we-as-a-society listen to girls when they tell us that stuff, and I love that Rookie is a place where they can feel safe sharing it and, in doing so, can see that they're not alone and can maybe even feel a little bit taken care of. But it's equally important, I think, to do something we aren't quite as wont to do, for so many reasons (including: healing seems more urgent, sad times are less talked about in general and we wanna fill a vacuum, as a group we tend to be maybe slightly more prone to depression/anxiety than a random sampling of the population—though maybe that could be said of any group of mostly young girls), and that is to CELEBRATE our VICTORIES. We are encouraged to be insecure. But it's like, you know Beyoncé doesn't give a shit if people think she's "stuck-up" or "too intimidating" or "full of herself." I see this month as VERY BEYONCÉ. Also: Gabby Douglas, Taylor Swift, Michelle Obama, Angelina Jolie. People who are unapologetic about how awesome they are.

I also see VICTORY as: Standing up to people. Standing up especially to AUTHORITY. Being proud of yourself, both for stuff that other people are impressed by and for stuff that other people might laugh at you for. SCHOOL SPIRIT—even if you're the black-eyeliner-wearing alterna-kid smoking weed under the bleachers, it's all right to have your heart filled with LOVE for and LOYALTY to the people around you, even the ones you don't know. Rookie is your virtual cheerleader this month, being all RAH RAH every time you accomplish something, big or small.

I like this idea for September because high school is so depressing!! I had forgotten exactly HOW shitty it was and then at some point this spring there was a day that Tavi and Ruby were both texting me photos from INSIDE THE WALLS OF THE AMERICAN HIGH SCHOOL and I was like OH MY GOD IT'S EVEN WORSE THAN I THOUGHT. And so September seems like a time when everyone needs a boost.

HATERS AND LOVERS OF HIGH SCHOOL ALIKE, this one's for you. Personally, I go back and forth (like most people?), but I'll save all those thoughts for some giant reflection at the end of the year when I graduate. *Graduate!* Senior year! WEIRD. I got pretty sentimental about it on my first day of classes last week, so here's a playlist I made of 13 songs about being between the ages of 13 and 18.

Enjoy this month, and this school year!

LOVE, TAVI

WONDER YEARS

1. Thirteen – Big Star
2. Fourteen – Beat Happening
3. Fifteen – Taylor Swift
4. Sixteen Candles – The Crests
5. Sixteen – No Doubt
6. Sixteen Going On Seventeen – The Sound of Music
7. What A Nice Way to Turn 17 – The Crystals
8. At Seventeen – Janis Ian
9. Anthems For A 17 Year Old Girl – Broken Social Scene
10. Seventeen – Ladytron
11. Dancing Queen – ABBA
12. Edge of Seventeen – Stevie Nicks
13. I'm Eighteen – Mr. Rosso

Design by Sonja. Title lettering by Hattie. Playlist artwork by Minna. Illustration by Allegra. Skater photos by Allyssa and Shriya. Dancer photos by Lindsey Rome.

GOODBYE GOOGLY EYES

I haven't been single in more than a decade.
By Anna M. Playlist by Pixie, artwork by Minna.

It was July, and the city was in the middle of a heat wave. This boy N. and I ducked into the air-conditioned Guggenheim to escape the heat. I was wearing a dress with no pockets and I did not want to check a bag, so I'd asked him to put all my stuff (ID, debit card, MetroCard, keys) in his pocket. So there's the setup.

We stood outside on line melting for a solid half-hour before we were allowed into the building, which is built like a giant spiraling maze. It was the Turrell exhibit, this light show that is super popular, so it was jam-packed with all these fancy people lying in the middle of the floor in their fancy clothes, staring at light beaming down from the ceiling, trying to have some transcendental experience or something. It felt like a joke to me, or like a big psychological experiment: *How can we get a room full of strangers in their fanciest duds to lie on a floor and stare at a ceiling?* N. and I lay down. Afterward, we circled up the spiraling stairs and there was a strip of white light emanating from a corner of a wall and a long line of people waiting to walk up to that corner and look at the light. We got on line.

"What's this line for? Does something, like, happen when you walk up to the light?" a young girl asked me. Her friend tittered.

"Ermmm, no. Nothing happens," I tittered back, feeling foolish for having joined the line.

I'll admit that I'm not great at appreciating contemporary art. I mean, I like the artwork just fine, but sometimes the whole museum thing throws me off. That's what I was thinking about as N. and I circled around that giant white maze—remember: me pocketless, him carrying all my stuff.

Right then this gallery attendant wearing a pin that said LET'S TALK ART walked over and started chatting me up. I babbled to him about how *weird* museums are and don't you think it's kind of *absurd*, all these people waiting on these long lines to just like *stare really hard*, and what do they expect will happen? And blah blah blah blah blah. I was just running my mouth, and he was running his

mouth too. Then I turned and saw that N. was waiting near the room's exit, staring me down. He and I made eye contact, but the dude was speaking and then I was speaking back and it didn't seem like that big of a deal? It was like four minutes total. I kept on trying to signal to N., *I'll be there in a sec*, and I swear it wasn't that big of a deal!?! (I admit it, I'm a flirt. I get a little close to people, and the attendant was hot.)

We talked for another couple of minutes, then I looked back and N. was gone. Gone. I scrambled frantically around the museum trying to find him. He wouldn't just *leave* when he had possession of my *everything*, would he? I ran around in my pocketless dress, searching for him, for over an hour, but he was just *not there*. I was all alone—no phone no money no keys no identification no water no nothing—abandoned in this big crowded lonesome city.

~ * ~ * ~

I know that not much happens in this anecdote, but I find it a little too perfect, too allegorical, not to use here. A boy and I were in this place and he had my everything—my identification and my ability to get around on my own and access to my own resources—in his pocket. This is a hilariously fitting metaphor for how I feel when I'm in a relationship with a guy. Through no fault of theirs (it wasn't N.'s idea to hold on to all my shit), it always ends up like this: The guy takes possession of my identity, my mobility, my everything, and I am rendered utterly dependent on him.

~ * ~ * ~

I found my way home eventually. I got there by sheepishly approaching the LET'S TALK ART attendant and explaining the situation, then following him to the coat check, where he brought out his laptop and I went on my Gmail and convinced my friend George, who lives a time zone away in Chicago, to call up N. and persuade him to come back to the

museum and return my stuff. I waited on Fifth Avenue, sweating in the heat, and then finally N. came storming up and said, "I'm going to get DRUNK," and he shoved my possessions at me and stomped off. And the strangest part of that strange day came at the end, when I was passing around a bottle of wine with my friends, and I found myself laughing. Laughing, not crying, because, duh, I was OK. I was always OK.

~ * ~ * ~

A year ago I wrote my first article for Rookie, about the philosopher Simone de Beauvoir. I talked about the figure she calls the Woman in Love, a woman who loses her identity and personality as soon as she's in a relationship. She drops all the activities she once took pleasure in, because she feels fulfilled simply by virtue of being loved by a man. It's what she was born to "do."

What I didn't say in that piece is that when I wrote it I was struggling with the fresh realization that from my very first kiss, I had spent most of my life as the Woman in Love. I got my first boyfriend when I was 15, and since then I had never not been in a relationship with a dude. I jumped from boyfriend to boyfriend, each one chosen because they had some quality I wanted for myself. When I wanted to become a Marxist, I dated one instead. When I got sick of hearing people talk politics with thin-lipped gravitas and wanted to try being a fun-loving fashionista, I dated a fun-loving apolitical hipster (and then another one). When I was tired of parties and wanted to believe that life was Realer and fuller of Permanent Truths than my life was at the time, I ran away with a hippie. Note: At no time during any of this did I go off on my own to read Marx, or shake my booty like an Independent Woman, or meditate alone in the desert. Instead I attached myself to some guy and hoped his qualities would rub off on me. I depended on him to hold on to everything I wanted to be, because I lacked the confidence to develop those qualities in myself, by myself, for myself.

If I date someone who is smart, well, that means I'm smart too, right? Because they're dating me? This went on for a decade.

~ * ~ * ~

When I'm in a relationship (i.e., almost all the time) I very quickly lose interest in pursuing my own activities or spending any time away from my lover. I'd rather spend my time *understanding him* (my new hobby). I get super attached to the role of Woman in Love, wanting to make non-stop googly eyes with the boy, wanting to say *I love you* and hear *I love you* back every hour on the hour, forgetting about my friends, forgetting about my own life separate from him.

I know that some of these symptoms overlap with those of the early stages of *real* true love, when you're busy fusing souls with another human being and you can't help thinking about them *all the time*; sometimes googly eyes are dead serious. But for me, all too often, they aren't. It's more like I'll see a guy that I want to be, and I'll make a calculated decision to fall in love with him, and then I pop in my googly eyes like a pair of contact lenses.

But if you never remove 'em, contact lenses dry up and get itchy and eventually shrivel up and die. After six or so months of dating someone, I'll wake up one morning and realize that I haven't spent a single day alone in my head for who knows how long, and I'll look at the guy and my googly eyes will malfunction, or maybe they slipped off while I slept. Then I become quiet, depressed, irritable—but I'll be too scared of the idea of being alone to end it, so I'll stay, and pretend. Finally, things fall apart. We break up. And then the panic sets in: How I am supposed to get by, day by day, and stand on my own two feet and *live a life*…on my own? I don't know how people do this, how do they live? How do they walk and smile and nod and talk and just survive and be a person? HOW DO YOU DO THAT?

That is what it feels like. It feels too hard. And so I set my eyes on another dude and put those googly eyes back on and focus all my energy on loving *him*. And then the cycle starts again…

~ * ~ * ~

Things have changed a lot in the year since I wrote that first Rookie essay. One of the biggest changes is that, believe it or not, I don't want a boyfriend anymore. I would actually rather be alone. I don't know when or how precisely this shift happened, but I think that a lot of it has to do with having published that article in the first place. For what felt like the first time, I had done what I wanted to do—to write about what I felt and thought—and I put myself out there, out in the world, and it was all right. I didn't collapse. I got positive feedback. And that gave me the confidence to keep writing, which I love doing and which makes me feel like the world is actually a fun place to be in. And when I am writing, I like to be alone in my head, so that the world can bubble up in prose.

So then I started wanting to hang out by myself, and I found out that it was actually great being alone, walking on my own two feet. I stopped wanting to give all my energy/time/love to one person; I stopped wanting to spill out all my emotions and words onto one dude. I wanted to save that energy, those words, for that quality time spent between me and my laptop.

In *The Second Sex*, Simone de Beauvoir says that one reason many of us act like the Woman in Love is that we're taught to be *objects*—we're here to be gazed upon, to be taken care of, to help other people achieve their goals in life while we are ashamed to admit to our own, and after a while we forget about them anyway. Boys, meanwhile, are taught that their value comes from *acting*, doing things, making things, shaping the world. *The Second Sex* was written in 1949, and things are not *quite* so bad anymore, and to tell you the truth, it never made sense to me that I was so scared of being an actor-upon-the-world that I chose instead to play a helpless, obedient '50s-style wife. It still doesn't make sense. But the point is that I was that scared, and I did choose to act that way. I lived fearfully.

And then I proved de Beauvoir correct in another way: I escaped the Woman in Love problem by *doing* something, instead of just *existing near* someone else

who was doing things. I had always wished I had more self-confidence and less fear, but you don't get those things just by wishing—at least I don't. But once I started writing—*doing* what I wanted, on my own, and in my own voice—I magically gained that elusive confidence without even asking for it. Just like that, my seemingly perpetual Woman in Love cycle was broken.

And I'm realizing something about myself these days. I'm kind of cool. I like myself. I'm ambitious. A good egg. A fun date. Frankly, the only person I'm interested in spending that much time with these days is myself.

~ * ~ * ~

When I pitched this article, I said that I'd write about how I want to be an Independent Lady for the first time in my life and how that feels great but I also feel guilty about it, like I'm worried that if I lose touch with the Woman in Love, I'll become loveless and unfeeling and morph into another gruesome female stereotype: the cold bitch in a power suit. After that incident at the Guggenheim, I tried to make up with N. because I felt guilty and nervous about chucking those googly eyes. But I couldn't force them back on, and I didn't want to. Plus, I think cold bitches in power suits are hot. So you know what? I don't feel guilty. *Eh*, I feel. *Suck it.* Maybe someday, when I've had enough time with myself, I'll be ready to share my love with another person, in a chiller, more mature manner than before. But for now, I feel good. I feel great. I feel victorious. 👁

BRIGHT LIGHTS
☆ FOR ☆
DARK DAYS

1. Fawkes the Phoenix – John Williams
2. Be Above It – Tame Impala
3. Gotta Get Thru This (D'N'D) Radio Edit – Daniel Bedingfield ☆
4. Shake It Out – Florence + The Machine
☆ 5. Bravado – Lorde ☆
6. Comeback Kid – Sleigh Bells
7. Roar – Katy Perry ☆
8. Obvious Bicycle – Vampire Weekend
9. Dear Prudence – The Beatles
10. Everything Will Be Alright – The Killers ☆
11. One Day Late – Sam Phillips
12. Waltz (Better Than Fine) – Fiona Apple

STAND FOR SOMETHING

Meet six girls who are changing the world.
Interviews by Jamia. Photography by Sandy. Styling by Mike and Claire.
Thanks to Arabelle for doing everyone's makeup and to Cote-Amour for lending us clothes.
All footwear by Dr. Martens.

Every once in a while I'll meet an adult who describes "teenagers today" as lazy, entitled, and narcissistic; apparently your brains have been numbed by hours of playing Halo and posting selfies to your Insta. But as an organizer who cut my teeth working with young female activists, I know firsthand how powerful you all are, especially when you band together to stand up against all kinds of injustice. You inspire me, for real.

That's why I was so excited to get to talk to Kisma, Francesca, Diamond, Alex, Kodi, and Nathania, the six young activists Sandy photographed for this album. Though their tactics—writing, dance, mentoring, speaking out, and organizing—differ, their refusal to accept things the way they are, and their commitment to making their communities and schools better, stronger, and more just and compassionate, unites them (and you, and me). I feel safer, freer, and happier knowing that these girls and others like them are showing up and standing up for what they believe in.

KISMA, 16
Sisters in Strength
(Girls for Gender Equity)

What do you stand for?
I stand for people having respect for one another and following their moral values.

What is Sisters in Strength about?
We are a group of young women of color organizing in our communities to end gender-based violence and harassment.

What does equality mean to you?
Equality means that people of all genders and races can live with the same rights. That's not the definition we have right now—our world is not equal at all.

How do you want your generation to be remembered?
I want to be part of a generation who try to make the world better and who actually use their lives to help someone else. I want

us to do something we can be proud of. It can be as small as making someone happy and as big as inventing something that helps people.

What is one thing students can do to positively change the culture at their schools?
They can take a vow to not encourage sexual harassment in their school—even better, they can vow to prevent it from happening.

What is your biggest wish for the world?
For everyone to have an overwhelmingly happy life—to have total bliss without any sort of anger.

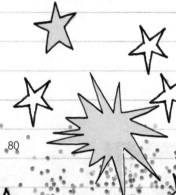

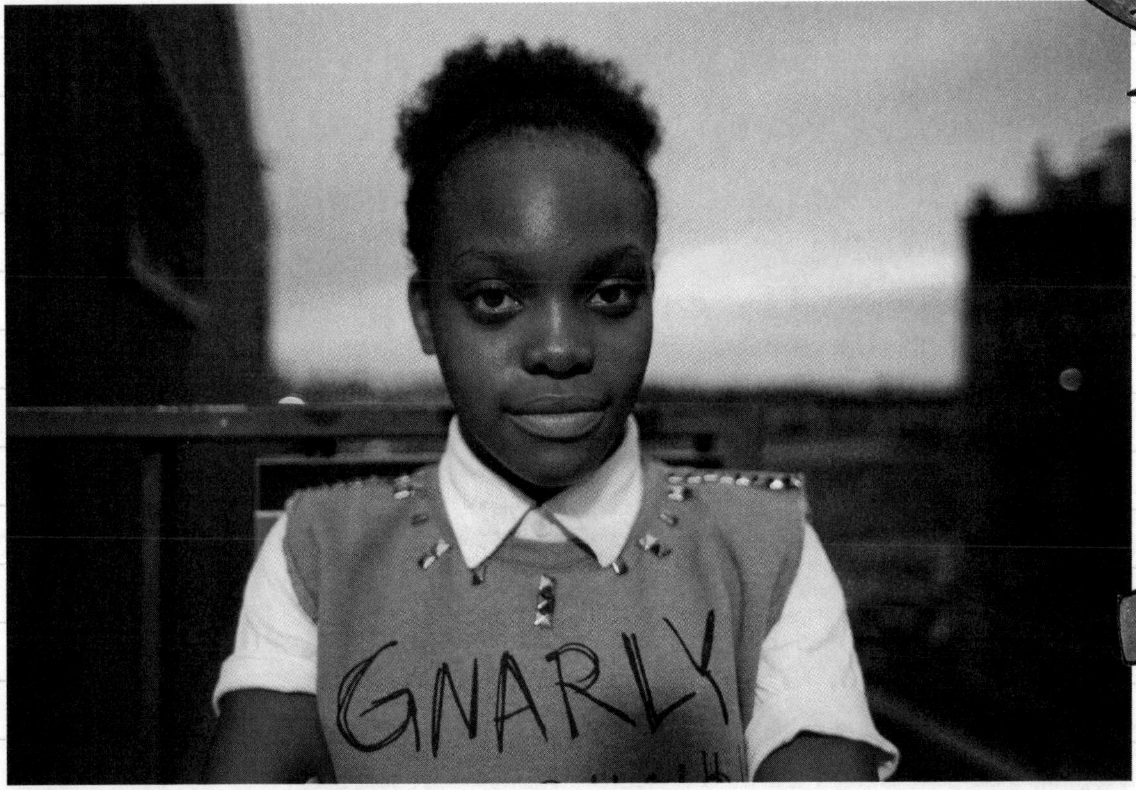
GNARLY

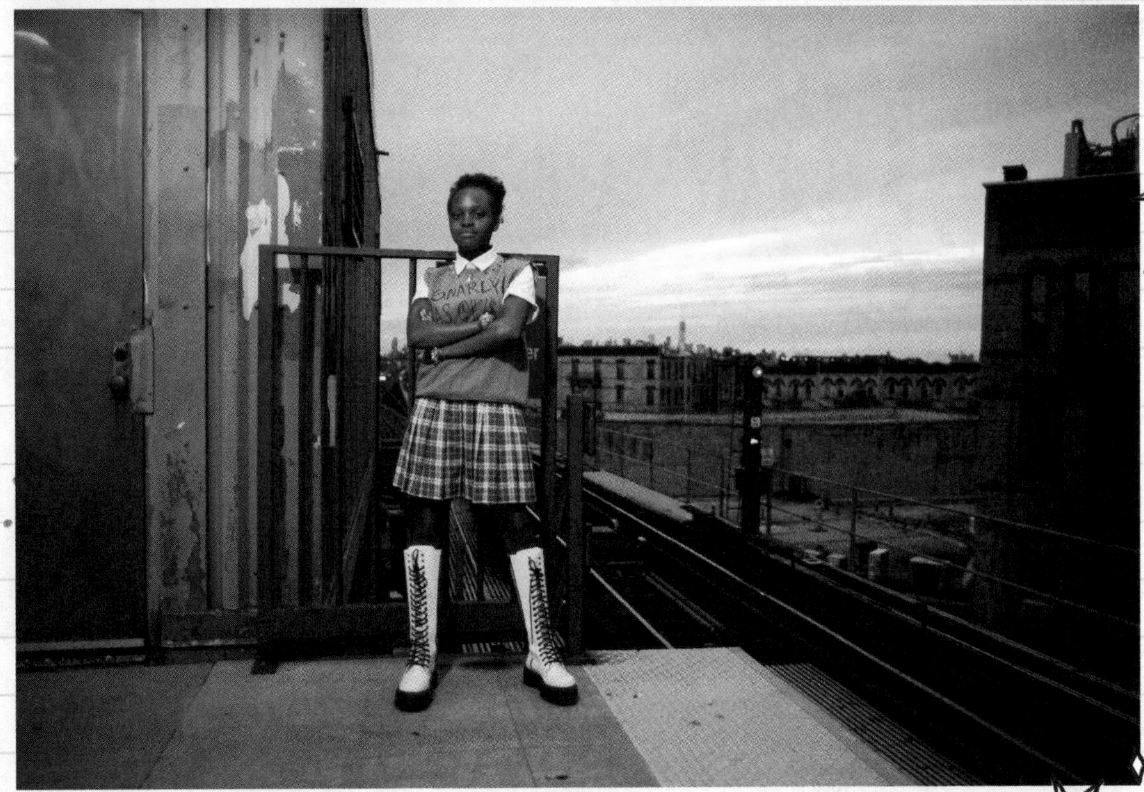

FRANCESCA, 17
Girls Advocating and Innovating the Nation (GAIN)

What do you stand for?
I stand for peace, positivity, and standing up for what you believe in. I also stand for self-expression.

How do you express yourself?
I express myself through the arts. I do a lot of creative writing. I write poetry. I sing. I dance. Anything artistic, I do that.

What's GAIN all about?
I started this organization to empower young women in my community. We focus on building self-esteem in girls when they're young, and to give them the tools they need to get their voices heard.

What led you to start GAIN?
I used to go to school in East New York, one of the tougher neighborhoods in Brooklyn. I noticed that a lot of the girls there seemed like they had low self-esteem. I asked a few friends if they wanted to get together and mentor some of the preteen girls to help build up their confidence, and they said yes. Soon other girls wanted to join us, and I noticed that the girls we were mentoring were starting to become more comfortable in their own skin.

What is the most important thing a mentee has ever taught you?
They all teach me to listen. When you're building a relationship with younger girls, you have to be an active listener. Everyone needs someone who will listen to them.

Adults need to understand how to listen to young people. We are more adventurous, and that makes us better at having the courage to rebel and to start revolutions. Adults can learn a lot from us!

DIAMOND, 18

Teen Activist Project, New York Civil Liberties Union (NYCLU)

What do you stand for?
I stand for freedom of expression.

What does freedom of expression mean to you?
Freedom of expression means that you have the ability to be who you want to be, or say what you want to say, or do what you want to do, without fear of being censored or silenced.

What's an issue that you're concerned about right now?
School bullying. Young people need to raise awareness about it. The bullying is going on among our peers. We go to school with them every day and we know how to speak their language. It is our responsibility to teach one another. New York just passed the Dignity for Students Act, which protects students against all forms of harassment, but a lot of kids don't even know about it. It's important that we educate one another about our legal rights.

What do you do when you're not out there speaking out about the issues?
I'm really into Irish dancing.

Has your experience as an Irish dancer affected your work as an activist?
I've learned a lot from Irish dancing. I've learned how to be an individual. Sometimes you have to do something out of the ordinary to get attention. Before, I was really shy. Irish dancing made me a lot more confident. I learned how to be more expressive in general.

Anything else you want to share with Rookie readers?
I feel like our generation is moving in a positive direction. The only thing is that we all need to learn how to stand up for each other. We need to find commonality with one another and learn how to work together. We are better as a team.

Teen Activist Project, New York Civil Liberties Union (NYCLU)

What do you stand for?
I stand for the power students' voices have to make schools safer, more effective, and more enjoyable places to learn.

Tell me about the Teen Activist Project.
We are organizers and peer educators. We meet once a week to learn about civil liberties and legal issues affecting teenagers in New York. We pass that information on to our peers and try to get them involved in fighting for their own rights.

Why is it important to educate young people specifically about this stuff?
Before I started working with the NYCLU, I had no idea about the amount of policing that happens in schools. We all know that students are walking through metal detectors every day, but it's shocking how many students are brought to court and arrested in schools. Police presence is supposed to promote safety in schools, and while I support safety, pervasive police presence is psychologically harmful for students.

Less than half of New Yorkers between the ages of 18 and 29 cast a ballot last year. It is really important that they know that there are issues at stake that target them very specifically and that their voice needs to be heard. Especially the ones who just graduated from public schools—they have a very important perspective on education policy.

What's the biggest misconception older people have about young people today?
Some people think social media points young people in the wrong direction. Social media is a great outlet for young people to find supportive communities and get involved in activism. It makes activism approachable for people who are any age.

What do you do when you're not informing people of their rights or urging them to vote?
I also co-founded an organization called Teen Concerts NYC that organizes concerts for young musicians in New York. We're still working to get in touch with more musicians, especially young female musicians!

Which freedom fighters have inspired you?
Jane Jacobs was a journalist in the second half of the 20th century who focused on urban planning and social ecology in New York City. She paid attention to nuanced things happening in different neighborhoods, and this is so important in a city as diverse as New York. Jacobs spearheaded the cancellation of the Lower Manhattan Expressway that would have run directly through Washington Square Park and many other things like it. She is inspiring! She didn't have a college degree in urban planning. Her work was so incredible because she was so observant and so involved in her community. This is an important message for activists everywhere—you don't need a formal degree, just a lot of love for your community.

KODI, 17
Girls Advocating and Innovating the Nation (GAIN)

What do you stand for?
I stand for every young girl's voice that hasn't been heard.

As a GAIN mentor, what do you try to teach young girls?
I aspire to be a role model who shows young girls that anything is possible, and that whatever they put their minds to, they can achieve in a positive way.

What's the biggest issue that teenagers are facing in your community right now?
In my community, stop-and-frisk is a big issue right now. There are some kids who are so focused on getting stopped, questioned, and frisked every time they're out in public that their minds aren't on anything else. They're afraid of leaving the house.

How are you taking action on this issue?
I spoke on behalf of New York Civil Liberties Union during the stop-and-frisk court case a while back.

Was that scary?
No. It felt good to speak. There were a lot of other teens there, so I didn't feel alone.

NATHANIA, 16
Sisters in Strength
(Girls for Gender Equity)

What do you stand for?
I stand for teen youth who deny who they really are because they are scared of being judged.

You and Kisma are focused on achieving gender justice in school communities. What can students do to change the culture in their schools?
They can strive to be open-minded and considerate of other people and their needs.

What project or campaign are you most passionate about right now?
I'm passionate about the Audre Lorde Project's Welfare Justice Campaign, which fights discrimination against gender-nonconforming people who are applying for welfare or public assistance. It is very important to talk about issues like this, which a lot of people overlook. It shouldn't be like that.

How do you want your generation to be remembered?
I want my generation to be remembered for being open-minded.

What is your biggest wish for the world?
My biggest wish for the world is for people to stop being scared of being judged, and to just be themselves. I wish we could teach our young men not to rape and abuse, rather than teaching our young women how not to get raped and abused. I wish the world could be a place where anyone and everyone can feel safe and welcome.

THIS IS MY THING:
An Interview With kathleen Hanna

On music, politics, and why cabaret is the most punk-rock thing out there right now.
By Lena. Illustration by Suzy.
Playlist by Dylan, artwork by Minna.

Kathleen Hanna formed the Julie Ruin three years ago in New York with Kathi Wilcox, Kenny Mellman, Sara Landeau, and Carmine Covelli. The band's first album, Run Fast, which came out this month, is full of joyful, rambunctious music. There are moments when it's reminiscent of Le Tigre or Bikini Kill, Kathleen's previous bands, both outspokenly feminist projects, but Run Fast is not a nostalgic or overtly political record. Among other things, Kathleen sings about love, hanging out, and letting your adult self say goodbye to your younger self.

It's the first music Kathleen has released since 2004—around the time she started feeling the horrible effects of Lyme disease. She was strictly private about her illness until Sini Anderson's documentary about her, The Punk Singer, premiered earlier this year. Around the same time, the Feminist Press published The Riot Grrrl Collection, which features some of the zines, fliers, and other work Kathleen made as a musician, writer, and artist in the early '90s.

She has been feeling better and working like crazy on the Julie Ruin's record release and tour, and she recently invited Rookie over to her apartment in Manhattan.

LENA With the new Julie Ruin record, the Bikini Kill reissues, and *The Riot Grrrl Collection* coming out, there's a lot of attention back on Riot Grrrl. You were a big part of that movement in the '90s, so obviously a lot of people want to talk to you about it. But I was reading on your blog that it gets old for you—

KATHLEEN HANNA [*Laughs*]

—because it's been 20 years and you are more interested in talking about new art and new activism. So, are there ways that people are merging art and politics that are exciting to you right now?

Yeah. I mean, Pussy Riot goes without saying. The first time I saw one of their videos I was really interested. I liked the music, I liked the energy, I liked the costumes. I didn't know they were going to get fucking arrested and all this shit was going to happen, but they're really exciting. And the worldwide anger and disgust at the way they've been treated because they're feminist art-makers—it's an intense wakeup call for me, and I hope people in the United States are like, *Wow, we could get away with so much more, and we're not. We're blowing this chance.*

I also see young girls like Grimes, who is so amazing. She's producing her own work and it sounds really great and it's really interesting to watch. And Savages. I don't know how "feminist" they call themselves or whatever, but feminism isn't something that you are, it's something that you *do*. I don't give a shit what you call yourself. If you're doing feminist work in the world, then it's exciting.

Compared with when you started, do you think it's gotten easier to be in a feminist band in the United States?

I don't really know, because I'm older, but I don't know a lot of bands who are like, "Yes! We are feminists!" besides Pussy Riot. There are definitely women who are singing about women's issues, and to me that's the most important thing. But I would love to see more female musicians—and male musicians—calling themselves feminists and not being nervous about that word. There are all these stereotypes about it—it means you're a man-hater, it means you have hairy legs, it means you're a lesbian—and I was like, "Yeah, and? So what if I am a lesbian? So what if I do have hairy legs? So what if, right now, I do hate men? Fuck off!" [*Laughs*]

There were people at Bikini Kill shows in the '90s who would be violent or really mean toward you and the band, but a lot of that type of thing seems to come out now on the internet—for people like Grimes, who gets rape threats on her Tumblr.

When we were playing in the '90s and men would come to our shows and yell, "Take it off!" or call us the C-word or the B-word—or, most commonly, they would just say, "Shut up!"—in a way, they were doing us a big favor. At the time, of course, I wanted to punch them in the face and drag them out of the club—and sometimes I did. But sexism exists in every room we're ever going to walk into. Racism exists in every room. Homophobia exists in every single room. When people bring it to the fore, it's like popping a blackhead. All of a sudden, everybody knows: There's sexism in the punk scene—we can't ignore this issue anymore. What's scary to me is that [people] aren't going to shows and being like, "Shut up! Just play your music!" or "Show us your tits!" or whatever—[they] just take to the internet and rip other people apart. Maybe it's safer for women to be at shows now, but it's not safer for women to be on the internet.

ON TOP OF THE WORLD

1. Cadillac — T. Rex
2. On Top Of The World — Cheap Trick
3. Working For A Living — The Nightgowns
4. Heavy Damage — Jeff the Brotherhood
5. Hey Hey, My My — Neil Young & Crazy Horse
6. Hard Workin' Man — Natural Child
7. The Working Man — Creedence Clearwater Revival
8. She's A Mover — Big Star
9. I'm On Fire — Dwight Twilley Band
10. How Are You — Cheap Trick
11. Born to Run — Bruce Springsteen

You've said that you don't want people to try to relive or repeat Riot Grrrl, you want them to use it to make something better. What do you think better could look like?

I know of these young women who are doing this really amazing zine called *International Girl Gang Underground*. It talks about Riot Grrrl—the great things about it and the shitty things about it. That, to me, is how something awesome is going to happen—that was the whole point. It was something that anybody could take over and say, "This is my thing. I'm starting my own Riot Grrrl group, even if there are only four people in it."

Before this new Julie Ruin album, you hadn't put out any new music since the last Le Tigre album in 2004, and you hadn't recorded under the name Julie Ruin since your solo record back in 1997. Why now?

I got very sick. I got Lyme disease—late-stage Lyme disease. I'm in remission now, but it was a really intense, awful two years of treatment. But getting sick was one of the reasons I started a band again, because it made me realize how important it is for me to perform and make music. I think I had taken it for granted. And because I was kind of told by my body and told by my doctors that I couldn't do it, I was like, *I have to do it. I have to get better.* It really gave me something to look forward to: being with my band and writing when I felt well enough.

But the thing that also happened was that I realized that I'd gotten into this role of writing these songs that should be there. They were the songs that I wanted when I was 15—I was writing to my 15-year-old self in Bikini Kill. And then I was writing to myself in my 20s. And then I was writing to myself when I was 25. And I was writing to the kids who wrote me letters, who said, "I'm trying to come out and my family's rejecting me and I feel suicidal." It was always coming from my heart, and it wasn't bullshit, but at a certain point doing that starts to feel like you're a waitress and you're asking people if they want cream with their coffee, and you're not an artist anymore. But once I got sick, I was just

like, *Fuck it, I don't want to do that. I don't want to do the thing I'm supposed to do—I just want to write for me.*

Having made a body of work that—a lot of it—was really personal, do you feel like you're ever going to want to go back and write your life story?

I'd love to write my life story. I just feel like it would be weird to do that before I'm like 60, you know what I mean? I'm still making work. Part of the point of *The Riot Grrrl Collection* was making [my papers] available for the next generation, who will do better than we did. I'm completely confident of that. Every 20 years, the people involved with a particular feminist movement have changed enough and grown enough as people that they've been able to be honest about the damage that happened near the end [of that movement]. I'm at that place now. I'm able to move on now and make new work. Then, hopefully, after I make a bunch of new work and have to get away from that, I can—you know, when I'm 60—have my one-woman show and my autobiography.

You've talked about bands and zines you like, but are there authors or filmmakers or artists you're into right now that you feel aren't getting a lot of attention?

Well, I loooove Bridget Everett, who is a cabaret performer. The thing she does that attracts me to her is that, one, she's a big girl—and she would say that herself—and she is constantly naked or in a bathing suit or showing her ass. And, two, she is just like a total sexual predator. I don't mean that like she should be in the registry of sex offenders—but as a performer, she goes out into the audience and finds men and pulls them onstage and puts her hoo-ha in their face. If the tables were turned, it would be a completely different thing. I'd be so grossed out by it. But they're not. It's different to be a woman in society—the way we're looked at, and the way we're put upon sexually. It is uncomfortable to see a woman be like that, and it does raise these really interesting questions about "Well, isn't it still just as gross when a woman does it?" There have been times when I've been like, *I don't know if this is OK. She's*

violating men's space like a million ways to Sunday. But it's punk rock—it's not supposed to be safe. It's supposed to leave you with questions.

There's something punk rock happening in the cabaret scene that I wasn't feeling in the music scene. There's a lot of music right now that I might like listening to while I'm doing the dishes or hanging out in my house, but I don't feel like "Oh my god—somebody might die onstage," or "Someone might get ripped offstage by their ankles," or "This is like really scary." And I miss that. I miss that excitement and fear, that feeling that anything could happen.

Do you think you would ever do cabaret? Or have you done it before?

When I'm older I want to do a one-woman show where I tell stories à la Henry Rollins—but way better because I would sing, too. And maybe do some exercises—Pilates onstage. [*Laughs*] Do a painting and sell it for $200 at the end of the show, I don't know.

That would be a show I'd watch.

Yeah, it'd be awesome for about the first five minutes. And then it would be like, "Okaaaay! Enough already!" [*Laughs*] ☆

Dancing with the Q-KIDZ

Behind the scenes with the Cincinnati troupe.
By Lindsey Rome

The Q-Kidz Dance Team was formed 28 years ago in the West End neighborhood of Cincinnati by Marquicia Jones-Woods, in an effort to give the kids in the area's housing projects something safe and productive to do after school. Over the years, Q-Kidz has become far more than a dance team: Marquicia and her twin daughters, Mariah and Chariah, teach the team members how to dance, but more than that, they teach them the importance of a good education, healthy living, and combating violence in their community.

OCTOBER 2013: HAUNTED

Hi, Rookies!

This month's theme is HAUNTED. Haunted by nostalgia, embarrassment, family history, love and breakups, past relationships of all kinds. And ghosts, too, of course. I like this bit from what Anaheed wrote to me when we were brainstorming about it:

Do you know what a palimpsest is? It's one of my favorite words just 'cause it means something so beautiful: Literally, it's a piece of parchment that has been erased and then reused, and you can see light traces of the old writing underneath the new. There are so many different kinds of palimpsests in life: architectural ones, where you can tell that your doctor's office used to be someone's home or like how there was this bar we used to go to in Chicago where they peeled back many layers of paint and wallpaper to reveal the most beautiful old wallpaper from the '30s; art ones, e.g., when a new picture is painted over an existing one and a trace of the old one shows through; emotional ones, like the way memory works in *Eternal Sunshine of the Spotless Mind.* Or my favorite one: How Johnny Depp turned his WINONA FOREVER tattoo into WINO FOREVER. Close second: How Pamela Anderson turned her TOMMY tattoo into MOMMY. Just anything where you can see traces of the past poking through to the present. Or even, if you wanna get , the way each day erases the one before so you can write a new one.

Isn't that fantastic? With that in mind, here's a playlist for getting over heartbreak when you have no reason to be angry or bitter, or for when you're done being angry and bitter and want to be able to appreciate whatever fond memories may remain. It's for looking back on love and feeling OK—not like Beyoncé–Robyn–Taylor Swift "don't need you" defiant, but not quite full of regret, either. These songs start a little more melancholy and end almost triumphant, with a new understanding that what happened, happened the only way it possibly could have. I love what we have in store for this month and I hope you will, too.

EVERY LOVE STORY IS A GHOST STORY

1. WEREWOLF – FIONA APPLE
2. STORMS – FLEETWOOD MAC
3. SAD BEAUTIFUL TRAGIC – TAYLOR SWIFT
4. FOR EMMA – BON IVER
5. IF YOU SEE HER, SAY HELLO – BOB DYLAN
6. APRIL COME SHE WILL – SIMON & GARFUNKEL
7. FIRST GIRL I LOVED – THE INCREDIBLE STRING BAND
8. IN YOUR LIFE (DO I STILL FIGURE?) – HONEYBUS
9. CONGRATULATIONS – THE CHANTELS
10. SOFT SANDS – THE CHORDETTES
11. SOMEONE LIKE YOU – ADELE
12. FORGET THE SONG – BEACHWOOD SPARKS
13. WONDER YEARS – REAL ESTATE
14. THE FAIREST OF THE SEASONS – NICO
15. GIRL FROM THE NORTH COUNTRY – LINK WRAY
16. GO YOUR OWN WAY – FLEETWOOD MAC
17. HOLY GROUND – TAYLOR SWIFT

LOVE,
TAVI

The Sex Crylebration

No matter what goes wrong, you will live to bone another day.
By Krista and Lola.
Illustration by Esme.

Close your eyes and imagine the most embarrassing thing that could happen to you during sex. OK, now come back here. What did you think about? Does it involve blood? Barf? Farting? Pain?…Pee? Someone seeing you naked and in a weird position for the first time and just backing away slooooowly and then grabbing their clothes and running out the door? OK. Get a good, horrible picture in your mind of what would be a worst-case scenario for you. Now take a deep breath, grab a cup of tea, sit down right here with us, and let us tell you a story.

It goes like this: Once upon a time, two people rubbed their genitals together, and nothing embarrassing happened. No one queefed or farted. Candles literally lit themselves all over the bedroom. No one's parents were home and everything smelled like roses and everyone felt sexy and didn't go past their limits, and when it was over, the sheets were still white as a snowy dove's wing and everyone high-fived and it was the best and that was what happened the end.

HAHAHA NOPE! The above scenario has probably happened like five times in the history of sex. Sex CAN be perfect and not make messes and not be interrupted by weird-seeming things, but—especially when you're starting out—that's unlikely to happen very often. Sex is a vulnerable and kind of strange thing: We get naked with one another and see each other at odd angles and…fluids happen, making it almost unavoidable that something we weren't necessarily prepared for right at that second will occur at some point during the proceedings. But take heart! While no sexual encounter is likely to be perfect, it's equally unlikely that all

of your WORST SEXUAL FEARS will come true. Some will, though, and here's what you need to know about those: They will not be nearly as bad as you imagined.

Sex is new and freaky enough as it is without having to deal with the idea of weird noises and barfing in the presence of your partner. So we put our heads together and thought of a few of the most common things that make people cringe during sexytimes. Things that cause rumors, things that cause your face to burn just hearing about them. And now we're gonna give you the true stories on all of them.

So, whatchoo afraid of, bb?

"WHAT IF I LOOK/SOUND WEIRD?"

KRISTA This one's easy: You don't. Or, you do, but it doesn't matter. Because *everybody* looks/sounds weird during sex. Looking and sounding weird during sex is like wearing a tuxedo to a ball. *Everyone* at the ball is wearing a tuxedo. Now, if you wore a tuxedo on the *bus*, you'd be awesome, but def out of place. If you *didn't* look and sound weird during sex, *that* would be weird and out of place.

When you're having sex, you and your partner(s) are doing things you would not normally do (hopefully). Would you normally, in your everyday life, put your tongue in someone's ear and then trail your hands down their chest, ending with your hands cupping that person's genitals, all while stark naked and making little happy noises? No. During sex? Yes.

So, the way you look and sound during sex is normal…for when you're having sex. Sex is all about what's happening in the moment. Not what happened last week, not what's coming (hopefully you, hyuk hyuk) later. Sex is about the present tense, and being into what you're currently doing and experiencing.

If you're still worried about how you look and sound during sex, here are three more things to keep in mind:

1. By the time you get to the having-sex stage of making out, your partner is already so turned on that they are NOT

thinking, *Huh, she looks really weird from this angle* or *She is really sweaty, ew.* NO. Here is what your partner is thinking: *Holy fuck, we're having sex, I am having sex with a girl, oh my god she's so hot, whoa, this feels great.* This is not a guess; it is a guarantee.

2. Your partner is into you, hardcore. That is why they are having sex with you. They are not having sex with you to find out if they think you're hot. They have already decided. They know what you look like and smell like and they are 100 percent on board with all of it.

3. Are you busy critiquing what your partner looks like from every angle? I'm betting you aren't. I bet you have never thought, *Huh, Skylar looks SO DUMB bent over like that, it's ridiculous, actually.* When they took off their clothes, you probably weren't like, *Oh wow, this is the opposite of what I thought this person would look like naked.* Your guess was probably pretty close to reality, right? What's going on in their head is not so different from what's going on in yours. What if you knew that your sweetie was feeling weird and self-conscious? What would you do to help them feel comfortable? How would you help them understand how hot you find, say, their butt, or their jaw? Do that!

"WHAT IF I FREAK OUT/ CRY?"

LOLA For me, good sex is about freedom from inhibition/anxiety/shame. The best sex I've had has been when I've been able to be my entire weird self with another person, because I know that person will be OK with—even charmed by—the parts of me I feel kinda vulnerable about. This kind of comfort with another person more or less guarantees that there will be mistakes, or messiness, or our putting ourselves in (wait, should I finish this sentence?) positions (oh well) where we aren't exactly comfortable.

So if you ask me, "What if I cry during/after sex?" I will answer, "Then cry!" It's not uncommon or "weird." Sexercourse should welcome laughter-cries and sad-cries.

"UM, ORAL SEX."

LOLA There are so many different things to be scared of here—let's break them down.

1. "During a blow job, what should I do when the person with the penis comes?"

KRISTA Let's assume that you're the blow-job-giver here, since what you do as the recipient seems pretty straightforward. There are generally four possibilities: (1) They come into the condom they're wearing. This is the safest option in terms of both disease and embarrassment. It's also the least messy. They just hold the condom around the base to make sure it doesn't slip off while they remove their penis from your mouth, then they slide the condom off, tie it closed to keep the semen from leaking out (ew), and dispose of it somewhere where it won't be found by parents or family dogs. (2) They ejaculate somewhere other than your mouth—onto the bed, onto your body, onto a towel, whatever. If they've come on your body, just run a wash-cloth under warm water and wipe it off. (3) They ejaculate in your mouth, and you spit it out into a paper towel or the bathroom sink. (4) They ejaculate in your mouth and you swallow. I should point out that the last two possibilities carry a slightly higher risk of STDs/STIs, but neither one is riskier than the other. If your partner is going to come in your mouth, it's totally up to you—NOT THEM—how you handle the situation. There's nothing wrong with liking to swallow come and there's nothing wrong with deciding to spit it out instead. It's not a judgment on your partner if you spit it out, either—you don't have to enjoy ingesting someone's every bodily fluid to prove that you love them.

2. "What if I gag—or even barf—on a penis?"

KRISTA This can happen, but only in three scenarios that I can think of: (1) Some-one—possibly you—is not respecting your mouth boundaries. If someone's penis is making you feel like you're going to gag, they're in too deep for you, or pushing too hard. Stop the blow job and explain what's

up, then either continue in a gentler way or move on to some other activity. (2) You are really, really sick. In this case, what are you doing giving a blow job? You shouldn't be working so hard, and anyway, you don't want to give your partner whatever you've got. Lie down, babe. Take a nap. Do you want some tea? (3) You are drunk. DO NOT HAVE SEX OF ANY KIND WHEN YOU ARE DRUNK. You are a thousand percent more likely to make self-destructive decisions when you're impaired in any way. Of course, this means it's hard for you to heed the advice not to have sex drunk, because you're drunk! This is why it is super duper important to be sure, if you know you're going to be drinking, to have a sober friend with you. And if you're with a drunk friend, be that person for him/her.

3. "What if my mouth gets tired during oral sex and I can't go on?"

LOLA Your mouth is going to get tired. Faking your own death is the only option; tell your sweetie you have to go to the bathroom for a second.

KRISTA When your tongue feels like it's going to fall off and you feel like you OMG cannot keep going for ONE MORE SECOND, just…take a break. As we have established, you are a human, with human limits. You are not an oral-sex machine, programmed to keep going nonstop for as long as it takes to get someone off. You can take little breaks, going and then stopping for a bit, then going again.

LOLA I like to get really concrete with people in this situation. "Do you want me to keep going?" is a good one, because sometimes maybe they DON'T want to come. Maybe they're just being polite, and are secretly like, *Oh my god when is this going to end.* Or you could just guide their hand onto their business as a hint that you need an assist.

"WHAT IF THE CONDOM BREAKS?"

LOLA If the condom breaks or comes off during vaginal intercourse, stop having intercourse and wash up like you normally would—DO NOT USE A DOUCHE to try to flush the semen out of your vagina, as

this will increase your risk of infection. Go to the drugstore or a Planned Parenthood and get some emergency contraception, aka the morning-after pill, which is effective for preventing pregnancy if taken within 120 hours of the broken-condom incident.

"WHAT IF I QUEEF?"

LOLA Whilst at rest, the vagina isn't "open"—the walls touch each other, like a balloon that's deflated. During arousal, the vagina lengthens and expands, creating space that air (and other things) can get into. If something enters the vagina in this state, it pushes out the air. And, staying with our balloon analogy, we all know what happens when you force the air out of an inflated balloon really fast: It makes a farting noise. The same thing happens when a pocket of air is forced out of your vag by an invading object. According to an article I just read on SexInfoOnline (www.soc.ucsb.edu/sexinfo), the risk of queefing is increased "the more times a penis is completely withdrawn from the vagina and reinserted," such as often happens when you change sexual positions. I think it's safe to extrapolate that this principle probably applies to other penetrative objects. I guess the question for you is: Is changing positions frequently more fun than queefing is embarrassing?

KRISTA No, I think the question is, what if you *don't* queef? THEN WHAT DO YOU DO???

LOLA Right?!

KRISTA There is no way to prevent queefing. Either it happens or it doesn't, and there's nothing anyone can do about it, so you can either laugh about it or just ignore it and act like nothing out of the ordinary happened. *Because nothing out of the ordinary* did *happen.* PEOPLE QUEEF. It is normal!

"WHAT IF THERE'S BLOOD?"

LOLA People bleed after sex for a lot of different reasons, ranging from the totally harmless (friction, not enough lube) to conditions that need medical attention, like chlamydia. If you experience this and don't know why it's happening, it's worth getting it checked out, even just to be reassured that nothing serious is going on.

A lot of people with vaginas bleed the first time they have intercourse because the corona (previously known as the hymen) has been torn or stretched out really fast, but the *vast majority* don't. If you don't bleed the first time you're penetrated by something (fingers, tampon, penis, toy, whatever), that doesn't mean you weren't a "virgin." It just means your corona was already torn or stretched or that it wasn't in the way or that it wasn't there in the first place.

KRISTA Sometimes, after rough or extensive sex with penises or fingers, or when there's not enough lubrication, the vagina can bleed just a little bit for no particular reason. Also, sometimes you're on your period, which is—you guessed it—NBD.

LOLA If having period sex skeeves you out, don't do it. Sometimes, even though a sex thing is normal and not medically dangerous and doesn't interfere with anything and many would find it of little to no consequence, people can't hang. That's your right. But know this: Sometimes, even with the best scheduling, the uterus is NOT havin' it. There is a sudden rebellion. The sheets get bloody anyway. If this happens, panic not. Here are a few truths about having sex during someone's period:

1. Being on your period can increase the sensitivity of your nerve endings, and that can make sex feel super nice for lots of folks.

2. Period sex also carries with it a couple more medical risks (I'm sorry I'm sorrrryyyy). For the menstruating partner, semen and menstrual blood both alter the pH of the vagina, which can make it more susceptible to infections, like yeast or bacterial vaginosis. For the other partner, there is some research suggesting that period sex may increase the risk of contracting HIV. Condoms or not having sex can be used as protection against these risks.

3. It's really easy to have sex while bleedin': Just say, "Hang on a sec, I've got to take my tampon/Diva Cup/whatever out, I'll be right back," head to the bath-

room, take it out, and come back. There are also a couple of options to prevent blood from escaping during sex on your period: An Instead Softcup or a contraceptive diaphragm can be used during intercourse to catch any overflow. But that's not necessary so long as the sight of your menstrual blood doesn't freak you or your partner(s) out. If you're gonna have sex during your period without a barrier, though, make sure to grab your...

4. Sex Towel. A Sex Towel is a towel you own that is specifically for sexy messes. Preferably black, red, brown, or navy, a Sex Towel is something you grab with studied casualness, shooing your partner over to one side while you lay it down and spread it out. It kills the moment for a sec, but you know what kills the moment worse? Suddenly realizing that you've gotten blood all over your sheets. Especially if someone else does the laundry (hi, Mom!).

KRISTA My sex towel was once pink and is now a horrible rusty-beige color. It's also fraying and torn in three places. Only the best for those I love.

LOLA My old sex towel's name was Old Filthful. By the end of my relationship it stiffly held its own form no matter how much we washed it.

"WHAT IF I SMELL BAD?"

KRISTA When I first started to have sex, I nervously asked my boyfriend how I smelled *down there*. "I think my crotch smells really sweaty and weird," I said. "How can you like that?" He laughed and said, "It smells like sex. That's why I like it—it turns me on." If you are washing yourself on a regular basis and you don't have any infections, your crotch will smell like...your particular crotch. And someone you're sleeping with is going to be very, very into that.

LOLA If a vagina smells very fishy, or has a strong odor of any kind, it might be a symptom of a totally treatable infection like bacterial vaginosis or yeast. But! There is a huge range of smells that are normal. Almost nobody smells "bad," but almost everyone thinks they do.

"WHAT IF I FART... OR POOP?"

LOLA In the words of one of our wisest staffers: "Never end up with someone who makes you hold in a fart. Life's too short and sex is too ridiculous." Another Rookie writer actually dumped her boyfriend the day after she farted during sex—because she was the only one who laughed.

As for pooping. As...for pooping...

KRISTA Here is my real-life worst-case scenario that actually happened:

One winter night, I went to bed with my boyfriend (we'll call him Jonathan). I wasn't feeling very well; we had eaten tacos for dinner and my stomach hurt and I was grumpy as I took off my clothes and climbed into bed with him. We ended up having sex, and then we both fell asleep, naked, with him spooning me. The windows were open—Jonathan and I both loved to sleep in really cold weather while being all warm with another person in bed. In the middle of the night, I sort of woke up, vaguely needing to fart really badly. Mostly still asleep, I farted—AHHH, SWEET RELIEF—and immediately felt 100 percent better. I rolled over and fell completely asleep.

Sometime around 4 AM, I woke up again, feeling strangely cold and wet. It felt like I was in a...puddle of some sort. Hmmm. What was going on? I put my fingers down into the puddle and touched—OMG OMG—cold liquid near my crotch. *OH SHIT*, I thought. *I'VE STARTED MY PERIOD IN JONATHAN'S BED*. I froze there in the dark for a second, quietly panicking about the apparently HUGE amount of blood that was pooling on his mattress, then got up (Jonathan could sleep through absolutely anything) and switched on the desk lamp.

OH SHIT. IT WASN'T BLOOD. IT WAS ACTUALLY *SHIT*. One hundred percent liquid shit, goldeny-brown in color. YOU GUYS, I SHAT MY BOYFRIEND'S BED.

It was everywhere. *Everywhere*. It was all over me, it was all over Jonathan, it was all over his sheets. There is really no way for you all to understand *how much liquid diarrhea* there was in that room, and it was freezing cold, because the window was open. What the fuck was I going to do?

My first thought was that Jonathan *could not be allowed to see this.* He was a germophobe—he'd never be able to recover. It would be the end of us.

He was still asleep. I went to his closet and grabbed a few washcloths. I grabbed his water bottle. Naked, covered in my own diarrhea, I inched toward the bed. Carefully, carefully, I pulled the top sheet off his body and threw it on the floor. He didn't wake up. I wet one of the washcloths with water from his water bottle. Slowly, and so gently it almost didn't work at first, I dabbed at the diarrhea on my boyfriend's body. It took me about 10 minutes to wipe him pretty much clean.

Now about the bottom sheet, the sheet *under* his body: What was I going to do?

I did what anyone would have done if they were in my position and dating a heavy sleeper: I loosened the fitted sheet around the mattress and tugged, gently rolling Jonathan to one side as I pulled the sheet out from under him. This maneuver took another 10 minutes, and I was terrified that any second he would wake up and see what was going on. But you'd best believe I GOT THAT SHEET. You guys, it *dripped* in my *hands.*

Now I had the bottom sheet, I had the top sheet, and I had several shit-covered washcloths. I bundled everything in my arms and crept into the bathroom. I got into the shower clutching the sheets and washcloths, turned the water on "scalding," and used shampoo to scrub at the poo all over everything until there was almost no trace of it. I scrubbed myself practically raw with soap, dried off, hung the sheets over the shower-curtain rod, and went back to the bedroom, where Jonathan was sleeping, naked, on a bare mattress, with the windows wide open on a winter night. I checked to make sure there was no trace of diarrhea on his gorgeous body, then curled up next to him and dragged the blanket over us. His skin was freezing.

He woke up the next morning, confused, cold, and disoriented. "Baby, what the fuck? Where's the sheet? Why are we on the mattress?" His beautiful, accusing eyes locked with mine.

For a second, I was speechless. If I told him what had really happened, he would break up with me (Nooooo!! I loved him) and then possibly kill himself, or at least spend the rest of his adult life taking 22 showers a day and the remaining two hours rubbing Purell into his raw skin.

So I did what I had to do to save our relationship and to save Jonathan from the ninth circle of a germophobe's hell and a lifetime of therapy. I looked him in the eye and said solemnly, "Jonathan, there's something I need to tell you. Last night…you peed the bed."

We dated for years.

IN CONCLUSION…

We're not saying that to be a happy and responsible member of sexual society, you should just GET OVER any and all fears/phobias/hangups IMMEDI-ATELY or NO SEX FOR YOU. In general, it's OK to be embarrassed about something, or think something is gross, or not want to do something because it seems weird to you (in a not-good way). You don't have to feel ashamed about feeling embarrassed about feeling ashamed, OMG, not in this busy modern world.

Embarrassing stuff happens in life, to everybody. You have two options for how to respond to that stuff: You can try to prevent it, or you can get over it. Luckily, if you choose "preventing it" and it ends up happening anyway (which it will), "getting over it" remains an option. For some people, getting over it is riding a motorcycle of DGAF off of the highest cliff of YOLO Mountain. For others, it means working around the stuff that embarrasses you—or finding a way to accept that something happened and you felt embarrassed and now it's over and you might as well move the heck on. If Krista did, so can you. 🐱

TWO kinds of MEMORY

STORY BY ROSE LICHTER-MARCK DRAWN BY MARIA INES.

I WAS SIXTEEN WHEN
I FELL IN LOVE FOR THE FIRST TIME.

AND ONCE IT WAS
WITH A BOY.

ONCE IT WAS
WITH A BOOK

THE BOY WAS TALL, WITH LONG, STRINGY LIMBS, A DANGEROUSLY SHARP ADAM'S APPLE, AND ICE-BLUE EYES. HE ASKED ME OUT TO LUNCH FOR SANDWICHES. LOOKING ACROSS THE TABLE, I FELT FLUTTERS IN MY STOMACH, AND TRIED TO CALM THE BUTTERFLIES I HAD ALWAYS ASSUMED WERE A FIGURE OF SPEECH.

HE SMILED AT ME AND I NOTICED THAT A SLIVER OF RED PEPPER HAD LODGED ITSELF RIGHT BETWEEN HIS CHICLET-PERFECT TEETH.

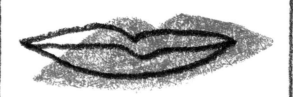

THAT WAS THE DAY OF MY KISS...

...
THAT WAS THE YEAR I READ VLADIMIR NABOKOV'S
LOLITA.

Lolita,
light of my life,
fire of my loins.
sin, my soul...

FROM THE FIRST SENTENCE I WAS HOOKED.
THE PROSE WAS PLAYFUL AND ERUDITE,
BUTTRESSED BY WORD GAMES AND ALLUSIONS
TO LITERATURE, ACADEMIA, HOLLYWOOD,
SCIENCE, ART...

I LOVED ALL THAT
BUT IT WAS THE WAY NABOKOV WROTE
ABOUT MEMORY THAT MADE ME FEEL
HE WROTE FOR ME.

I WAS ALREADY OBSESSED WITH THE IDEA
THAT THE EXPERIENCE OF ANY SENSATION
IS ACCOMPANIED BY THE KNOWLEDGE
OF ITS IMPERMANENCE.

THE VERY FACT OF MY NOTICING ANY PARTICULAR
PLEASURE OR PAIN MEANT THAT THE MOMENT

HAD PASSED.

I WAS IN LOVE FOR A WHILE

AND THEN
IT ENDED

IT'S NOT A REMARKABLE STORY EXCEPT FOR THE
FACT THAT IT HAPPENED TO ME.

IF I DON'T HOLD ON TO WHAT IT WAS LIKE
TO FALL IN LOVE FOR THE FIRST TIME, THEN
I HAVE ONLY MYSELF TO BLAME FOR THE LOSS
OF WHAT WAS ONCE THE MOST PRECIOUS THING.

I CAN'T SUMMON THE FEELING OF BEING IN LOVE.
IT'S TOO BIG.
IT WOULD BE LIKE TRYING TO MEASURE THE OCEAN.

INSTEAD I THINK OF:

THE TASTE OF HIS MOUTH.

THE SMOOTHNESS OF HIS SKIN BETWEEN
THE BRIDGE OF HIS NOSE AND HIS CHEEK.

THE ELECTRICITY
BETWEEN OUR PALMS
WHEN WE HELD HANDS.

THE ROPEY SHADOWS OF STREETLIGHTS THAT FELL
ACROSS OUR BODIES WHEN WE ROLLED AROUND
IN THE BACK OF MY STATION WAGON.

THE LOOK HE GAVE ME
WHEN I STOOD UP FROM HIS BED.

THE ACHE IN MY CHEST
WHEN I RACED HOME
TO MAKE MY CURFEW.

WHEN I THINK OF HIS FACE,
I REMEMBER WHEN WE LAY IN THE GRASS

AND HE LET ME
GARLAND HIM
WITH DAFFODILS.

HE KEPT HIS EYES CLOSED
AND TRIED TO FIX HIS FACE WITH THE
SERIOUSNESS OF A DEATHMASK

BUT MY TICKLY FIDGETING
GOT THE BEST OF HIM

AND HE COULDN'T PREVENT
HIS MOUTH FROM

STRETCHING
INTO A BROAD SMILE

LOLITA WAS THE FIRST TIME I HAD ENCOUNTERED A BOOK THAT SO PERFECTLY DEPICTED THE EXQUISITE FUTILITY OF USING ART TO PRESERVE SOMETHING

THAT IS ALREADY GONE.

THROUGH NABOKOV'S LENS,

HUMBERT'S PASSIONS, THOUGH LOATHSOME,

WERE FUNNY AND TRAGIC,

FOR NABOKOV, STORYTELLING, LIKE TAXONOMY, IS THE ACT OF COLLECTING FOLLOWED BY THE ACT OF ORDERING.

EACH WINGED INSECT IN THE AUTHOR'S NET WAS BOTH THE THING HE WAS SEARCHING FOR AND YET ONLY A SMALL PART OF A BIGGER STORY.

IN LOLITA NABOKOV CATALOGUED TWO KINDS OF A VISUAL MEMORY:

THE PORTRAIT OF A BELOVED

AND THE FREEZE FRAMES OF PRECIOUS MOMENTS THAT STAY WITH US LONG AFTER THE PERSON LEAVES OUR LIFE.

In reading, one should notice and fondle details

NABOKOV WROTE.

HIS PROSE COLLECTS THE DETAILS OF EXPERIENCE AND PRESERVES THEM LIKE BUTTERFLIES PINNED IN PLACE.

(THAT'S NOT AN INCIDENTAL PARALLEL. HE WAS ACTUALLY A TRAINED LEPIDOPTERIST WHO SPENT HIS BREAKS FROM TEACHING LOOKING FOR RARE BUTTERFLIES.)

NEITHER BRINGS BACK THE THING THAT HAS BEEN LOST.

HUMBERT DESTROYED A REAL GIRL

Dolores Haze

AND THEN TRIED TO SAVE HER BY TRANSFORMING HER INTO HIS LOLITA, CREATION OF HIS ART.

I ENDED THAT LOVE AFFAIR AND BROKE HIS HEART.

ALL THESE YEARS LATER I RETURN TO THE SCRAPS OF MEMORY, THESE WORN BUT STILL IRIDESCING BUTTERFLY WINGS, AND TRY TO MAKE SOMETHING FLAWED YET BEAUTIFUL.

THIS WILL BE MY ONLY CONSOLATION:

THE REFUGE OF ART.

GIRL-ON-GIRL CRIME

If only there were a 12-step program for misogynists.
By Brodie. Playlist by Tavi.

When I started high school, I despised a girl named Elle* who had recently joined the small group of friends that had come with me from my primary school. She seemed to appear from nowhere, instantly fitting in with the popular group I had worked hard to join, getting invited to all the parties, and being the object of my crush's affections. These things gave me enough reason to hate her. At one of the first high school parties I attended that included drinking, kissing, and sleeping over, Elle hooked up with a guy under a sleeping bag in a room full of people too terrified to touch one another. I had no feelings for the guy she slept with, I didn't see what happened, and it didn't affect me AT ALL, but none of this stopped me from judging her really harshly. While IMing with a friend the day after the party, I took it upon myself to detail what had happened and how "slutty" Elle had acted at the party. I vividly remember calling her "dirty" for what she'd done. As I ran down a list of misdeeds I knew nothing about (I was a 14-year-old kiss virgin), I felt totally justified: Elle had done something I didn't like, and I had a duty to register my disapproval with our peers.

*Name has been changed.

The next day, the girl I'd been IMing brought a printout of our conversation to school and showed everyone. But rather than revile me for being a gross, unfair, jealous gossip, people took my side. I still feel guilt over how I treated Elle, and other girls like her, back then. It's really difficult to get over the shitty things I thought, said, and did 10 years ago, and it's not like I can go to a Misogynists Anonymous meeting and embark on a 12-step program to deal with them.

As a teenage girl, there was nothing I wanted less than to be a teenage girl. I mean, I thought *I* was pretty great, but I held the very misguided idea that my fellow girls were less awesome than I was. I felt no greater pride than when I was considered "one of the boys." I made it my mission to let adolescent high school boys know I wasn't just another dumb *girl*, because there seemed to be nothing worse. I was a chronic girl-hater.

I know I didn't come to that behavior on my own: Girls are basically trained from birth to hate one another. Even kids' shows have plot lines about one girl stealing another girl's boyfriend; and we still are encouraged to look down on women we think are "sluts," to see every other female as a threat to our relationships and self-worth, to disparage the looks of women we disagree with politically or intellectually, and to regard successful women as "bitches."

When I was 16, I discovered feminism on a very basic level when my modern-history teacher used Pink's "Stupid Girls" video to introduce the concept to my class in a way that made a lot of sense to me and got the wheels going in my brain. But it wasn't until I was 19 and in my second year of university, where I was exposed to revolutionary ideas and surrounded by new friends who supported, encouraged, and agreed with my fairly new worldview, that I began to really develop the feminism that I call mine today. It's always expanding and evolving as I get older, but one thing never changes: I will always feel some remnant of guilt and shame for the myriad things I said and did during my PF (pre-feminism) years in the service of making Elle and other girls feel bad.

Every feminist has a different story about their journey to feminism. Some people change perspectives as a response to a specific event; others grew up in really socially conscious environments and can't imagine anything else. I built my feminism LEGO-tower-style, brick by brick, adding, removing, and changing components as I went along. Kathleen Hanna did an interview with The A.V. Club last November in which she described how her particular feminism evolved from a knee-jerk, man-hating breed to something more universal after she was exposed to the effects of the patriarchy on all people, including men. This quote really stuck with me:

When you first step into the Feminist 101 personality, you're like, "Get the fuck out of my face, men!" I was just sick of it. Every movie I saw, everywhere I looked, I saw sexism. I had never been looking before. And once I had that lens on, I just got more and more rageful. But then I started getting more nuanced. […] I'm more interested in a feminism that ends discrimination for all people. It's not just about a woman becoming the CEO of a company or something. It's connected to racism and classism and gender issues that go beyond the binary…It's more about [the] intersection.

That word—*intersection*—was a turning point that moved me beyond Feminism 101 and into something "more nuanced." Basically, intersectional feminism acknowledges that people can be subject to more than one kind of oppression at the same time. Women, racial minorities, LGBTQ people, and people with disabilities, for example, experience multiple systems of oppression all at once. So you're never *just* a woman—you're a woman who is Latina, or a woman who has a disability, etc. Becoming aware of intersectionality made my feminism feel more solid and important; it taught me that ableist, racist, and classist words and actions are as destructive as the sexist, homophobic, and misogynistic behaviors I'd slowly unlearned over the years. And I was comforted to know that, while my feminism was morphing into what it is now, I had role models like Kathleen Hanna to guide me.

When the holy princess of music Grimes apologized on her Tumblr earlier this year for having worn a bindi, I saw it as a way for her to reconcile the guilt she felt for doing something ignorant before her feminism had evolved. While he's not exactly a feminist role model, I was really glad to see the rapper A$AP Rocky, in *Interview* magazine, reconsider homophobic things he'd thought and said growing up. When I was younger, I too said and did some pretty shitty things, out of a combination of social conditioning and sheer ignorance. I grew up in a small town in Australia where calling someone "gay" or "retarded" was par for the course. As much as I despise these behaviors when I look back on them now, they mark an integral point in my feminist journey. They gave me things to move on and learn from, habits to unlearn, and intolerances to overcome.

It's important to me to resist the urge to deny these phases I went through, no matter how much I want to. I'd much rather forget the years I spent hating on girls like Elle in attempts to impress boys, but that wouldn't get me anywhere. To really learn and move on from our experiences, we need to admit to them and understand why they're problematic. Not everyone's feminism will follow the same path or end up in the same place, but if we start by being honest about ourselves and our own prejudices, at least we'll be headed in the right direction. ⚘

GHOST PROM

1 BLUE MOON - ELVIS PRESLEY

2. BASEMENT SCENE - DEERHUNTER

3. I ONLY HAVE EYES FOR YOU - THE FLAMINGOS

4. YOU KNOW WHAT I MEAN - CULTS

5. WHO DO YOU LOVE - THE SAPPHIRES

6. I FOLLOW YOU - MELODY'S ECHO CHAMBER

7. IN DREAMS - ROY ORBISON

8. SLEEP TIGHT - THE KID

iN the STACKS

A reader's photo diary of the two months she spent living in a bookstore in Paris.
By Molly Dektar

Shakespeare and Company is an American bookshop on Paris's Left Bank. A former monastery for Notre Dame Cathedral, it has been a center of Paris literary life since the 1950s, thanks to the late George Whitman, the bookstore's eccentric, bohemian founder. Since it opened, thousands of writers and artists, from Allen Ginsberg to Rachel Antonoff, have lived at Shakespeare and Company for free, working in the shop during the day and transforming its benches and lofts into the Tumbleweed Hotel at night. You can't make a reservation at the Tumbleweed—the only way to get a spot is to show up at the store, track down George's daughter, Sylvia, and ask. I did so twice this year, in January and June.

116

Above the shop, in George's old quarters, is the writers' studio.

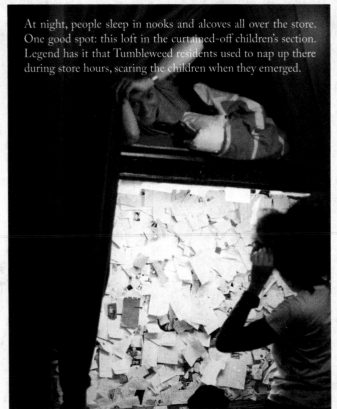

At night, people sleep in nooks and alcoves all over the store. One good spot: this loft in the curtained-off children's section. Legend has it that Tumbleweed residents used to nap up there during store hours, scaring the children when they emerged.

OLD SMOKY READING ROOM

Portraits of literary heroes in the stairwell.

George's rules for the Tumbleweed still hold true: In order to stay there you must work in the shop, read a book a day, and write an autobiography (and include a picture) before you leave.

Visitors leave notes on the "Mirror of Love" in the children's section.

THE SAFETY CLOSET

Coming out is not for everyone.
By Krista

It was a Thursday morning a few weeks ago. I started the day the way I always do: by grabbing my phone and, still blinking my eyes open, scrolling through email from six different accounts (work, personal, freelancing job #1, freelancing job #2, blog photos, blog). This is not the most relaxing way to wake up, but it works.

On this particular morning, I got the usual meeting announcements, updates from my day job, and LGBTQ press releases (I write a humor blog about lesbian stereotypes). But there was also something else: an email addressed to my blog from an unfamiliar address. I opened it and started to read, and my stomach dropped.

> Dear Krista,
> I recently realized I'm gay, but I live in a very small, very religious, very closed-minded, and very not-gay community. I haven't told anyone about my eureka moment, mainly because my parents are very vocal and a bit violent about their opinions. I'm in high school and I live with them; plus, they are the kind of people who would disown their kid for something like that, or send them to a so-called "treatment center." Should I tell them?
> —Danni*

It's the second such letter I've gotten this month. Last month there were three. Letters like this scare the shit out of me.

Today, October 11, is National Coming Out Day. It's a day when LGBTQ folks

---

* Name has been changed.

celebrate the power of going public with their queerness. The idea behind Coming Out Day is that the more gay, lesbian, bisexual, transgender, and queer people come out of the closet, the more our sexualities will seem normal to everyone, the less we'll all have to hide, and the safer and more accepting our world will be.

Danni's email jolted me awake. I stumbled into the bathroom, peed, popped in my contacts, and headed over to my computer, where I started tapping out my reply. I've adapted that response into this article, because I think you all need to hear this.

~ * ~ * ~

When I was 15, I didn't have a clue that my obsessive feelings about other girls were in fact romantic crushes, but even if I had known, I would never, EVER have come out in high school. I was too afraid. My school was full of kids from rural Wisconsin who drove pickup trucks to go "muddin'" (which is where you drive a truck at high speeds through muddy fields for no particular reason) and who seemed obsessed with things like homecoming and football games. My parents are strictly observant Mormons who weren't, let's say, "cool" with what they called the "gay lifestyle." Had I known then that I was a lesbian, I'm sure I would have stayed in the closet until I left that town and my parents' house. I wasn't brave enough to come out.

Today, of course, I realize that, statistically speaking, a number of those mudders and football players and cheerleaders were probably gay too, but back then I couldn't fathom it. As far as I knew, there were *no*

queer people in my school—hell, in my whole town! I had no queer role models in my community, or even on TV. In those days we didn't have *Glee*. There weren't any out gay rappers, country singers, or basketball players. I didn't have access to queer YA novels, nor anywhere near the number of informative websites there are now for queer youth. And not only couldn't we get married, it didn't even seem like a possibility in my *lifetime*.

Y'all are lucky to be growing up in a time when the message from so many sources is suddenly "IT'S OK TO BE GAY, WE REALLY MEAN IT THIS TIME." With visibility comes knowledge, which makes you better equipped to recognize romantic feelings for your same-gender friends and to adopt labels for those feelings if you want them: *I am gay. I am bi. I am queer.* The average coming-out age for queer and trans people has gone from 20-something in the 1980s to about 16 today. Because of the stuff I write about on my blog, I often get emails from 12- and 13-year-olds identifying themselves as queer or gay. I talk to 15-year-olds who are *completely open* about being queer—their friends know, their parents know, their grandparents know, their teachers and coaches and neighbors know. This is amazing to me. It's a wonderful thing, and it deserves to be celebrated.

But here's what I'm worried about: Because a lot of kids are coming out while they're young, there's increased pressure on ALL queer kids to come out ASAP. It's like, "Look! Everyone's coming out now! It's safe to be queer! Be yourself! Everything's OK!" If you stay in the closet, not only do you have to watch some of your peers celebrate the freedom of being out without getting to experience it (yet) yourself, but you're also made to feel like some kind of *weirdo*. On top of that, a lot of well-meaning LGBTQ organizations and publications tell us that we have a *responsibility* to come out. We owe it to our *community* to be seen, to be heard, to *increase LGBTQ acceptance*! And in case guilt doesn't work, they throw in a curse on your love life: Until you come out, they say, you'll have a hard time finding a partner.

The problem is that many of you live with people—and depend on people—who remain untouched by all this new queer-positivity. Danni, for example. What would Danni gain by coming out today? Well, she would be claiming her identity in a way that is positive, meaningful, and powerful for her, and she'd increase her chances of finding like-minded friends. These are all big pros. But what would Danni *lose* by coming out today? She could be verbally or physically abused. She might be sent to some kind of "treatment center" aiming to "cure" her of gayness. She may be ostracized by her community, attacked at school, and/or get kicked out of the house. Uh-oh—that cons list is getting mighty long. Coming out right now is actually dangerous for Danni, and for thousands of teenagers like her.

Everyone's family has a different reaction to a kid's coming out, but they tend to fall into a few very general categories:

1. **It goes really well.** They love you no matter what! They already knew, or they didn't know but it's fine with them! Do you want to march in the Pride Parade next year?
2. **It goes OK.** They're not mad, but they're not thrilled. Of course they still love you, but they're hoping this is "just a phase."
3. **It goes badly at first, but then it gets better.** At first they're all, "WHAT DO YOU MEAN YOU'RE GAY THIS IS NOT ACCEPTABLE YOU KNOW WHAT THIS FAMILY STANDS FOR AND THIS IS NOT IT," but

then you leave them alone for a while (maybe a very long while) and maybe slip a booklet or a flier for a PFLAG meeting under their door, and after a while they come around and support you—or at least finally come to terms with it.
4. **It goes really, really badly.** As in "Get out of my house, you are not my child." This is the option I'm talking about when I say that letters like Danni's terrify me. It's thankfully not very common, but the consequences are dire. Among homeless teenagers, the percentage of LGBTQ kids is disproportionately high: While they make up between 5 and 10 percent of the general population, they account for 20 to 40 percent of homeless youth. There is a reason for that statistic. These are kids who have been kicked out of the house for coming out or being discovered to be queer or trans.

My own coming out was of the third variety: terrible at first, then gradually better. I came out to my parents when I was 20 or 21, when I was already living in another state and paying for my own schooling. My mother FREAKED OUT and told me not to tell my father. "He will love you less," she said. My father ended up guessing anyway; he seemed disappointed but not surprised. My mother barraged me daily with hurtful emails and phone calls until I stopped speaking to her altogether. Ten years later, we're only beginning to repair the rift my coming out created between us. Or, no—the rift that my parents' intolerance and general rudeness about my gayness has created between us. We've lost an entire decade together. I still haven't totally forgiven them.

But I know that in the scheme of things, I'm lucky. I wasn't in a position to be cut off from my only source of shelter and financial support, and all I had to do to avoid my mother's verbal abuse was ignore her phone calls and delete her emails.

Danni is not as lucky—but she will be if she just waits a couple years, till she lives on her own and is supporting herself. When I wrote back to her, I strong-

ly urged her not to tell her parents that she's gay right now, and told her why I felt that way. And now I'm saying the same thing to any of you who are in a similar situation.

Queer/trans Rookies, listen to me: If you suspect that your parents will be violent toward you in *any* way, kick you out of the house, yell at you, be hurtfully angry with you for a long time, threaten to send you to a "treatment center," force you into religious activity/"therapy" for being queer, cut you out of their lives, shun you, or just generally make your life hell until you move out, please, please, **DO NOT COME OUT.** Not now. Not yet. Wait until you have ceased living with them. Your safety is more important than your gay pride or your allegiance to the LGBTQ community. It's really OK not to tell them. Protect yourself first.

Then: Leave home after high school. Move away. Tell your family then, if you want to. And if you don't want to tell them, if you *never* want to tell them, that's fine, too. You are not obligated by your queerness to tell anyone, ever, that you're queer. It's not a law. You get to decide who knows what about you, forever, amen.

Please don't misunderstand me—it's awesome if you know you're queer, or think you might be, and want to come out to your family. If you're sure your parents won't be horrible to you, then by all means, come out whenever you're ready! Being honest about who you are can bring you closer to your family, and it can be a huge relief not to have to worry anymore how they might react. Your parents may become your biggest supporters. And you could help others around you feel more comfortable with themselves, too.

But if you think coming out will place you in any kind of risk, there is no shame in waiting. National Coming Out Day is about honoring who you are, and making a decision to live a freer future. That means keeping yourself well today, so that your future self can join the queer family that is waiting for you out here when you're ready. We're counting on you to take care of yourself, until we can take care of you.

Stay safe, Rookies. ♥

Ouija Board, Ouija Board

What was it trying to tell us?
By Tavi

Ella and I met in a seventh grade writing class. We became best friends based on a shared interest in Bob Dylan and a resistance to the popular idea of what it means to grow up. It was middle school, the time of coed hangouts and touching tongues and wood-paneled basements becoming scary in a way that was not spooky-scary but more like "I can smell my B.O. and I don't really like this guy and wasn't I a child like just last year?" scary. I couldn't even tell you how many times I pretended my parents were calling so that I had an excuse to leave a gathering of acquaintances, or how badly I wished I could just go back to the dreamy fun of crushing on a particular boy once we became "boyfriend–girlfriend." In Ella I found someone who preferred spooky-scary, who wanted to grow as a person but also liked to build fairy houses and take photos in the woods and try to talk to ghosts. We could confide in each other, but we could also make the good parts of childhood last as long as possible. Things that otherwise made us feel strange seemed perfectly normal when we were together.

One of our favorite things to do was the Ouija board. After a couple rounds of "Who will I marry?"–type questions, we decided to try contacting real-live (dead) ghosts. We found her dad's board from when he

was a kid, waited till everyone was asleep, and sat on the floor of her living room, surrounded by candles. (One ghost, Mary, asked us to bring her white roses, so we once decorated the board with those. Another time, we were trying to reach a six-year-old girl we'd previously contacted who loved Ella's garden, so we used daisies, gems, and a plastic unicorn.)

In our second year of high school, Ella became busy with theater, singing in a band, and hanging out with a long-term boyfriend. I became busy with Rookie. We found different friend groups. We never lost touch, but we did fade away, hanging out less frequently and, for me, never telling her the whole story as to what was going on in my life. My new friends were dark and tortured, and Ella seemed so happy—I didn't know what she would think if I told her I was depressed or developing unhealthy eating habits. Having problems was too grown-up for our sleepover agenda. It was easier to sit in the dark, ghosts of who we used to be, trying to get in touch with the bond we used to have.

At the end of 11th grade, Ella and I got together for the first time in a long time. As we lay side by side in her family's guest room—white walls, white blankets, white sheets, white pillows—about to fall asleep, Ella asked, "What happened to us?" It turned out we'd been going through a lot of the same stuff at the same time and simply never reached out. I still wonder how things might have been different, how our respective pains might have been alleviated, had the Ouija board spelled out that we should have just *talked* to each other.

These Ouija board conversations are from the time of our falling out and our periodic attempts at reuniting. (They end last winter, before we realized how much we could have shared.) I promise that nei-

ther of us ever tried forcing any of these answers, because, first of all, we would've made them a lot scarier and weirder, and, second, we believed this stuff for real. I think I still do, although, looking back through these notes, I would not be surprised if one very popular theory turned out to be true: that the answers on a Ouija board actually come from your subconscious. So many of our shared interests made their way into the ghosts' sides of these conversations: movies we'd watched in Ella's basement, songs we'd sung together and played on guitar. These exchanges feel more like a record of our time together than like any third party's wishes and commands.

This past summer, Ella and I ran into each other at the airport. She had just returned from an acting program in France and was on her way to a family reunion. I was with my dad, heading to a friend's wedding and college visits. My boyfriend and I had broken up not even two hours earlier, and the first thing I did when I saw Ella was burst into tears. She gave me a big, long hug and I realized how many other kinds of love exist and that they are often just as rare as the romantic kind we hear so much more about.

We're both seniors now, applying to colleges and planning our futures. We still get together occasionally to catch up, erupt into fits of giggles, and watch trashy TV. We also tell each other the stuff we wouldn't before. It's still cool to think that there was something about our relationship that was so special it could be manifested only through a supernatural presence. While there would have been better ways for us to communicate with each other, I like the idea that our subconsciouses were trying to remind us of the good times we'd had, and of good times yet to come.

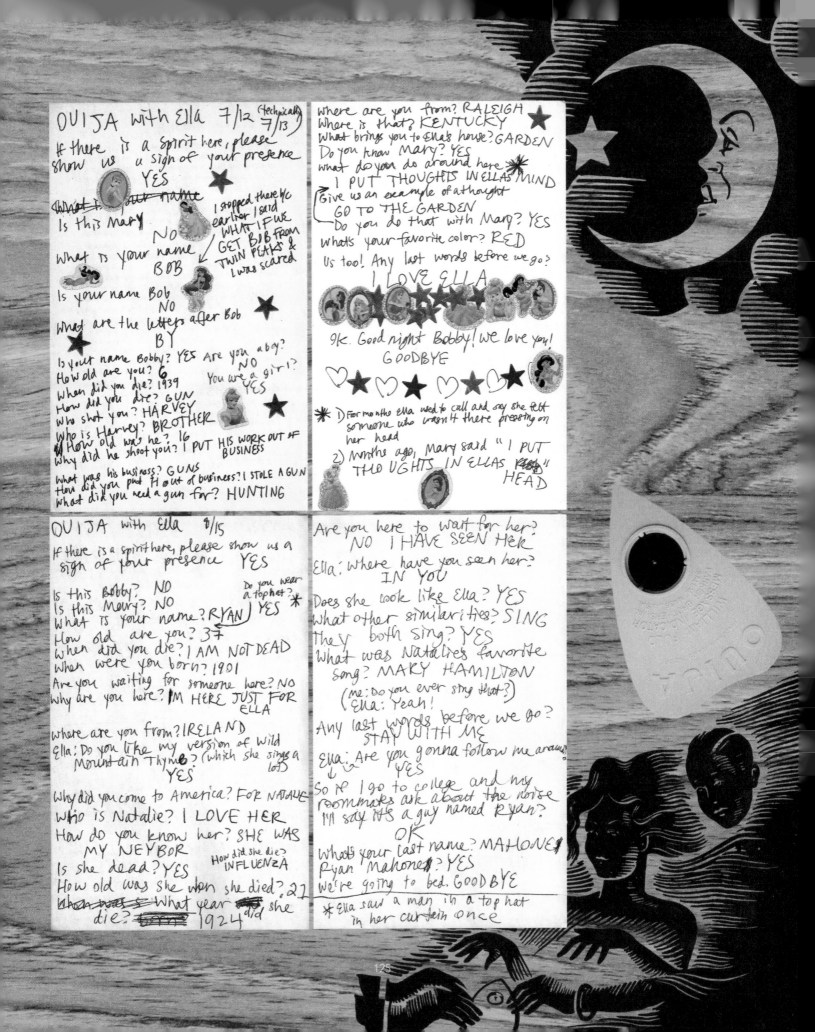

OUIJA with Ella 7/12 (technically 7/13)

If there is a spirit here, please show us a sign of your presence
YES

~~What is your name~~ I stopped there b/c earlier I said WHAT IF WE GET BOB FROM TWIN PEAKS & I was scared

Is this Mary
NO

What is your name
BOB

Is your name BOB
NO

What are the letters after Bob
BY

Is your name Bobby? YES Are you a boy?
NO
How old are you? 6 You are a girl?
When did you die? 1939 YES
How did you die? GUN
Who shot you? HARVEY
Who is Harvey? BROTHER
~~How old was he?~~ 16 I PUT HIS WORK OUT OF
Why did he shoot you? BUSINESS

What was his business? GUNS
How did you put it out of business? I STOLE A GUN
What did you need a gun for? HUNTING

Where are you from? RALEIGH
Where is that? KENTUCKY
What brings you to Ella's house? GARDEN
Do you know Mary? YES
what do you do around here ✴
    I PUT THOUGHTS IN ELLAS MIND
Give us an example of a thought
    GO TO THE GARDEN
Do you do that with Mary? YES

What's your favorite color? RED

Us too! Any last words before we go?
    I LOVE ELLA

9k. Good night Bobby! We love you!
    GOODBYE

✴ 1) For months Ella used to call and say she felt someone who wasn't there pressing on her head
2) Months ago, Mary said "I PUT THOUGHTS IN ELLAS ~~head~~ HEAD"

OUIJA with Ella 8/15

If there is a spirit here, please show us a sign of your presence YES

Is this Bobby? NO
Is this Mary? NO Do you wear a top hat? ✴
What is your name? RYAN YES
How old are you? 37
When did you die? I AM NOT DEAD
When were you born? 1901
Are you waiting for someone here? NO
Why are you here? I'M HERE JUST FOR ELLA

Where are you from? IRELAND
Ella: Do you like my version of Wild Mountain Thyme? (which she sings a lot)
    YES

Why did you come to America? FOR NATALIE
Who is Natalie? I LOVE HER
How do you know her? SHE WAS MY NEYBOR
Is she dead? YES How did she die? INFLUENZA
How old was she when she died? 27
~~When does s~~ What year ~~did~~ she did
    die? 1924

Are you here to wait for her?
    NO I HAVE SEEN HER
Ella: Where have you seen her?
    IN YOU
Does she look like Ella? YES
What other similarities? SING
They both sing? YES
What was Natalie's favorite song? MARY HAMILTON
    (me: Do you ever sing that?)
    (Ella: Yeah!)
Any last words before we go?
    STAY WITH ME
Ella: Are you gonna follow me around?
    YES
So if I go to college and my roommates ask about the noise I'll say it's a guy named RYAN?
    OK
What's your last name? MAHONEY
Ryan Mahoney? YES
We're going to bed. GOODBYE

✴ Ella said a man in a top hat in her curtain once

125

OUIJA with Ella 8/27/11

If there is a spirit here please give us a
sign of your presence. YES

What is your name? BELLA

How old are you? 25

What year were you born? 1957

When did you die? NO

Sorry. Where are you from? ROANOKE

What brings you here? MUSIC

whose music? I CAN SING

Do you sing along with Tavi? YES

To what? HOLE

Awesome! You like HOLE? YES

Do you like Courtney Love? NO

Why not? SHE IS ON SOMETHING

What's your favorite Hole song? DOLL PARTS

What other music do you like? ELLA

What's your favorite movie? JUST KIDS

Do you mean the book by Patti Smith? YES

what's your favorite movie, though? BIRDS

The Birds? YES   Do you like Twin Peaks? YES
Who killed Laura Palmer? BOB

Is there anything you'd like to tell
       us? MY DAUGHTER IS GONE

Where is she? HOME

In Roanoke? YES

How old is she? 58 NOW

How old was she when you last saw her? 12

What's her name? JESSICA

Last name? MARVIN

Why aren't you with her? I LEFT

Why? I WANTED TO SEE THE WORLD

Do you feel that you have? YES

What was your favorite place? MOROCCO

Meet anyone interesting? KATE JERIAH

Where? ORIENT EXPRESS

Met any famous people? YES

Who? AUDREY HEPBURN

Are you just like everything Ella and
     I like materialized in the air? NO

Where did you meet her? SOMALIA

Did you work with Unicef? YES

What was she like? BEAUTIFUL

Do you mind if we pause to write
    all this down? I WILL STAY

We're back. What's your favorite color? BLACK

If I were to make an outfit of you, what should
    I be sure to include? A SUN HAT

What if I don't have one? A CAMERA

Do you like Joni? YES

What's your favorite of her songs? LITTLE GREEN

Is there anything you DON'T like that I do?
                  COURTNEY

We've established that.
Anything else? KIRSTEN DUNST

Why not? SHE IS ANNOYING

That's invalid! Have you
ever met her? NO

Well, do you like the
Virgin Suicides? NOT SURE

OK Bella, ultimate question:
Edward or Jacob? ALEX

Like in "Alex Reads Twilight"?
YES

what the hell! Do you like
Bob Dylan? YES

Favorite song? BRINGING
IT ALL BACK HOME

That's an album. Favorite
song on that album?
SHE BELONGS TO ME

Why do you come to MY house?
I LIKE TO READ

My books? YES

How often do you come here?
DEPENDS

Where else do you go in oak park?
BOOK TABLE

Do you just follow me around?
YES

Ella: Do you put thoughts in her
head? NO

We're off to bed. Any last words?
GOODBYE

OUIJA with Ella 11/26/11

If there is a spirit here give us
a sign of your presence
        YES

Is this Ryan Mahone?
        YES

Prove it. What do you wear on
your head?
        TOP HAT

Ok. Have anything to say to us?
        COME

Where?
        TO YOUR GRAVE

(Ella:) Why don't you like me
anymore?
        THE NIGHT

Ok we're leaving now

OUIJA with Ella 1/22/12

If there is a spirit here, please give us a sign
of your presence YES

Is this Ryan Mahone? YES

How are you today? I BROKE MY PROMISE

What did you do? I DID NOT HURT ELLA

So you promised that you would hurt
    Ella? YES

To who? NATALIE

We thought she was dead. How did you talk to her?
    SHE SAW THE KNIFE

Can you elaborate? ELLA WAS HOLDING IT

You were gonna hurt her with the knife? YES

Why didn't you? SHE SAID SHE SAW ME

Was this when Scott was over? YES

Are you gonna keep your promise? YES
What J Natalie's last name? KELLENGER
Kellenger? YES
Anything else before yf we go? WAIT
What? AM I DEAD
I don't know. Are you? I THINK SO
Anything else? DO YOU THINK I SHOULD DIE
No! Anything else? WATCH OUT FOR
    MARCH 15
What's gonna happen? IT WILL BE A SCARY DAY
Why then? Why not the 14th or 16th? NATALIE
    WILL COME
Ok. Bye! GOODBYE

OUIJA WITH ELLA 2/8/13

IF THERE IS A SPIRIT HERE PLEASE
GIVE US A SIGN OF YOUR PRESENCE
    "YES"
DO YOU MIND IF WE WRITE THIS DOWN
    "NO"
WHAT IS YOUR NAME?
    "EZRA XAVIER FYRE"
WHAT YEAR WERE YOU BORN?
    "1914"
WHERE ARE YOU FROM?
    "KENTUCKY"
HOW OLD ARE YOU?
    "61"
WHAT WAS YOUR JOB?
    "AVIATOR"
WHAT IS YOUR FAVORITE PLACE YOU WENT?
    "NO"

WHAT DO YOU MEAN?
    "I WILL ONLY TELL IF YOU BRING
    ANSWERS TO MY QUESTION"
WHAT IS YOUR QUESTION?
    "CAN YOU SEE ME"
NO. NOW THAT WE'VE ANSWERED,
WHAT IS YOUR FAVORITE PLACE?
    "ARABIA"
HAVE YOU EVER BEEN IN LOVE?
    "WITH NENA"
HOW OLD WERE YOU?
    "MY TURN WHERE WILL I REST"
DO YOU MEAN IN OAK PARK?
    "NO"
WHAT DO YOU MEAN "REST"?
    "I AM DEAD"

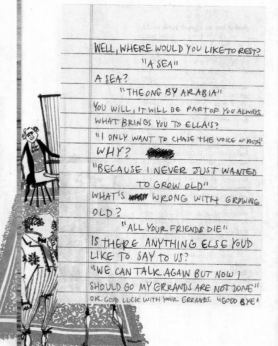

WELL, WHERE WOULD YOU LIKE TO REST?
    "A SEA"
A SEA?
    "THE ONE BY ARABIA"
YOU WILL, IT WILL BE PART OF YOU ALWAYS.
WHAT BRINGS YOU TO ELLA'S?
    "I ONLY WANT TO CHASE THE VOICE OF YOUTH"
WHY?
    "BECAUSE I NEVER JUST WANTED
    TO GROW OLD"
WHAT'S WRONG WITH GROWING
OLD?
    "ALL YOUR FRIENDS DIE"
IS THERE ANYTHING ELSE YOU'D
LIKE TO SAY TO US?
    "WE CAN TALK AGAIN BUT NOW I
SHOULD GO MY ERRANDS ARE NOT DONE"
OK. GOOD LUCK WITH YOUR ERRANDS. "GOOD BYE"

ALL BROTHERS

A-42269-I
Time: 2:34

KIDS ARE PEOPLE TOO!

1

Design by Sonja. Title lettering by Vanessa Han. Portrait of Jackson 5 and watercolor suspenders by Brooke Nechvatel.

NOVEMBER 2013: Family

Happy November, Rookies!

This month's theme is FAMILY. We'll be talking a lot about those people who are raising us, the ones we live or lived with, and the families we build for ourselves. And the families we only *feel* like we know, like the ones from *The Royal Tenenbaums*, *The Squid and the Whale*, *Sesame Street*, the Muppets, *Fraggle Rock*, *The Cosby Show*, *Family Matters*, *Full House*, *Who's the Boss*, *Diff'rent Strokes*, *Little Miss Sunshine*, *Parenthood*, *Bob's Burgers*, *The Simpsons*, *Gilmore Girls*, *Six Feet Under*, *The Addams Family*, *Freaky Friday*, *Fun Home*, ETC., FOREVER, BECAUSE WOWEE, there are SO many stories about families, and people always talk about family like it's this sacred institution, or like you're not allowed to question your family's unconditional love for you, and you have to love them unconditionally, and huuuuugs all aroooouuund for everyoneeee.

But…unconditional love is stupid? A person should meet certain conditions to be deemed deserving of your love! And also, what about the episode of *Boy Meets World* where Shawn's half-brother is being weird and Shawn says to Cory, "Eddie's only blood. YOU'RE my family"? And also, WHAT ABOUT THE EPISODE WHERE SHAWN ADOPTS A PIG?

When we wrote our contributors about this theme, Anaheed included this quotation from a Joss Whedon interview (*Sidney Morning Herald*, 2005):

> I am a great believer in found families, and I'm not a great believer in blood. Although I love my family, even the ones I grew up with, to me I've always felt that the people who treated you with respect and included you in their lives were your family, and the people who were related to you by blood might happen to be those people, but that correlation was a lot less [strong] than society believes it is.

So this month is neither a big happy Thanksgiving dinner nor a massive bedroom-door slam accompanied by a "LEAVE ME ALONE"—it's a bit of both, plus an ode to the people whom you *choose* to love and include in your life. Enjoy this month!

LOVE,
TAVI

Let's Be Friends

How to find your people in a new city (or anywhere).
By Estelle

I just moved to New York from Melbourne, Australia, where I'd lived all my life. Living in a new city for the first time is really exciting, but I miss my friends and family back home. Movies, meals, walks, and new discoveries are not as fun when I don't have anyone to share them with. And living in a big, overcrowded city, it's really easy to get lost in the shuffle. Somehow being alone in the middle of a crowd feels even lonelier than physical isolation.

So now I'm on a quest to make new friends! I have never had to do anything like this before—in Melbourne, I just naturally got to know people through school or work, and some of those people became my friends. Now that I'm out of school and freelancing from home, I have to go out of my way (i.e., actually leave the house) to meet people, and then explicitly ask them to hang out, risking rejection and embarrassment. I can be really shy and a bit awkward, so I was wary about approaching people like that.

But when I thought about it some more, I realized that even in my hometown, I'd gone through lots of little transitions over the years—between primary and secondary school, entering college, starting a new job, even just going to parties where I didn't know everyone—and I'd been able to make friends with at least one person in each new environment. So even if I wasn't the bubbliest social butterfly in the world, I obviously wasn't *completely* devoid of friendship skillz. Now I just had to figure out what those were, and then hone them.

I've been in New York for a month now, and my friendship quest has forced me to test out some friend-making strategies. You don't have to be born with this innate knowledge—anyone can learn how to make friends, no matter how old you are or how inhospitable your surroundings. It's not even that hard, I promise. Here's what's worked for me so far.

1. START WITH PEOPLE YOU ALREADY KNOW.

This is a good first/baby step, because you're not really making *new* friends, but reaching out to people you already know, but not super well: acquaintances, people you've lost touch with, Facebook friends, that kind of thing. I was lucky in that when I moved to New York, I had a cousin who already lived here. I hadn't seen him in 10 years, but I contacted him over email shortly before I arrived. As soon as I'd settled in, I invited him out for brunch. It was great! We filled each other in on our lives and laughed about how alike our moms (who are sisters) are. He also told me where to get the best food in my new neighborhood. Over a handful of friend dates we went from cousins-at-a-distance to actual buds, and now we meet up every couple of weeks for a meal or a movie. He was my first New York friend. Making just *one* friend in a town makes all the difference, and the good news is it doesn't take too much to achieve this.

2. NEXT STEP: FRIENDS ONCE REMOVED.

Another thing that's great about people you already know is they'll have a ready-made set of friends for you to meet! One of my old university friends, Al, has lived in New York for a while, and he knows a bunch of great people. He invited me to a party at his house and introduced me to a couple who had also just settled in the city. When I texted them to catch up last week, they invited me and my boyfriend over for dinner. They were so nice, and we found we had a lot in common—we'd lived in some of the same places, and one of them is a big reader like me—and I definitely want to hang out with them again. I couldn't believe how easy and straightforward it was to meet new

people. It turns out that all you have to do is ask!

But what if you don't know *any*one in your new city? Well, do you know people elsewhere? They might be able to help you out. Rack your brain for every time anyone has ever mentioned that they know someone in your new town. You can literally just say, "I haven't met anyone I really click with here; if you know anyone you think I would get along with, can you introduce us?" Charlie from orchestra is originally from Cleveland? Ask him. Your brother's girlfriend used to work in London? Hit her up. Don't be worried that you're hassling them; if they're your friends, they'll want you to be happy wherever you are! You and your friends' friends already have one thing in common (your friends), and chances are there'll be other stuff too.

Another thing that helped me was a blanket announcement/request. If you tell people that you're moving—in person, by email, or on Facebook, and add, "If you know anyone fun in [wherever] I should hang out with, let me know!" people will start sending you names and numbers. Humans are so naturally social! If you want to be more specific, you could say, "I'd love someone to go see Fiona Apple with next month!" and your peeps will let you know who their other music-lovin' friends are. After I did this, the names started pouring in, and I now have a huge list of New Yorkers to meet—and I hardly had to lift a finger.

Now, contacting the people on this list presents another challenge, because of the aforementioned shyness. If you have trouble making friends, I'm guessing you might suffer from the same affliction? Well, email was *made* for us, my friend. Writing an email to a stranger is a lot less intimidating than calling or texting, and it puts less pressure on them. Here's an example—an actual email that I wrote when I moved here:

Dear Dan,
I hope you're well!
Our mutual friend Ian—who is the best—kindly put us in touch. As he mentioned, I've just arrived in NYC and would love to meet

you and hear about what you do. As I'm new in town, I would love for you to suggest somewhere fun or delicious where I can buy you a coffee (or other treat)!

Bestest,
Estelle

This email does a few different things: establishes contact, reminds the potential friend who you are and whom you have in common, invites them to suggest when and where might be convenient for them to meet, and subtly acknowledges that they are doing you a favor by taking the time and the risk to meet up with a stranger. Also, it's short! The people you'll be contacting probably already have busy lives, and it's considerate to be brief, I think.

Dan responded to that email, and we have since had a couple of fairy-tale coffee dates where we literally talked about Rookie, so it's worked out pretty well so far. I'm meeting some more people this week, too! Cross your fingers for me.

3. FIND YOUR TRIBE.

If you don't know anyone at all in your new school/city/whatever, you'll have to push up your sleeves and do a bit of work. I love books and literature, so I've been looking up New York book events. I'm planning to go to a few of them and just say hi to people who look friendly. This might sound scary, but all you have to do is say hello (and maybe smile)! You don't have to make friends straightaway. It's all about getting used to the vibe and the faces around you. Eventually, you might see the same faces again and again. Then, try to get beyond hi—these could be the people you eventually ask to see a comedy show with you, or to grab a bite to eat after a reading.

I haven't done that last part yet, but I will. It will require me to swallow my shyness and just go for it. Maybe if someone's holding a book I've read, I'll ask them what they thought about it. If I overhear a person chatting in a non-American accent, I'll ask them if they're from out of town like I am. People flying solo might be the most approachable, because they could be in the same situation as me. Groups might

have their own thing going on, but still, if you overhear a conversation about a topic that really interests you—someone's having trouble with their sewing machine, or abstaining from watching *The Mindy Project* when they have buckets of studying to do—why not try politely jumping in?

I realize that the strike-out-on-your-own path might not be for everyone. That's why clubs and social events are so great. There are heaps of sports teams you can join, for example, and lots of themed meet-ups that are arranged online. And then there are less-formal groups you can be part of. A new friend has just asked me to join a baking club. I don't even have an oven, but I'm joining as a guest eater. I mean, I love to put carbs in my face. That qualifies me for friendship with bakers, RIGHT?

If you can't find an event, team, club, guild, or league that appeals to you, why not start one of your own? Create a Facebook event for a talent show you want to run, or let it be known that your *Buffy* Binge-Watch Brigade is open to new members. When I'm in charge of something, I feel more confident, and I find it's easier to talk about something I'm *doing* rather than about myself per se. And when you create an experience with a bunch of other people? That's some intense, satisfying bonding right there.

4. HELLO: THE BASICS.

Then there are the connections you can make just by being in the world. When you move to a new city or start at a new school or a new job, you're thrust into a whole new social milieu. It can be tricky to stay cool in such circumstances, because every situation is so different. You won't know anything about pre-existing social allegiances or rules, and the risk of doing something you'll feel embarrassed about is higher than if you know where you stand.

But you know what? At a minimum, all you really need to do is say hello, introduce yourself, and ask your companion's name. Smiling helps! After that, if conversation doesn't seem to be flowing, just ask a simple question or two. "How long have you worked here?" or "Who's that band on your T-shirt?" will work fine. It doesn't

have to be rocket science—you're just two people being friendly. If they don't reciprocate, it's probably not your fault: People can be closed up for personal reasons, or they might have had a bad day. Even really awesome people sometimes have terrible friendship chemistry. But don't give up on being interested in others. Someone who will be curious back is right around the corner.

~*~*~

I know I could live my life safely alone in my apartment, ordering delivery and never having to leave or speak to anyone. But new friends do stuff like crack jokes with you and support you and teach you new things, and that's all stuff I'm willing to work for. If that means I have to open my tender, fragile little heart to strangers, so be it! Some people might peek in and find nothing of interest there, and that's OK. But a couple of people might open their hearts to me, too, and I'll be so grateful and excited. This is how it works for *everybody*, yourself included! Say yes to friends, friend. ✿

Hanging Out With
Rory Gilmore
by Hazel

1. There She Goes - The La's
2. Here's Where the Story Ends - The Sundays
3. Tea or Coffee - Gaze
4. My Favourite Book - Stars
5. I'm a Cuckoo - Belle and Sebastian
6. Questions and Answers - The Apples in Stereo
7. Here Comes Your Man - Pixies
8. Favorite Food - Bunnygrunt
9. I Just Do - Go Sailor
10. This Is Not a Test - She & Him

DIY FINGER-KNITTED SCARF

Cold, gloomy weather = the perfect time to wear a rainbow everywhere.
By Marlena

For this cozy, fall-themed DIY, I'm gonna show you how to make your very own faux-knitted scarf. I say "faux" because for this project, you'll be using just your fingers to knit—no knitting needles! It's super-simple to do, and the result looks totally rad.

WHAT YOU'LL NEED:

- **Lots of yarn.** Any kind, from medium to bulky weight, will work, but yarn described as superfine or lightweight is too thin. I went for a rainbow theme with my scarf, so I used yarn in a variety of colors, plus some white for clouds.

- **Scissors.**

HOW TO DO IT:

1. The base of the scarf will be made of long finger-knitted "ropes." Start off with a piece of yarn that's still attached to the skein.

2. With your palm facing you, clasp one end of the yarn between your thumb and your index finger, as shown at left.

3. Wrap the yarn under your middle finger, over your ring finger, and under your pinkie. Bring it back over your pinkie, under your ring finger, over your middle finger, and under your index finger. Repeat this over/under wrapping process two more times, until you have what looks like two dashed lines of yarn across your fingers, like in the far left corner below.

4. Now it's time to start knitting! Pull each loop from the bottom row of yarn up and over the top row of yarn and your fingertips.

5. You'll be left with just one row of yarn along the palm side of your fingers. Push these loops down your fingers a bit as shown.

6. Repeat steps 3 and 4. Continue repeating those two steps until you have something that looks like photo 6a, below. If you kind of tug on the end a bit it'll start to look more like a rope.

7. When your finger-knitting reaches the length you want it to be, finish the end off by weaving the tail into and out of the loops on your fingers, removing the yarn from your hand, and tugging the end again to tighten it up. Photo 7b shows much shorter versions of what your finished ropes will look like. For reference, my finished ropes were about 60 inches long.

8. Pair off your ropes in whatever color combinations you like, such as red/orange, yellow/green, and blue/purple, and tie the loose ends on each side of the ropes together.

9. Using a crisscross pattern, lace each pair of ropes together with a piece of matching or contrasting yarn. Gently tug on the yarn as you go along to help close up the gap.

10. Once you've laced the entire thing up, tie the loose ends together and snip off the excess.

11. To make this scarf actually look like a scarf, you'll need to lace up all three rope pairs. If you don't want to bother with the lacing, you can braid the ropes together instead, or even just wear them as-is! It's up to you.

TO MAKE AND ATTACH THE POMPOMS:

1. Wrap some more yarn around your hand (or a small piece of cardboard) multiple times to create a bundle.

2. Lay that bundle on top of a length of yarn about three times longer than the length of the bundle (see photo 2 at right).

3. Triple-tie that loose length of yarn around your bundle. Tie it tight! This will create a bunch of loops on either side of the knot.

4. Mark the ends of the yarn that you used to tie your bundle with a piece of tape or a marker so that you won't get them confused with the rest of the yarn—you're gonna need these strings in a minute.

5. Cut all of the loops open with your scissors and give the pompom a trim. Remember: Don't cut the yarn that you marked in step 4! But otherwise, don't be afraid to cut off a lot—pompoms usually look more pompom-y once you've cut away a good portion of the yarn.

6. Weave the strings that I told you not to snip through the ends of the scarf and tie them together to secure the pompoms in place.

And there you have it! Your new scarf is perfect for gloomy fall days, wouldn't you say? R

that's what friends do

The best kinds of buddies make you better.   Interviews by Maddy Ruvolo. Photography by Lauren Poor.

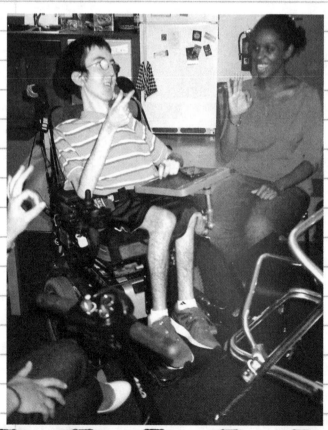

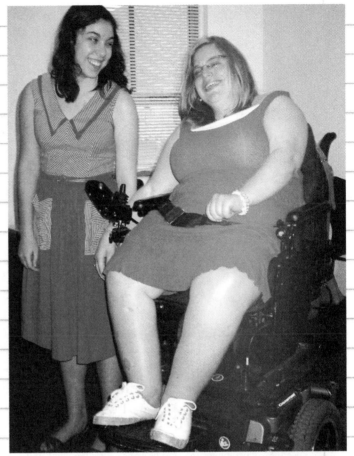

This past summer I was in an internship program with other disabled students. We all lived together and worked in various offices across DC. I asked my buddy Lauren to come hang out with us and take pictures for a day, and then I talked to my friends about their experiences with disability.

If you look for depictions of disabled folks in the media, you are likely to come across one of two portrayals: the bitter, evil disabled person or the Super Crip, who is portrayed as "inspirational" in the most dehumanizing way possible. The goal of this project is to give people another view, to show you what our lives are actually like.

[OPPOSITE PAGE, BOTTOM LEFT]

ALEX (LEFT), 20 I like teaching American Sign Language because it is thrilling to teach a language that is not well known in the hearing world. It allows me to personally connect more with my hearing friends. To be honest, sometimes it can be hard to be friends with hearing people, but it really depends if they are willing to accommodate to my communication method. There are some people who are very busy with other friends, like at college. But there are also people who will move mountains to communicate and be friends with me.

[OPPOSITE PAGE, BOTTOM RIGHT]

JASMIN (CENTER), 24 I got my disability about three years ago. I'm legally blind, and my vision is getting progressively worse. I'm learning how to deal with and accept my disability. I found it easy, at least with this group, to transition from being "able-bodied" to now being a person with a disability. I'm able to accept a new identity.

[THIS PAGE, TOP RIGHT]

KARIN (RIGHT), 23 You and I were roommates this summer, and we became really good friends. The best part about living with someone else who is disabled is that you don't have to worry about being judged or being treated like the charity-case roommate. I never had to pretend or hide parts of my disability because I thought you would be uncomfortable.

I have cerebral palsy, which affects my muscles, and I have this thing that gives me medicine to help relax my muscles, which makes it easier for me to do things like pick up my purse or put on my makeup.

I wish people got that disability isn't this weird thing that makes me a freak, it's just part of who I am as a person; and when they stare at me they're just seeing me in ways that reflect their own ideas about disability—they're not seeing me as a person, as an individual.

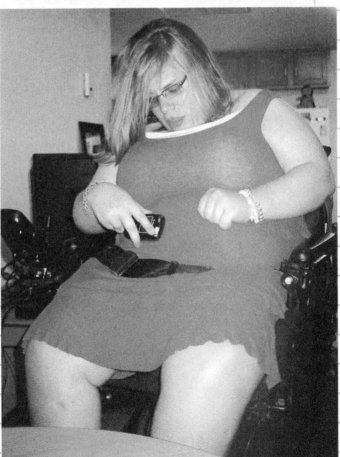

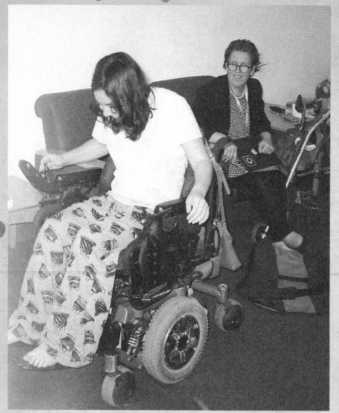

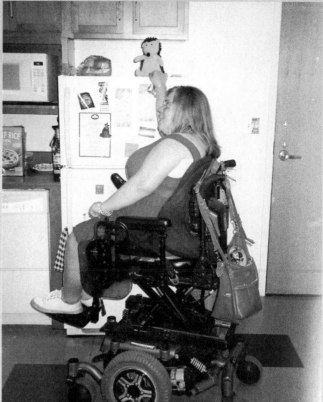

KARIN For the most part, I don't let people play in my chair because they don't understand that it is not a toy. They don't understand what it represents, what it means to me, and what it gives me. It can be really frustrating when people look at a chair as just something to have fun with. I'm like, "No, it's the difference between having a life and not having a life." It's different with us because we're friends and we both are disabled, so we both understand what the chair means. But most people don't get that the chair is a part of me, and without it, I don't go anywhere.

The fact that my wheelchair can elevate allows me to reach things and be more independent. I used to not use parts of my chair that could do all these things because I thought people would think it was strange, but now it's just like, why should I care about what people think of how I do things, as long as I get things done? It's either embracing who you are or not living your life, and I choose to live my life.

[THIS PAGE, RIGHT]

ROSE, 23 I have been legally blind since birth. I use a monocular, which is like binoculars but just one, since I only see out of one eye. I feel most self-conscious using my monocular at fast food restaurants, because everyone is standing around looking at the menu and I feel like there's more of a chance that they will notice me. I memorize one or two things that each restaurant serves and I limit myself to those choices, just so I don't have to use my monocular. I'm holding myself back, but I shouldn't.

Technology is rapidly improving, but it is very difficult for me to read the small font on the small screen. When I check Facebook on my iPhone, I use a magnifying glass.

I like who I am today, and my disability

ROSIE (BELOW, RIGHT), 20 A few months ago I started wheelchair dancing after a friend recommended it to me. It's a really cool way to express myself.

KELLI (BELOW IN THE YELLOW T-SHIRT), 23 I've been disabled all my life, since I was born. After my junior year of high school, I did the California Youth Leadership Forum [for Students ▶

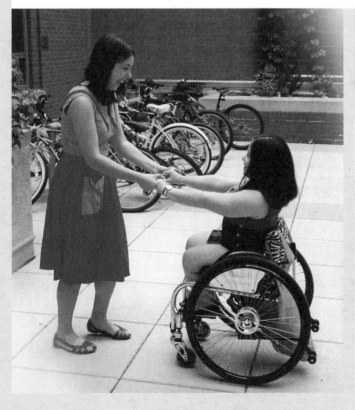

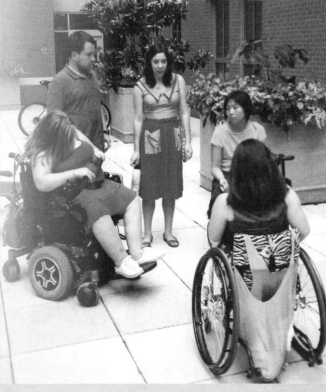

has played a really big role in shaping that.

It's about communicating with your partner and meeting in the middle.

with Disabilities], and that kind of got me into working in the community and knowing so many people here. I met people who have had the same experiences as me, who know what I'm going through, and I learned how to be an advocate for other people. I really love hanging out with other people who have disabilities, learning about their experiences.

ROSIE We have "walkers" and "rollers" partner with each other. It's a new way of figuring out how to accommodate each other. Some dance moves, people in power chairs can do but people in manual chairs can't. So it's about communicating with your partner and meeting in the middle.

[THIS PAGE, BOTTOM]
MICAH, 29 I have an intellectual disability. Before I had this voice-recognition software called Dragon, I would have to wait for my parents to come home to write emails. Now I can send emails and do everything on my computer. It's very cool.

[OPPOSITE PAGE, TOP LEFT]
LILI (LEFT), 21 I have a complicated relationship with my walker because it's not the perfect piece of assistive technology for me from an efficiency standpoint, but it's been with me for so long and it's such a part of how I think about my disability. I learned to walk on a walker just like this one. Sometimes I decorate it for Halloween or for school plays. I try to make it part of my look.

[OPPOSITE PAGE, TOP RIGHT]
MADDY This is me, counting out my pills for the week. I have a chronic illness called dysautonomia. People forget that not all disabilities are visible—if you looked at me you'd never know that I spent the last three years of high school in bed, and you probably wouldn't guess that fatigue and pain continue to be major factors in my life. I wish people would remember that the healthy-looking person taking the elevator up one floor or sitting down on the bus might really need to do those things.

[OPPOSITE PAGE, BOTTOM]
MADDY Finding the online disability community was transformative for me. Before, when doctors and school administrators told me I was lying or faking or being dramatic, I knew they were wrong, but I still took in their judgments. Realizing that the problem wasn't me or my body, but rather social stigma and discrimination and ableism, was super empowering. I like who I am today, and my disability has played a really big role in shaping that. ☺

I'm able to accept a new identity.

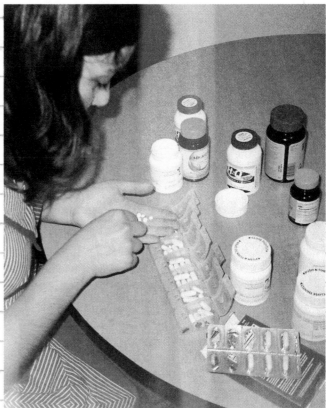

AFTER-SCHOOL SNACKS: A TAXONOMY

Pantry ignorance = social death.
By Dylan

The after-school snack is the most important meal of your social life—friends go where the snacks are, after all, leaving memories and crumbs to be ground into the carpets and cushions of our lives. The afternoon snack is the pillar of the adolescent weekday, a tall and steady totem of three o'clock refueling for the wobbling soldiers of sixth-period math. Since the selection of a designated after-school chill spot corresponds directly to whose house has the most appealing pantry selection, it is crucial that we study and learn the relative merits of the most common snack foods out there today.

It is in this spirit that I present to you these 14 staples that no good pantry can do without. Ignore them and risk social disaster!

1. Cereal

What is it about the combination of processed grain-product and sugar, soaked in milk, that soothes us and makes us want to pound multiple bowls? Cereal is the ultimate snack food, mostly because it is appropriate at all times of the day, from normal morning until *It's already 5 AM?* morning. And the pinnacle of cereal-discovery bliss is opening a friend's cupboard to find rows of Technicolor boxes containing the likes of Cinnamon Toast Crunch, Trix, Honey Nut Cheerios, Chex, and Lucky Charms. Sugar cereal was banned in my house, so trips to my buddies' houses were crucial—without those excavations I wouldn't be the proud sweet tooth I am today.

2. Costco 86-Pack Individually Wrapped Snacks

Costco families take the after-school snack seriously. Why else would you need 14-pound tubs of Twizzlers, triple-jumbo bags of Doritos, and screw-top buckets of chocolate-covered nuts? These kinds of quantities suggest apocalypse prep, but they're just enough to accommodate an afternoon stampede of hangry youths. Some items may be more thrilling than others—individual cups of applesauce are fine, but 50 small bags of Cheetos = the snack dream fully realized.

3. Candy Disguised as Fruit Snacks

The difference between fruit snacks and gummy candy is in name only. We have marketing to thank for keeping Gushers, Fruit Roll-Ups, and squishy fruit-shaped globules in the snack zone. Real candy is often prohibited until dessert time, but when the package says a product contains two to three servings of *real fruit from a plant*, there's room to negotiate with the parentals.

4. Candy Disguised as Trail Mix

Rustic! Hiking! People who walk around in nature eat this mix of granola and candy, so we will overlook the fact that it is really just a deconstructed chocolate-and-nut candy bar mixed into some grains, and categorize it as food for children. As a still-school-age person who enjoys walking around in nature, I'm not complaining.

5. Candy Disguised as Granola Bars

These are sad excuses for sweet treats. Listen, Kudos and Chewy Bars: Sandwiching a thick slab of chocolate and mini M&M's between two layers of puffed oats or rice isn't going to make that center stripe any less the candy that it actually is. Figure out who you are and then get back to me.

6. Candy Disguised as Nothing, Allowed to Be Itself

Adults who put out communal snack bowls of M&M's are key-holders to the golden kingdom. One of my aunts does this, and when my extended family gets together, guess whose house I choose to stay at? Her heaping bowls of bonbons may be a trap to see who the greediest guests are, but I'm not interested in conspiracies—I'm interested in CANDY. It's also great when parents really don't give a rip and `just go all *c'est la vie* and *carpe diem* on this business by keeping their cupboard stocked with straight-up full-size candy bars. I salute you, carefree spoilers of supper!

7. One Part Vegetable, Five Parts Ranch

Here's the one vegetable-based option everyone can agree on. Mom and Dad are happy because you're consuming something that comes from nature and might supply a vitamin or two, but you win because celery is nothing more than a slightly more respectable vehicle for dip than a spoon. We know this—even Mom and Dad know this—but no one seems to mind. Could this be the peacemaker of after-school snacks?

8. Chocolate Milk

Most people seem to outgrow their taste for plain milk drunk straight from a glass, but almost anyone is down to drink the chocolate kind. Some families use Hershey's syrup and others prefer Nesquik, but the best houses have Ovaltine, that sweet malted-chocolate powder. It's like a 1950s American diner in a glass, and in a pinch it can fill the milkshake hole in your life. Bonus points if your friend's house has plastic straws—everyone knows chocolate milk tastes better that way.

9. Frozen Pizza Items, Miniature Variety

This is an incredibly nuanced field of snack. Practically anything that involves dough, cheese, and a tomato-based substance can be considered pizza flavored, so there are a vast array of options: Pizza rolls, Bagel Bites, and Hot Pockets all qualify. Your after-school pizza craving can be taken care of in a matter of minutes! These are foodstuffs in a category all their own, separate from Pizza World, but close enough to be neighbors.

10. Processed Vegetable Products

Some of these are acquired tastes, but nori sheets, root-veggie chips, dehydrated snap peas, and green-bean crisps can do wonders to maintain/enhance a salty addiction. You'll usually find these in the homes of hippie or gourmand parents. I especially love sweet-potato chips—they sound healthier than regular chips/crisps, so I can eat *all of them*. Honorable mention goes to nori sheets—they're salty and thin and crackly, so if you're into sushi or tasting the salty breeze of the ocean on your lips, it's the best snack of all time.

11. PB&J

It would be a crime to neglect this classic. The combination of soft white bread, smooth peanut butter, and fruit jelly has earned OG status in the realm of comfort foods, but the variations are fun too, and an exciting snack house is one that offers multiple spreadable options. When I'm craving texture, for example, I use chunky peanut butter instead of smooth, a whole-grain, hippie-ish variety of bread, and raspberry preserves with all the seeds. As your tastes develop, I encourage you to experiment—try raw almond butter or Nutella, apple butter or marmalade. Step it up times two with some HEAT—toast the assembled sandwich on a panini press or in a grill pan, and eat it with your pinky out 'cause you're a classy sandwich eater.

12. Fancy Fruit Beverages

Just like fruit snacks get a pass as candy, so do fruit drinks dressed up like soda. Those 24-packs of what is basically sugar water were a special bulk-bought concession in my no-junk-food home, and I drank a lot of Orangina, Izze, and Juice Squirt. When you're a kid, fizzy juices in glass bottles make you feel very fancy. My San Pellegrino Limonata phase was exciting for me, but my friends found the drink too tart. I didn't concede defeat, though: I took this as an opportunity to demand that my mother supply our house with *options*. "Don't you care about my social life?!?!?" was as effective an argument as I needed.

13. Homemade Cookies (Bonus: Leftover Dough)

Absolute game changer. Cookies will bring kids from a mile away to the yard, where they will press their noses to your kitchen window, peering inside with begging eyes. The fresh-from-the-oven gooeyness is a treat in itself, but leaving some of the dough around in the fridge to be eaten with a spoon is NEXT-LEVEL SNACKING.

14. Small Animal-Shaped Bites

Small things baked in the shapes of animals are incredibly delicious, even for vegetarians. Animal crackers, Goldfish crackers, Trader Joe's Cats Cookies, Hello Panda, Teddy Grahams, and the like are standard in any snack cabinet. They are consistently under about one inch wide—perfect snack size—and have cute little faces that stare up at you as you crush them with your teeth. Dang, cuteness is delicious!

Between Two Beats

No matter what I listened to, I felt like I was betraying half of myself.
By Brittany

One day, when I was in kindergarten, I came home from school and asked my mom why I was lighter than the black girls at my school but darker than the white girls. "If Kimmy is black and Amber is white, what does that make me?" I said.

My mom paused for a beat. She would later explain that she had spent that extra breath figuring out how to explain why my dad wasn't in my life. Impatient, I beat her to the punch and crafted my own conclusion: "I think I'm golden." She looked relieved.

I lived with the three white people who had raised me—my mother and her parents—and had attended mostly-white Catholic schools in the suburban Midwest since pre-K. I don't know why I hadn't thought about the difference between my skin color and the rest of my family's before, nor what prompted me to do so on that particular day. I don't remember anyone ever mentioning race at school, but my best friend at the time was mixed like me, and we came to this question at the same time, suggesting we'd been wondering together: Why were we darker?

I was a well-kept only child, spoiled beyond what my family's lower-middle-class lifestyle probably could have afforded. My mom and her parents were my world, and I theirs. My mother worked part-time as a teacher's aide at my elementary school and fixed her schedule to make sure she had time to be with me in the evening too. When she went off to her second job in the morning, her Polish-American mother babysat me and taught me how to read. On school-vacation days my grandfather, a proud Greek-American man with a belly and beard as big as his personality, took me to his job at a pest control business he co-owned. In his blue pickup truck, we'd listen to the oldies station and he'd sing along to Joe Cocker, Johnny Cash, and his hero, Elvis Presley.

As kids do, I adopted my family's tastes as my own. Papa's oldies station became my automatic car request (as he would proudly tell everyone as I grew older). My mom liked the oldies too, but hers were from the '80s—she could never turn off the radio when either of her teenage crushes, Michael Jackson and Prince, were on. She was 21 when she had me, and maybe the angst of being such a young mother is what drew her, in the '90s, to that decade's wave of indignant female singer-songwriters: Tori Amos, Alanis Morissette, and Tracy Bonham. Amos's "Silent All These Years" and Bonham's "Mother Mother" were played on repeat on our desktop Dell computer in the dining room as my mom cleaned or paid bills. As soon as I figured out how to work our car's CD player, I played those songs on repeat, too.

It wasn't until I was seven that my kindergarten question was answered. My mom had been doing a great job of hiding the court battle she'd been fighting for a year against my father over visitation rights. But then he won that case and was granted biweekly visits. Suddenly I was required *by law* to spend time with a man who had until then been a stranger to me.

My parents had begun their toxic on-and-off relationship when they were both 13. They had me eight years later. They never married, and my mom left my dad when I was six weeks old. He saw me a couple of times when I was an infant. I don't remember it.

At first he seemed like an alien to me. His complexion was much darker than my mom's, which wouldn't be hard because she has the type of pale skin that instantly turns red in the sun. I could tell right away that he really wanted to build a relationship with me—he was unfailingly nice, and he even dressed up in a suit for our first few meetings. After that, though, he relaxed into his usual wardrobe of black T-shirts emblazoned with the names and logos of heavy metal bands. I was just starting to branch out from my family's musical preferences to develop my own, which tended toward Radio Disney and its endless bubblegum-pop goodness, and my father's Metallica shirts scared me. With their imagery of skulls and graves, they looked nothing like my Backstreet Boys tees.

Desperate to get to know my father, I overcame my fear over time. I never talked to him about race because I was too busy learning about who he was as a person. His identity as a metalhead seemed more integral to his personality than his blackness. Not that his race was irrelevant—it was just lower on the list of the things that made him *him*.

As I got to know him over the course of the next couple of years, I was also evolving as a music listener. Ages seven through nine were devoted almost exclusively to 'N Sync. The band's breakup in 2002 and Justin Timberlake's subsequent maturity—as manifested on the solo album he released that fall and in his scandalous Super Bowl halftime performance with Janet Jackson 15 months later—were too much for a Catholic-school-attending nine-year-old to handle. They ignited the most intense bout of preteen angst my young life had ever seen. Deepening my sorrow, my grade school closed down at the end of fourth grade due to low enrollment, so I began fifth grade at a new private Catholic school. It felt like heading into the great unknown, leaving behind life as I knew it and a slew of familiar faces, and I was terrified.

Going to a new school just before junior high did have one advantage, though: It meant I could "reinvent" myself. I was pretty much known as a dork in grade school, and I longed to be, or at least seem, cooler. I was starting to rebel internally against my own self-image; I felt rough and bratty and whiny. Lucky for me, this was all happening in the mid-to-late-'90s, when a pop-punk revolution was taking place in America. Acts like Avril Lavigne and Good Charlotte spoke to my suburban angst. I began exploring MTV and watched *TRL* religiously. Q101, Chicago's excellent (but sadly now defunct) radio station, became my respite and my truest love.

My new school was even whiter than my last one. I was one of three people of color in my grade. Race wasn't brought up, because there was nothing to talk about—three people don't cause so much as a ripple in the majority's consciousness. It wasn't until sixth grade, when a required Spanish-language class was added to our curriculum, that I realized everyone had assumed for a full year that I was Hispanic. This came to light after our teacher, a white woman, asked in class if I spoke the language at home. When I told her I wasn't Latina, people seemed shocked.

By then I had fully adopted the persona of "the rock girl." I talked about Linkin Park and Blink-182 with the boys in my class who played in bands and had rock & roll dreams. My favorite music also helped me bond with my dad—the guy who had seemed for so long like an alien being was now my most valuable resource. I asked him to play me his Metallica albums, which I had previously rejected as "too loud." We'd listen to System of a Down's "Aerials" every time it came on Q101; I would later steal his copy of *Toxicity*. Young dudes in 2002 loved System of a Down, so I always had something to talk about with these new friends and classmates.

By seventh grade, I had marked my territory as my class's resident music snob. I began collecting full discographies of my favorite bands and subscribed to *Rolling Stone* and *SPIN*. My homeroom teacher, a hippie with a small peace sign tattooed on his hand, would play Bob Dylan and Pink Floyd CDs for us in class. Eventually, he let me bring in music I had been discovering on VH1, Fuse, MTV, and through my magazine subscriptions. When I played

Bright Eyes for the class, our teacher seemed to appreciate Conor Oberst's talents more than my classmates did.

That year two new black kids enrolled in our school, bringing the grand total of people of color to five, and the number of black kids, including me, to three and a half. This must have been some kind of tipping point, because suddenly race became an issue. My classmates learned a new word that year: *Oreo*—not in the sense of the delicious cookie, but to mean a black person who is "white on the inside." This word was used to describe not just me but also my mysterious father, whom no one had met but who loomed in everyone's imaginations as "the black guy who likes metal." For the second time in my life, I felt that eternal mixed-girl struggle: not quite black, not quite white, but still pressed to choose sides. This time, however, I didn't feel as confident proclaiming my golden uniqueness. I was getting insecure about my identity, mostly because there was this very visible other half of me I didn't know if I was allowed to claim, because I was "the rock girl."

One of the new black kids was a girl named Amber who was obsessed with R&B, soul, and hip-hop, the last of which had recently been discovered by the upper-middle-class suburban white boys in our class. Amber's pride in her own culture made me step back and take a look at the music I had been consuming. After two years of a steady rock education, I hadn't realized how blindingly white all of it had been. Outside of Eminem's single "Lose Yourself," a song that was

almost unavoidable in 2002, hip-hop didn't appeal to me, and I had been prevented from buying the *8 Mile* soundtrack because my mom found Eminem's past lyrics misogynistic.

I befriended Amber, and my new education began. I began actively seeking out music that strayed from the grunge self-education I had been focused on and added artists like Mary J. Blige and Common to my iPod. From there I moved on to 50 Cent, Kanye, Outkast, Usher, and Lil Wayne. It was wonderfully surprising how much this music appealed to me, even if I cringed whenever the N-word came up in a song. Amber and I are friends to this day, and she still loves thanking me for introducing her to rock and pop artists like the Yeah Yeah Yeahs and Lana Del Rey.

At some point, you have to learn to love what you love outside of the roles you feel you need to play. Rock & roll never left my heart, but the moment I learned to love hip-hop for the sake of the music and not to prove anything to myself or anyone else, I realized that my race, my skin color, and my own anxiety have nothing to do with what I look for when I put my headphones on and get lost in a really epic playlist. Instead of segregating my iTunes according to my two racial halves, I started to see the connections and similarities among all the different kinds of music I liked. I took ownership of who I inherently was—a mixed girl who just happens to love a lot of music. This was the beginning of the future I had daydreamed about for myself as a music writer, which is what I am today. I've never felt more golden. ★

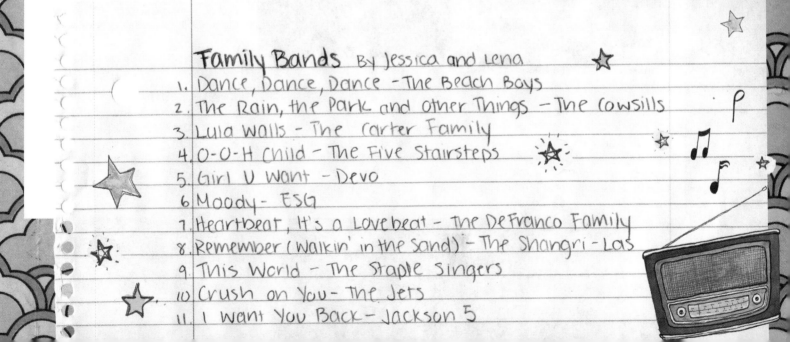

Family Bands By Jessica and Lena
1. Dance, Dance, Dance - The Beach Boys
2. The Rain, the Park and Other Things - The Cowsills
3. Lula Walls - The Carter Family
4. O-O-H Child - The Five Stairsteps
5. Girl U Want - Devo
6. Moody - ESG
7. Heartbeat, It's a Lovebeat - The DeFranco Family
8. Remember (Walkin' in the Sand) - The Shangri-Las
9. This World - The Staple Singers
10. Crush on You - The Jets
11. I Want You Back - Jackson 5

DIY PET PHOTO SHOOT

How to take the kind of picture that makes people go
"AHHHHH OMGGGGGG LOOOOKIT HIIIIIMMMMMM."
By Krista

Since our theme this month is FAMILY, we're thinking about our relatives and chosen friend-families a lot. But there's a V. IMPORTANT someone that we haven't talked about yet: the unsung heroes of our daily lives who always make us feel happeeeeee. That's right: our pets! I myself have a three-year-old dwarf bunny named Timothy Maxwell Thumperton, and HE IS THE BEST AND CUTEST AND MOST PERFECTEST BABY McFLUFFERSON EVER. If you have a pet, I bet you feel exactly the same way about him or her. Someone you love so much deserves a tribute, right? A mark of respect! Something like…*a customized, elaborate photo shoot that shows off their intrinsic animal beauty*, perhaps?

This is my first bunny, Midgeon P. Bundlesworth III, enjoying an Oktoberfest celebration. NO PHOTOSHOP.

See, there are pet pictures and then there are *amazing* pet pictures. A regular pet pic is something you probably have hundreds of stored in your phone:

Your pet was doing something cute, you stealthily grabbed a camera and snapped a picture, and there it was. Fun and adorbs, to be sure, but probably of interest to you alone. An *amazing* pet picture is one that makes you stop, clutch your heart, and make audible high-pitched squealing noises like "AHHHHH OMGGGGGG LOOOOKIT HIIIIIMMMMMM," or "EEEEEEE HIS LIDDLE HAAAT AHHHH DYING." For this DIY, I tried capturing my best friend in a totally new light. It's deep autumn here in Chicago, and I thought, *Wouldn't Timothy Maxwell Thumperton look SPECTAC as a little north woods camper?*

WHY YES, HE WOULD.

AHHHHHHH OMG. A good pet picture is universal: All people, everywhere, are powerless in the face of True Cute. It's the language we all speak, and achieving this level of greatness isn't even *hard*—I don't care if you've got a hamster, a dog, a cat, or a lizard, you have the power! A quick note, though: If your pet is SERI-

OUSLY NOT FEELING IT when you're setting up a shoot and fights you every step of the way, don't force her or him to do it. There's no reason to make a pet really unhappy about something that's supposed to be fun—if your cat is hiding under the bed and scowling in the dark, it's not a good time for a photo shoot. But if your pet seems willing enough to model their tail off, prepare to ABSOLUTELY SLAY PEOPLE WITH CUTENESS.

1. PICK A THEME.

A theme can revolve around a time of year or a holiday like Valentine's Day, Halloween, or Hanukkah. Or you can base it on an activity, be it as fancy as a tea party or as ordinary as breakfast. Just keep in mind that the best themes usually are the ones where the pet in question is photographed in a human situation, e.g., wearing a sweater or playing an instrument. Other ideas: the first day of school, meeting a new friend, a trip to the beach. The world is your adorably dressed pet oyster!

2. ACCESSORIZE.

Make/find pet-size accessories to photograph Fido or Fluffy with. Thrift- and dollar-store toy sections are gold mines for props, but you can also look for stuff around your house. Is your pet big enough to sit at the table like a person? Set the table for a fancy dinner party and photograph her wearing a tie. Is Fluffy about to be the guest of honor at a birthday photo shoot? Make him a cat-size b-day hat, frost and stack three cookies so they look like a cake, and add a candle (don't light it)! HAPPY BIRTHDAY TO EVERYONE.

I got Timmy accessorized and prepped for his camping shoot for under $1. For the fire, I picked up some twigs outside, hot-glued them together, cut up an old ribbon to make it look like flames, snipped off a strip from a flannel shirt for the scarf, and fashioned a tent from an old pillowcase. All I needed otherwise was mini marshmallows, wooden dowels to hold up the tent, and a dish towel tied with string for Timmy's bedroll. We all have imaginations, so why shouldn't we make a miniature ice rink for a gerbil to "skate" on, hmm?

3. DRESS TO IMPRESS.

Little pre-made outfits for animals typically cost $10–$50 at pet stores. Let me just give that a NOPE! Thrift stores, dollar stores, and garage sales are your best bets for finding clothes that will fit your pet. Animal companions are easy to clothe because many of them just so happen to be the same size as human children. This is clearly fate telling you to put your dog in a toddler's dress. Some species-based suggestions:

Hamsters and mice: If you can get a teensy hamster or mouse to wear clothing, I bow to you. I'd stick with cute li'l hair bows and hats.
Lizards, guinea pigs, and rats: Add leg holes to part of a cut-off sweater sleeve to make a form-fitting and chic onesie!
Rabbits: Buy a whimsically outfitted secondhand stuffed animal that's approximately the same size as your pet and steal its clothes for your model.
Cats and dogs: Many cats and small dogs will fit into baby clothes labeled NEWBORN or 0–3 MONTHS. For medium-size dogs, try toddler

T-shirts labeled 3T. Hoodies and T-shirts made for children up to about eight years old are good for larger dogs, and if your dog is GIGANTIC, *your* clothes might look fetching on her.
Pets of all sizes: TINY HATS ARE ALWAYS A GOOD IDEA.

4. SET THE SCENE.

This is a cellphone picture I took of Stevie Wonderbun, the baby bunny my friend Jen just adopted. Where are we? In a professional photography studio? On set at *Vogue Animaux*? Nope! We were in Jen's bedroom, where I swept everything off her dresser, covered the top of it with a down comforter, and put a drinking glass down next to Stevie *to show that she can fit in a drinking glass*. The background for your scene doesn't have to be that elaborate! Neutral backdrops like white walls and solid sheets draw the viewer's eye right to where you want it.

If you do get fancy with your backdrop, arrange everything *exactly* just so before introducing your pet to the set to reduce the amount of time she has to wait (or decide "I'm over this" and bounce) while you fix, fuss, and rearrange things. Less time spent being made to wear a silly hat and sit still = happier pet. For Timmy's photo shoot, I made the props and scouted the set location ahead of time. I even took a few practice shots so I would know which angle would best hide the street behind the pine tree and the apartment building two feet away. And no matter where you're taking your pictures, natural light is best: Shoot during the day, near a window, or outside.

5. GET YOUR PET READY FOR THEIR CLOSE-UP.

Brush your pet so they are looking their fluffiest (Or polish their scales? I have no idea who you're working with), then gently put the outfit on him. Tip: It can be helpful to get your animal used to the idea of wearing something before you put them in it. Run the clothes over their fur several times—snuggle them with the outfit, then let them smell it with their scent on it. (Most animals are rampant narcissists.) Again, stop if they're really resisting you.

6. TAKE SOME PICTURES!

First, BE PATIENT. Timothy Maxwell Thumperton is no supermodel. He's an *animal*. He runs, hops everywhere, moves too quickly and blurs pictures, and sometimes he absolutely REFUSES to put on his special outfits. Rude! Timmy actually sucks at posing. I have to take lots of shots for every one picture I'm pleased with, and that's completely normal. But is it worth it? OK LOOK AT THE TINY MARSHMALLOWS AGAIN AND THEN YOU TELL ME.

Photographing animals is not like photographing humans. Don't give up! Keep your finger ready on the shutter button, and keep going! If your pet is motivated by food, make sure you have a supply of tiny treats on hand at all times to bribe them into sitting, staying, or looking at you. And get as close as possible, allowing us an intimate view of a seriously cute li'l critter—get on your pet's level and put the camera on the floor if that's where your dog is, or hold it on the same shelf your cat is lying on.

Amazing pet pictures are within your reach! So have fun, and don't forget to give your bestie a treat when the shoot's over. Just don't let the Insta-fame go to her head! 📷

Sister, Sister

Some friends are born, not made.
By Eleanor. Styling by Verity Pemberton.

Thanks to American Apparel, Aries, Calvin Klein, Casio, Clarks, COS, House of Hackney, Lacoste, My Crazy Scrunchie, Sophie Hulme, Topshop, Urban Outfitters, and V. Pemberton for lending us clothes and accessories.

BETH I don't think you can ever love anyone like you love your sisters. They're like best friends who sometimes make you want to cry, but also make you feel like the luckiest person alive. I remember secret clubs, games with our cats, gross home-made breakfasts for our dad, bedroom dance parties, dressing up, and makeovers. My sisters and I are the best girl gang to ever grace the planet, in clothes borrowed from each other (not always with permission) and the same size feet. (We all have really small feet.)

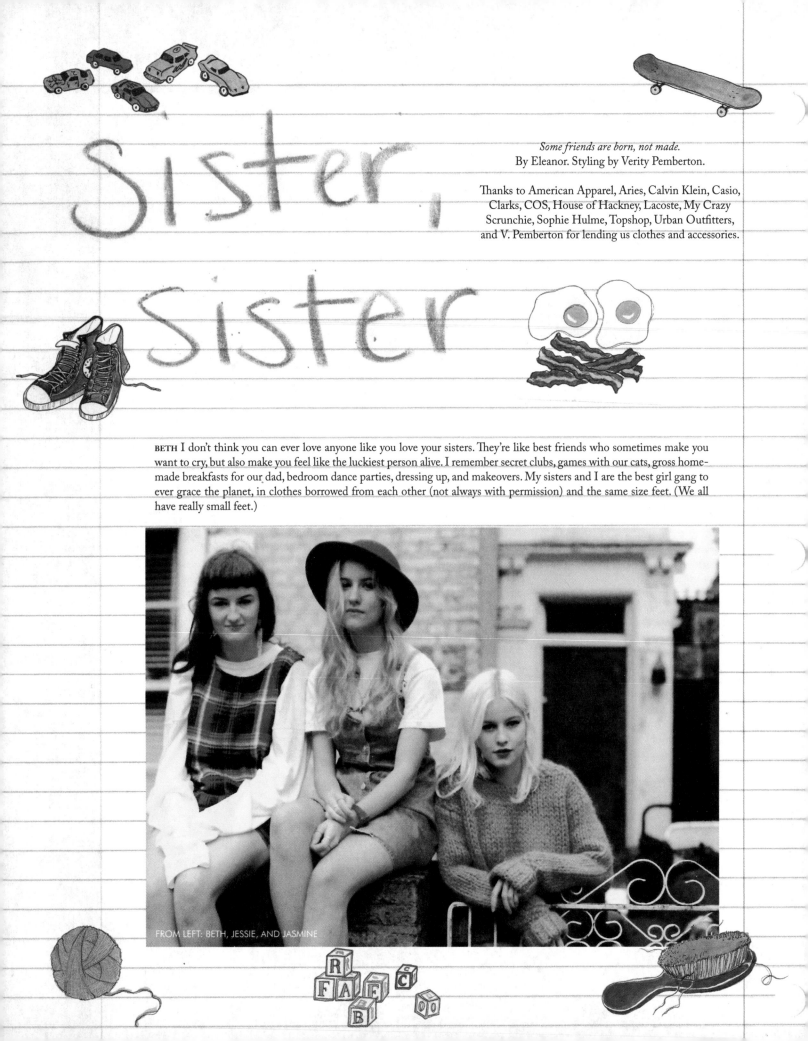

FROM LEFT: BETH, JESSIE, AND JASMINE

I have someone to look up to and someone to look after.

My sisters and I are the best girl gang to ever grace the planet.

REBA (IN RED) AND JESS.

REBA Me and Jess were born three years apart in the same hospital in Oxford. We grew up surrounded by really strong and glamorous women. We both feel really lucky to have grown up in an environment like that. It couldn't have been better for two young girls!

SANAA (LEFT) AND SABAA

MICHELLE (LEFT) AND BAITONG

SABAA AND SANAA We like spending all day watching fighting over clothes and rolling our eyes at each other. Like most twin sisters, we've developed our own language and sense of humor that are meaningless to everybody else. We hate it when people ask if we can feel each other's emotions (no), whether we share a room (no), if we like being a twin (do you like being alive?), and who our parents like best (Sanaa).

BAITONG Michelle and I didn't start off on the right foot. We had a few good years of bickering and teasing before we became what we are now, which is pretty much best friends. We have this thing where whenever we make promises to each other, we have to do a pinky swear, and we have to kiss our thumbs while we do it, to seal the promise—otherwise it can be broken.

REBECCA (TOP) AND RACHEL

RACHEL Rebecca is the best sister ever and my best friend! Everybody assumes she's older than me. I sometimes feel that way too—probably because she acts like it. She does so much for me. I very much look up to my sister (literally too), and I miss her all the time.

We were really naughty when we were younger, and double the trouble when we were together!

NANCY (LEFT) AND LOTTE

LOTTE Before Nancy was born, I enjoyed two dreamy years of solo attention, kisses, and cuddling from our parents. Then this bundle of joy appeared to light up my life with her blond curls and sweet voice.

We both live and work in London (best place in the world). I throw parties for a living, and Nancy works for our grandparents at their antique and prop rental business. She lends out to the dopest period dramas (errrr, heard of Harry Potter?).

SIDONIE (LEFT) AND ZAZOU

SIDONIE AND ZAZOU We were really naughty when we were younger, and double the trouble when we were together! At school we would set all the clocks forward so we could go home early. We also used to go 'round the school licking the teachers' elbows because they wouldn't notice.

We're really close and hang out all the time. We love skateboarding, surfing, the '70s, and Bill Murray. The only thing we argue about is clothes and who used to be the bigger Miley Cyrus fan! 🌷

Design by Sonja. Title lettering by Lisa Maione. Portrait of Layla from *Buffalo '66* and Elvis sign by Brooke Nechvatel. Playlist by Gabby, artwork by Minna.

DECEMBER 2013: *Forever*

I. A BRIEF HISTORY OF FOREVER

Forever is the state, exclusive to those between the ages of 13 and 17, in which one feels both eternally invincible and permanently trapped. When my parents were young, Forever was expressed through promise rings, names carved into trees, and photographs you could hold in your hands. In the years since, Forever has inspired many phrases and ideas popular among adolescents: Best Friends Forever, Together Forever, Forever Young. In more recent years, Forever, with its cousins Always and Infinity, has dominated young adult literature, differentiated the internet from the more fleeting IRL, and, one could argue, explained the popularity of the galaxy print. Nothing lasts forever, of course, but Nothing doesn't resonate with a teenager the way Forever does, because, for better or worse, it's hard to imagine ever not feeling this way, being this person, having this life.

I waited my whole life for Forever. I started reading *Seventeen* at age seven and regarded my camp counselors, babysitters, older sisters, my sisters' friends, and my dad's high school students with more reverence and awe than I did any actual grownup. And really, truly? My Forever didn't disappoint. It wasn't perfect, but therein lies its perfection: I've been lucky to come up in a time when there are enough teen movies that make high school's terribleness into something interesting at worst and beautiful at best, so even the darkest times were not lonely, but strangely magical. John Hughes said that "one really key element of teendom" is that it "feels as good to feel bad as it does to feel good," so really, I've had a solid run. Forever is not meant to be the *best* time of someone's life, but it is certainly the most Forever-y. So I'm not sad because I think post-Forever seems terrible, I'm sad because Forever is remarkably peculiar, and I've really enjoyed trying to understand why, and I will miss it.

I've often worried that this ambition to understand my own teenage existence has lessened its sincerity, made my experiences too self-aware, but it's been quite the opposite. Chris Kraus writes in *I Love Dick*, "The Ramones give 'Needles & Pins' the possibility of irony, but the irony doesn't undercut the song's emotion, it makes it stronger and more true." The self-awareness or irony or whatever you want to call it made it easier for me to appreciate the awful parts of Forever because I had the rose tint of nostalgia in real time. It granted me a sense of humor about even the most resentful teachers. I was careful not to hang out in the alley behind school often enough to find it redundant and oppressive. I let myself write bad poetry and diary entries because I knew they'd at least be funny to look back on. Of course, the idea of a time when I'd ever be looking back was nebulous to the point of being unimaginable, because Forever, Always, Infinity, etc.

Technically, I still have quite a bit of Forever left. I won't be a legal adult until April. According to science, adolescence now lasts until age 25. If we use high school as a timeline, I have six months left. But because my friends have already graduated, because I'm in the midst of planning my future, because I feel like I hold more memories of who I have been than an understanding of who I am now, I say with certainty that my own personal Forever is over. And I'm terrified.

II. A THEORY OF FOREVER'S REMARKABLE PECULIARITY

Forever is when you have the height and width of a miniature person with the density of an alpha-person. Forever is when you're a human cartoon with every vein and skin cell as exaggerated as Minnie Mouse's gloves. Forever is when you experience all kinds of things for the first time, as do your hormones, which will never again be this crazed, never again experience things as either so bleak or so Technicolor. Forever is when your brain is still developing, so everything sticks, like a lot. Forever is when you have tunnel vision because you (I) have not yet understood that you (I) are not the center of the world, so you (I) grant yourself (myself) permission to see things as though you (I) are (am). I don't recommend it as a lifestyle, but there's something to be said for having this much time to just think about you, what you like, what you believe in, how you feel. When I asked Sofia Coppola why she continually writes movies about teenagers, she said, "It's a time when you're just focused on thinking about things, you're not distracted by your career, family. [...] I always like characters that are in the midst of a transition and trying to find their place in the world. That is the most heightened when you're a teenager, but I definitely like it at the different stages of life."

III. DIFFERENT STAGES OF LIFE

Like Sofia said, Forever is not the only time a person is transitioning, finding their place in the world, finding their identity. Forever is not the only time in which a person feels things strongly, or for the first time, or in a way that is central to their forming who they are. It's maybe a crazy concentration of that time, but that doesn't mean it's a great time. Sometimes the awful parts are beautiful, but sometimes they're actually just awful.

The good news is that most people's lives get better after Forever. The bad news is that some people's lives don't, or they do, but those people themselves become cold and bitter and nostalgic for Forever, whether or not their own Forever was really worth pining for. Or, as Allison says in *The Breakfast Club*, "When you grow up, your heart dies."

One way to avoid killing your heart is to decide that you will spend your whole life growing up. I am not saying you should

aspire to the maturity level of the characters in *Hot Tub Time Machine*; I am suggesting we resist a life that looks, in line-graph form, like it goes up and up and up and then it stops, and then it levels out, and then it stays on that flat plane until death. I hope to live a life that goes up and up and up until the end, with the inevitable dip here and there. I hope to continue to learn and change.

Coveting youth also needs to be dealt with. I'm not afraid of being old; I'm afraid of being afraid of being old, which for some reason appears to be an inherent part of being old, because the examples out there of adults who aren't trying to turn back time are few and far between. But a fear of aging turns every second into your enemy. It means that your worst nightmare is constantly coming true, unless you choose to die, which is a terrible choice to make. I generally like life—it lets me do things like eat good food, watch good TV, and have good friends—so I'd hate to have a bitter relationship with it, to hide from it, to dread it. I'd rather not romanticize a lack of knowledge. I'd rather be a wizard or a mad scientist or a walking encyclopedia. I'd rather get on with things than spend every day super pissed that we haven't yet figured out time travel.

Finally, it's important to take time to mourn Forever. I know this doesn't have to be so tragic, I know I don't actually want to stay in this place—but to effectively move on, I have to effectively wrap things up. Because I don't want to long for Forever in small, unhealthy ways later, I have to honor it in big, creative ways now. Reflecting and archiving is not the same as dwelling on the past. It is not anti-living, but a part of life, even a crucial one. We do this to highlight one thing above others, so that a special moment can take up more space in our brains than an inconsequential one; so that, by plain math, our personal worlds contain more good things and fewer bad ones. Or more interesting things and fewer blah ones, since you have to record the bad, too. Like I said, Forever is not about being the best years of your life, just the most Forever-y.

IV. GRIEVING PERIOD

I remember learning in eighth grade that you could be alone without being lonely, and enjoying many nights of watching *Freaks and Geeks* in my parents' bed, zine- and collage-making materials at hand, soft yellow light coming from the lamp on the floor in the corner.

I remember sitting in social studies with the lights out and a movie on the projector. The boy I liked sat right at the front, backlit against a bright screen, so although he was turned around and facing in my direction, I couldn't tell if his eyes were looking at me or not. This still drives me nuts.

I remember being in a play freshman year that brought an unexpected group of people together, prompting the, yes, *Breakfast Club* question of *Will we all still talk to each other in the halls on Monday?* We didn't really, but that turned out to be OK. We helped one another change, and then we moved on.

I remember sleepovers with Ella, the shadows in her family's white guest room as we lay on our backs, able to share secrets only when staring up at the ceiling.

I remember a family trip where my two tools of escape were a mixtape called *Tomorrow I'll Be 16* and a novel called *Girl*.

I remember the school's music festival, knowing deep down that it was hopelessly lame but reveling in the opportunity to feel part of the pimply, heaving organism of the student body as it moshed in the cafeteria to a band that may or may not have actually been any good.

I remember twirling Emily to the Pixies' "Where Is My Mind?" that night and letting go upon realizing that she was like Angela and I was like Rayanne, this comparison generously heightened by Emily's floral dress and red hair.

I remember walking home from school with Amelia, asking her about that boy I still liked, excited by the realization that I was like Angela and she was like Rayanne, this comparison generously heightened by Amelia's colorful wardrobe and impossible charm.

I remember meeting Claire. She was a lot nicer than she had been that time I followed her into the school before first period, drawn to her Doc Martens and teal hair, only to be met by a suspicious scowl. We realized we liked the same music and disliked the same people. A few weeks later we'd visit a psychic to learn about our futures.

I remember sitting in biology and imagining myself getting a hall pass, suddenly looking like Audrey Horne, and tracking down that boy I still liked. I remember going to his house a few months later and watching a reality show about a rifle competition. Things did not work out, but I got what I wanted out of it: a deeply emotional experience with the song "Thirteen" by Big Star.

I remember the way Chicago looks from the top of an Oak Park parking garage, a cluster of LEGO buildings against a sky orange from the city lights, a soundtrack of gossip between two kids I only kind of knew but had already decided I really liked.

I remember sophomore year, sitting on the walking bridge over the Eisenhower the night Claire told me everything. An elderly man went by one way and smiled, and on his way back, stopped in front of us and said, "If I don't see you again, I hope you have a happy rest of your lives."

I remember liking a new boy, and thinking he liked me too, and then he didn't, and I decided that this was better, because now I could listen to Heart and Carole King records and light candles and gaze out my window and feel sorry for myself.

I remember my 16th birthday, dancing to my favorite songs with my new friends under the pink balloons and silver stars that clouded our dining room, eating waffles made of cake batter, and then taking a communal clothed bath at Claire's (my friend Claire's house, not Claire's the store). We fell asleep in a pile and woke up dreading the walk home, because even though it was a beautiful spring day, it meant the night was over.

I remember when Petra visited with her camera and I realized just how special the suburbs could be.

I remember Anne's birthday when we went to the cemetery, a wacky adventure for a bunch of people who are too young to realize that they'll end up there, too. Most of us chickened out and went to the strip mall across the street. Claire claimed they saw a ghost inside the graveyard. We then went to an elementary school playground and were promptly asked to leave.

I remember junior year, liking a new boy, and changing my hallway route so it would coincide with his. It never did, because, as I'd later find out, he was trying to do the same.

I remember walking down Anne and Lizzy's alley with Galaxie 500's "Here She Comes Now" on my headphones, each garage's sensor light going on in sync with the song as I went past.

I remember the New Year's Eve when I finally, officially met that new boy I liked, looking for him at a dank basement show we were all at, the room filled with red light and cigarette smoke that followed me through a narrow hallway and turned it into a tunnel of love. He stood alone in the crowded room at the tunnel's end. His conversation starter was: "If you got married, and your husband went bald, would you be mad?" I said no, just in case we ever got married or whatever.

I remember the roller rink on Claire's birthday, and Anne's roof on Siobhan's. I leaned against Anne's lipstick-covered mirror and smiled as everyone sang along to "Satellite of Love" by Lou Reed. They would all graduate weeks later.

I remember seeing Petra in Toronto a few weeks ago, listening to all our favorite songs and crying on a mattress in the center of her living room because we could feel the end. She gave me a book of her photos of me and of our time together throughout my adolescence. The cover reads "Nothing Lasts Forever." We woke up the next day and learned that Lou Reed had died that morning. I came home and wrote this.

I don't remember prom or homecoming. I don't remember being very involved in my school's community or extracurriculars after freshman year. But I do remember Rookie prom, and other Rookie events, all these amazing gatherings of the kinds of people I would LOVE to populate a school with. I remember getting to watch them all meet and bond, asking two girls how long they'd been friends, and them answering, "Just now, right here."

Since I started this thing, lots of people have asked me if I feel like I lead a double life, but my Rookie memories have fit in so seamlessly with all the others described here, and I feel incredibly lucky for that. Thank you so much for reading our website and our books, for supporting us, for coming to our events. Thank you for creating the most inspiring community. Thank you for being part of my Forever, and part of one another's. I know this one doesn't end here.

Enjoy this month of early valentines, BFFs, and fuzzy nostalgic holiday feelings. And really, seriously, thank you again.

Love, Tavi

Sitting Pretty

1. Sittin' Up in My Room — Brandy
2. Little TV — Dressy Bessy
3. Girl Left Alone — Dolly Parton
4. Waiting by the Telephone — Bleached
5. Here I Sit — The Ronettes
6. In My Room — Best Coast
7. Girls Like Me — TV Girl
8. I Wanna Dance With Somebody — Whitney Houston
9. Take It As It Comes — Vivian Girls
10. Built This Way — Samantha Ronson

Rescuing moments from the tides of time.
By María Fernanda

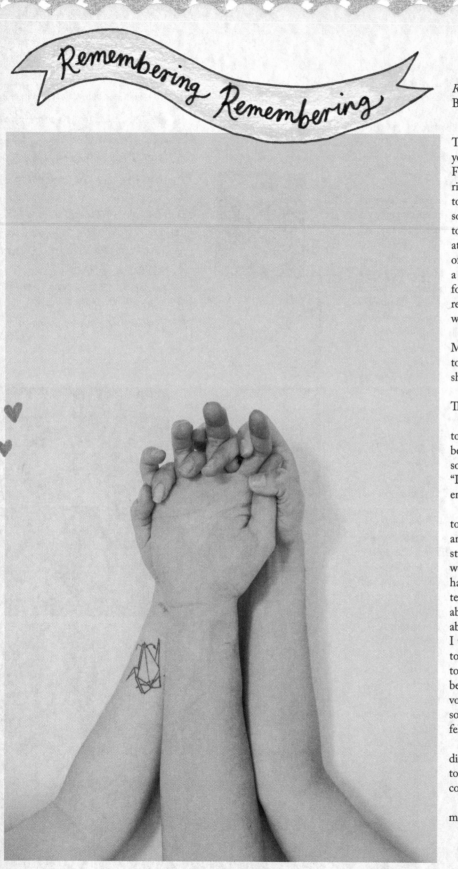

Time passes, people vanish. Some die, some you just don't talk to anymore, not even on Facebook, and all you're left with are memories. I always wish I'd taken more pictures to preserve my memories of certain beloved souls, but by the time regret has set in it's too late—they're gone. These pictures are an attempt to re-create the moments that some of my friends and I wish we'd photographed—a kind of do-over. They are a defense against forgetting, a remedy for regret. They are visual representations of the contents of our hearts, which feel heavy because they are full of love.

Thanks to Carmiña, Leo, Mayte, Cuauh, Manolin Adrián, and Zaid for their help, and to Zaid, Fera, Allz, Lalli, Elvia, and Ricky for sharing their memories with me.

This first photo is about my dad and me.

It started with a phone call. My mom told me I had to come home right away because my father was going to be "leaving soon." I took a bus to Mazatlán with my sister. "Do you think he's going to die this weekend?" she asked me. I said no.

When we got there, we all ate lunch together in his hospital room. My mother and my sister had some errands to run, so I stayed alone with my dad that evening. I was wearing a Police T-shirt, a gift from him. He had lost his ability to speak, and I remember telling him that that scared me. I told him about the guy I was dating, and that we were about to go to Veracruz for a Björk concert. I told him about my plans to make music. I told him all of my plans. I ended up singing to him—"Fade Into You" by Mazzy Star—because he always said he loved hearing my voice. I started to cry and couldn't finish the song. He squeezed my hand and I felt safe. It felt like time had stopped forever.

We were still holding hands when you died the next morning. I was the one who had to let go. I didn't let go until your hand was cold.

I love you for 10 thousand years, maybe more. Definitely more.

ELVIA AND NACHO

We met in middle school in 2005 and became best friends very quickly. We were both 15 years old. I could always count on Nacho to protect me. He always had my back. I remember I'd started seeing this "bad boy" that my parents didn't approve of, and Nacho helped me hide the relationship from them. They eventually found out anyway, though, and I ran to Nacho's house and into his arms, sobbing. He told me that everything would be OK. The next day he took me to a pet store to cheer me up. I fell in love with a bunny there and brought it home with me. I still laugh when I remember all the times that rabbit peed on Nacho's lap. We had so many good times, the three of us together.

My bunny died in 2007, and a year later Nacho died too.

I'll always miss you. I love you forever.

07/08/2010

Por siempre Mae

ALLZ AND ALÁN

I celebrated my birthday in 2010 with my best friend, Alán. He was leaving that night to go to London for a six-month photography course, but he didn't want to miss my party. He gave me a card with a picture of Beyoncé and Jennifer Lopez. We liked to jokingly relate to them, like they were hawt bitches who hung out together and so were we! They were the secret language through which we expressed our friendship and love for each other. On the back of the card he wrote, "Por siempre Mae" ("Forever Mae") and my birthdate. (Mae was the nickname we used to share.)

The night was a roller coaster, from being soaked in the rain, dancing, drinking, and going back home extremely late, worried that he would miss his flight. When we said goodbye he gave me another card with another picture of Bey and J.Lo.

That was the last birthday I spent with Alán. He died in 2011.

Alán, you know that I am not a person who keeps things. But I have kept those two cards you gave me in a safe place. They remind me how close you can feel to another human being and how deep your love for a friend can be, even if it doesn't make sense to anyone else. I miss you.

RICKY AND HIS UNCLE

I never met my dad; my male role model was my uncle. He was the best uncle anyone could ever have. He was the one who raised me, who looked after me. He also organized all of my birthday parties. When I turned nine, he brought home the most beautiful birthday cake I have ever seen in my entire life. It was a five-tiered cake like the ones you eat at a quinceañera. I couldn't believe my eyes. It was all covered with icing and was topped with a huge rocket ship made out of sugar. I kept that rocket for years. I will always remember my uncle, the birthday parties, his warm hugs, his words of wisdom, and all those amazing cakes!

I love you, I love you, I will always love you.

ZAID AND HIS GREAT-GRANDMOTHER

The last time I saw my great-grandmother, we were on a road trip from Mazatlán to Guadalajara to spend Christmas with my mother's family. It was a few months before my parents divorced, so our whole family was riding together in the car. My bisa (that's what I called my great-grandma) was sitting between my brother and me in the back. I got into a fight with the rest of my family, and I was really upset, and my bisa told me that I had two options: to either let go and get along with everyone, or to be bitter and miserable. I decided to let go and enjoy the trip, and I ended up having a lot of fun. That was the last time we were a family.

Later that day, I gave her a chocolate flower I had gotten her for Christmas. She really loved it—not because she loved chocolate flowers, but because it was from me. Right after we got to Guadalajara, we drove her to my aunt's house, where she was going to stay. She died the next afternoon.

She was cremated, and her ashes are kept in a cabinet with a letter my brother and I wrote to her... and that chocolate flower.

I still think of you often, of your stories about your travels around the globe, and how you made me feel whole and accepted.

FERA AND PTOLOMEO

Ptolomeo was my beautiful Pekingese dog. He had one blue eye and one black one. He was the best company a girl like me could ever hope for. I remember one night when I got home really late after a party. I knew immediately that something was wrong when I didn't see him at the window, waiting for me. I walked into the house calling his name, I looked in his hiding place under my bed, but he was nowhere to be seen. I started to panic, and I must have cried out, because my whole family suddenly woke up. I ran outside, yelling his name. It was the middle of the night, and the streets were silent and empty. I started to cry.

The next morning, still teary-eyed, I called my best friend, and together we printed posters and walked through the neighborhood until our feet hurt, looking for Ptolomeo. I even borrowed a megaphone and broadcast a request that all my neighbors be on the lookout. "Please give me my dog back," I said into the megaphone. "He's mine and I'm his. I love him so much, and we need each other." I was sure I would find him.

A lady from the beauty salon told me she'd heard that a woman who lives three blocks from my house had found a weird-looking Pekingese. I went straight to her house, but no one was home. I left a note on her door and went back home, sad but still hopeful.

Two hours later there was a knock at the door. The woman had come to return Ptolomeo to me. I hugged him so close. I served the woman a big piece of cake as thanks.

That scare showed me how important Ptolomeo was to me, and how much it would hurt to lose him. After that, I spent as much time with him as I could, loving his company, caring for him as much as possible.

My best friend is in heaven now.

I know you're up there, Ptolomeo, looking for me with your little blue eye. I will always be with you.

LALLI AND HER MOM

I'll never get over the death of my mother, but I can feel her presence when I think about her. Sometimes when I go to bed, I close my eyes and jump into another world—the world she showed me, of creativity and imagination. She was a prolific playwright, and invented many wonderful stories. I particularly remember *Red Riding Hood 2000*, in which Red Riding Hood uses a cellphone and visits her grandmother with magical biscuits. The play had an ecological and pro-animal-rights message that made a lasting impression on me as a child. I spent hours playing the lead in my red cape, with my dog Orion taking on the role of the wolf. I value the connection I still have with her through her writing.

I love you, Mom. ♥

The Long Goodbye

A belated apology. By Joe. Playlist by Dylan, artwork by Minna.

S.,

It's been more than three years since we talked, way longer than we were even together. The end, in Texas, was anticlimactic. Our last words were probably awkward, but I don't remember much, to be honest—I just knew Justin and I had to get the hell out of there because we'd poisoned your new house with more than enough testosterone and negative energy. If you cried, I didn't see, although by that point I already knew too well what it looked like.

You were an angel to host us—your ex-boyfriend from high school and his loud, loving bully of a best friend—the minute after you'd moved to a faraway place for your first real job, but it was a terrible idea. We'd driven across the South, not necessarily aiming for you except out of convenience, staying in $35 motel rooms, subsisting on sunflower seeds and energy drinks, and not showering much. Our attitudes could only be described as bad, and our skins were thick from needling each other with oafish insults to pass the time. You had let us tease you for years and always took it, even after you and I split, but it was beyond insensitive to trample on your new life with old jokes. You were vulnerable; we were crass.

I heard you whispering on the phone in the middle of the night to what sounded like a new boy. We left in the morning. I didn't know you'd never call me again, but I'm glad you didn't. I deserved it.

—Joe

I fell in love over smoothies in her mom's sedan. We'd spent sophomore year in English class whispering, and a few days secretly passing back and forth the issue of *SPIN* with Karen O on the cover. Soon after that, we climbed a tree and kissed, saw *Spider-Man 2*, traded mix CDs, and hid from the Florida humidity in air-conditioned cars that always made hugging uncomfortable. She straightened her bangs, but when they got sweaty—and they always did—they stuck to her forehead and curled upward. They had blond streaks, because of course they did. It was summer, because of course it was.

She was the first person I texted with, among other things—we shared a lot of firsts. I was 15 when it started. I was 22 when what was left of our friendship finally, officially ended after way too long. The years in between were messy, and many of them unnecessary. It's hard to let go, but sometimes holding on hurts more.

It went so well for a while, and that probably made the rest worse. We became friends, then, quickly, we became like family, close with each other's parents and always included on holidays and vacations. But each memory we made was one more to forget, or at least push aside when the end came. A clean break proved almost impossible: We had learned everything at the same time or from each other and shared so much, especially music. There's no period in life when records mean more than when you're a teenager in a stupid town with one ally—when you feel like two special-snowflake dreamers surrounded by people who just *don't get it*. The songs understood us when no one else did, and we loved them together, never alone. Our actual time together was limited—we lived at home with curfews (and school)—so we clung to things like books, movies, and MP3s that knew our romantic plight and kept us feeling connected even while we were apart. That and endless phone calls about nothing, so we were both out of it for school the next day.

We made tentative plans for the future, six months at a time, never more. We weren't crazy.

S.,

We had to stay friends after we broke up. It was senior year of high school and everything was about to change. We had to at least see our joint mission through and make it out of there. Besides, we had so many classes together.

Maybe we jumped into it too fast, the friendship part. There were still a lot of emotional instant-message chats, late-night calls, and tears—lots of tears—when we started driving to school together again. But at least we had a buffer—he was friends with both of us. They all were, because we'd been a pair for so long. Who else were we supposed to eat lunch with? I probably should have made myself scarcer—that was on me as the one doing the dumping—but how could I? Then I'd really be alone.

We had to stay friends, at least until the end of the year, for both our sakes. That's what I told myself. We probably didn't have to stay friends when we went to college. Dorm room beds are too small to share with visiting exes.

—Joe

The breaking up is the hard part. The moving on is the hard part. The not getting back together is the hard part. It's all the hard part.

Two years together felt like so long, especially considering that it coincided with all of the most exciting parts of life up to that point—sneaking around and staying out late and getting to know how bodies work and learning to drive and acting like we thought grownups were supposed to act. Hitting every teenage milestone in the presence of one person means they will be with you forever in the abstract, a witness to your important inaugural experiences. And later, it can be hard to understand that while the memories are forever, the physical human pres-

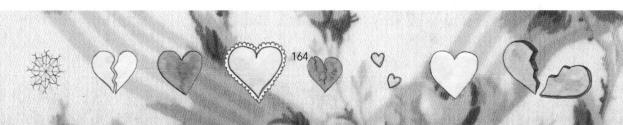

ence of the person probably shouldn't be.

And so the prospect of saying good-bye for real was too painful for us to deal with. In that sense, I was extremely selfish: I was 17 and I wanted to feel free, with time to focus on my friends and the ability to kiss another girl if the opportunity ever presented itself, but I also wanted to keep around the one who thought the most of me in the entire world. I tried to have it both ways—I broke up with her, but kept hanging out with her "as friends."

I recognized the advantages of that arrangement: Because she still wanted us to be together, I got to control when and how much we hung out, and how much like dating our friendship would be at any given time. But I ignored the festering ugliness that this arrangement was creating: Over time, she lost self-esteem and started to resent me, while I was becoming a power-hungry master manipulator.

S.,

I'm sorry for turning off my emotions when they started to make me uncomfortable. I'm sorry for acting like everything was fine in front of people when it so wasn't. I'm sorry I kept your hopes up by being more open in private than in front of our friends. I'm sorry I couldn't control my carelessness. I'm sorry I dated two of our mutual friends. I'm sorry I kept saying I was sorry just to make you feel better. I'm sorry I didn't mean it. I'm sorry you accepted my apologies. I'm sorry I let you accept my apologies. I'm sorry.

—Joe

A few weeks after the breakup, I started spending serious time with a girl I'd known before I met S. I was needy and confused, used to having a constant companion, and C. was both new and familiar, an old friend but a fresh love interest.

It was the wrong thing to do. By high school, C., S., and I were all friends, part of a small group of relatively innocent kids who studied and saw movies together, but didn't dare try drinking or smoking. There weren't that many of us, and we all knew one another's business, probably because we didn't have much business to begin with. Compounding the wrongheadedness (and

the hurt): Because my breakup was so fresh and we knew we were being insensitive, C. and I decided to keep our rushed relationship a secret. We got ice cream after doing homework, watched football on Sundays, and sometimes squeezed each other's hands in the hallway when no one was looking.

Around everyone else, though, we acted the same as we always had. Or we tried to. But S. wasn't stupid. One day she asked me and C. to go out for food after school, and we agreed, because that's what friends did and we were all pretending, in our own ways, to be friends.

Maybe we were asking to get caught. When C. went to the bathroom, she left her cellphone on the table. S. picked it up casually, flipped it open (cellphones flipped open back then), and all her fears were confirmed—probably by a flirty text from me. Her face dropped and she stormed out, leaving her artichoke dip untouched on the table. In yet another in a series of massive mistakes, I followed her.

We spent the next few hours in the parking lot of a TGI Fridays, sobbing in her backseat. "How could you do this to me?" she asked. "Didn't I mean anything to you? I thought you loved me." I thought I did, too. I apologized over and over again, drowning in guilt, but with no good answers. It wasn't our last such argument, but it should have been. Somehow it took a thousand more *sorry*s for us to move on.

Looking back, I realize the best thing for both of us would have been for me to cut things off completely, since she couldn't. I probably knew it at the time, too, but I rationalized our on-again, off-again intimacy by telling myself *she* was dictating the terms—like, if she didn't want me around, wouldn't she just tell me that? I certainly gave her the chance to tell me to eff off and die. Instead, we'd start the "let's be friends" cycle over again. When I would halfheartedly suggest we stop because it always ended in one or both of us crying, she would insist we avoid talking about "us" and stay lighthearted. But when someone tells you they can't imagine life without you—that they'd rather have *some* contact, anything you're willing to offer— it's a sign things are no longer equal, and

that they're not equally free to choose. If one person picks independence over commitment, they should give up the right to interfere in the other's new life. In our constant bargaining, the deal always came out lopsided. Still, on vacations from school, it was too easy to return to the comfort of old, familiar patterns.

We had some good times during our five years of attempted (and often, to be fair, successful) post-romance friendship, but we'd been there before, and retreading the past wasn't worth the prolonged pain. It's possible for exes to restart as friends (or even try again for more) later in life, but only if the original wounds have had a chance to become scars of tough tissue instead of constantly re-torn scabs. The cuts were hers more than mine, and my mere presence picked at them.

Put back into situations from their past, people will usually revert to the roles they're used to playing. On that visit in Texas, on the eve of becoming real adults, we were still acting like the kids we once were when we'd promised to never stop being there for each other. But sometimes the best way to show someone you'll always care is to just leave them alone.

S.,

I couldn't stand the idea of being the bad guy. I let your constant forgiveness cover up my guilt. How bad could I be if you still wanted me around? Now I know for sure I was wrong. Maybe the only right thing I did was to never send you these letters.

—Joe

1. Say You Won't Cry – Television Personalities
2. Goodbye Summer Girl – Desolation Wilderness
3. Spit on a Stranger – Pavement
4. A Fond Farewell – Elliott Smith
5. Beautiful Bye-Byes – Red Kross
6. Take Care – Big Star
7. Star – Hallelujahs
8. Goodbye Little Darlin' – Johnny Cash
9. I Won't Be the One – Dead Moon

the dead celeb DINER

lunch · dinner · dessert

OPEN 4 EVA

The famous last meals of stars on the other side of forever.

By Esme

the Jimi Hendrix

tuna fish sandwich

red wine

d. 1970 - London, England

the Jim Morrison

sweet-n-sour chicken

beer

d. 1971 - Paris, France

the *Marilyn Monroe*

gazpacho

meatballs
guacamole refried beans
veal parmigiana

d. 1962 – Los Angeles, CA.

the *James Dean*

slice of apple pie

glass of milk

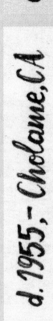
d. 1955 – Cholame, CA.

the *Elvis Presley*

four scoops of vanilla ice cream

six chocolate chip cookies

d. 1977 – Memphis, TN

DIY BFF Earrings

Put your heads together in the name of friendship. By Gabby

Power couples are cool and everything, but if you ask me, nothing tops a POWER FRIENDSHIP. What's more beautiful than two talented people hanging out and supporting each other's brilliance? Celebrating a power friendship requires something special, like a pair of extra faces that you can wear on your head!

Here's how to make a pair of earrings to commemorate your favorite BFF duo, whether that's a pair of celebrities, fictional characters, or you and your own best friend. The same technique can be used to make rings and pins, too!

WHAT YOU'LL NEED
- Printable shrink film. (You can find it at craft/art-supply stores.)
- Scissors.
- A baking sheet.
- Aluminum foil or parchment paper.
- Superglue.
- Earring posts (available at craft stores).

- A paper plate/magazine/anything that will protect your work table from errant drops of glue.
- Photo-editing software (Photoshop, Preview, and Microsoft Paint all work for this).
- An inkjet printer.
- An oven.

STEP ONE

Find and save a picture of each member of the best-friend duo. Straight-on pictures of their heads work best. Open the pictures in your photo-editing software and crop them so that just the heads are left.

STEP TWO

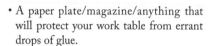

Resize the images. Because you're going to be printing these on SHRINK film, make them about twice as big as you want your earrings to be. (I made my images about half an inch long by half an inch wide and set the resolution to 300 dpi.)

STEP THREE

Copy and paste your images into a text document. If you plan on making multiple pairs of earrings, try to fit as many heads as you can onto each page, so you can make the most out of your shrink paper.

Sidenote: Why wasn't I invited to this party?!

STEP FOUR

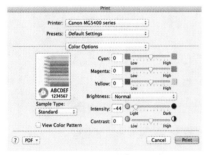

Adjust the color intensity to just above minimum—the colors will intensify as the paper shrinks; this adjustment will keep them from getting too dark.

STEP FIVE

Insert the shrink paper into your inkjet printer according to the instructions on the package, then print out your pictures. Let each sheet dry for a few minutes before you touch it. Then cut out each head.

STEP SIX

Preheat your oven to 325º F. Line a baking sheet with foil or parchment paper. Before baking your heads, test out a scrap piece of shrink film to see how long it takes for your oven to shrink it. You'll know it's done when the film is about half its original size and completely flat. Mine took about a minute, so keep a close eye on it! (The packaging for the shrink film should also give you guidelines for shrinking in the oven.) Once you've done your test, place your heads on the covered sheet, evenly spaced, and bake. They should look like this when they're done:

Let them cool for a few minutes before handling.

STEP SEVEN

Over a paper plate or other table covering, carefully superglue the earring backs to the head pieces.

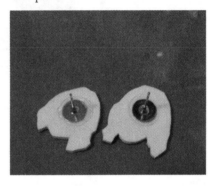

To avoid getting superglue on your hands, place a dot on the head first, then press the back piece onto it.

Let those babies dry for an hour and they're ready to go! When you're wearing best friends on your ears, three heads are definitely better than one.

Best Friends Forever

A visual ode to the greatest love of all. By Eleanor. Styling by Nao Koyabu.
Thanks to Desiree and Julie for modeling, and to Beyond Retro, the Pocket Library, Tabio, and Topshop for lending us clothes and accessories. All eyewear by Warby Parker.

when all other LIGHTS go out

If you can't imagine a future with you in it, please hang on.
By Pixie.
Playlist by Pixie, artwork by Minna.

When I was 17 or so, I started feeling like it was raining every day. There were no rainbows in my world, only dark clouds, and they never seemed to lift. I remember taking a quiz in a magazine, something like "Are You Depressed?"—and even though I knew the answer (YES), I was still a little scared when the results told me I should maybe consider seeing a doctor, because what I was feeling wasn't "normal."

Instead of asking for help like I should have (easier said than done), I started looking around at my classmates to try to figure out what "normal" meant. Did *they* cry all the time? Didn't other people think about hurting themselves on a regular basis? This was just, like, typical teenage angst that I was feeling, right? It would go away, wouldn't it?

Of course, I never actually asked anyone any of these questions—the idea of exposing myself as "crazy" was too much to bear. I told myself to keep the sadness and anxiety inside, to bury it and bear it, to wait it out the way you wait out the flu: Eventually, the sickness will disappear and everything will go back to normal. But that's not the way clinical depression works, of course: Instead of growing out of it, I fell deeper in, to the point where I began to see death as a viable option. Everything just hurt so much—even getting out of bed required Herculean strength—and I doubted I had it in me to keep going.

In the darkest times of my life, I found myself thinking about different ways of dying. It was the only thing that seemed to give me a measure of peace: the idea that I could, if nothing else, control my own mortality. It hurt so much just to exist that I came very close to extinguishing all lights, inside and out, and disappearing into an unknown, all-encompassing darkness. Darkness, I figured, was something I was good at, anyway.

But something stopped me—an almost invisible spark of defiance that I had to dig very deep to find and fight very hard to cling to. For a time, 99.9 percent of me wanted to die, but there was that .1 percent that kept flickering alight, the most distant of stars in the universe, and though it was hard for me to see it on a daily basis, I decided to find some kind of faith in the fact that it was there at all. Most of my brain insisted that this was just cowardice disguised as hope—that I was just afraid of death or physical pain or failure (oh, perfectionism, you are ever so much fun). When your mind turns on you, it is hard to fight it. But you don't have to battle it to the ground all at once. Fighting back is an incremental process, and all it takes is the smallest effort—waking up and saying, "Not today"—to send your depression the message that you will not be easy prey.

These small, quiet victories added up for me, and here I am, several lovely and weird years later. They are years I am so glad to have lived, inhabited by people I never even knew existed in my darkest days, people who were worth waiting for—worth living for—and the help I needed (and need) to keep my mind healthy and filled with good things. Of course, you don't get from "I want to die" to "I feel so glad to be alive" in one step. My steps may be different from yours, but regardless of the path you take, I know that you are capable of making this trek on your own, and that recovery is possible in all things.

If you are where I was a few years ago and are considering suicide, I have a few things to say to you. First of all, I would like you to know that somebody out there loves you. Some of you won't believe me, and some of you already know it but aren't sure it's enough. You can't feel it, and you can't believe in it, because you don't understand how anyone would look at you and see anything worth loving. Everything seems dark and sad and lost, and lately there's one thought that you can't shake from your mind: *Maybe everyone—including me—would be better off without me.* What you are feeling is a sadness beyond sadness, and it's hard to picture any other way to escape it. Daydreaming about disappearing becomes a source of sad relief.

People who have never been there do not understand it. They will tell you to "snap out of it" or that you're "going through a phase" or that "*everyone* gets sad sometimes." These people aren't evil, they just don't have the experience or the information or the imagination to conceive that other people's brains don't work like theirs do. But trust me: There are many people who know how you feel, including me. And that's why, even though we've never met, I can tell you: Somebody out there loves you. You may not even know they exist yet, but I promise you that they do. I am telling you, telling you, telling you, as someone who has been at the bottom of the lowest pit, with no lights and no ladders:

You are not alone, you are not worthless, and you are stronger than you think. Did you get up this morning? Did you open your eyes and take a deep breath and try to get through one more day? Then you, my love, are tough as nails. You are a fighter. Do not ever forget it.

So, how do you keep going? How do you fight those urges and those thoughts and that feeling that nothing is worth anything? I suppose for each person there's a slightly different answer. But I can tell you that the path out of darkness almost always begins with help from someone else—one of those aforementioned people who understand what you're going through. Here comes the hard part, though: You have to ask for help. You have to be willing, for one moment, to let someone else in. The scariest part of mental illness is how isolating and consuming it can be. It will try to shut you out of the world, to keep you away from help and hope. To just say, out loud, even something as simple as "I don't feel good, and I think I need some help" is a huge step in the right direction. You do not have to suffer alone. There are people who understand, who will not judge, who will not belittle you or dismiss your pain. The major thing is to let someone else in, so that you don't spiral out of control within your own mind.

Please do not hold these thoughts inside. I speak from experience—they don't go away on their own, but with a little help (and I don't mean just medication, because some people need it and some don't), they DO go away, and it is such a marvelous and miraculous thing that I can't even express how amazing it feels. For me, it was as if someone had come in and polished up my mind, removing cobwebs and ink spills and leaving everything sparkly and new. Colors were brighter, sounds were clearer, love was deeper, and life, in general, was worth living. It took me a long time to admit that I needed help, but once I told my parents how I was really feeling, they made sure I got what I needed. If your parental situation isn't great, that's OK—you can open up to anyone you trust: a friend, a counselor, a relative, etc. If you don't have anyone in your life you feel comfortable talking to, call a suicide hotline, a crisis center, or a hospital, especially if you are actively suicidal. Here's a number you can call from anywhere in the United States, 24 hours a day: 1-800-273-TALK (1-800-273-8255). Suicide.org has a list of resources outside of the U.S. You can also always call 911, or the emergency number in your country, on yourself if you feel like you have no one else to turn to. When they answer, simply tell them that you are feeling suicidal, or that you feel you are a danger to yourself, or just that you're having an emergency and need help. There is no shame in reaching out. Some of the bravest people in the world are the ones who picked up the phone and decided to save their own lives.

If this piece doesn't apply to you directly, but makes you think of a dear friend, understand that your friend is hurting, and that they may withdraw from you as things get worse. There are classic suicidal warning signs to look for: giving things away, isolating themselves, talking about suicidal plans, self-harming. If someone tells you they are considering suicide, take them seriously. Speak to someone you trust and voice your concerns. If you have any reason to fear they are close to making an attempt, don't leave them alone. Call your local emergency number, or take them to the emergency room. And tell a family member or a friend what's happening, so you're not in this alone.

Sharing your friend's secret may feel like a betrayal, but a serious situation calls for a serious response, and you have to trust that your friend will understand that your heart was in the right place. It may take months, it may take years, it may take forever, but if they get the help they need, they will look back one day and remember that when everything seemed hopeless, somebody out there loved them. Maybe they'll be struck by the revelation that they actually love themselves, something they once thought impossible. I've met many people in treatment who started out very bitter that they were "forced" to get help by loved ones, then I watched them heal and recover and remember themselves and thank those who helped them get the treatment they needed, without which they'd probably be gone. I also struggled with accepting help for a while before I got well enough to see how beautiful recovery is.

I'm not sure I can tell you how to find that little light inside of you to cling to, but I know, simply because you're reading this, that it's there. You are looking for someone to tell you that it's OK to need help and it's OK to *want* help, that you can get better, that you *will* get better, and that all of the things that seem so heavy and painful and impossible now will eventually lift and life will seem worth living again. Let me be that person. You are worth something. You are worth saving. Your life matters. Maybe you can't see all of that now, but you will. Because you can get better. You will.

Maybe someday you'll remember all of this and you'll write about it online and share it with a bunch of strangers, hoping that whomever needs it will read it and will know that they are not alone, that it's possible to get up every morning and look in the mirror and laugh and think, *I'm still here, motherfuckers*, and dance down the stairs into another day. Maybe you'll be able to tell them what they need to hear, and maybe they'll believe it, because it's sincere and true and worth believing: *Somebody out there loves you.*

Hopelessly Devoted to you

1. Moonlight Serenade – Glenn Miller
2. Our Love Is Here to Stay – Ella Fitzgerald
3. (I Love You) For Sentimental Reasons – Sam Cooke
4. Come Softly to Me – The Fleetwoods
5. Eternally – Sarah Vaughn
6. My Dearest Darling – Etta James
7. True Love Ways – Buddy Holly
8. It Had to Be You – Doris Day
9. Only You (and You Alone) – The Platters
10. You Belong to Me – Patsy Cline
11. Every Breath I Take – Gene Pitney
12. Love of My Life – The Everly Brothers
13. I'll Never Let You Go (Little Darlin') – Elvis Presley
14. Time – Nancy Sinatra
15. Something Good – Julie Andrews & Bill Lee

JANUARY 2014: **VISION**

HAPPY NEW YEAR, ROOKIES!

If last month, Forever, was all about nostalgia and savoring precious moments, this month is about GETTING ON WITH YOUR LIFE. I'd be lying if I acted like this wasn't a theme that's more personal for me. See: my journal entry from December 4:

> My Forever editor's letter went up on Monday and it's been so heartening to see the response, to have it out in the world, to feel a sense of closure. […] I am no longer afraid of not experiencing moments of Strange Magic; I am finally able to look forward to what's ahead…Like on the walk to school today, I decided to try out the Replacements for the first time, and the first song I listened to was "Alex Chilton" off *Pleased to Meet Me*, and I played it like four more times, throughout the whole rest of the walk, because it filled me with the most amazing dancing + crying feeling, and I know *nothing* about them but the chorus *slayed* me. [They cannot be printed here for copyright reasons, but I'd highly recommend looking them up: starting with "I'm in love," ending with "With that song." Butterflies, in my stomach.]
>
> It's such a teenage feeling, that moment of discovery followed immediately by obsession. But I decided this morning that it can be a *me* feeling, too, a simply *human* feeling, if you go about being a human in a fulfilling way. Instead of following this magical feeling with a mournful one like I have been lately—*ENJOY IT, SOON YOU'LL BE OLD AND JADED AND EMOTIONALLY REPRESSED*—I followed it this time with one of excitement, anticipation, just plain positivity. Not because I'm depending on the future being great, but because I know it will at least be *itself*, aka more living, aka more feeling.

Rookie will always be for teenagers, even as I get older, so this month is not about growing from a teen into an adult. It's about growing from less of yourself into more of yourself. Anaheed and I had a nice exchange about this month as we were planning it:

ANAHEED We've done a lot of stuff about indecision, and how it's OK not to be sure. But we haven't really covered those times when you just KNOW YOU'RE RIGHT. What does that do for you, what kinds of decisions do you make when you're sure? How does your relationship to fear change? How hard is it when you're young (and female!) to convince people that you're right? There's real value in normalizing indecision and heralding the courage it takes to change your mind, but when that's all that's talked about, it can make you start to doubt your own convictions—especially since young people are constantly told that their perceptions and beliefs are worth less than older people's. When you're a teenager people are always like, "You think that now, but you'll change your mind," so I think it's valuable to put some words and images and heft behind validating the surer moments, when you just KNOW. I wanna support those kinds of insights, because they lead to greatness.

ME Such as Rookie! When I started my blog, at first people questioned whether I wrote it myself. Then, once it was understood that it wasn't a scam, they questioned whether I really *got* what I was talking about—like, *Do you even understand that designer's history or how important that band is???* Then once people were like, K, she knows what she's talking about, it was like, *Well, isn't that BAD for a CHILD to KNOW ALL THAT? Shouldn't she have time to BE A KID?* It went through some more cycles and then I started Rookie and now people seem to get it and no one really bothers me anymore. Or at least I don't read what they have to say anymore because I am too busy executing my ~VISION~ and preserving my own bubble of stuff that inspires and motivates me.

My point is that there is always a reason why you are in over your head, but you have to POWER THROUGH IT and literally not have time to deal with it because you are too busy being ON THE MOVE. When Comme des Garçons first showed in Paris, fashion critics were so confused by how dark it was because it was the '80s and everything else was bright/colorful/gaudy/flashy/YSL/Versace. Then the '90s came and everyone caught on and minimalism and asymmetry and all-black was everywhere. Rei Kawakubo said she's concerned when people love her collections right away, because that means she isn't ahead of the times. Greatness is often first met with suspicion; sometimes you know what you're doing is interesting and new precisely *because* people don't like it. I think it's good to carefully consider criticism, but once you've done that and you're sure of yourself, you need to really develop a habit of shoving doubt to the side and moving on, and this month should inspire our readers to do so.

ANAHEED A while ago I read that almost half of young Evangelical Christians support marriage equality, while something like 12 percent of older Evangelicals do. This is true of so many issues—younger people see the issues clearer and are more right-er. Which is why I can't wait till you babies take over the whole world. And I'm psyched, after the intense month-long farewell to youthful ideas about the future that was Rookie in December, to spend January embracing the next moment, when you suddenly see the (near) future really clearly, and it makes sense, and you make sense in it. It's the moment when you emerge from a long and important hibernation/gestation period of looking inward, to look out at the rest of the world a little more. I like the paradigm of growing up as getting lighter instead of being weighed down, so you can fly higher. It's still part of being young, but it's the part of being young that = freedom. I dunno, I just feel like this will be a month of EXCITEMENT about THE WORLD OUTSIDE.

ME Yes yes yes. December was a good bittersweet nostalgic month, fitting with the holidays and the year ending and all that, but by January it will be time to move on. A lot of the stuff I was mourning in last month's editor's letter is no longer having these teenage moments of INTENSE CRAZY FEELING. That stuff can feel really strangely great in the moment or—especially—when looking back and romanticizing the moment, but there's a different kind of happiness that is less fleeting and more substantial.

I go on and off antidepressants depending on my schedule and how much I can afford to ~feel everything~ at a given moment, and every time I am off them for too long and then start taking them again and get clear-headed, I'm able to be like, *Oh, right, I am a more complete me when I can think clearly and execute my ideas and* make *something of my feelings, instead of just having these sporadic bursts of extreme chemical joy or sadness.* Like the episode of *Girls* where Hannah stays at Patrick Wilson's house and is like, *Wait, what if I don't have to be CRAZY and FEEL IT ALL? What if simple boring stuff like reading the paper and having friends makes me happy? Isn't that OK too?* At the same time that this month is about how old people CAN'T HANDLE THE TRUTH, it is also about how it does not make you boring to grow up a little and value stuff like your health and your family and what have you.

When Danielle interviewed the comix artist Ellen Forney for us last fall, she asked about the trade-off between being healthy and stable and not having those end-of-the-world moments anymore. Forney said:

You know how it is when you first totally fall in love with somebody, and you're just like still crushing, like HEAD over heels, like, *Awwwww!* Like, *I can't even believe this experience would be happening!* Right? And then let's say that relationship extends into years. And then, ideally, four years down the line, you have this sense of deep love. And it's still an extremely strong sense, and you can say that it's even stronger because

your feet are on the ground, and you can say, "I have this great thing." It's like that.

So this month is like, yeah, it's special to have those great moments of intense feeling, but it's also cool to not hate the world and to be productive and to know what you want and to get it done.

And, from the email I sent our staffers, to get a sense of this month's vibe:

SPORTY GOTH TIME. The dark minimalist asymmetry of Martin Margiela, Rick Owens, Yohji Yamamoto, early all-black Comme des Garçons, Rihanna's style of late. My Bloody Valentine, David Byrne, Lorde's *Pure Heroine*, Jay Z's *Magna Carta Holy Grail*, Arcade Fire's *Reflektor*, Joy Division's *Unknown Pleasures*, Beach House's *Bloom*, Kanye's *Yeezus*, Grimes's *Visions*. *The X-Files*, *Born in Flames*, and, of course, *THAT'S SO RAVEN*. Neon lights in the suburbs, tennis courts lit up at night, pavement and concrete, skyscrapers and city lights (empire state of mind <33), ALIENS AND UFOS, the people who spot them, prophets and poets.

And HEY, while I'm pasting little scraps of Vision inspiration, some of our staffers have been sharing New Year's resolutions. Some of my favorites include:

• "Start a female astronauts' club called Ladies Who Launch."—Amy Rose
• "Make a list of enemies and outlive them."—Lola
• "Learn choreographed dances from late-'90s/early-'00s hip-hop videos."—Marie
• "Remember that I'm still a beginner."—Brodie

To a VISIONARY new year,

LOVE, TAVI

Design by Sonja, Vanessa Han, and Kristin Smith.

THE GREAT BIG BEYONCÉ ROUNDTABLE

We just needed a week or so to digest the new album.
By the Rookie staff. Illustration by Suzy.

On Thursday, December 13, just after midnight, in our staff Facebook group, this happened:

TAVI BEYONCÉ JUST DROPPED A "VISUAL ALBUM" WHAAATASJBDFK

Then, pandemonium:

ERICA What
HAZEL HOW
JULIANNE Fourteen tracks?!
TAVI OMG and 17 videos?! *She is the future.*
GABBY Doesn't she know I have finals right now??
DANIELLE Beyoncé just snatched Christmas from Santa Claus like a bawse.
NAOMI I didn't know what was missing in my life until right now. I don't have to leave my bedroom today, for the world is in my bedroom.
AMY ROSE My eyelashes are in my bra. VERY VERKLEMPT.

Then we all calmed down a little but had SO MANY THOUGHTS 'N' FEELINGS ABOUT BEYONCÉ that NEEDED TO BE SHARED. So we commenced a casual, late-night roundtable discussion on the album:

TAVI WHERE SHOULD WE START? What were your first reactions?
HAZEL I was like WHAT, album out of nowhere?! Which is pretty fucking cool, but then when I realized there was a video for *every single song*, it took it to a whole new level. And then, when I started watching the videos, I was kind of in shock, because each one is SO GOOD, and to have them all together—that

was like WHOA. And then it was 1 AM and everyone was talking about it on the internet—I mean everyone. It just felt so important!
TAVI It says so much that she could release it without having to follow the industry protocol of taking out lots of ads, doing lots of press, releasing single after single and then video after video—she just said what she had to say, all at once, how she wanted to say it.
DANIELLE I was floored that she pulled it off, particularly filming the videos—and not even like a background dancer said anything about it?
AMY ROSE My first reaction, as a person who likes Beyoncé a lot but never LOVED one of her albums before this one, was to swoon and be like, "Why did I never get her before this? This is a multimedia masterpiece." I was completely blindsided by how gorgeous all the videos are and how her sense of humor is so present in them. Her grace is immense.
LAIA I just rewatched "Pretty Hurts" and started tearing up.
TAVI The part where Harvey Keitel asks her, "What is your aspiration in life?" really chokes me up on two levels: (1) It makes you think about Beyoncé's own life aspirations and how this album is such a definitive self-portrait (this feeling is intensified by the clip at the end of her winning a contest when she was very little), and (2) we (I) always forget that prettiness doesn't = happiness, and it was just very real to hear it plainly put—like, "OK, but what is your *actual aspiration in life*?" (this is intensified when she sings, "Are you happy with yourself?").
JULIANNE I really admire how explicit she was willing to be, even mimicking bulimia, which was kinda triggering, but as a SURVIVOR or recovered E.D. CHICKADEE or whatever, it was important for me to see that, because usually bulimia (and anorexia,

see: the girl eating a cotton ball to feel full) is treated flippantly, as a joke, or at least without a decent understanding of it. Seeing it put in context with the pressures surrounding it—not just "look beautiful" but "you feel like total shit about everything, therefore you are barfing up your food"—was pretty real.
HAZEL Can we talk about how different each video is, just aesthetically?
TAVI EVERY SINGLE ONE is impeccably art-directed—none of them feels like filler—and the progression is so amazing, getting to see all these different dimensions of her life unfold and make up this unreal (but SO REAL) self-portrait. "Blow" is one of my favorites, vibes-wise, plus I love seeing Solange in there. And the lyrics! We so rarely hear about female pleasure like this. I mean, movies will get an NC-17 rating for oral sex performed on a woman but stay PG-13 for oral sex performed on a man. Plus, the song is called "Blow," so I wasn't expecting it to be about the former.
JAMIA It is interesting to see some of the critiques of "Blow" and "Drunk in Love"—some people are calling the content "pornographic." I get a sense that a lot of that stems from judgment and shaming because Beyoncé is a mother, which is supposed to make her a different kind of "role model."
HAZEL Do people actually know what pornography is? I'm tired of people using the term *pornographic* for things that are not unsimulated sexual acts created for the viewer to get off to. It's a really sensationalist way of describing sexual expression that is actually pretty tame, especially in terms of pop music videos.
Anyway, why is being covered up associated with empowerment? Why is the universe so afraid of women being erotic? Beyoncé cage-dances in front of her husband in a music video and people cry to

ban it LOL maybe they're just jealous I can't even.

ANAHEED I mean, on one hand, we live in a patriarchy, and in many contexts a woman will be more successful if she plays up her attractiveness to men, which is unfortunate and unavoidable. But, on the other hand, does being a feminist mean taking no pleasure in your sexuality and never (god forbid!) profiting from it? There's really no winning here, and that's where the conversation should START. I don't see how it's cool or smart or "feminist" to dog on women for using the system to our own advantage, or for taking pleasure in something that happens to also sell. Being a woman is a trap, full stop. And there's something especially gross about scolding a black woman for being too bodily, for taking too much pleasure in her sexuality. Like she should remember her "place" and be "modest."

TAVI I don't easily buy the argument that a pop star's putting forth a sexualized image is automatically some kind of feminist act, but this album addresses so many different kinds of sexual desire, and you can tell how personal it is for her. (Consider "Drunk in Love" vs. "Rocket" vs. "Partition.") You can't simply say she's selling sex or whatever when it's all part of a self-portrait of who she is as a wife, a mom, a friend (especially in female friendships), an artist, a public figure, etc. It's incredibly personal. And if she is "selling sex," it's not up to anyone else to give her shit for it, and it feels especially UGH for white feminists to insist that a woman of color cover up and stop letting everyone know that she's hot and beautiful. Or to insist that she sing less about relationships when it's clearly a big part of her life. Honestly, those are usually the songs a lot of people want to hear and relate to, and I'm just thankful we get them from someone who delivers them through a lens of ultimate independence and self-assurance.

I think it's also important to note that this album is about so many kinds of love. In "XO" she is singing about love with one person, but in the video she is surrounded by people at like a Coney Island love fest, dancing with everyone, making everyone so fucking happy. Then there's the first line in "Superpower" about how feeling her palms together is different from feeling her hand in someone else's hand, how that's a different kind of power—it reminded me of this one time when my boyfriend and I were having a rough patch and I was walking outside in the summer and felt this huge gust of wind and it felt, legit, like a HUG. And I thought, and probably wrote in my diary, *The world is hugging me!* She covers spouse love, mom love, friendship love, self love, world love—it's so inspiring, my god!

JAMIA Beyoncé is in charge, which I don't think some of the critics get—she's in control of her own image and her own body, and it isn't up to us to police her.

TAVI And it's so lazy and out of context to fixate on the songs about sex and say that's all she's about, when this is an album of many songs and videos about LIFE. She didn't release these videos individually and over time like people normally do, because it should all be considered part of one package. You cannot get mad that she sings, "I just wanna be the girl you like" on "Partition" and not acknowledge the first lines of "Superpower." These aren't "singles"; this is a fully fleshed-out work, released as a whole. To be simplistic about it does it a disservice. I guess some people would accuse her of trying to have it both ways or whatever, as though "Blow" invalidates the message of "Flawless"—but why are we denying her right to explore her own complexity? She isn't saying women have to be all things, she is saying they can be if that's who they are, just like her.

HAZEL I love the video for "Partition." The mirror dance, that lavish mansion—it's all so beautiful. Also, just from a fashion perspective, the clothes/lingerie are incredible.

TAVI That napkin drop while she has tea at like VERSAILLES is just one example among many from this album where she turns racial power dynamics around so that she is the one in power.

JAMIA I love the French lines in that song. Translation: "Do you like sex? I'm talking about physical activity. Coitus. Do you like that? Men think feminists hate sex., but it's a very stimulating and natural activity that women adore." That gave me chills. I love that she is taking ownership of her sexuality, when some of her critics have been challenging her agency and objectifying her body for so long. She's owning and embracing sexuality and pleasure. I'm also moved by her vulnerability on "Jealous." Making it must have been so cathartic and painful.

TAVI In that video, she says something about looking in the mirror and going, "I've still got it"—and it's like, she's "still" got it?! I feel like this is just the beginning! To hear BEYONCÉ singing about feeling jealous was like, OK, so this really is something everyone feels—OK. The whole album has this energy of, like, she just knows what is important to her and doesn't have time for BS. It is thrilling to think of ever being in that place (being a teenager has never felt like being in that place).

HAZEL "Mine" feels like an homage to ARTSY FARTSINESS, with Beyoncé playing Pieta, and then there's a reference to *The Lovers* by Magritte, and the group dancing on the beach feels super Pina Bausch. Compare all of that with Lady Gaga just being like, "I AM A KOONS."

TAVI I get what Gaga is trying to do with all the *ARTPOP* stuff and asking people to take pop music seriously, but I feel that it's more effective to make something that demands to be taken seriously for its quality and not because you're like, "I'm on the red carpet at the AMAs on a giant fake horse, clearly I am an artist." Though I would like to include a disclaimer that I am not pitting Beyoncé and Gaga against each other just because they are both women. They

have done songs and videos together—they are obviously not enemies. But with all of December's "year in music" stuff and considering that the past two months alone have brought us new albums from Miley, Katy, Gaga, and Britney, it's impossible to consider Beyoncé's album in the ~pop music landscape~ without also looking at what else has dominated it and forced people who don't even care about it to pay attention.

JULIANNE On a different note, people were pissed about Beyoncé naming her tour "The Mrs. Carter Show" and about how much she talks about her love for her husband in her documentary, but that stuff is important. It is really reinforcing of black love/marriage, which some people reduce to "just his little wife" but which actually has real-world implications, such as the financial stability marriage provides, especially considering that single black women are on the lowest rung of the income ladder and earn less as a whole than any other group in America. WHICH MAKES BEING MARRIED A FEMINIST ISSUE. The song "Mine" reflects that.

DANIELLE She's fully recognizing that she is at the top of her game and deserves massive respect, but also telling people to GET ON HER LEVEL. "Flawless" is the perfect anthem for that state of mind. She's reaching back and pulling people with her as she goes by, inciting them to feel their own power.

GABI Bey is one of the few people on her level in the industry who have consistently been humble and kind to everyone, and I feel like she just needed to have a moment to be like I AM THE FUCKING SHIT and acknowledge that she is a queen and was doing big things before most (all?) of the other big female pop stars right now were even on the scene. The fact that she included, in "Flawless," this sample about how it can be a good thing to be competitive in career/accomplishments makes so much sense in this context.

We teach girls to shrink themselves, to make themselves smaller. We say to girls: "You can have ambition, but not too much. You should aim to be successful, but not too successful—otherwise, you will threaten the man." Because I am female, I am expected to aspire to marriage. I am expected to make my life choices always keeping in mind that marriage is most important. Now, marriage can be a source of joy and love and mutual support. But why do we teach girls to aspire to marriage and we don't teach boys the same? We raise girls to see each other as competitors, not for jobs or for accomplishments—which I think can be a good thing—but for the attention of men. We teach girls that they cannot be sexual beings in the way that boys are. Feminist: a person who believes in the social, political, and economic equality of the sexes.
—Chimamanda Ngozi Adichie at TEDxEuston, 2012, and sampled on "Flawless"

TAVI I love imagining Beyoncé watching that TED Talk and being like, "I should put this in a song." And I love looking to that as an example of how accessible information on feminism can now be outside of, like, academia. It's important to note that, in the video, she is moshing while this all goes down.

DANIELLE And recognizing black punks! I've felt deeply alienated by feminism lately, and am trying to work out why I feel that way. A lot of it is that before anything, I'm a black woman, so I go into feminism already racialized and somewhat on the outside. But this album has REINVIGORATED ME.

JULIANNE OMG, me too, Danielle. I have been feeling so bad about feminism (mostly because #whitefeminism), but Beyoncé just WIG-SNATCHED the term/concept from the people who would exclude her from it. Like, it's hers now.

DANIELLE It's so important that she is not just talking about feminism on this album, but black feminism specifically. Her race informs and enhances her feminism. Black women are the most undervalued population in our culture in so many ways, and it's so, so important to me that this feminist message is being heard by black girls too.

I've really enjoyed watching her relationship with feminism evolve, because she seems to come to it in the way that a lot of people do—not with jackbooted certainty, but with a lot of questions that she works out in her own way. Her earlier songs about love are still great love songs, and no less feminist in scope, but here she's saying, "I can have all of this, and you can too, and still be a feminist, and still be a boss."

TAVI Too often, when people dip their toe into feminism, they are scared away because people start to ask too much of them, and I think the impulse then is to just be like, "If that's what this feels like, I don't actually want to be in your club, thanks." But Beyoncé not only made this amazing song where she not only reminds us that SHE ALREADY DOES SO FUCKING MUCH, YOU CANNOT COMPLAIN THAT SHE TALKS ABOUT LOVING HER HUSBAND, but also warms up to feminism even more, and on her own terms. I mean, to have a definition of a feminist explicitly stated in this song is so huge!

DANIELLE There are a bunch of girls who listen to Taylor Swift who will never identify as feminist, but who get some sort of personal empowerment from hearing her sing about breaking up with guys who are bad for her—that's still important. My own feminism evolved when I realized that being a feminist means I support the rights of all women, even the ones who don't give a shit about feminism. Of course, it would be amazing if everyone could access femi-

XO

nism, but I'm not going to stop fighting for rights just because they can't, and I won't devalue the lives of women who just aren't feeling it.

HAZEL You cannot argue that Beyoncé is not being a role model when she LITERALLY IS a role model. When a young feminist says, "Beyoncé empowers me," how can you argue with that? I'm tired of feminism's rigid rules and restrictions. We have to abolish those. A major point of this album is to underline this idea of feminist growth and acceptance and to hair-flip restrictive haters.

AMY ROSE "XO" expresses how I feel about everyone that I even remotely like.

DANIELLE That video wrecked me, unexpectedly—like, why am I crying at someone having fun at Coney Island?! But she's so generous, and showing us how important it is for her to be a real person in that moment. It's so genuine. Like, she accepts love, gives love, all in a way that makes her more capable of doing her work. It isn't a distraction, it's an enhancement. And what really ruined my mascara was seeing a carefree black girl, because we so rarely do.

TAVI In a recent interview, Beyoncé talked about how she'd been thinking about how hard she's been working since she was a child, and how she wanted to basically "blow that shit up" and make an album about what is truly important to her. It totally comes full circle, starting with "Pretty Hurts," being reminded that she's been competing and performing her whole life, and then ending with "Grown Woman."

JAMIA I saw someone tweet today that Beyoncé is at that place in your 30s when you start feeling like a grown-ass woman, owning your strengths and failures, when you stop giving a fuck about what other people think. Bey and I are about the same age, and I'm feeling so much of this album and its message.

TAVI Ooh, YES. Not that I directly relate, but as y'all know I've been having funny feelings about growing up. But this song/album makes me excited to be a real-person grown woman motherfucking boss ruler of my own world. I've been jittery all day because I'm just so excited for the future in general! I love Beyoncé I love myself I love being a young woman OMG.

JAMIA This album is about being the CEO of your own life, not rising to the top of someone else's industry. Beyoncé moves the conversation from "run shit within someone else's institution" to "RUN YOUR OWN SHIT," and that is the goal for real.

TAVI This album is the perfect sound-track for both lovetimes and world domination. It covers all the ground.

AMY ROSE This album is making me feel more like myself.

DANIELLE This album is a tax write-off, because I need it to live.

JAMIA I think this is the feeling that e.e. cummings was talking about—that the "hardest battle which any human being can fight" is "to be nobody but yourself." Every year I resolve to preserve my imagination and my child-mind. When I'm feeling like I'm fronting or losing myself or martyring myself, I imagine my five-year-old self, with ashy knees and a big snaggle-tooth, smiling at me and reminding me who I am—and I just can't lie to her.

JULIANNE I have been a huge fan of Beyoncé since Destiny's Child, but this album was a total surprise to me in terms of its openness and the adventurousness of its sound. It has only reinforced my love for Beyoncé, "flaws and all," as she once sang on another one of her many feminist anthems! If she has contradictions, and I do for liking her, so be it. We are human women and I'm a better, stronger person because she exists. ⚡

SPORTING LIFE

Let's go down to the tennis court.
By María Fernanda. Styling by Zaid Díaz.

Thanks to Caro, Luciana, and Paula for modeling; to Adrián Glez for styling assistance, hair, and makeup; and to Cynthia Buttenklepper for lending us clothes.

LIFE SKILLS 301

Advanced-level techniques for being a person.
By Krista

Holy crap, another year has gone by. The planet slowly but surely completed one more revolution around the sun. We lived 365 more days on Earth. And in that astonishingly long yet unbelievably short time, somehow we wised up. We know things now that we didn't know this time last year. We are smarter. More experienced. We made it! And that means: It's time for a round of Life Skills. Advanced level. Here we go!

1. ENTERING AND EXITING A CONVERSATION (POLITELY)

Entering: You know how when people are talking at a social event they stand in a tight circle, and it looks intimidating? You know how it can sometimes feel weird to be alone at a party and want to be in the talking group but you don't know anybody or have any idea how to join a conversation?

It's OK, lemon drop! Everyone (EVERYONE) feels a little awkward in a situation like this, but we can handle it!

So you don't know anyone. So what? You are an interesting and cool person, and other people, if they are not total jerks, will listen to what you have to say, or at least be willing to let you join their group. If you are alone at a social event and don't know how to enter a conversation with people who are already talking, just get a little closer to their group and eavesdrop in a non-hover-y way. Find an excuse to stand near them—fiddle with a book on the bookshelf or get a beverage nearby. What are they talking about? If you hear someone mention something you like or know about, that's your in. Maybe someone is showing someone a picture of their dog on their phone. You say, "Whoa, is that your dog? It's so cute!" And, BOOM, you're talking to someone in the group! Maybe you hear someone say, "Wait, you haven't heard of the Breeders?" and the Breeders are your favorite band—jump in! Say something as simple as "Aaaah, I love the Breeders!"

and people, if they are not snotty, will move over and make some room for you.

The key, though—and this is real—to entering groups of already-talking people is to not apologize for yourself. No "Sorry, I couldn't help overhearing you guys talking about the Breeders" or "Sorry, I don't mean to interrupt, but…" *Nuh-uh.* It is natural for you to talk about shared interests with other human beings, so just act like it's the most normal thing in the world for you to casually join a group of people already conversing, even if it is a big deal for *you.*

Exiting: Maybe a conversation has gone on… a little too long. Perhaps it's just run its course, and there's nothing left to talk about. Or maybe someone has cornered you and is boring you to tears about a subject you care nothing about; or they're persistently hitting on you, and you're completely uninterested. You don't want to be impolite or hurt anyone's feelings, there's no escape route that doesn't seem super awkward, etc., so you're stuck talking to this person, desperately scanning the room for anyone who might come and rescue you, blinking SOS signals at everyone who walks by.

You know what, though? You're not stuck. You can leave this soul-sucking convo *any time you want!* Here are some of my favorite strategies:

- There's always "Excuse me, I have to go to the restroom." So tried and true that it's a cliché at this point. NO ONE can argue with your need to pee. This is my go-to for getting rid of people who are conversationally irritating me. And it's not even a lie! I really do have to pee—practically all the time! *You do not have to come back to the person*, especially if you're at a party or in another social setting. Clearly you meant to come back, but you were distracted by someone else. You're a social butterfly, flitting airily about!
- If that feels too abrupt, do what my friend

Jen does and offer the person something. Say, "Hey, do you want some chips?" or "I'm getting a drink, you want one?" If the person says yes, go get it, cheerfully bring it back, and then wave goodbye and vanish into the crowd. You have now done them a favor. You are obvs not rude, and now you are freeeee.

- If you're dying to get out of a conversation with a person you know, you can *try reminding the person of a future event.* This maneuver involves trying to wrap up the conversation quickly by saying something like "Hey—Kara's show next week! Are you going?" If the person says yes, say, "Awesome, I'll see you then!" and smile while backing away. However, this is a risky social move, as it may serve only to delay, but not prevent, further misery. This person may approach you again at Kara's show—after all, you both just agreed to see each other there! But you do have all these new ways to politely avoid talking to them, so maybe it's not such a big risk after all.

Anyway, remember: If someone has backed you into a corner, cutting you off from all other people, and is going on and on about something that does not interest you, *they* are being rude. It is *not* rude of you to make a prompt, polite, and effective exit.

2. MAKING SMALL TALK

Small talk is when someone talks to you in a polite way about something unimportant. Small talk is when a friend's mom says, "Hi! How are you today?" and you say, "Fine." It's when a bus driver opens the door, looks down at the slush on the road, and says, "Cold out there, huh?"

A lot of people hate it and find it annoying, but small talk has its place. It smoothes out social interactions and makes simple exchanges between strangers (e.g., you and the bus driver) more pleasant. It can also serve as a launching pad for actual conversation.

The worst kind of small talk, though, is when you *have* to do it with a stranger—like when someone introduces you to another person at a party and then leaves, or when you and your friend go out for breakfast with her friend from out of town, and your friend gets up and goes to the bathroom, leaving you with a stranger you must be friendly to. What do you say now?

Don't panic! Just repeat after me: "So, what did *you* do today?" Emphasis on the *you*. Ask this question while forming your face into an I-am-so-fascinated-by-and-interested-in-you expression, and you have yourself the perfect small-talk opener.

It works every time. You're not asking something boring or trite, like "So…what do you do?" or "Where are you from?" or "Uh…do you have any hobbies?" No. No one likes answering those questions. But if you ask something too specific, like "Read any good books lately?" a lot of people won't have an answer for you, because they can't think of the last good thing they read, and they wind up feeling like total idiots even though they totally read great stuff all the time (ugh!). Instead, you are asking them a pointed question that everyone has an answer for—often a really interesting one!

But let's say their answer is not exactly a thrilling tale of derring-do. Usually, it isn't. Most people will give you a really banal laundry list: "Well, I went to school, and then I had dinner, and now I'm here, ha ha." Your job is to seize on the one thing that sounds even vaguely interesting to you, and then drag the details out of them. For instance:

YOU Oooh, what'd you have for dinner?
THEM Pizza.
YOU What *kiiiiind* of pizza?
THEM Ha ha, um, pepperoni.
YOU Is that your favorite?
THEM Yeah. But I like sausage, too.
YOU So you're not a vegetarian, I take it?
THEM Nope. But my sister is.
YOU Oh, that's cool. Is your sister older or younger?
THEM She's older.
YOU I have an older sister, too. Did yours used to beat you up?

OMG, LOOK, YOU ARE TALKING!

Small talk is not hard—it is 100 percent about being (or even just faking being) super interested in another person. Most people are *really good* at talking about themselves—all you have to do is ask questions. You can do that!

3. GETTING WRINKLES OUT OF CLOTHES REALLY FAST

You're going somewhere and you have to look nice NOW, but the places you usually keep your clothes are on the floor, wadded up in drawers, and in backpacks. Welcome to my life (no need to take off your shoes).

Because we don't have time for irons or steamers (and even if we did, let's be real, would we be ironing and steaming?), I have a trick for you. You know that Downy Wrinkle Releaser stuff that's like eight bucks? You spray it on clothes and they become magically unwrinkled. That stuff is amazing. It's a miracle. And *you can make your own version at home in less than 30 seconds, for almost no money*:

1. Combine two cups of water with two teaspoons of liquid fabric softener in a spray bottle.
2. Shake it hard.
3. Spray a fine mist over your wrinkled-as-hell garment.
4. Gently tug on the hem and sides, then smooth the wrinkles out with your hand.
5. Walk out the door wrinkle-free.

Gosh, you're always so well-groomed!

4. GETTING YOUR PARENTS/ GUARDIANS TO LOOSEN THEIR VISE-GRIP

OK, you screwed up. Your parents finally just started allowing you to borrow the car on the weekend, and what did you do? You piled all your friends into the backseat, *drove to another town*, went to a party your parents didn't know about, and *massively* underestimated the amount of time it would take to get back, meaning you missed your curfew by miles. One of your friends smoked in the car, and even though the windows were down, your parents can definitely smell it.

You are *grounded*. You are so grounded you will never again see the light of day, and you are definitely never, ever, ever going to have your mitts wrapped around the steering wheel of your parents' car. *Help.*

Well, honey bun, you earned this. I know. I'm sorry, it sucks, but seriously, come on. Look at it from your parents' point of view. They were hesitant to let you borrow the car because they weren't sure if you were ready for that kind of responsibility, and you basically just waved neon red flags that say NOPE, NOT READY in front of their faces. They were sooo right, and they're not going to give you another chance to blow it for a loooong time.

Here's a way to *maybe* make things a little better:

1. Meekly accept the grounding. You are, after all, in the wrong.
2. Keep meekly accepting the grounding for a surprisingly long time. *Shock* everyone with how calm you are about it. No whining, no crying, no begging. Just stay quietly grounded and lead a responsible life doing what your parents tell you to do.
3. When it's been a good long while, and you've accepted that you blew it, and you feel *confident* you will not screw up like that ever again…seize on the right moment to approach your parents and say you'd like to talk to them.
4. Begin by sincerely apologizing for your behavior that night. You know how.
5. Follow the apology by stating what you will do in the future if given a similar opportunity. For instance: "I know I don't have car privileges right now, and that's OK, but I want you to know that I understand that what I did was wrong. If you give me another chance, I will not take the car anywhere without telling you where I'm going, because that isn't safe. I will be home by curfew, because I know it's only there to protect me. Also, I will never allow anyone to smoke in the car, period."
6. Here is the kicker. It's the most important part. Follow your sincere apology and statement of future intent with this little gem: "I would like the opportu-

nity to show you that I can be responsible and trustworthy sometime in the near future. In order to show you that, **I need the freedom to improve myself and to be able to make the right choices**."

And then leave it alone. Don't beg for the car, don't make wild promises. Just try this. My friend Lexi taught me the part about "needing freedom to make the right choices" and she is *onto something*. Parents like it. It's mature and well thought out. If they say no, don't argue. Concede defeat gracefully, like the super reasonable person you are. You gave it your best shot, and becoming *less* mature now certainly isn't going to improve anything.

And when you do get the car back, don't shoot yourself in the foot like that again, OK?

5. ERASING YOUR INTERNET FINGERPRINTS

Most of you probably already know about clearing your browsing history, but I think *completely erasing all traces of your internet activity* is a vitally important tech skill we all need to have. I mention it because I know what it's like to have to share a family computer and not have a smartphone.

Maybe you have a really embarrassing question you have to google? It happens. Do you really want your dad to know you searched for "chunky period blood normal"? (It is, btw.) If you're just clearing your history, what you looked up might actually still be findable. Ahhhh, unacceptable!!!

To erase your online activity forever, you need to clear your browsing history, download history, search history, cookies, and saved passwords, as well as empty the cache on whatever browser you use, like Firefox, Safari, or Chrome. All of it! To learn how to do this, step by step, go to ComputerHope.com, click on "Help," and then "Questions and Answers." It only takes a minute. Go forth and google, friends.

6. RETRACTING AN EMAIL AFTER HITTING SEND

Disclaimer: This one is for Gmail users only. Sorry! But it's a good one.

Let's say it's 1 AM and you're in a fight with your boyfriend or girlfriend or best friend. It fucking sucks, and everything hurts, and it's late, and you can't sleep, and so…you decide to write this person an email. People always say to write down how you feel, right? *Fingers flex over keyboard*

You begin the email by listing their flaws, both huge and petty. You call them terrible names. This feels magnificent. YOU are the champion of Truth and Right; THEY represent everything that is wrong in this world and they have been fucking with you for MONTHS and you are not going to take it anymore. You go on to outline every horrible thing they have ever done, then you wrap it up by telling them just how very wrong they are and how much you despise them and how, right at this moment, you feel like seeing them never again would be juuust fine.

You are not going to actually *send* this email—certainly not. You just wanted to get that all out of your system. And it's kind of fun to imagine the damage hitting Send would wreak in their world.

You finish the email, shaking with rage. You reread it. Its rightness brings tears—actual TEARS!—to your eyes. You know what? You know *what?!* EVERYTHING YOU SAID WAS TRUE, THIS PERSON NEEDS TO READ THIS.

You hit Send.

It feels tremendous for 2.5 seconds. *You are mighty and powerful.* And then: OH MY FUCKING GOD WHAT DID YOU JUST DO?!

But it's too late. The email is sent. *The email is sent.* Oh no oh no oh no oh no.

If only there were a way to take back that nasty little missive you never meant anyone to see, and for there to be NO TRACE of its having ever been written!

Friends, there *is*. A little-known feature on Gmail allows you to retract emails up to 30 seconds after you've hit Send. It's not technically withdrawing an email that's making its way to your bestie's/honey's computer; it just delays its flight for half a minute in case you change your mind. All you have to do is click Undo, and, like magic, the email NEVER SENDS AND YOUR WORLD IS 10,000 PERCENT BETTER.

If you have Gmail, go to your settings, choose "Labs," scroll down till you see "Undo Send," and enable that feature on your email account. It takes less than a minute. AND IT HAS SAVED MY LIFE COUNTLESS TIMES.

7. LOOKING (AND BEING) GENEROUS WHEN YOU HAVE LESS MONEY THAN YOUR FRIENDS

Do you have friends who always, *always* have spending money? Friends whose parents give them credit cards to just *us*? Friends who constantly and casually pay for things like meals and snacks and movie tickets, sometimes taking care of you in the process?

Hiya. This was—and is—me. In the past, in the present, and probably for all time. I grew up with less money than any of my friends. We weren't flat-out broke, but I certainly did not have casual spending money, and there was no way I could wander into a store and just buy something like a cool T-shirt. All purchases had to be carefully plotted in advance and saved and schemed for. A lot of my friends, having always had access to plenty of money, simply did not understand that if I went to the movie, I could not go for pizza, and that was that.

It's still like that today. I have friends who make six figures and are always ready to go out for fancy drinks, who casually drop $250 at Whole Foods in 20 minutes, and who want to go to that new award-winning restaurant where entrees *start* at $35

AHEAD OF THEIR TIME
BY THE ROOKIE STAFF

1. IMAGES OF A WAYWARD SOUL — NINA SIMONE

2. KEEPING UP — ARTHUR RUSSELL

3. TABETAI — YOKO ONO / PLASTIC ONO BAND

4. SHOUT, SISTER, SHOUT! — SISTER ROSETTA THARPE

5. BRIDGE — FLORA PURIM

6. HIT — THE SUGARCUBES

because it just opened and they're hungry and it's Tuesday. If I say, "Umm, could we maybe go somewhere…less spendy?" they're all over it. "Oh, I've got you," they say, waving their hands in the air. "Baby, don't worry, I'll get you. Just come."

That's nice as hell, but a lot of times, it makes me feel like an asshole. I don't want to *always* be on the favor-receiving end. It skews the balance of our relationship in a way that makes me feel like I owe the person covering me something, but I can't afford to ever make good on this debt. I feel this even though I know my friends don't think I owe them anything, and that they're offering to pay out of total friendliness and love. It's just that it doesn't always feel so great to *me*, in my head. Know what I mean?

If you have wealthier friends who are constantly doing you monetary favors, I have a way to feel better, seem generous, and balance the friendship scales: *Spring for the small stuff.*

When the opportunity arises, use your limited funds to pay for little things, without announcing it or making it a thing in *any* way. If your friend with a great allowance constantly buys your lunch, buy her coffees when y'all go out. If someone insists on getting your movie ticket, hop quick like a bunny and pay for the popcorn. Even tiny things, like buying *two* orange juices from the vending machine and silently handing one to your friend, make a huge difference.

These are small things you can do to show that someone's generosity does not go unappreciated, and believe me, your friends will notice. You are showing that, while you may have less $$$, you are willing to share what you have, and that makes for a balanced and mutually generous friendship.

And if you don't have any money to spring for the small stuff? It's really OK. Don't be afraid to say, "Hey, I'd love to do that, but I can't afford it, and I don't want you paying for me all the time," and then stick to your guns. On the occasions when you do accept a favor, thank the friend who

spotted you and try to think of a way to help them. Maybe you're really good at algebra, which that person sucks at. Study with them. Maybe you're just an awesome listener who gives amazing hugs. You can still pay them back in your own way, free of charge.

8. ASKING A STRANGER OUT

You notice a cute new person working behind the counter at a your regular coffee shop. Or you see a cool someone at a library/concert/reading/museum/restaurant. They're in your line of vision, and suddenly, BAM! All of your radiant energy is directed like a laser beam on this person whom you don't actually know. OH MY LORD, NOW YOU KNOW WHAT PERFECTION LOOKS LIKE. You want to talk to this person; you are *filled* with a desire to know them. But they might leave at any moment! And *you may never see them again*! This is your one chance in life to ask this person out. Do it. DOOOOOO IT.

"But Krista!" (That's you.) "I don't know anything about them! What if they've got a girlfriend or boyfriend already? What if they're gay? What if they're *not* gay? What if they're asexual? What if they get it on every day (OBVIOUSLY THEY DO, LOOK AT THEM!!!) and are totally sick of it and want to be left in piece?

Guess what? I DON'T CARE. These are all useless details, clouding your shining, brilliant nerve. Get ready to become instantly bolder, because I'm going to teach you how to ask a stranger out in the quickest, politest way possible, with *way* fewer rejection possibilities than usual. You won't have to have any prior knowledge of the object of your sudden affection's situation—and the ball will stay COMPLETELY in *their* no-pressure court. Here's what you do:

1. Scan your crush-target for headphones/work/body language that says DO NOT APPROACH. Don't ever bother someone who's wearing headphones (the

international sign for "leave me alone"), or who's hunched over a book or a laptop, or who looks super-busy, like a café worker who's got a big line. Would you like that? Course not. Respect people's body language, space, and time.

2. If you've determined that now is possibly an OK time, gather all your stuff. Get totally ready to go. Use the restroom, put your coat on, everything. Asking someone out will be the last thing you do before leaving this place.

3. Find a slip of paper and a pen. Write down your name, your phone number or email address, and a short description of who you are and what you look like. Example: "Krista—the blond girl with cat-eye glasses who asked you out at Swim Café. You can reach me at kristaisawesome@fakeemail.com." Be brief! What you are about to do will be memorable.

4. Take a deep breath and approach this dreamboat.

5. BE BRAVE! Smile and say, "Hi, my name's [your name here]. I don't know what your situation is, but I think you're really cute. I'd love to hang out sometime, if you want. Here's my info."

6. Hand them the prepared slip of paper with your information on it. Smile again. You are a brave and confident person who has no fear!

7. VANISH. Seriously. Vanishing is the secret to asking a stranger out without too much awkwardness. If they try to talk to you, cheerfully say, "Sorry—I have to go!" One more smile, then *get the hell out of there*. This makes it so there is absolutely NO PRESSURE on your new crush to respond to you. They have a way to contact you. If they're interested, they'll get in touch. If they aren't, who cares? No harm done/no feelings invested.

Guys, this really works. It does! I've been doing it for years, and I've also taught it to every shy friend I've ever had, with excellent and sometimes even astonishing results.

Go get 'em, killer. ✳

7. EL GATO BLANCO (THE WHITE CAT) — MELTDOWN

8. — — MIRANDA JULY

9. BAM BAM — SISTER NANCY

10. CAME TO GIVE LOVE (OUTRO) — AALIYAH

11. FADE — HOLLY HERNDON

12. GALANG — M.I.A.

13. FLOWERS — SWEET FEMALE ATTITUDE

REALLY FUNNY

I wish TV shows and movies didn't make me feel like being fat is a joke.
By Brodie

When the movie *Shallow Hal* came out in theaters, I didn't know how to articulate why I didn't find it as funny as my friends did. Why I, 11 years old in a baggy T-shirt and squeezed into my cinema seat, wanted to hide, while everyone around me guffawed at the onscreen hijinks. But now I know: It was the first time I looked at a movie screen and saw an image that looked like me. And that image fucking sucked.

For those of you who haven't seen it, let me save you the pain: *Shallow Hal* is about a guy called Hal who falls in love with Rosemary, a fat woman played by Gwyneth Paltrow in a fat suit. The "joke" is that Hal has been hypnotized to see Rosemary as thin, but everyone else knows her true size. She breaks every chair she sits on and her cannonballs empty a swimming pool (LOLOLOL fat people, amirite? Why do they even bother leaving the house!), but he thinks she's hot. When Hal finally sees her as she really is, he becomes a better man and learns not to judge people on appearances—because he fell in love with a fat girl he thought was thin and therefore learned that fat people actually have brains and hearts and feelings and personalities! What a hero!

The reactions Gwyneth's character got from people (aside from Hal) were very familiar to me. I've gotten the same reactions all my life: at the pool or at the food court or in the school gym or on a plane when I, too, had the gall to be FIP (fat in public). This movie, though not deep or heartfelt, also touches on something that is very real for a lot of fat girls: the idea that a thin, pretty version of yourself exists underneath your fat, and if you only bothered to excavate her, you might be happy/loved/successful. I call this the "but you've got such a pretty face" syndrome, based on comments I've heard my entire life—from relatives, from movies, from TV—that say in no uncertain terms, "You're not good enough now, but with a little work, you *could* be."

We (people, women, Rookie) talk a lot about media representations of women and how they affect the lives of real, non-famous women and girls. We celebrate Beyoncé's power and her unapologetic, take-no-prisoners attitude (in her life and her art) and the messages these things send to young girls. We talk about the pressure that unrealistic beauty ideals in magazines and other mass media puts on girls, and how that affects their self-esteem. But it's harder to talk about the way fat women are represented on TV and in film, and how these representations affect fat women (like me) IRL, because there are so few examples of our being seen as anything besides comic relief. It's hard to work out how to do something properly when it's so rarely been done at all. And it's really, really hard to be OK with your body when you're constantly being reminded that it's something for other people to laugh at.

The "pretty face" message was heartbreakingly brought to the screen in the British TV series *My Mad Fat Diary*, one of very few shows on the air ever that have featured an authentic and multidimensional fat female character. In the second episode, that character, Rae Earl, a 16-year-old girl, has just been released from a psychiatric hospital following a suicide attempt. We see her get into an argument with her best friend, Chloe (who is thin, conventionally beautiful, and outgoing), then we see Rae weigh herself and hear bits from her diary in voiceover: "I am a body dysmorphic, without the dysmorphic. I am bulimic without the sick. I am fat." What follows is a dream sequence in which Rae lowers a zipper that runs down her back and sheds her "fat self," revealing a curvy lingerie model underneath. She drags her flabby shell down the stairs, takes it into the backyard, and sets it on fire.

I followed Rae's story obsessively through the show's first season, because it brought back so many memories of my own teenage years. When Rae lies down on the grass near the boy she likes, tugs at her T-shirt, and positions her hands across her stomach in a subtle attempt to hide its size, I replay in my mind scenes of myself doing those exact same things. When Rae struggles to find a swimsuit to wear to a pool party, I'm transported back to tear-filled changing rooms, where I relive my terror at the thought of anyone from school seeing me without my clothes on.

But Rae is more than her insecurities and issues. She loves music and tells jokes. She's a supportive friend. She occasionally acts out as a bratty teenager. Rae is a wonderful fat female character because her weight is important to her backstory, but it's never more important than her obsessive love of Manchester bands or her kind, sensitive personality. She makes us laugh by telling jokes—not by eating, struggling to walk, falling over, breaking chairs, or doing other Fat Person Things. She is Rae first, fat later.

In this, Rae is kind of the inverse of the roles Rebel Wilson has been playing lately. After appearing briefly (but memorably) in *Bridesmaids* (more on that movie later), Wilson went on to star in the a cappella comedy *Pitch Perfect*, in the dark comedy *Bachelorette*, and on her own TV series, *Super Fun Night*, which is on the air now. In those three roles, Wilson's weight informs her character. *Pitch Perfect*'s Fat Amy hates exercise and, in the movie's uplifting climax, tells the thin girls on her singing team that she loves them because they have "fat hearts." Becky, Wilson's character in *Bachelorette*, is a mope whose friends tread all over her and tear her wedding dress in half when *two* of them get inside it and express their jealous disbelief that she's about to marry a handsome guy. Kimmie Boubier, Wilson's character in *Super Fun Night*, is the butt of almost every joke (many of them about Spanx—I counted five in the first episode alone).

I wanted to love *Super Fun Night*, but it just left me feeling shortchanged. After all the years of crappy role models, I was so psyched to see an actress—who, like me, is a fat Australian girl obsessed with Salt-N-Pepa and improv comedy—make it to the top of the comedy world, where she could've pitched any show she wanted to. Imagine my disappointment when I saw her, *Super Fun Night*'s star and one of its writers and executive producers, telling the world to keep laughing at the miserable fat girl who loses the handsome love interest to her skinny rival.

I read a while ago that Jodie Foster seeks out roles that were written for men but could be played just as well by women. I think the same mentality should apply when writing and performing fat characters: If you switch them out for thinner actors and can't tell the difference, you've probably got a successful, non-offensive character who's not going to remind girls that fat bodies are ugly and the people in them unlovable.

The character I always come back to when I'm thinking about representations of fat ladies on TV is Sookie St. James from *Gilmore Girls*. Played by Melissa McCarthy, Sookie was lovable and cool and funny and successful and clever. She was a businesswoman, an amazing chef, and a great friend. She was adored by her husband, her children, and everyone else who knew her. In all 153 episodes of *Gilmore Girls*, I cannot remember one single occasion when

Sookie's weight was a point of conversation. It was never framed as a positive or a negative: The dudes who were into Sookie never fetishized her for her weight, and the ones who weren't never used it as a deterrent. Her friends never discussed her size behind her back. She never attempted to change her body nor collapsed in a heap with a bag of cookies when things didn't go her way. Her body mattered less than her personality and talent.

Melissa McCarthy changed the game again in *Bridesmaids*, in which a bride, Lillian, played by Maya Rudolph, is kind of obligated to include her fiancé's sister, Megan (McCarthy), in the wedding party. Megan tags along on all the bridal party activities, stealing every scene. She is brash and kind and intelligent and loyal. The actress's weight in no way influences or alters who the character is at her core. The third time I saw *Bridesmaids* in the theater, I became aware of how totally my reaction to this character differed from those of the people around me. When Megan came on to Air Marshal Jon (played by Ben Falcone, McCarthy's real-life husband), I laughed—because a woman hitting on an air marshal by suggesting they "go into the restroom and not *rest*" is funny.

But a group of people sitting near me in the theater could not contain their disgust at the sight of an aggressively flirtatious fat woman daring to even mention sex in a movie. Instead of laughing, they groaned, and when the credits rolled over a "leaked" tape of Megan and Jon engaging in sandwich-centric foreplay, these audience members faked vomiting noises and declared, "I can't watch this!" I'll never know for sure what they were thinking or feeling, but I'd be willing to bet my collection of Swatch watches that they were disgusted—rather than amused—by the couple's behavior, purely because Megan was a fat woman, and these people had spent their movie-going lives being trained to either laugh at or be disgusted by people who look like her (and me).

In a way, I can understand how that happened. Plotlines have reinforced the message to *me* my entire life that I am unlovable, that anyone who pays any romantic attention to me is doing it for a

dare or a bet, or they're a fetishist who gets off on fat girls. Most movies tell me I'll only find love with the most desperate dudes, like Kyle Edwards, DJ Qualls's dweeby character in *Road Trip*—a shy nerd who genuinely sees fat women as boast-worthy sexual conquests. Get a load of this loser: He's treating all women equally, no matter their size! His douchey friends are quick to remind him that fucking fatties is a pastime best kept secret. When Kyle produces a girl's plus-size animal-print underwear after losing his virginity to her, Seann William Scott proclaims, "Did you kill a cheetah!?"

This shit matters to me. If we're trained to mock the idea that fat women can be desirable, or make barfing noises every time we see someone Melisssa Mc-Carthy's size in a sex scene, we're going to think it's OK to act like jerks if we see a fat girl dancing with her friend in a club. If we're taught to laugh at women if they're the size of Paltrow's character in *Shallow Hal* or Wilson's in *Pitch Perfect* or *Super Fun Night*, we're going to treat a fat person differently next time we're given a seat next to them on an airplane. On the opposite hand, seeing fat people represented as real people in the media would have a positive effect on how *real* fat people are viewed and treated. When fat female characters are allowed to be more than just one thing, it convinces people that real fat women can be, too.

I'm lucky to be surrounded by people to whom I'm like Rae, Sookie, or Megan: My weight is incidental. It's a huge part of who I am (pun intended), but it doesn't define me. Even still, this is personal. If and when fat women on TV and in movies stop being presented as sad, lonely, dateless, hopeless, lazy losers, people might stop calling out fat "jokes" from their cars as I walk down the street, and I won't have to pretend not to hear them as I try not to trip over my feet. Dudes might stop hitting on me based on an assumption that I'm desperate or that I will jump into bed with them if they just say, "I like bigger girls." Maybe my mind and my personality and my dance moves and my sense of humor and who I am as a person will be the first things they acknowledge and (dare I say it) respect. ★

AFTER SCHOOL SPECIAL

Let's go anywhere or nowhere.
By Petra. Styling by Laia.

Thanks to Amery and Diana for modeling and to Girasol Bakery in Brooklyn. Thanks also to Adidas Originals, Nasty Gal, Ohne Titel, Rachel Antonoff, Rodebjer, Screaming Mimi's, Y3, Zara, and Zero + Maria Cornejo for lending us clothes and accessories.

KIDS WON'T LISTEN

Why I'm sick of articles about teenage girls written by grown-up men.
By Hazel. Playlist by Suzy.

"Whoa, impressive taste for a teen-girl mag!"

This comment, in one form or another, often gets directed at Rookie on Twitter, especially on Friday nights, right after we post our weekly playlists. It's also something I hear a lot in real life when I tell people—especially grown men—who I write for. "Wow!" they'll say. "Good work, ladies!" Their surprise might be based on our staff's working knowledge of punk rock history (yes, we know who the Wipers are) or on the fact that Rookie's articles are actually thoughtful and well written, but it's always condescending and insulting, and never itself much of a surprise.

I know I'm coming dangerously close to generalizing about ALL men in the exact same way I'm complaining that SOME of them generalize about young women. There are, of course, many male critics who celebrate teen-girl fandom and our voices as cultural consumers and analysts and don't roll their eyes when we gush about 1D or whatever. Thank you for that, dudes. But because men have more power across the board than women in our culture, they get the message, from birth, that their opinions about things are the Most Important Opinions. Whether they choose to believe this is up to them, but rejecting it is a lot harder than sitting back and enjoying it.

So I can hardly blame the many, many adult males who seem to have this cute assumption that all girls are dying for their approval of our cultural tastes, though we never actually asked for it. And I guess it's kind of understandable that they might assume we have shitty taste—but I still

don't totally understand their need to vocally *criticize* us for liking the things we like. When Tavi posted a link on Twitter to an excerpt of a piece she wrote about Taylor Swift for *The Believer*—a highly detailed and laborious work of pure love for Swift's music—a male cartoonist called her out for liking what sounded to him like "the soundtrack to getting a froyo and then stopping at Target for a new pair of Crocs." Not that she asked him!

When I wrote a long piece for Buzzfeed about discovering Animal Collective and falling in love with that band as a 12-year-old girl, dudes in the comments section made fun of my musical taste! Apparently, my enthusiasm and knowledge meant nothing, because this band's music wasn't on the sacred list of Music Men Approve Of. And that's just one example in a long history of criticisms lobbed against me and my apparent TEEN TASTES! Once, I was talking to an older male friend about the brilliance of *Mean Girls*, and he kept dismissing it as an airheaded comedy "for teens." Obviously, he hadn't seen it, because I think we all know that *Mean Girls* is a classic for people of any age. It wasn't until I told him that the movie was written by Tina Fey that he seemed willing to reconsider his first reaction. Because *30 Rock* is cool, but young women are NOT.

When you applaud or critique a young girl's taste based on how well or badly it aligns with yours, you are suggesting that your taste = THE RIGHT TASTE, because you are the one IN THE KNOW. I sometimes rate movies on the website Mubi, and I can't count the number of times an older male cinephile has urged

me to rewatch a film I've given a low score to, because obviously I "didn't understand it" the first time around. "How do you even know about this?" they sometimes ask. "You weren't even *born* when this movie came out." Dude: I have the internet.

This kind of cultural superiority complex extends to the makers of culture as well. For evidence, look at almost any piece written by a grown man about a young female artist. Here's one: When Jody Rosen wrote about Taylor Swift for *New York* magazine last November, rather than ask this funny, smart, world-famous young pop star anything interesting about her work or her views on the world, he pitted her G-rated pop against Beyoncé's and Rihanna's more risqué work and let us know that Swift has never "writhed across a stage wearing a negligee, or less." Rosen found Swift "witty," "despite her public persona." Because, what, cute girls can't be funny? He marveled at the mostly female crowd at her concert for a full paragraph, but was careful to point out that there were "creepy dudes from Oklahoma" among the screaming young females, to illustrate…what? That Swift is so versatile that she appeals to both (a) females and (b) male creeps? The whole piece came across as the work of someone deeply out of their element. I mean, he described the male gaze as an "old feminist bugbear." Why is this the person who was assigned to the Taylor Swift story?

Following the U.S. premiere of Chris Lilley's television show *Ja'mie: Private School Girl*, which has Lilley playing a highly exaggerated mean-girl archetype, several think pieces popped up to criticize not the show itself, but rather…the sorry state of REAL YOUNG WOMEN in the world. In one such article on *The Atlantic*'s website, Jake Flanagin took a look at a work of over-the-top campy fiction and posed, in all apparent sincerity, this question (about real people!): "Why are young women turning into monsters?" I repeat: *monsters*. Ooh, scary! I'm sure we're a big threat to straight white men who write for magazines like *The Atlantic*, what with all our *dangerous* selfies and Snapchats and sexts. Flanagin went on to wonder whether the average viewer was smart enough to tell that the show is satire: "Presumably, Lilley poses this array of amusing insecurities and prejudices as a critical device, not face-value comedy," he sniffed. "But it's difficult to say whether the audience can discern the difference."

As a member of that audience *and* a teenage girl (aka future monster), I'd like to ease his fears, at least on that last point: Teenage girls know that *Ja'mie: Private School Girl* is satire; it's by *Chris Lilley*, for god's sake. Have you ever met a teenage girl, Jake? We don't act like Ja'mie. Just like how you, a guy in his 20s, don't act like Van Wilder. Or so I assume (insert a thousand winks here).

I know I have a vested interest in this whole thing because I'm an aspiring cultural critic and a current young woman, but I think I speak for all girls and women between the ages of 13 and 19 when I say that grown-up male journalists are probably not the best choice to assign stories about teen-girl culture to (keeping in mind those aforementioned exceptions). What they come up with, too much of the time, is a lot of off-base and frankly clueless speculation about what girls think, what we do, what we want, and what we need.

It's not these dudes' fault that they believe they know everything. They were raised that way. But they really don't know much about us at all. Here's a tip for them: Next time you're musing on what girls are all about, try to shut up and listen. ☽

COSMIC LOVE

1. LADIES AND GENTLEMAN WE ARE FLOATING IN SPACE - SPIRITUALIZED
2. MESMERISE - CHAPTERHOUSE
3. HEAVEN OR LAS VEGAS - COCTEAU TWINS
4. FIVE MOMENTS - THE FIELD MICE
5. UNDER THE MILKY WAY - THE CHURCH
6. SPACE AGE LOVE SONGS - A FLOCK OF SEAGULLS
7. COPACETIC - VELOCITY GIRL
8. OUTER SPACE - SOUR PATCH
9. GINGER - LILYS
10. GIRL FROM MARS - ASH
11. SOMEONE LIKE YOU - MANNEQUIN PUSSY
12. (PLEASE) LOSE YOURSELF IN ME - MY BLOODY VALENTINE
13. I LOVE YOU - SPACEMEN 3

SUPER HEROINE:
AN INTERVIEW WITH LORDE

In which we talk about songwriting, Tumblr, Beyoncé, Kanye, Raymond Carver, haircare, clothes, insecurity, and…pretty much everything.
By Tavi. Photo by Petra. Illustration by Suzy.

Although she had no music out at this time last year, by now Lorde requires no introduction. Seventeen years old, from New Zealand, with a richly hushed voice that she lays over minimal beats—you've heard all this. You've probably also heard her portrayed as some kind of alpha-Daria. According to one YouTube commenter (I SWEAR I WASN'T READING YOUTUBE COMMENTS, THIS ONE WAS ALREADY AT THE TOP OF THE PAGE), "She's like that awkward-ass girl in the back of your class lol." According to many of the writers who have profiled her, she's the patron saint of Weird Girls Everywhere.

What these people don't realize is that her reach goes far beyond a very hip sect on Tumblr. In fact, Lorde's song "Royals" was #1 on the radio for nine weeks straight. Her debut album, *Pure Heroine*, got her four Grammy nominations. She is not niche. She is huge. But despite the commercial and critical success of her music, and the fact that she was signed to Universal at the age of 13, Lorde is continually portrayed as an underdog. Adult journalists tend to see only "edgy"-looking outsiders in the backs of classrooms identifying with her music, and totally miss the fact that hordes of Snapchatting normies understand her, too, and vice versa. This is not only because they tend to underestimate Lorde's ability to appeal to the masses. They also underestimate the capacity of "normal" teenagers to appreciate thoughtful, unflashy music.

Sure, Lorde dresses like a witch and drips with sarcasm in interviews. Her best-known song denounces the materialism that other artists

show off and other ones say things like, "I'll let you in on something big: I'm not a white-teeth teen." But they also declare, "I'm little, but I'm coming for the crown. I'm little, but I'm coming for the title held by everyone who's up." And "We're bigger than we ever dreamed, and I'm in love with being queen." And "I'm doing this for the thrill of it, killing it, never not chasing the million things I want. And I am only as young as the minute is, full of it, getting pumped up on the little bright things I bought." Do not for one second mistake her stoicism for self-deprecation, or think it's only goth girls who relate.

The album is a delightful cluster of such contradictions: Lorde is content with the world she's created for herself but eager to make waves in the one outside. Bored by the suburbs but endlessly in love with them. Critical of the other songs on the radio but wondering if she's any better (follow up a listen to "Royals" with "Still Sane": "Only bad people live to see their likeness set in stone—what does that make me?").

It's also insanely beautiful. A thorough listen feels like driving with shadows shifting across your face, quiet and thoughtful, in a car full of rowdier friends. Lorde elevates her suburban experiences to the level of mythology, becoming an empress surrounded by hounds, marking underpasses as her territory. She fixates on blood and veins as well as on the simple wonder of connecting with someone and wanting to experience everything with them. You can tell by the sound of her haunting voice that she means every word,

and that she knows she's on the edge of erupting, as if to say: I've been taking notes and keeping secrets, and I want to share them with you now.

I met Ella (her given name) in October, after we'd both discovered via online interviews and social media that we shared a mutual admiration (she's a Rookie!), so this interview got pretty conversational, but I liked that we could talk to each other as peers. We gave it a try on the night we met, but we were on a noisy restaurant rooftop and my recorder wasn't working. (I was also nervous about meeting her and embarrassed when she called me out for humming "Royals" under my breath subconsciously.) (She was nice about it.) (It is a really catchy song.) She was generous enough to agree to a do-over on a snowy day last month, and we talked for more than two hours on Skype. She addressed, among other things, the pervasive line that journalists dole out about her: "While I dress and talk somewhat differently from other people whose songs are in the Top 40, I feel like more people dress like me than the media makes out." Instead of letting a few random sartorial choices narrow our expectations of music and music listeners, let us appreciate what Lorde's popularity says about all sorts of people, which is the only way to describe her demographic. And let us see what she has to say for herself, right here.

TAVI I want to start out by saying that what I want to do with this is…I'm in a unique position in interviewing you because we're the same age—

LORDE Holla.

LORDE AND TAVI

And I feel like everything I read about you is like grown men writing—

Oh my god, that tweet you made where you were like, "She laces her Converse…" I was like, "This is so accurate!" There's a definite viewpoint of the think piece by an adult writing about kids.

It's true! The end is always like, "She does [this childlike thing] but she also does [this adultlike thing]. Whoa!"

Mine is "She squeals…"

Yeah! So I just want this to be, like…a lot of our readers really relate to you, and I want this to be for them. Not music-journalism-y or about "the pop music landscape."

Aw, yeah, yuck. Well, this is fun!

I asked Rookie readers on Twitter if they had questions for you, and someone wanted to know what you thought of Beyoncé's new album. We could start there.

I will admit that I haven't purchased it yet, so I haven't seen all the videos in full, but I was just blown away by the creativity. I would cry if I had to make that much visual content for an album! Just on that level, it's phenomenal. But it also just feels like the album that I have wanted to hear from Beyoncé for such a long time, and I'm so happy that it has happened. I liked what you guys said about her not being afraid to let her feminism evolve, and you can hear that in this record, which I think is so important and such a hard thing to bare. It feels really personal. It meant a lot to me—I was just like, *Shit, I'm so happy that this exists right now and also I'm so glad that no year-end lists matter anymore.* [*Laughs*]

I'm so happy she exists now too! Some guy on Twitter said, like, "Oh, I'm so sad for your generation that you don't have the Smashing Pumpkins and Soundgarden."

I saw that! [*Laughs*]

I was like, "Ugh, no, we're fine. We don't need testosterone-y bands to worship…"

[*Laughs*] People always say I was born in the wrong era. And I'm like, just don't. Stop.

I like being alive now, because I can appreciate things from the past without having to actually live in the '50s or whatever. Can we go way back for a moment? Tell me what some of your influences have been, not just in music, but writers, movies…You've been interested in all kinds of culture from a very young age, so I want to know what you feel has shaped you the most.

Reading has always been the thing that I've done the most, apart from sleeping and stuff, so I guess that's a good place to start. I am one of those people who read everything, regardless of whether or not it's shit. I don't know why, but I will have just as much fun reading something really awful as I do something really good. Anyway, three or four years ago I had, like, my *moment* with short fiction. My mom gave me a Raymond Carver book and I was like, *This is so cool*. Before that I'd been into Roald Dahl short stories and stuff. Tobias Wolff's writing has had a big influence on me. There's this guy called Wells Tower who has only one collection, but when I read it at the age of 13 it was the best collection I had ever read. It was so good! That book that I gave you, by Claire Vaye Watkins—I think she's incredible. And Kurt Vonnegut—he's way sassy, but I love that.

Short fiction appeals to me because of the necessity of conciseness—that's what writing songs is about, but times 20. I like people who can build something great and huge with a very limited amount of time or space. It's difficult to do. Kurt Vonnegut is a good place to start if you haven't read a lot of short fiction, because he's fun and his humor is really black. Raymond Carver will put you in a sad, dire mood for sure.

You're asking about stuff I'm not used to talking about in interviews, so I don't have a stock way of driving the question.

OK, then: "Do you feel 17?"

AGHHHH! What do you even say to that, honestly?

It's kind of a trap, because if you say yes you're shitting on their question by making it seem obvious, but if you say no you seem like you think you're older and better. I always get these weird people being like, "Oh, she's growing up way too fast, she looks 30." Oh, god.

People always say that. I remember—not to be all mother hen—

No, go for it!

I remember when people started paying attention to what I was doing, and it was like, "She should be getting knocked up like all the other kids her age!" It's like, you complain when you think teenagers are stupid, and then when they try to do something, you're all, "Oh, they're growing up too fast, they don't know what's good for them."

It seems like a double standard to me. And there's another part of it which I find really strange, which is that so many interviewers, even ones that I consider really intelligent and good writers, will do the, like, "Oh, you're not taking your clothes off like Miley Cyrus and all these girls" thing, which to me is just the weirdest thing to say to someone. But then people will say, "She's always talking about being bored, that's petulant," which I feel like is kind of taking the piss out of teenage emotions—just, like, making light of how teenagers feel. When people react that way about things that every teenager experiences, how can you expect to make anything good?

Is it hard to have your particular style and aesthetic in an industry where it'd be easier to wear the "opposite" thing—the dress and heels?

People have been surprisingly much more accepting of my vibes than I would've expected, which is awesome. I think that when I step onto a photo shoot, I probably have a fearsome reputation of not letting anyone tell me what to do, so they're like, "Let's just let her wear whatever she wants." I love dresses, and I wear a lot of dresses. But lately I've just been more drawn to a really nice pair of pants and a white shirt. Patti Smith vibes.

I didn't answer your question—I'm sorry! I have found that there is a lot of stuff, particularly on photo shoots, that people expect of girls, like, "Pop that hip out a bit more! Can you just give me a wink? Can you just look a bit more sexy?"

[*Laughs*] Or, if it's an outdoor thing they'll be like, "Oh, you're in a long, beautiful dress? Let's get you sitting in this field and looking confused." Some of the stuff, I'm like, no one would ask this of a guy.

I hear that loud and proud. I think having to assert yourself in that way—it's on a different scale with you, but it's something a lot of girls our age have to do anyway. Do you have any advice for girls about getting yourself to that headspace where you trust yourself and can tell people what you want? What helped you trust your instincts?

I'm actually a super nonconfrontational person, and I hate having to assert myself. I find it difficult and really awkward. But the way I see it is, it's 15 or 20 seconds of discomfort, and then a product that you are truly happy with. Which is a lot better than being like, "Dammit, why did I not speak up?" I just tell myself that the reward will be good, considering it's usually just a small amount of stress.

Does being singled out as the kind of outsider repping the "weird girls" ever feel like a double-edged sword? Because then you become responsible for representing the "real" teens... Sorry, that was just me talking to myself, ugh.

[*Laughs*] No, it's OK! I have definitely felt that sort of pressure, and it's strange, because while I dress and talk somewhat differently from other people whose songs are in the Top 40, I feel like more people dress like me than the media makes out. You know what I mean? I'm not an anomaly, so it feels weird that I get treated like one and have that pressure of "You represent all teenagers in the Western world. No stress!" The easiest way of dealing with that is just to try not to think about what your art might mean for others. I know that sounds bad, but honestly, if you want it to be meaningful to other people, you need to just totally not even think about that part and make something that will mean something to *you*. Then other people will be able to live inside it too and understand it. But if you're making something like "this is for this demographic" in the hope of "they will get *this* from it," it's not a healthy way of creating.

Right. You can't plan ahead to mean a specific thing to any specific group—that comes after the fact, if at all.

Definitely. It's a weird one. I read a piece the other day that said "Why Lorde is this generation's Nirvana," and I was like, PLEASE DON'T! Don't do that to me! They meant it as a compliment, obviously, but what's the point in even making the parallel?

That's a lot of pressure! I also think it's limiting to define an audience ahead of time. This is something I've brought on myself, by being like, "There are no REAL teen publications! That's what I'll do!" But then it's like, well, if I want Rookie to be successful and popular, then people will invalidate the realness by saying it's popular and mainstream—

Oh, fuck that. No. That's—don't even. I've had that as well, and it's so much worse in pop music, because there's such a stigma to [the genre]—as soon as you make pop music, what you do isn't art and it's not real and it's a product of old people or whatever. It doesn't mean anything. Don't worry about those people.

OK! Thank you! [*Laughs*] Now, I have some questions that are just about writing. I really like that your music has become so popular, and I like hearing about your experience of writing music, because it's an example to me of how being an observer or being introverted can pay off. I don't know if you feel that way, but—

Totally. A hundred percent.

So, what taught you to look for the moments that you write about? Do those moments have anything in common?
I've been trying to figure out what links those moments. They often are such an inconsequential thing, but they happen to

kind of pin down a whole concept for me. I don't know if there's a common element, though. I wrote this song called "Biting Down" which was on my first EP, and no one really knows what that song's about and I never really talk about it, but what I meant by "biting down" was small moments of intensity that help you understand something greater, whether that be intense pain or shock or even being super cold or something. Sometimes those things, whether or not they're pleasant, can really tell you something about yourself or what you're feeling. So that's what that song was about for me. But, yeah, I don't know. Sometimes something will come along and it's almost like you made it up because it's that perfect. Those little serendipitous moments.

I think it can also be good to not know what the common element is, because then you'd start to look for it and lose the mystery. *The Love Club* is so different from *Pure Heroine*. What is the biggest lesson you've learned about songwriting through all of this? Do you have any rules for yourself?

I think with those two records, I was writing within a very simplistic pop structure, which felt like the purest way I could get across what I was feeling. Lately I've been writing a lot of instrumental music and like 10-minute jams where one tiny part of the beat is repeated over and over and over and over and over again—I've been having kind of a moment of musical discovery. But, yeah, I try to stick to that same rule.

This next question is very nerdy.

Go.

A lot of your lyrics use functional shifts, where you use one part of speech as another—a noun becomes an adjective or vice versa. Like in "World Alone," when you say, "this slow burn wait," or in "Buzzcut Season," "It's so easy in this blue, where everything is good." And I love this, and Shakespeare did it a lot too, so you're like Shakespeare.

[*Laughs*] That's *so* nerdy, Tavi. I love it.

It gets nerdier! I took a standardized test last weekend where one of the passages we had to read from explained how these functional shifts trigger things in different parts of your brain.

Amazing.

So, your lyrics stimulate multiple parts of the brain. Do you do this consciously, when you go more for how something feels than how it might typically be described?

I know that's something that I have always, always done. I didn't even know it had a name, but it's not something I've ever thought about—"Ella, stop using so many functional shifts!" [*Laughs*] But when I do those little things that you're talking about, a phrase will click into place and it will mean something to me. Like, I know that that's a good mechanism for me. I don't know the context for using them, but I'm conscious of the fact that it lights up a different part of my head, and sometimes a phrase like that will feel incredibly visual to me—I can see it as I'm writing. That is really important to me, and that's how I know that I have done something cool.

You also write fiction, or you used to. Do you still?

The thing is, when I write now, it comes out as songs.

Oh, interesting!

Yeah, it's in that format. Whereas three, four years ago when I would write, I would write a passage and then I would kind of have to fight to wrench it into the form of a song. I had a weird kind of emotional moment where I was like, *Aw, it comes natural now! It's part of me!* It was so weird! But I felt the feels. So I haven't really been writing short fiction, just lots of songs and stuff.

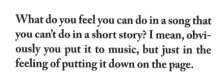

What do you feel you can do in a song that you can't do in a short story? I mean, obviously you put it to music, but just in the feeling of putting it down on the page.

With songs, you listen to the lyrics and you know that not all the words and not all the details and not all the exposition have been included—you kind of expect to take leaps of faith. One sentence can illustrate an entire experience or concept in a song, which I think is really cool. There's a song called "Afterlife" on the new Arcade Fire record—I don't know if you've listened to it yet, but you should, it makes me incredibly happy—and it goes, "After all the […] fires that burn," and it takes you right through that idea and extends it, then it snaps you right back: "After all the ambulances go." It manages to make something huge in that first verse without really saying much at all. That was the last thing I listened to the lyrics of and I was like, *Fuck, I am so glad I am in this medium. This is what you can do with it, this is the potential.* It rejuvenated me.

Can you talk to me about Kanye, who I know you've said you love? What do you love about him?

First of all, I just really like the music that he makes, apart from anything else. I've been listening to it since I was a little kid. I think his ability to evolve from album to album and still make something that I think is really incredible is super cool. That's way harder to do than

people think. I heard someone say that Kanye will do something first, and everyone will think it's weird until six months later, when everyone else is doing it. So Kanye kind of takes the fall by being the pioneer. Like with *808s & Heartbreak*, everyone was like, "We don't understand this." Kanye kind of predicted something, but because he was the first one, people thought it was weird. I love how he is just such a single human being—he seems to not have much creative dependence. He just seems so at one with who he is creatively, and that is really admirable, I think. And then, just as a performer, I often find myself telling people, "Can we just make this a little bit more like a Kanye performance?" His dedication to the classic nature of a single person on a stage, as a performer, I find really inspiring.

When people started to look at "Royals" as a critique of hip-hop, how did you feel?

I mean, it's one thing for kids who fight in the comments section of YouTube and who use "gay" as an insult to take offense at what you're doing; but when it's highly intelligent writers, all of whom you respect, you start to question what you're doing and if you have done something wrong. I have grown up in a time when rap music is pop music, and I do think people were maybe a little bit selective about the parts of that song they used to make those arguments, because a lot of it is examples of rock excess, or just standard pop culture "rich kids of Instagram"–type excess. But I'm glad that people are having discussions about it and informing me about it. Also, I wrote that song a few months into being 15, and now I'm a 17-year-old looking back on that, and I didn't know then what I know now, so I kind of am not too hard on myself.

There's a dedication in the liner notes to James [Lowe] where you thank him for the "truest, purest friendship [you've] known," and I just think that's so beautiful, because people rarely talk about romantic relationships as being friendships. How has even just the friendship part of that relationship inspired your writing?

I'm quite solitary by nature, I guess. I don't have heaps and heaps of friends. Often I can appreciate a place regardless of the people I'm sharing it with, which I know a lot of people can't do, but for me…this is really personal, but James and I spent a lot of time, and still do spend a lot of time, driving around all over our city, and that for me was enlightening, because for once, the company that I'm keeping is affecting how I feel about these places, and in a positive way. I think that was kind of what drove me to write a lot of the stuff on *Pure Heroine*, because I really thought about where I was in conjunction with who I was in conjunction with who I was with.

That makes me want to cry!

Stop it! It's the snow, you're just emotional!

That's not how snow works, Ella!

It's not like the full moon? [*Both laugh*]

I know that you identify as a feminist. How did you discover feminism, and what does it mean to you?

I think I'm speaking for a bunch of girls when I say that the idea that feminism is completely natural and shouldn't even be something that people find mildly surprising. It's just a part of being a girl in 2013. That kind of normal, non-scary, chill vibe that you had with it, and that Rookie has, was really encouraging when I was like 14. Even now, I find a lot of feminist reading quite confusing—often there's a set of rules, and people will be like, "Oh, this person isn't a *true* feminist because they don't embody this one thing," and, I don't know, often there is a lot of gray area that can be hard to navigate. It's just something that I'd assumed was natural for a long time. It's not some crazy kind of alien concept to me. Did you ever have that problem of getting into feminist writings and then feeling confused about all the ways people's opinions differed and all of the weird rulebooks and you're like, *What?*

Oh, yeah. Ultimately, I think we are all here for the same reason. I think it's so personal,

though, for each person who identifies as a feminist, and it can be related to the hardest shit that they've had to put up with in their lives and all of these different ways in which they've been oppressed and marginalized. It can be so delicate and hard to navigate that sometimes I just feel like "I never want to write about this again, because how can you ever know enough?"

Totally.

"How can you ever have read enough to be able to talk about this in the right way?" What I've learned is that the answer isn't to retreat into ignorance, but to find the ways in which it's important to you and talk about that and help other women talk about their experiences too. Just finding the human part of it is what I find myself coming back to when I feel disillusioned with feminism as a community. It's complicated. Ultimately, I'm a feminist, yes, but I certainly have moments where it has to feel like something that is mine, and…

And not something that a hundred different people can define in exactly the same way.

Yeah. Finally, I have some more questions for you from Rookie readers. One of them asked, "Is your hair big because it's full of secrets?"

I love that. Um, yes. But also, I'm on this crazy hair vibe right now where if you ask me when I last washed it I couldn't even tell you, because it's summer here and we swim all the time, so it's mad in there, dude. It's just dry and awful.

It's working out, it looks great, don't wash it.

OK, these are really dumb things to be talking about, but a lot of people ask me about my hair, so: The trick for me is, *don't wash your hair that much.* I wash my hair a couple times a week, sometimes once a week, sometimes once every two weeks. You shouldn't do that, readers at home, 'cause this is a unique type of straw I've got going on here. But also I use product: I use one called Potion 9 by

Sebastian, but it's expensive, so just find some sort of like creamy situation and scrunch it into your hair when it's wet and then let it dry. No blow-drying, no brushing. Peace. Hair tips with Ella. Getcha hair on.

I'm sure people will appreciate it. Eugenia asked, "What relieves you when you're sad?"

I live by the beach near a mountain, and if you walk around the side of the mountain, there are lots of succulents and kind of aqueous plants that grow on the rock base and they all drift in the water, and there's always sound there but it's also always quiet. Walking along the beach over a bunch of rocks and just hanging out there is really nice for me. I walk heaps and heaps and heaps, and sometimes just a good two-hour walk through my neighborhood listening to some rollicking music will make me feel happy. But often if you feel like crap you're just gonna feel like crap, and you have to write it out sometimes. Yeah, being creative is a good way to fight those blues. Do you like these like super-corny '70s-dad ways of talking about sadness?

It's wonderful. I have one last question from Twitter. One girl asked for advice on not caring what people think. Which, no pressure, even though it's advice.

Oh, man. I mean, I don't wanna be unhelpful, but this is something that I still totally struggle with to this day. Throughout my high school years and my intermediate school experience—which is like the two years before high school—everyone would tease me for wearing weird clothes and reading weird books and liking stuff that other people didn't like, and that was hard for me, but I also had this attitude of, like, "I'm above these people." [*Laughs*] But I've also had trouble with it with music. Just the other day this guy who I don't know but who I have mutual friends with posted a photo of James and me at the beach. This guy is

quite famous on Facebook and Tumblr and stuff, and suddenly there were like hundreds of people from my city looking at my picture and making fun of me [in the comments]. That affected me much more than it should have, because I was transported back to high school, when you get to school and everyone has been talking about something that happened to you maybe the night before or whatever, and straightaway you feel like you're on the outside of something. I surprised myself at how stressed out I was about it. OK, sorry, that was totally like the opposite of what you asked…

No, I think it's helpful to hear that you feel that way.

It's so hard, especially when you put yourself out there creatively. Just take pride in what you do. Take photos of yourself wearing super weird clothes and love how it looks and be happy with that and be happy if other people hate them, 'cause sometimes there's some fun in that too. [*Laughs*] But that's a hard one, and everyone deals with it on some level.

When I was more interested in fashion and wore weird stuff to school, I had to resist the urge to feel trumped by people by taking delight in wearing stuff that looks like dead Muppets, you know? It's like this appreciation for more exciting and interesting and less boring things that makes it easier to go with yourself.

Yeah, and knowing that that's what you want—what the you, the *inner* you, really wants. And the outer you being true to inner you—there's something kinda cool about that.

Plus, now the stuff that they were making fun of you for has really worked in your favor.

I used to get called "monobrow." I *still* get stressed out about that. I was always like, "Guys! Frida!" ★

FEBRUARY 2014: ESCAPE

Hey, Rooks!

Hopefully last month got you all inspired/motivated/pumped for 2014. For February, we'll take a step back from 24/7 go-getting to explore the theme ESCAPE. Imagination, fiction, travel, adventure, losing yourself in order to find yourself. Finding ways to escape your situation even when you can't physically leave (hi, school). Escaping obligations, standards, and stereotypes. Escaping arbitrary expectations as bestowed upon us by society. Escaping danger and damaging situations, and understanding the radical act of self-care.

Think storybooks, fairy tales, postcards, and Maurice Sendak, but do not mistake Escape for something precious. We still want you all to take over the universe! This month's theme is about living outside convention, and defining happiness and success for yourself. Consider this quotation from Beyoncé (who is always relevant) from an interview with *Complex* magazine (August/September 2011):

> There is room on this earth for many queens. I have an authentic, God-given talent, drive, and longevity that will always separate me from everyone else. I've been fortunate to accomplish things that the younger generation of queens dream of accomplishing. I have no desire for anyone else's throne. I am very comfortable in the throne I've been building for the past 15 years.

So, although this month will pay its respects to daydreaming, I'm not suggesting we all cut ourselves off from the rest of the world. Personally, I'd like to build my own world within the one outside. I have no desire for anyone else's throne; I am proud that I started Rookie, I am lucky that we are independent and that I've gotten to do it my way. But I want us all to examine and change the rest of our culture, too. I want to make sure the earth's many queens get the opportunities to assume their rightful places.

A year ago, after feeling overworked and overwhelmed by how many eyes were on Rookie and on me, I thought the only way to escape the pressures that come with a conventional idea of success was to disappear completely. I seriously contemplated calling it a day, moving to the woods, and "nobly" becoming some reclusive artiste. The problem with that mindset is that I was still giving in to the voice of conventional success that I'd been denouncing. I was considering giving up my aspirations because I was scared of failing. I nearly convinced myself that the only way to feel free and confident in my work was to dismiss everyone else entirely.

Half a year ago, simply out of the natural personal backlash we have with our own ideologies, I mercilessly re-evaluated this line of thought, and came to the conclusion that the only way to escape the pressures that come with a conventional idea of success was to meet them. I contemplated skipping college to focus solely on my work. I no longer knew how to talk with friends who were not feeling as motivated as I was. I began to see myself as someone too devoted to killing it to have human relations anyway. The problem with this worldview was that once again, I was giving in to the voice of conventional success that I'd been claiming I'd conquered. I began to covet meaningless forms of validation, and nearly convinced myself that the only way to feel free and confident in my work was to make everyone else happy.

Yesterday, while working all this out, I wrote in my diary:

What do I care about?
- Being the CEO of my own life (copyright Jamia). Climbing to the top of my own ladder. Building my own throne.
- Changing who gets to speak and why. Finding opportunities for Rookies, changing the journo game. Understanding the power of my platform, and sharing it. Lifting up people who deserve a greater audience.
- Giving thought to the projects I choose. Not doing anything I will feel silly about promoting. Having dignity, integrity, good taste: "Build a good name. […] Eventually, that name will be its own currency." —William S. Burroughs
- Expressing myself effectively. Giving artistic endeavors my all. Being honest but not attention-seeking, compliment-fishing, or pitiful.

Design by Sonja. Title lettering by Lisa Maione. Portrait of Suzy Bishop by Brooke Nechvatel. Playlist by Tavi, artwork by Leanna. Photographs by Eleanor.

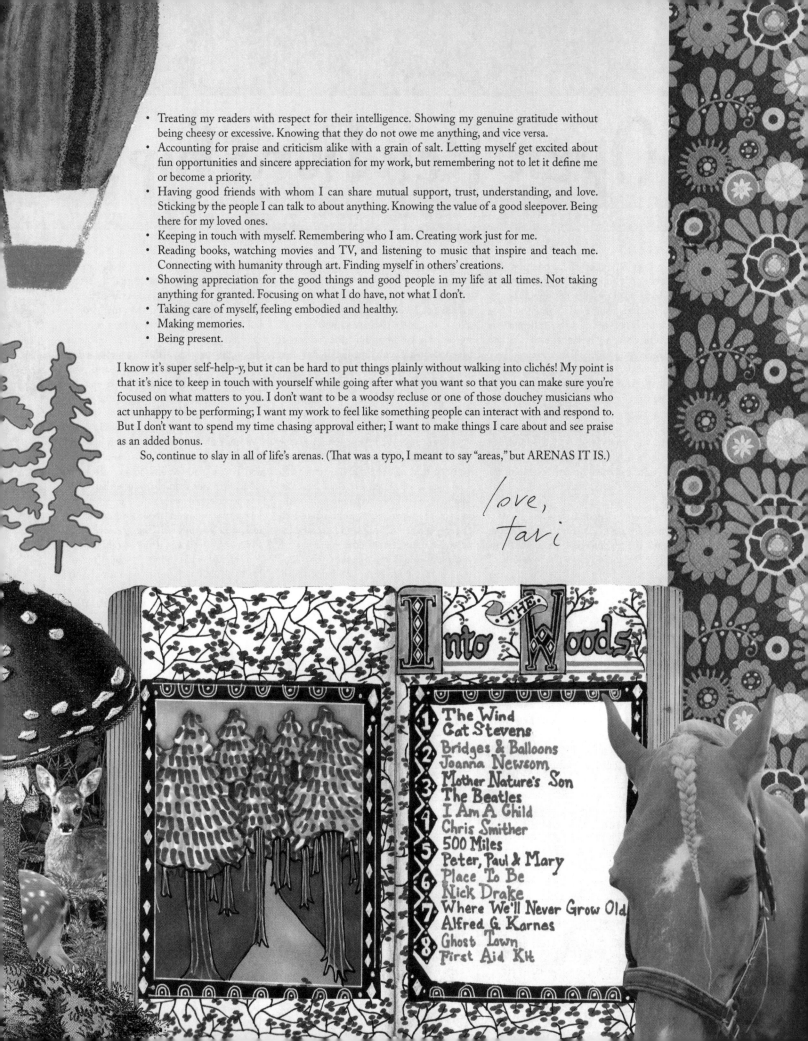

- Treating my readers with respect for their intelligence. Showing my genuine gratitude without being cheesy or excessive. Knowing that they do not owe me anything, and vice versa.
- Accounting for praise and criticism alike with a grain of salt. Letting myself get excited about fun opportunities and sincere appreciation for my work, but remembering not to let it define me or become a priority.
- Having good friends with whom I can share mutual support, trust, understanding, and love. Sticking by the people I can talk to about anything. Knowing the value of a good sleepover. Being there for my loved ones.
- Keeping in touch with myself. Remembering who I am. Creating work just for me.
- Reading books, watching movies and TV, and listening to music that inspire and teach me. Connecting with humanity through art. Finding myself in others' creations.
- Showing appreciation for the good things and good people in my life at all times. Not taking anything for granted. Focusing on what I do have, not what I don't.
- Taking care of myself, feeling embodied and healthy.
- Making memories.
- Being present.

I know it's super self-help-y, but it can be hard to put things plainly without walking into clichés! My point is that it's nice to keep in touch with yourself while going after what you want so that you can make sure you're focused on what matters to you. I don't want to be a woodsy recluse or one of those douchey musicians who act unhappy to be performing; I want my work to feel like something people can interact with and respond to. But I don't want to spend my time chasing approval either; I want to make things I care about and see praise as an added bonus.

So, continue to slay in all of life's arenas. (That was a typo, I meant to say "areas," but ARENAS IT IS.)

love,
tavi

Into the Woods

1. The Wind
   Cat Stevens
2. Bridges & Balloons
   Joanna Newsom
3. Mother Nature's Son
   The Beatles
4. I Am A Child
   Chris Smither
5. 500 Miles
   Peter, Paul & Mary
6. Place To Be
   Nick Drake
7. Where We'll Never Grow Old
   Alfred G. Karnes
8. Ghost Town
   First Aid Kit

Open Relationships

Is nonmonogamy right for you?
By Amy Rose. Playlist by the Rookie staff, artwork by Leanna.

I'm not at all proud to admit that I've cheated on almost every boyfriend I've ever had except my current one—although that doesn't mean I've stopped hooking up with other people. The difference is that nowadays, my foremost love associate knows about (and is cool with) my liaisons. It's taken me a while to admit this, but in the past few years I've come to accept that I mostly prefer romantic relationships that don't require me to be sexually faithful. I think a lot of people find this "deviant" or weird, but, unlikely as it may sound, it's actually not that complicated.

Monogamy has always been hard for me, even in the context of loving, committed relationships. In the past, the trouble usually began after a few months, when some new heartthrob would swim into my life. Although I knew my then-boyfriends wouldn't be cool with it, I would start lying about how often I saw said heartthrobs, flirting with them on Facebook and in person, or secretly having "sleepovers" with them that involved a lot of physical contact but no official "fooling around." I rationalized all of this behavior as just *friends bein' friendly*, even though my motivations were decidedly less pure.

Once I started being dishonest, it was hard for me to stop. Although my cheating usually didn't involve anything more serious than some furtive makeout sessions, I'd always wake up the next morning smothered in guilt, which quickly morphed into resentment: *Why should I feel bad about wanting to fool around with people while I'm young?* The answer, of course, was BECAUSE YOU ARE LYING TO A PERSON WHO CARES ABOUT YOU, JERKUS, but I also had a point: It's totally OK to feel like kissing basically everybody, if you can find a way to do it without being deceitful and/or disrespectful to anyone

else. I just hadn't figured out that way yet.

In my last monogamous relationship, which included a lengthy and serious engagement, I vowed not to cheat, and I didn't. But after two and a half years, I started backsliding into the realm of backdoor Facebook encounters. When I caught myself typing double entendres to people whose profile pictures I found achingly cute, I broke up with my then-fiancé rather than violate his trust, which I could tell I was about to do.

Even though I was the one who chose to end that relationship, I was overwhelmed by despair and grief when it was over. I wondered if I would ever be able to love someone without emotionally fucking them over with my constant tail-chasing and tomcatting, and I decided the answer was no: I had tried my very hardest with someone I was prepared to spend the rest of my life with, and I had failed. Clearly, I was incapable of curbing my desire to freaq a sizeable fraction of the world's population, and that, I felt, made me worthy of contempt.

Then I met Ben. We were introduced by a mutual friend on a beach trip two years ago, when I was 21, right before I made the choice to leave my fiancé. Over the course of an afternoon, we discovered that we had the same favorite animal (squid) and compared our imitations of the director Orson Welles. We separated from the rest of the group for a while, and I told him secrets that not even my best friends knew at the time, like why my engagement was ending (and that it was even ending at all). I felt closer to him than I had to anyone else in a very long time.

I broke up with my fiancé not long after that day. Even though wanting to be with Ben wasn't the reason for that split, I'd be lying if I said I wasn't totally jazzed when

we started dating just a few weeks later. I tried to keep things super casual for a few months, during which time I refused to call him my boyfriend and dated other people. I didn't want to get too involved because, as I told him one morning after we'd spent the night together, I didn't believe in the whole "love" thing. He told me that he was a longtime cheater, too, and, like me, he felt some shame about that, but he didn't think it exempted us from falling in love with each other, which, yo, we totally were! We mutually decided that nonmonogamy was the best option for us as a couple, and I'm so glad we did, because it's been working better than anything either of us has experienced before. And guess what? I was very incorrect about love not being real, which is probably the greatest thing I've ever been proven wrong about.

Here's what nonmonogamy means for us: Like many people who are deeply obsessed with their main squeeze, as I am with Ben, I want to spend as much time with him as I possibly can without our driving each other crazy. *Also* like many others who are deeply in love with their person, I occasionally want to french people who aren't him, as does he with not-mes. The difference between monogamous relationships and our thing is that we act on those feelings, and we don't want to sob, scream, or murk each other afterwards. There's none of the sinking dread involved with cheating that I'm all too familiar with. I get all of the action, with none of the harrowing doubt about whether I'll ever be able to truly love someone without fucking them over. Doesn't that sound kind of nice?

There are some drawbacks to non-monogamy, of course. I'm very happy with the mechanics of my romantic situation, but that doesn't mean others agree with my choices. Maybe you're one of those people, in which case, get bent! Just kidding, my dude—I like you just the same, and I'm going to do my best to clear up any misconceptions or stigmas that you, a person who is maybe curious about open relationships but skeptical that they can really work, might be harboring. The truth is that it's more than possible to be in such a relationship without having it wreck your life, and that wanting to try nonmonogamy doesn't make you a misguided perv who doesn't understand how to do love "right." For your perusal, I now present this not-comprehensive but still probably kind of helpful list of things worth knowing when you're figuring out how to screw the world without screwing up your relationship.

1. DON'T FEEL LIKE YOU NEED TO "IDENTIFY," BUT FEEL FREE TO CHECK OUT PLACES WHERE PEOPLE DO.

I've never identified as a "polyamorous person" or involved myself in communities based on a shared rejection of monogamy—I don't like to assign names to anything about my love life, period—but if I had to pick a descriptor for my situation, *nonmonogamous* probably fits best. I'm just not that into the identity-based language I've seen used by other non-monoggos (ooh, I'm actually kind of into this newfound term after typing it just now—it sounds like something a cute cartoon caveman would say).

This is not to disparage "polyamorous" or what-have-you communities—I understand that the big city where I live, and my friends in it, afford me the comfort of knowing others who just happen to also be non-monoggo (sticking with this), and that giving a name to any non-mainstream thing you do can help you find others who are into it wherever you are. Polyamory, which most often refers to having more than one long-term partner at a time, just isn't what I do—but continued blessings to anyone who chooses that.

To say I'm in an "open relationship" also feels like a misnomer, because, although I'm talking about it publicly here in the service of this article, for the most part, my bond with Ben is really private—we're in love, and our particular love is just for the two of us. We keep our extracurricular sex casual—it never impacts the inside jokes he and I make about our stupid-looking cat, or the way we confide in each other about the stuff we were scared of as kids, or how we always seem to want to do the same things at the same time (doing crosswords at the diner, playing Boggle, performing impromptu Roy Orbison duets—everything) without talking about it first.

There are lots of other nonmonogamous permutations, from marriage-like unions among a group of people to "monogamish" situations, where a couple is mostly monogamous, but give each other a little leeway for occasional extracurricular fun, either together or separately. The internet is full of information on these and other relationship structures; just google "nonmonogamy" and away you go!

2. SET CLEAR GROUND RULES WITH YOUR PARTNER.

Being upfront with each other about what you can and can't do outside of the time you spend together is hands-down the most important factor in maintaining an open relationship—like, the whole point of nonexclusive arrangements is to absolve yourselves of the deception and guilt that come with "cheating." I think starting a relationship with the understanding that you'd like it to be nonmonogamous is probably far easier than trying to open a monogamous relationship, but the template for bringing the subject up is the same either way. Saying, like, "GUESS WHAT? I want to fool around with other people!! Fun, right?" is a great way to hurt somebody's feelings, put them on the defensive, and/or make them think that you're not attracted to them anymore. Instead, start by telling your partner why committing (or staying committed) to each other is a priority for you—e.g., "I love being with you in all ways, so I don't want you to think that what I'm about to tell you means I'm not into you anymore. I'm bringing this up because our relationship is important to me, and I want it to last for a long time." Then explain how you're feeling, why you think your connection would be strengthened by nonmonogamy, and what ideas you have about how to incorporate those ideas into your romantic life together.

Some important things to not only think about, but actually *discuss* with your heart-person, are whether it's OK to see other people more than once, and in what context (Can you go on dates? Are you only cool with one-time, strictly physical encounters?), whether there's a limit to what you can do with your side-pieces (maybe kissing is totally peachy by you, but sexing other people is more of a moldy, rotten banana that you'll break up with someone for eating?), and how cool you are with telling each other about your external entanglements.

Be respectful: Trying to force someone to relax their boundaries is just gonna end in tears. Locate a happy medium and stick to it. You love this person, so don't do things you know will hurt them. There's no simpler or truer aspect of romantic love than that one, for real.

Important side note! Nonmonogamy doesn't necessarily mean you're having full-on SEX with strangers (or whomever else you're seeing on the side). Even if you're not having sex yet, you might want to kiss other people, or go on occasional dates, while still considering yourself half of a couple. This is doable, so long as you and your partner set ground rules early on. For me, nonmonogamy is more about circumventing a general discomfort I have with being told not to do something—the classic reverse psychology of "I didn't want this thing until you told me I couldn't have it!"—than it is about getting down with some new person every night of the week.

The number-one tenet of my own nonmonoggo relationship is: Don't tell me anything unless I ask—but be honest if I do. Like, let's say I'm on my luxury yacht, the *Amy Rows-Your-Boat-Ashore*, with my two biggest celebrity crushes, Martha Stewart and Kendrick Lamar, and after a few glasses of rosé, things get frisky, and we have a three-way makeout (this is *just a hypothetical* and not a true story, so DROP THOSE PENS, *Us Weekly*!). The next day, I'm hanging out with Ben, and he asks, "So, did you get with anyone last night?" Not even maritime law exempts me from telling him the truth about this stuff, so I say yes. He is either satisfied with that answer and moves on or is feeling a little jealous and would rather know the reality of what happened than let his mind start spinning out paranoid fantasies. If he asks for more information, I answer him factually, but only to the extent to which I feel comfortable. I draw the line at describing nuanced details of physical encounters or identifying characteristics of the person (or celebrity businesswoman-rapper duo) I was fooling around with, for the sake of both our brains. While some people are cool with spilling everything about whose hands were on which deck, we know we're not OK with hearing all the salty details, and we respect each other's limitations.

Our final rule is that we involve ourselves with other people only when we're not physically available to each other. If I felt like Ben was prioritizing spending time with someone else instead of me, I would be devastated and probably key his car, and he's told me he would feel the same way if the sheets were swapped (and if I had a driver's license, which I don't). Luckily, when we're together, we feel a nuclear-grade infatuation toward each other that makes that potential difficulty and automotive disfigurement a non-issue.

3. ACCEPT JEALOUSY AS AN INTRACTABLE FACTABLE OF LIFE.

From time to time an acquaintance will see me macking on someone other than my boyfriend or overhear me waxing feverish about some new person, and look confused. When I explain my romantical arrangement, they almost always gasp, "I can't believe you don't get jealous!" But it's like, YO, OF COURSE I DO, ARE YOU KIDDING ME? I am one of the most jealous broads on the planet, if I let myself be!

In some of the "monogamous" relationships of my teenage past, I would get paranoid every time one of my boyfriends went out without me. Since I was a cheater, I suspected everyone else of the same behavior. Even though I knew on an intellectual level that I was being waaaaay too sensitive, I still did things like sulk if we were watching TV and a deodorant commercial came on and I thought the girl in it was prettier than me, which, of course, was a totally valid and logical reason to give my mystified boyfriends the silent treatment for the rest of whatever *South Park* episode we were probably watching at the time. I also remember, on one occasion, ripping up a drawing that a mutual female friend had done for a guy I dated in high school and blaming it on "a dog" like an uncreative homework-hating second grader, despite the fact that it was in his car and neither of us had pets. (I think the fictional canine was owned by an equally fictional neighbor who came over to talk while I was sitting in the passenger seat with the door open?) You would think that a seasoned two-timer like me would have come up with a better lie! Of course, no one believed me, and it was real embarrassing.

Thankfully, I outgrew this jealous-fugue period in my mid-teens, when I realized the extent to which it made everyone miserable. Every now and then, though, I still feel a diluted version of the self-doubt that incited it. But here's the really great thing about nonmonogamy: Having realized that my issues have far more to do with my own brain than with what my partner chooses to do with his D, it's actually the hugest relief to me that, on the surface, the reality of my relationship with Ben (he and I sleep with other people) is the exact worst-case scenario I would have imagined in my previous history of loving people. The difference is that back then, these dalliances would be hidden, and if I found out about them they would break my heart (and then I would break everything he's ever found comfort or enjoyment in) (maybe); whereas now, I'm secure in the knowledge that none of that affects how massively in love we are with each other. Instead of feeling cataclysmic, sex is just fun, and if I ever feel jealous, we just talk about it. I don't let it melt my brain into a rage-magma that overwhelms all my rationality, empathy, and happiness.

4. IF YOU'RE HAVING SEX WITH MORE THAN ONE PERSON, BE SAFE.

I mean, be safe no matter what kind of sex you're having with *anybody*, as I know you are smart enough to always do, but if you have multiple partners, USE CONDOMS AND/OR OTHER BARRIER METHODS OF PROTECTION AND COMMON SENSE 357 PERCENT of the time, with everybody, including your #1 paramour. I cannot stress this enough. Putting your partner's sexual health at risk is not only inconsiderate, it can be harmful to them in the long run. So please make a custom of being extra-safe.

5. BE FAIR TO THE PEOPLE YOU'RE SEEING OUTSIDE THE RELATIONSHIP.

I feel like all the best romantic wisdom comes from down-home country and blues singers, so here is a mournful old-timey ballad that I just wrote about telling a potential hookup that you're seriously involved with someone else (imagine that I am casually holding a banjo but not really knowing what to do with it and also I tried to put spurs on my Keds):

> *Tell them as soon as you can without presuming*
> *That something's gonna happen with your mouths or other parts*
> *But definitely before getting physical or going on like 12 dates*
> *And breaking their doggone heartsssssss*

Wow. That definitely sounded like the kind of time-tested profundity that can only come from living off the land and your own salty tears and probably there's a pickup truck involved. I *reckon* (OK I promise this stops here) that you should do what my awesome song tells you, *partner* (sorry this really is the last time for real) (more like sexual partner!!!!!!!! hahah) (please don't go).

Obviously, this doesn't matter as much for one-time flings. If you play tonsil hockey with a girl you meet on vacation or at a party out of town, you don't need to recite your autobiography before getting down to biz. But if you're more socially connected to a person, or intend to see them more than once, the time to let them know is *as soon as possible*. Some people you might want to mess around with are not going to be receptive to the idea that they're one of the many ships in your various ports, especially when one of those is a yacht (I'm talking about your main squeeze, not the old *Amy Rows*, here). Don't try to wheedle anybody into changing their mind. Not everyone is going to have the same attitude toward casual hookups as you do, and that's their prerogative.

Some people might think you're lying about being nonmonogamous just to try to get them to help you cheat. (The unfortunate reason for this is that there are horrible d-bags in this world who do exactly that.) It helps to disclose the realities of your relationship clearly as soon as it feels like something's gonna happen between you. The longer you keep it a secret, the more it'll seem like you're being deceptive, because why would you not mention it if you're not doing anything wrong? You don't have to give them the WHOLE ENTIRE HISTORY of your relationship and the philosophical reasoning behind your nonmonogamy, as I have here! Just say that you're in an open relationship—even if you don't like the term, this is the easiest and most direct way to get your point across.

6. BE PREPARED TO BE CRITICIZED.

Can I be honest with you for a moment? (Because everything I wrote before this sentence was a series of CRAFTY LIES, PRANKED YA, LIKING SEX IS ACTUALLY BAD!) Even though I'm comfortable with the way I choose to live my life, this is probably the most nervous I've ever been about writing something for Rookie, because there is still a giant stigma attached to being a youngish female person who is not willing to conceal the fact that she likes sex and all its related behavioral trappings.

The criticism often comes in the form of slut-shaming, which sounds like: "How

could you *do* that to him/her?" or "If you really loved each other, you'd be faithful" or the more concise "Don't you feel like a *slut*?" I almost admire that last one for its frankness, except I really don't at all. The implication behind all these comments is that it's "natural" if *men* want to sleep around, but when (young) women do, it's seen as self-serving and immoral. And you know what? I would like to politely invite such naysayers to go suck an egg, as long as we're in the business of telling people what they can and can't put their mouths on. Even if you find the idea of opening your own relationship abhorrent, it's shitty manners to treat those who choose nonmonogamy for themselves like they're BAD or WRONG—both of which I can totally be at times, but never for this reason.

A less damning, but still undermining, backhanded compliment that people sometimes give me is: "Wow, I guess you're really just more *evolved* than I am—I could *never* do that." It's one thing to ask questions or be curious about nonmonogamy, but entirely another to make a judgy comparison between two completely unrelated personal preferences about love. My response is usually to say, "Nah, different people are just comfortable with different things." People are not Pokémon—non-monoggohood isn't something you "level up" to when

you *free yourself from society's shackles, man*. It's a personal choice about what makes you happy, and it's not for everyone!

The key to maintaining a healthy outlook about nonmonogamy is not letting other people's dumb attitudes about it impact your mindset, so I mostly deal with the aforementioned situations by not worrying about them too much. They're so far from the reality of my life that I don't feel the need to explain myself—why bother clearing my name of some made-up wrongdoing I don't even believe in?

All told, the only advice you absolutely need to follow when you're figuring out your own relationship configuration is to always be aware and considerate of your own and your partner's feelings. Keep talking! Do a little state-of-the union every so often to make sure you're both still feeling happy and loved, and if one of you isn't for whatever reason, make some adjustments and see if things improve. All relationships require communication and a genuine desire to be sweet and kind to the person you're dating.

Hold these things at the forefront of your mind when you're deciding if you want to open your relationship. If you both decide you do, go get it, and above all, have fun and be respectful of the people you care about. If I know anything about you guys, that part'll come real easy. ♀

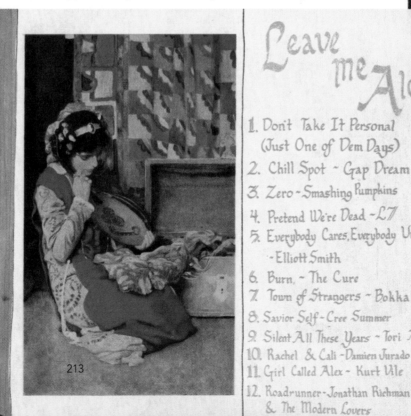

213

Leave me Alone

1. Don't Take It Personal (Just One of Dem Days) ~ Monica
2. Chill Spot ~ Gap Dream
3. Zero ~ Smashing Pumpkins
4. Pretend We're Dead ~ L7
5. Everybody Cares, Everybody Understands ~ Elliott Smith
6. Burn ~ The Cure
7. Town of Strangers ~ Bokka
8. Savior Self ~ Cree Summer
9. Silent All These Years ~ Tori Amos
10. Rachel & Cali ~ Damien Jurado
11. Girl Called Alex ~ Kurt Vile
12. Roadrunner ~ Jonathan Richman & The Modern Lovers

Follow Me

We'll know where we're going when we get there. By Olivia. Illustration by Leanna.

Thanks to Janine and Marie for modeling.

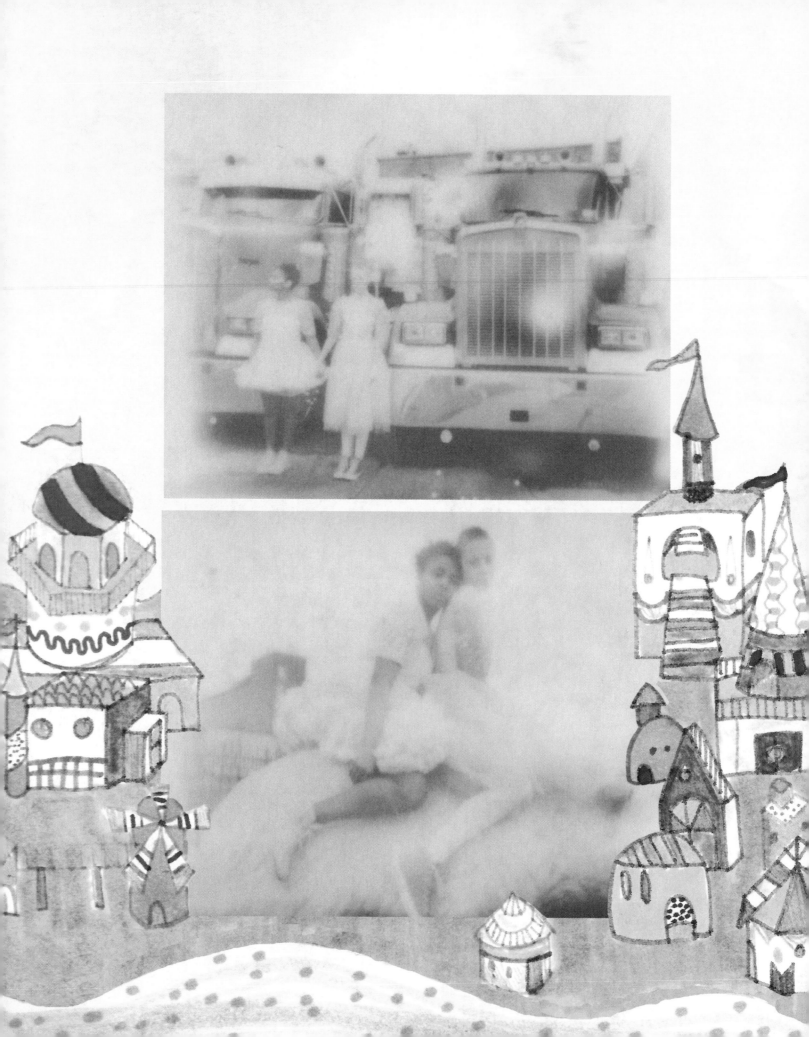

You Have the Answer:
An Interview With Lara Setrakian

The founder of Syria Deeply (and our personal Oprah) tells us how to steal her job.
By Anaheed. Playlist by Dylan, artwork by Leanna.

The first thing that Lara Setrakian ever said to me changed my life. It was last fall, and we were both on a "new media" panel at an event for women journalists. Part of the reason I said yes to participating was that I have an extreme fear of public speaking, which I'm trying to overcome by forcing myself to do it over and over and over. So when I walked into the venue, I was in a state of high anxiety. Lara came over and introduced herself, and I told her how scared I was. She kneeled in front of my seat, looked me in the eye, and said, "Anaheed, you have to *fall in love with them*"—"them" being the audience. It's the only thing that has ever calmed my nerves about public speaking, and I'm passing it on to you today. IT WORKS, you guys.

The project she was there to talk about was her latest (and coolest), the immersive-

news website Syria Deeply. Before creating it, she had spent five years reporting on the Middle East as a correspondent for ABC News and Bloomberg and had grown frustrated with the limits of TV news: You can't dive too deep into any one subject in a three-minute on-air dispatch. So she quit those jobs and started a website that would use every tool available—including interactive maps and timelines, Soundcloud news reports, and Google Hangouts where a bunch of experts could talk to one another while the public watched—to help people understand what was going on in Syria.

Lara's speech at the panel that day, by the way, was a full-on barrage of unadulterated inspiration. Like, when someone asked her what to do if you've created something and it's not all you

wanted it to be, she said, "Did you make it? Then it's great. It didn't exist, then you had an idea and *you made it real*? Then it's great, it's great, it's great." Sigh. She is basically my Oprah, so I was very honored to get the chance to interview her about how she got to where she is in her career. Unsurprisingly, she was full of all kinds of inspiring advice not just for journalists, but for anyone who wants to make something and send it out into the world.

ANAHEED Can you explain to us what Syria Deeply is?

LARA SETRAKIAN So, I started a news company where we focus on one place, and we take some of the most important stories and the most difficult issues in that place and put them all on one website, so we can explain *everything* about what's happening there. The idea with Syria Deeply was that, for something like the war in Syria, which can be so hard to understand, the best approach would be to add more explanation: Who's who? Why did this thing start to begin with? What is going on in that country? How are we gonna piece it all together? We wanted to help people understand all of this by piecing it together for them.

What were you seeing in the news that made you think this was needed?

Right now, the way the news works, you only get stories in a two-minute TV report or in an 800-word newspaper article, right? We wanted to do the news in a totally different way, where we would use technology to help people put the story together. But we needed to start our own media company to do that. So, Syria Deeply was a chance to create a different way to approach journalism. It was a dream of mine, and I got together with some friends and we just made it happen. And now, a year later, we're a media company! Pretty awesome.

In the early stages, what keeps you believing that it can happen?

You have to have a *lot* of faith in yourself. Use a journal every day, and every day you write in that journal, you know, "Here's what I want to do for the world, and here's what I'm dreaming, and here's what I hope will happen." Go back to that journal to remind yourself why this is so important to you. And find other ways to keep your energy high: Do yoga or run or do something to maintain your energy, you know? All it takes is persistence and commitment. That's it. And a little bit of courage. Because when you start putting it out there, magic things will happen.

That sounds awful to me, because I know people *always* say, like, "Keep going, be persistent." It sounds like it's gonna be just a lot of heavy lifting for a long time.

But the truth is, the reason you have to be persistent is that you're always getting ever so much closer to the right answer. That's why you keep going—because you figure things out along the way. It's a long, lonely journey to figuring out how to build your dreams.

But also, you have to remind yourself that ultimately, it's not about you! It's about what you want to create. Focus on what you want to *give* the world. That's so important. Give the best of you, and really great things will happen.

You mean instead of focusing on what *you* can get from what you're doing?

Yeah! If you have five people reading your blog, you dedicate yourself to those five people. And you dedicate yourself to giving those five people the best gosh-darn thing to read that you can give. And those five people will become 15, and 50, and 100, because you focused on the people you have. You focused on them, you were grateful for them, and you did your best, and they stuck around because of that. Focus on what you have, and it will grow over time.

I go back and forth on that idea of serving your audience. I mean, obviously that's important, and we try to give as much as we can to our readers. But at the same time, if I am only working for the readers and not for my own pleasure and enjoyment, I can burn out really quickly. I sometimes have to remind myself that we should be making what we want to make, what we would want to read, regardless of whether anybody else likes it. Because you can kind of drive yourself crazy trying to please everyone.

I think especially as women, we are really hard on ourselves. And we can be really mean to ourselves! We would never be as mean to our friends as we are to ourselves. If you can be aware of that and stop yourself from being so critical of yourself, or from doing something and then regretting it and beating yourself up,

that will help so much. It will make you a happier person! And everyone will be better off. I mean, listening to what you just told me—that you want to serve your users—you're being so hard on yourself! You're imagining that your users won't be satisfied with something that you're really satisfied with. Maybe you're misreading your users! What if they're just like you? And what *you* love to write and what *you* love to do—that's the best you can give. So why are you imagining that someone out there doesn't like what you love?

I mean, I'm telling you this, and I'm also saying it to every reader of Rookie: You need to be *really nice* to yourself. Like, *shockingly* nice to yourself. So nice to yourself it makes you *gasp*. Because you deserve it! And we do the opposite— we bring ourselves down. And that does *nothing* good.

This is reminding me of another question I had, which is, first of all, you are one of the most straight-up inspiring speakers I've ever seen.

Thank you!

You clearly have a natural talent for public speaking, which is probably why you were so successful as an on-air correspondent. I wonder if the public speaking part of it is really easy for you, and if what you're doing now is way harder because it's not based on a magical gift of yours.

[*Laughs*] You nailed it. Speaking in public, being a television journalist, was easy; building a startup was a challenge—but maybe that's why I like it! The truth is that I think my career will ultimately be a fusion of being a tech entrepreneur and being an on-air correspondent. I think journalism and technology are going to *really* start to intersect beyond anything we've ever seen. I think it's fundamentally good to do what doesn't come naturally to you every once in a while, because you learn a lot about yourself along the way.

I did what I had to do to build the things I believed in building. As glamorous

and as exciting as it was to be on TV, sometimes an idea moves you that requires your immediate attention. And if you're in a place in life where you can make that idea happen, you *have* to try. At the end of the day, it's exciting and fun to be in the spotlight, but it's just television—it will always be there, you know? You have to remember what you're in it for. As a journalist, you shouldn't be in it to be on television. You should be doing it because you believe in your story, and you want to help people get smarter about what's happening in the world. And if the best place to do that is on the internet, then that's where you'll find me.

Do you think college was necessary for you to get where you are?

I think college was necessary because it got me on the college radio station, which is where I really discovered my passion for this. But I think the most important thing that young women should do with their time in college is to pursue what they feel passionate about. Not to study what everybody else says to study, and not even always to listen to your parents' opinions on what you should do with that time. Because everyone—especially if you're a girl—is always telling you what to do. It's like, really, give it a rest! [*Laughs*] Listen to what everybody has to say, thank them for their advice, reflect on it, and then do what you feel is right. That's the process. Trust yourself, listen to yourself, and go for it. Do what *you* love. You don't ignore people's advice, but you don't just jump at it either. They don't have the answer. You have the answer.

I think it's easy when you're aspiring to something to look at people who have achieved that thing and feel that they're just lucky, or that it was dropped into their laps, and to feel jealous, and to dwell on the fact that the world is unfair. I mean, the world *is* unfair. What do you say to people who are feeling that way?
The world delivers knocks to everybody. It's all relative. And it's very important not to judge. Everybody says that in media it's

not what you know, it's who you know. But I didn't know *anybody*. The truth is that you can do *anything*. The possibilities are endless.

The way I rose in journalism was, first, I leapt at the opportunity to do an internship at ABC News, but that could have been anywhere. The more important thing is that once I got there, I always brought ideas to the table. Diane Sawyer met with all the interns at the beginning of the summer and said, if you have ideas, send them to me. So I would go online and look at what was going on in the world and send her my ideas. I emailed her very politely and very gratefully and said, "Thank you so much for meeting with us. Here are five ideas." She wrote back and said, "Thank you. These don't really work." So I tried again and sent other ideas, and after a while some of them started to get on TV! That was pretty cool.

So eventually when I applied for a job at ABC, they all remembered me as the girl who had all these great ideas and got them

on TV, you know? I got recognized just for trying to make something out of nothing and putting myself out there and really respectfully and politely writing emails to a lot of people and sending them my ideas. People are always thirsty for ideas.

Always have something to offer. Even if you come from nowhere and have nothing, you also have something to offer. Your ideas will get you as far as you want to go! Your hard work and the quality of what you bring to the table are what's gonna attract people to support you. And then really great things are gonna happen.

Do you have a final message that you want to deliver to the teenage girls of the world?

You're *amazing*. You are actually amazing! Be really nice to yourself.

That is great. You're awesome.

You're awesome too. 🎲

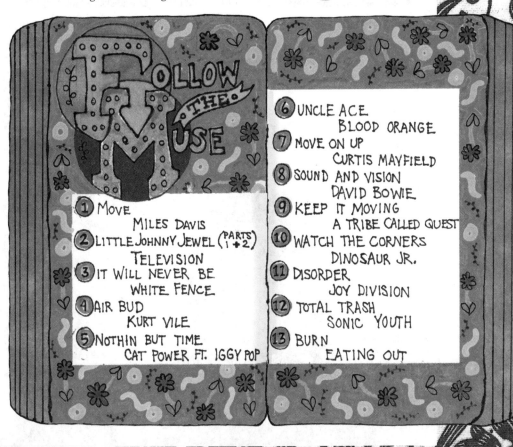

Fast Car

Got a ticket for anywhere.
By Amanda Leigh Smith.
Styling by Tashina Hill.
Illustration by Leanna.

Thanks to Olivia for modeling.

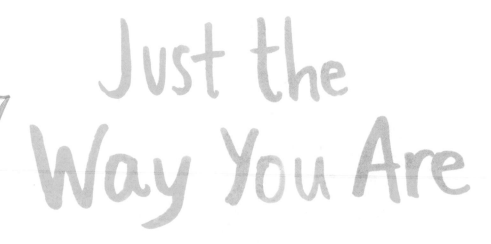

Just the Way You Are

In the throes of an eating disorder, loving yourself can feel practically impossible.
By Pixie

Your body is scrutinized and assessed from the moment you're born. You spend nine months swimming around in a womb and then—bam! You're out in the world, and someone is already scribbling down your height and your weight, which are broadcast to your parents' entire Facebook friends list. Even as a newborn, your body's dimensions are public information. It doesn't really get easier from there.

If we paused to notice every message we receive all day long that our bodies are flawed, that they need work, and that no matter how hard we work they will never be "perfect," we would never get anything else done. Companies take advantage of our insecurities and aggressively market to them, trying to convince us that we'd be so much happier if we just lost "those last five pounds" or bleached our teeth to Ross Gellar levels of whiteness or devoted ourselves to the noble cause of minimizing our pores, and they are aided and abetted by fashion magazines that sell us an unattainably perfect fantasy. It is almost impossible to love yourself when the entire world seems to be suggesting that you aren't good enough.

Here's the creepiest thing, though: Even if you're totally aware of the manipulation going on (I think we've all seen a Photoshop job that goes beyond reality and into the realm of WTF?), it's still possible to subconsciously absorb the majorly toxic messages that are constantly repeated by the culture at large, and to begin questioning whether we're doing something "wrong" by being, you know, actual human beings with flaws and such. I mean, I've been professionally rolling my eyes at commercials and being grossed out by red-carpet commentary and "bikini body" crap for decades now (history lesson: If you were a teenage girl circa 1995, you had to read at least 25 celebrity profiles that began with "the petite actress ordered a chicken Caesar salad" and then spent two more paragraphs describing that salad, its ingredients, how much dressing was used, how much was eaten and in what manner), and I'm STILL susceptible to this garbage. I recently saw a television commercial that was all about loving your armpits, and my first thought wasn't *Hey, this is dumb*, but rather *Oh man, now we're going to obsess over armpit smoothness? What if I DON'T LOVE MY ARMPITS ENOUGH?*

Thankfully, the armpit crisis was short-lived—I had settled on *Nope, this is dumb, I don't care* before the ad was over— but resisting the diabolical messaging took years of practice, after years of horrible self-destruction. For most of my late teens and early 20s, I had severe anorexia, and it

wasn't always so easy to push perfectionist thinking aside and recognize that society-at-large's messages that I needed to "be better" were actually super harmful and ruining my life.

As a Nobel Prize winner in the field of self-loathing, I can assure you that the very same energy a person puts into hating themselves can be harnessed for good. I spent years looking in mirrors strictly to find things to feel bad about. I noticed every lump and bump and felt ashamed of myself for not being absolutely flawless (which, btw, no one is, except Beyoncé). I was convinced that I was ugly and gross and that nobody would ever love me, because I didn't look like I'd just stepped out of a magazine. I compared myself to my friends, celebrities, strangers on the street, seeing the beauty in everybody but myself.

Self-loathing is easy, once you get the hang of it. I couldn't see anything positive about myself, mentally or physically, and I refused to consider an alternative viewpoint until I was forced to many years later, after my poor body image had developed into a full-blown eating disorder and I was hospitalized for a while. It was in the hospital that I learned how to fight back against negative thinking by doing something that sounds like it should be simple but is still something I struggle with: loving myself.

I am well aware that "loving yourself" sounds like some corny inspirational stuff that your aunt Debbie posts on her Facebook, accompanied by pictures of boring sunsets and recipes for okra bran casserole or whatever. But it's actually an extremely powerful move that essentially gives the finger to an often cruel world while celebrating all that is good about life itself. To love yourself is to recognize your own worth, beauty, and strength. Here are a few ways to get started:

1. REFRAME YOUR THOUGHTS.

This is one of the most important lessons I learned in the hospital. I was already using a ton of energy to hate myself, and when the opportunity came about to challenge that mode of thinking, I decided to give it a shot. I figured that at the very least, I could allow myself to expend a tiny bit of energy on treating myself a little better. If it was too hard or unpleasant, I could always quit and have one more thing to loathe myself for, right?

Reframing is a process that asks you to pay attention to the constant negative thoughts in your head and eventually to challenge—and finally change—those thought patterns. Every time my brain shot out something like "Your thighs are huge and ugly," I immediately came back with something positive, like "My thighs are strong and help me swim." By taking the power away from the negative thoughts, you remind yourself of the truly remarkable things your body can do. It takes a lot of practice, but eventually you'll find yourself able to compliment your body as fast as your brain can insult it, which changes the way you look at yourself and quiets the negative voices that try to bring you down. Steering away from body talk altogether can also be helpful—if your mind wants to make you feel awful about your physical attributes, reframe things by focusing on the other beautiful, weird things about yourself, like the power of your laugh or your superior ability to impersonate a disappointed Alex Trebek after everyone blows the answer on Final Jeopardy. You are more than what you see in the mirror. You are lovely in ways that cannot be mapped or described.

2. SOOTHE YOURSELF.

There are times in a person's life where the only appropriate thing to do is to be a complete cliché. Is it totally cheesy to sit in a bubble bath, surrounded by candles? Of course it is. But it is also the greatest, and a perfect example of self-soothing—allowing yourself to feel comforted and relaxed by doing something specifically kind for yourself.

Self-soothing is a perfect way to flip the script on negative thinking. If your mind wants you to engage in destructive behaviors, self-soothing can distract you from harmful patterns while replacing them with something positive. A bath, for example, gives you the opportunity to both relax and focus on the lovely things your body can do, as it is a sensory experience. Instead of concentrating on things you think are "wrong," concentrate on how the water feels, how the candles smell, how the music you're playing sounds, and how good your muscles feel as they get the chance to just chill for a second. These are tiny, lovely experiences that people often overlook. Slow down and pay attention. Give your body and your brain a chance to feel a bit of peace, and you'll carry that feeling with you for the rest of the day.

Self-soothing doesn't have to be so literal, though: You can soothe yourself by drawing, watching funny movies, dancing, taking a drive, calling friends, writing, playing games—anything that makes you feel good and encourages positive vibes instead of negative ones.

3. REMEMBER: SIZES ARE GARBAGE.

Sizes! They are the worst. They are also completely meaningless, as there's no standard throughout the industry. I've actually bought like four different sizes at the SAME store on the SAME day, because there's just no consistency in anything. So if you are obsessing over sizes, please don't. Just concentrate on how things fit and how they make you feel. And if you're still a bit numbers-obsessive, you can always cut the tags out of all of your clothes so that you can get used to just putting things on that fit, rather than that Size Whatever dress in your closet.

If clothes shopping is a major trigger for you, it also helps to bring little sticky notes with happy, positive affirmations on them, which you can make yourself or grab from the girls at The Dressing Room Project. Sometimes it helps just to have a friendly visual reminder slapped on the mirror to combat those ever-looming negative thoughts that tend to thrive in dressing room situations.

4. START SMALL.

When I was hospitalized, I didn't even want to *look* at my body. It was going through (necessary and healthy!) changes, but I wasn't in a mental place (yet) to deal with them. Instead, I decided to focus on a part of my body that I did like: my eyes. My eyes had always been the same, regardless of my weight, and though I'd never been into makeup before, I became a bit obsessive, buying mascaras and eyeliners and shadows—beautifully packaged things that had no size designation—and spending hours in my room trying on different looks. For the first time ever, looking in the mirror was actually *fun*!

For about a decade now, I've maintained my obsession with products—shampoos, perfumes, lotions, lipsticks, etc.—because they make me feel happy. I don't pay attention to the undermining advertisements that say this magic potion or that miracle serum is going to "fix" my "flaws." I don't buy this stuff because I hate myself and think I need fixing—I buy it because I *like* myself and I *love* red lipstick and I don't care what anyone else has to say about it.

Even if you start with something as tiny as "You know? My big toe is gorgeous," you're on the right track. You have to give yourself a break, and be able to say "So what, who cares?" when things aren't perfect, because perfection is super boring, and you are a shining light of all things marvelous, weird, and beautiful. ◊

Design by Sonja and Vanessa Han. Title lettering by Lisa Maione. Illustration by Brooke Nechvatel. Status symbols by Esme. Playlist lettering by Suzy.

MARCH 2014: CONSUMPTION

Hi, Rookies!

This month's theme is Consumption: foooood, consumerism, materialism, processing ye olde popular culture. Inspirations: *The Queen of Versailles* and the rest of Lauren Greenfield's work, *Spring Breakers*, *The Bling Ring*, Baz Luhrmann's *The Great Gatsby*. Rich Kids of Instagram. Madonna's "Material Girl." Kanye's "All of the Lights." *So much Kanye.* He's done so many great songs about the complexities of materialism and status that it was hard to pick just one for this playlist. Here, I give you 14 songs about money, cars, substances, le secks, and other pleasures/necessities/indulgences.

Thank you, as always, for being here.

LOVE, TAVI

MORE, MORE, MORE

1. CAN'T TELL ME NOTHING — KANYE WEST
2. GLORY AND GORE — LORDE
3. ASHTRAYS AND HEARTBREAKS — SNOOP LION FEAT. MILEY CYRUS
4. SUPER RICH KIDS — FRANK OCEAN FEAT. EARL SWEATSHIRT
5. MALLRATS (LA LA LA) — THE ORWELLS
6. I'M IN LOVE WITH MY CAR — QUEEN
7. WILD SEX (IN THE WORKING CLASS) — OINGO

8. MONEY — SHARON JONES AND THE DAP KINGS
9. MORE, MORE, MORE — ANDREA TRUE CONNECTION
10. SUGA MAMA — BEYONCÉ
11. LET'S GO GET STONED — LOWELL FULSOM
12. MOST WANTED — CULTS
13. NATIONAL ANTHEM — LANA DEL REY
14. CASHMERE THOUGHTS — JAY-Z

THANK YOU HAVE A NICE DAY

CLASS ACTRESSES

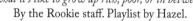

An occasionally uncomfortable, undoubtedly polarizing, but ultimately satisfying talk about what it's like to grow up rich, poor, or in between.
By the Rookie staff. Playlist by Hazel.

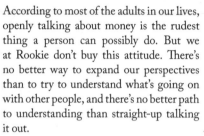

According to most of the adults in our lives, openly talking about money is the rudest thing a person can possibly do. But we at Rookie don't buy this attitude. There's no better way to expand our perspectives than to try to understand what's going on with other people, and there's no better path to understanding than straight-up talking it out.

So we decided to have an open conversation about class as a staff. Sure enough, we all learned a ton about not only the ways other people think about money, but the real-world implications of "class" in all its blatant and sneaky permutations. And guess what? No one said "HOW DARE YOU" or "I NEVER" even one time, even though we were talking about *that paper*!

We had this conversation over Facebook, where a few of us instigated new threads by asking questions (in bold below). We hope you find our not-so-master class on class as *valuable* and *enriching* as we did.
—Amy Rose

AMY ROSE **Let's start off with a very basic question: What class did you consider yourself growing up, and why? What class do you consider yourself now, and why?** Growing up, I considered myself lower-middle-class, because while my family struggled financially, I was a white person growing up in a wealthy area, and I was able to go to school because of financial aid and scholarships. Now, though, I'm solidly middle-class: I can take care of my bills, pay my rent, and have some semblance of a disposable income despite working in a creative field and living in an expensive city.

SUZY It's fluctuated so much throughout my life! Until I was in middle school, my family was low-income. Then we were middle-class for a while, then the recession hit and my parents had a hard time finding steady jobs, and we sank back down to where we'd been. Now that I'm on my own, though, because I have a full-time job, a college education, and an apartment in New York, I would consider myself middle-class.

CHANEL I have had a similar trajectory: lower-middle-class until about middle school, then my mom went through a series of promotions at work and I would say we entered the middle class? Right now, though, if I had no help from my family, I would definitely be on the low end of the spectrum, because I barely make enough money to rent an apartment (I stay with my sister for this reason).

STEPHANIE Same here! My parents are both college-educated nurses, but when I was younger, they were just beginning their careers and their jobs didn't pay well. We lived in a working-class neighborhood in St. Louis. Then, when they were making a bit more money, we moved to a middle/upper-class suburb of Chicago. I could really tell the difference: They were able to buy a house, and suddenly I was asking my mother to buy me certain things to measure up to my peers at school. My mom didn't understand why I needed them, and honestly neither did I, but I wanted them. She never bought me lots of status-y things, but to this day, when I can't pay my student loans or my dentist bill, she helps me out. I know what a huge privilege that is, and that freedom probably defines my class status more than the amount of money I'm currently making.

ANAHEED My parents moved to this country as immigrants in 1970, and for a long time my family was probably in the lower half of the middle-class, but they were both doctors, so pretty soon they were making good money and we had all the trappings of an upper-middle-class life. That's where we were for most of my upbringing, and it gave me a sense of (material) safety and freedom and expectation that I think still defines me as upper-middle-class even though I personally do not make enough money to classify as such in a strictly financial sense.

DYLAN I will probably always feel like I'm in the upper part of the middle class, for the same reasons as Anaheed: My family and how I grew up gave me the freedom to pursue a creative profession despite the lack of any guarantee of its ever "paying off." Even when we were almost broke, I still felt like we were upper-middle. Whatever struggles any of us went through, they were considered a temporary dip in our normal quality of life. To me that's the difference between *poor* and *broke*. *Poor* is the place you go when all the safety nets have fallen through, or you don't have the resources in place to stay afloat—like family who can help or schools with scholarships. *Broke* is when I had to live without my smartphone for a couple months. Poor is never having a damn smartphone! The difference is less about dollars and numbers and more about resources and access.

PIXIE **Yeah, I think it's important to remember that class isn't always synonymous with financial status; there are signifiers that allow people to maintain class privilege even when they're struggling financially. Can you think of any such signs you've noticed?** I'd agree with Dylan that access is a big one—particularly in the digital sense. Being able to have internet at home is a huge deal that a lot of people take for granted.

CAITLIN D. Obvious ones: education and membership in any of the networks of rich white people who enjoy perpetuating themselves. (There is some overlap between these two things.)

ARABELLE Access to libraries and public programs helped me prepare for college and stuff. I got farther along academically because I had amazing public school teachers and librarians. That accounts for a HUGE part of my privilege.

CHANEL At my high school, if you were in AP classes and excelling, you were assumed to be higher-class. When I got into the University of Virginia, a lot of my classmates said they couldn't possibly understand how I got in (while they were rejected), because I was black—which I think to them meant I was inherently lower-class and therefore could not be as smart or successful as them.

DYLAN CREDIT.

PIXIE BRACES.

ANAHEED Health insurance! I have had checkups, vaccinations, dental care, a gyno, birth control, an eye doctor, THERAPY, meds, etc., for my whole life, and I would be a completely different person, physically and psychologically, if I hadn't.

PIXIE Yeah, access to mental health care/medication is a big one.

ANAHEED The way people speak is a huge indicator. Also cultural references. Also personal style.

JAMIA No joke about speech! My cousins used to tease me for "talking white" and I'd say, "Call me when you need someone to talk to the debt collectors." They'd always laugh and be like, "Ooh, good idea!"

AMY ROSE **When did you become aware of hierarchies of class and your place in them?**

For me, it was when I was about nine—that year, my mom cried when I asked her to buy me a paperback that she couldn't afford, but also got upset when the well-meaning people in our rich suburb left groceries and gift cards to department stores in our mailbox.

SUZY I think I was six or seven. My mom would sometimes send me to school without lunch money; as an immigrant she didn't know that there were free or reduced-price meals available to low-income students. I think children carry class bias too, even though they don't know any better—I got bullied out of a pool once because the kids noticed that I'd had the same faded swimsuit for years.

JULIANNE I remember becoming aware of poverty and generosity when I was five, going grocery shopping with my grandma. She was always on the lookout for the cheapest deals on food, but she spent the quarter she had left to buy me an Archie comic. She couldn't read or write, and she lived off Social Security and selling tortillas by the dozen, but she knew I loved those comics.

ROSE A really formative moment for me was when I was about six. My dad left a pile of cash on the counter to pay our nanny for the week. I took some twenties out of the pile and kept them for myself. When the nanny went to count the money, it wasn't the right amount, and everyone was awkwardly confused and quietly alarmed. My dad gently asked me if I took it (probably because I am a terrible liar and was most likely slinking around like the guiltiest creature alive) and I fessed up. It was the first time I remember understanding that you can't take things just because you want them; it was also the first time I fully understood that my parents *paid* people to help them, that the monetary exchange I had witnessed created a particular power dynamic between humans, and that my parents had more power in that arrangement.

PIXIE I thought we were rich because we could afford brand-name soda as opposed to generic soda.

CHANEL I had free/reduced lunch in elementary school and thought it was some kind of cool perk. Around the same time, I visited Louisiana for a family reunion and saw the literal "other side of the tracks": There was a geographic dividing line between races, and the white part of town was cleaner and prettier.

PIXIE **Can you think of any behaviors (table manners, for example) that were instilled in you as a means of establishing your class?**

SUZY Saying please, thank you, and excuse me for EVERYTHING. I am still regularly shocked by how most of the wealthy people I've come across don't say please or thank you…ever.

MAGGIE I was taught: *Never say please, but always say thank you.* No one was more scorned than the nouveau riche who didn't say thank you and didn't treat their "help" well. Even at Taco Bell, my mom screams, "THANK Y'ALL!" to the entire kitchen staff. But you don't say please to waiters or the "help," because they're not doing you a favor, they're doing their jobs.

PIXIE My mom was really anti-swearing and hated us using words like *sucks* and *crap*, even. We had to say *crud*. And she was not a fan of chewing gum. Her favorite saying was "Were you born in a barn?" and now I'm so mad that my childhood self never thought to come back with "No, but *Jesus* was!"

AMY ROSE **How did your class background affect your ability to pursue the career and education you wanted?** In my case, the privilege of going to school in a major city for a vastly reduced cost due to financial aid/scholarships was instrumental to my being able to make a living doing what I do.

ANAHEED My class background is 100 percent responsible for every job I've ever had. Potential employers assume the best even when I am totally fucking up in job interviews. They never question my credentials because I went to good schools, and they "like" me because I know how to talk to such people, because I am comfortable with them, because of my privilege.

STEPHANIE I definitely am where I am because of my class background. My parents encouraged me to be a writer even if that meant borrowing money from them. I've always had a safety net, and I'm very aware that it would have been a lot harder for me personally to have any of the professional and creative success I've had without it.

CHANEL I'd seen my mom and sisters work hard for what they wanted, even if it took them a long time to get it. So even though I didn't have the ultimate privileges (e.g., getting tutored for SATs), I made do with what I had: the public library, after hours at school, so I could get into a good college so I could build a good career (though now I'm like LOL is "a career" even a real thing anymore?). I had to apply for financial aid; without it, I would not have been able to go to college. Then came internships, which were such a bitch because of the whole unpaid thing! If I couldn't stay at my sister's place in Jersey while I'm interning, I wouldn't have been able to say yes to these unpaid (or very-low-paying) positions, almost all of which, I have to admit, helped me shape my current hustle. Most of the other interns at all my jobs came from well-to-do families, because unless you're holding down a paying job in addition to the internship, you have to be rich to be able to afford not to be paid for that long. Some of my fellow interns would buy takeout lunches *every single day* of *every single week*. I was like, "Wow, how do you pay rent?!"

JENNY Yes, so true in re: internships! To do an unpaid internship in New York City, you need to have a couple thousand bucks at your disposal, so it weeds out the vast majority of people from step one. I always felt like the rise of the internship industrial complex was another way to make sure talented poor folks don't get a chance to get their foot in the door, because even if you work your ass off and are talented as hell, you are like 100 connections behind if you can't afford to spend your summers working for no money.

AMY ROSE **How did race inform (a) the financial realities of your class, (b) your perception of your class, and/or (c) the class-based ways others treat or treated you?** Coming from a white family, I quite obviously had tons of privilege even when we were at our poorest.

SUZY It's not just limited to white people! Many members of my family have adopted racist rhetoric in the hopes of better assimilating into white American culture.

CHANEL I had a weird mix of experiences with race and class growing up. On one hand, as a black girl, there were definitely some assumptions about how I was raised and that I was probably low-income. I remember that this white kid in one of my classes laughed at me because I was reading *Candy* (that book about heroin addiction) and he said of course I would read something like that, since most black people are lowdown drug addicts. My mother didn't really raise me to see characteristics based on race, even though she had it *rough* growing up in the '60s (there was a "slave day" at her high school and she participated in a sit-in because of it, because she's a badass). On the other hand, I often got flak because I was in band and wrote for the literary magazine and stuff like that, I wasn't "black enough" or part of "the black community." Even my own family mocked the way I talked because it was "proper" and I came off as "affluent" (which is like, get the fuck outta here).

AMY ROSE **What preconceptions did you have of people in other classes growing up?** I had/have an ingrained prejudice against people who grow up wealthy that I am trying to work past. Like all prejudices, this one is based more on my own insecurity about money, class, and my worthiness/abilities than on anything real, and I often catch myself trying to invalidate the achievements of people who grew up with privilege ("Yeah, of course you're an editor at the *Paris Review*, YOUR PARENTS STILL PAY FOR YOUR APARTMENT PROBABLY" or "If I grew up with what you did, I'd have SO MUCH MORE to show for it").

But everyone's life, experience, and pain are valid, even if I don't immediately relate to them; and anyway, my unfair attitude benefits no one, least of all me. Do any of you grapple with these kinds of feelings?

JULIANNE I had the exact same feeling for a long time, and while I still get pangs of it, as I've grown older I feel it less—maybe because by the time people are my age, most of them aren't really supported by their parents anymore and have had to experience the shock of doing it on their own.

SUZY I still don't think I can shake it. I think living in New York has exacerbated it.

CHANEL I also have a little prejudice against wealthy people, which actually didn't come about until college. I just saw how rich people at my school walked around so entitled, as if their money did everything for them, and the way they treated "the less fortunate" was something that I just didn't like to see. But my senior year, I became really good friends with this girl who is a great deal wealthier than I am (family-wise), and she showed me that rich people are also humans, and some do work hard for what they have, etc. (We're still friends today.)

PIXIE I remember watching *Tiny Furniture* and being like, *What is the point of this? I am so pissed!* But after I thought about it, I was like, *Welp, I don't relate to this at all, but I appreciate a view inside a world that I don't live in, because it makes me understand it a tiny bit more.* So I dunno. People can be sheltered in millions of ways.

AMY ROSE Did those of you who grew up comfortably, money-wise, ever feel like you want(ed) to hide it because of attitudes like these?

ANAHEED I was embarrassed about not being working-class like most of my friends when I was a teenager, but I grew out of that the way I hope to grow out of all pointless, faultless insecurities. I mean, what is more useless and tiresome than a privileged person's guilt over their own privilege? It's a waste of everyone's time.

MAGGIE I was always surrounded by people richer than me. No one felt bad about it. No one was ever challenged to feel bad about it. It's really hard to describe the cognitive dissonance we all had at my high school. It was like, we felt sorry for poor people, but at the same time there was NO awareness of how lucky we were. It's very disturbing for me to reflect on how disjointed and deranged my worldview used to be...

ROSE I never identified with "rich people," in part because I grew up in a context (Hollywood) where there were always people around with much more money, living more-extravagant lifestyles, with tons of fame, fortune, and privilege. Still, my parents were very successful at their jobs in the entertainment business, so we had a nice, big house, people to take care of us when my parents were working, all the clothes, toys, and athletic gear we ever wanted, fancy hippie private school educations, fun family vacations, and no worries about where money for gas/electricity/food would come from.

I can see now that I lived/live with a tremendous amount of privilege, but at the time it wasn't as visible to me as the extreme wealth displays I saw all around me and how those contrasted with the rest of the city we lived in.

I've avoided addressing the issue of shame head-on, but it's pretty painful to consider that someone would dismiss me outright without getting to know me. In terms of the question of wealth and morality, I think the moment I realized how spoiled I was, I also realized I never wanted to *act* spoiled. I feel incredibly lucky that I grew up with economic privilege, but even luckier that I was taught that it's what you do with your gifts (helping people, connecting people, making the world a better place however you can) that matters more than what you come from.

ANAHEED I think it's pretty easy for most of us to pay attention to (and possibly resent) people who grew up with more privilege than we did, but why aren't we as comfortable looking in the other direction: at those with a lot less?

I mean, everyone here is on a computer, and there's a certain amount of privilege associated with that. We all have time to sit around and have a DISCUSSION ABOUT CLASS, which also requires some degree of class privilege. So, what makes it so hard to see ourselves as privileged?

STEPHANIE We're definitely all privileged to be here. I know I'm privileged because I could have had this conversation in an AOL chatroom in 1995 because I had a computer and internet access back then. But now that I've owned that, where do I go with it? I think that it is great that we're having this conversation, but that doesn't do anything for the people who have neither the access nor the time to read it...

JULIANNE I was never hungry growing up, and I always knew that if something terrible happened, I had 11 aunts and uncles we could go stay with. The occasional Archie comic notwithstanding, I didn't have a lot of extras, nor, more important, did I have the resources or the guidance to go to college, but I was never hurting for any of the essentials. We regularly sent money and toys to my cousins in Mexico, whom I never got to visit but who I am sure were worse off than I could imagine.

CHANEL I'm definitely privileged relative to most of the population of the world, but often I don't see that until something is taken away from me and I am confronted with my own entitlement. Sometimes I need to jolt myself out of my own head and my own problems and recognize what's going on around me.

SUZY My family is actually pretty comfortable these days, even if some of my family members have to squeeze into my grandparents' apartments to make do. That's the thing—there were many instances in which some of us could've ended up homeless, but we try really hard not to leave each other behind. Not every family has that strong of a bond. However, I don't agree that talking about class is a privilege. People in poverty are very much aware of what's going on—they experience class struggle every day. Some of them are very present in movements for fair housing and labor practices. Some of them read the internet on mobile phones or go to public libraries—just like I used to.

ARABELLE Even though I am chronically ill and queer and whatever, I have had it so easy, comparatively speaking. I went to an amazing public school, have both of my parents in my life, and have always had a home to go back to when needed. I've also had health insurance for most of my life, which, because of my health conditions, I literally couldn't live without. But this conversation has helped me realize how often I have disregarded my privilege, so thank you.

I think we tend to overplay our hardships to make ourselves less accountable to the people with less than us. Like, if we're hurting a lot then other people can't be hurting more than we are, or something. That's when we start playing Oppression Olympics and getting defensive and not listening to each other. I am still pretty quick to defend myself, but I used to be a lot worse. I am still learning. ☆

24 HOUR
PARTY PEOPLE

Festival NRMAL + running around Monterrey, Mexico + getting
kicked out of McDonald's + dancing like crazy = one perfect day.
By María Fernanda. Styling by Zaid Díaz.

Thanks to Alma and Cheryl for modeling, to Adrián Glez for doing hair and makeup, and to MANCANDY and MILKBBI for lending us clothes.

KICK 'EM TO THE CURB

Getting rid of toxic friends.
By Hazel

Once upon a time, I had a friend. I had read her blog for years, and she read mine. She lived in the city I was moving to for school, and we were excited to meet and finally be IRL pals. But the more I hung out with her, the more wary I became. I started to notice some troubling patterns: Sometimes I would try to tell her something I thought she'd think was funny, and she'd cut me off midsentence to tell me how stupid it was. She rarely asked me to hang out, and when I asked her, she often flaked on me or wouldn't answer my texts. On top of all that, she would legit insult me on a regular basis. She'd make digs at me for being uncool (because I rarely went out) or for writing for Rookie, which she liked making fun of. She even started subtweeting disparaging things that were obviously about me.

If we'd been closer, I would have confronted her and tried to save the friendship, but, things being as tentative as they were, I decided instead to cut my losses. I stopped trying to contact her, and, unsurprisingly, she never picked up the slack.

I recently broke up with another friend, someone I'd felt close to, because he was always questioning my personal choices (like where I go to school) and actions (like my writing). One day, I couldn't take it anymore. He was saying mean things about my then-boyfriend, and I was like "fuck this" and told him to never contact me again.

Yeah, so maybe I'm a li'l dramatic, but I live by the great Amy Poehler philosophy of "anybody who doesn't make you feel good, kick them to the curb." It seems so simple, right? Don't be friends with jerks. But, as much as I wish I were the kind of person who doesn't give a damn what anyone

thinks of her, if someone I think is awesome tells me I'm uncool for liking Grimes or caring about school or not knowing a certain artist or *anything*, it makes me wonder if they're right and I'm actually really stupid and horrible. Even worse, I start changing my opinions to match theirs. When you're surrounded by people who dismiss you for being you, you're going to start to dismiss yourself.

I'm not talking about constructive criticism. Friends call out friends. Friends can get into arguments. But a friend saying, "Hey, please don't be so hard on yourself about your weight" is completely different from someone saying, "Stop talking about how fat you are—nobody wants to hear about it." When a so-called friend makes you feel bad, it's hard to stop holding out hope that *one day, this person will be nicer to me*. Sometimes, we don't want to admit that someone's laughing at us and not with us, so we laugh too and try to shrug it off.

I spent most of my teen years accepting this kind of garbage behavior from "friends." People would insult my intelligence, my introverted nature, my clothes, whatever—and I would just keep hanging out with them! In my tiny high school, I had a limited choice as to whom I could even hang out with, and I figured if I wanted to be "normal" I needed to have friends, even if they weren't actually right for me. I was also worried about being "mean" to people who were hurting my feelings. I mean, what? They sure weren't worried about that vis-à-vis my feelings, and anyway, there's nothing mean about protecting yourself.

Once I'd reached a point in my life when I'd found what I call "true friends,"

people who value and respect me, I learned that I'd rather not waste my time hanging out with underminers, snootypantses, and saboteurs. Those are the people who may seem like friends on the surface, but who get angry at you for being successful, happy, or confident (often out of jealousy). It finally dawned on me that this is my life, and I get to choose who gets to be part of it.

I'm lucky that I learned this lesson at a relatively young age, but I wish I had learned it at, like, age two. So let me bonk you on the head now: THIS IS YOUR LIFE, AND YOU GET TO CHOOSE WHO GETS TO BE PART OF IT. You will never stop running into people who are jealous and insecure and who thrive on pulling other people down to their level. But you don't have to listen to them. You are entitled to kick anyone out of your life, for any reason! It's not elitist, stuck-up, or "too picky" to weed out those who BRING YOU DOWN. Seriously, some people are just mean, and "I don't like her/him" is a good enough reason to cut ties with a person.

Not to sound like a L'Oreal commercial, but you deserve great friends because you're worth it. If someone insults you on the internet, feel free to block them. Is someone starting shit in the comments under one of your status updates? Unfriend them. It's not ridiculous or an overreaction, it's being true to what's comfortable *for you*, which is all that counts, because you are you! Life is too short to waste your time on people who bring bad vibes into your life. Let's all pull a Poehler and kick 'em to the curb for good. ✹

OUT OF (MY) BODY

I totally wanted liposuction—until I got it.
By Katie McMahon

I had liposuction when I was 18 years old. While many people choose to have cosmetic surgery for their own totally valid reasons, my reasons were based in shame. I was fat, and I hated being fat. I hated my body, and I had surgery to get rid of it and replace it with one that wouldn't embarrass me every time I looked in the mirror or stood on a scale.

That was a decade ago, and this is the first time I've told anyone I'm not very close to about my surgery. I've been too embarrassed to talk about it, because I feel like I'm supposed to be "above" that kind of body shame. I'm a feminist who is always telling people how beautiful *they* are at any size or age, in any shape, and I truly believe that all bodies are "good" bodies. So why couldn't I exercise this kind of acceptance toward myself?

My mom has told me that as a baby, I was happiest when I was naked, playing in the sandbox and crawling around the backyard without a care in the world. That's the only evidence I have that there was ever a time when my body was just a *body* to me and not a reflection of my inner "goodness," which boggles my mind, because as far back as I can remember, my inner and outer selves have been so inextri-

cably linked that they feel like they came that way.

The trouble began just before my 10th birthday. My mom took me shopping for a new bathing suit, and in the dressing room, she casually mentioned my "thunder thighs." I tried to figure out what she meant: Was she saying the earth shook when I walked on it, and it sounded like thunder? When she saw my face, she realized how upset I was and tried to comfort me by assuring me I would outgrow my "baby fat," but the damage was done. I looked at my body in the full-length mirror, pushed out my stomach, and pinched the flesh around my belly button with my hands. Suddenly everything about my body felt *wrong*. What was I to do about this? If I stayed the same size, I would obviously be "fat," which I was old enough to know meant "bad" in my family. And what if I got *bigger*? The thought filled me with terror, which, along with my "baby" fat, increased as I got older.

My mom continued to bring up— and try, unsuccessfully, to manage—my weight throughout my adolescence, mostly through constant criticism. She was diabetic and, even though she was relatively thin, struggled with her own body image,

and she projected her anxieties onto me. When I was 11 or 12, my parents told me they were afraid I would become diabetic too, and they put me on a diet. I wasn't allowed to eat pizza, chocolate, soda, butter, ice cream, cheese, or basically *anything* I liked. I was signed up for basketball, soccer, softball, and swim team, all of which I loathed and was terrible at. In desperation, I started secretly hoarding my "forbidden" foods. I would binge on them when no one was around, then immediately beat myself up for doing so.

By the time I was 14, I was eating all the time, whether or not I was hungry. I ate when I was bored, angry, frustrated, or sad, and kept eating until my stomach felt like it was going to explode. I didn't know how to stop.

Mother-daughter shopping trips, which used to be pleasant experiences, had become almost unbearably painful. On one such outing, when I was 16, we stopped at my favorite plus-size store. I couldn't find anything I liked that fit me, and I became overwhelmed with frustration. My mom and I walked out empty-handed and sat down on a mall bench, where I tried not to cry. That's when my mother asked if I had ever considered liposuction, the surgery where they basically vacuum fat out of different parts of your body. That knocked the wind out of me, and I started to openly sob.

"Sometimes dieting and exercise don't improve the parts where you need the most help," she said, trying to be supportive. She told me that she'd had liposuction herself after giving birth to me—something I hadn't known—and that she was happy with the outcome. She advised me to "think about it" and said she'd pay for the surgery as my high school graduation present. Even though her suggestion that I might "need" lipo hurt my feelings, part of me immediately wanted badly to do it. *Mom also hated her looks once, but she did something about it*, I thought. *Maybe I should, too.*

She didn't bring liposuction up again, but I kept thinking about it. I was ashamed of my body, and it felt like I couldn't keep my weight down, no matter what I tried. I ate lettuce all day and started smoking cigarettes, which I had heard made people skinny. When I couldn't control my cravings, I binged on huge amounts of food and then threw it up. Over a few months, I lost significant amounts of weight and gained it all back more than once. I ended up sad, frustrated, and still fat. I couldn't handle it anymore.

When I told my dad I was accepting my mom's graduation present, he said it was fine with him as long as I felt absolutely certain that that was what I wanted. I was. Any trepidation I may have felt about going under the knife was quickly replaced by excitement. I watched shows like *The Swan* and *Extreme Makeover* and saw the "magic" that plastic surgery could work for unhappy people like me. The people on those shows became so sexy and desired after their operations; their past selves were unrecognizable. I thought I would be transformed that way, too. I obsessed over a future free of "thunder thighs," dressing-room meltdowns, and bathing suits with T-shirts over them. I was moving

from Michigan to California for college the following fall—if I had lipo, I thought, no one there would have to know I was ever fat. In mere months, I would be lying on the beach in a bikini, waving at surfers as I dug my toes into the hot sand.

At my first pre-surgery consultation, the doctor told me the procedure wouldn't change my actual weight by much; it was more about "shaping"—a push in the general direction of thinness, as opposed to an instantaneous *Swan*-like transformation. But as he drew circles and *X*es on my body with a blue marker, all I heard was that I was about to get rid of *fat*. Even when he warned me about the potential health risks—including death—that came with such an invasive surgery, I wasn't afraid. I was ready to do whatever it took to make my visions of thinness a reality.

The surgery removed fat from my thighs, arms, and stomach. But when it was all over, I didn't look the way I thought I would. My arms were the same size, but with extra skin flaps, little white stretch marks, and oozing scars. My stomach had loose skin in new places, and I couldn't see my belly button without moving folds of hanging flesh away with my hands. My thighs were smaller, but my knees now looked swollen instead of just chubby. The physical post-op pain was extreme, but it was nothing compared with how heavy my insides were with confusion and regret. After all I had hoped for, I felt *worse* about myself after liposuction.

By then, my parents had gotten divorced, and my dad stayed in our family home, where I recuperated for a few months. I thought I would feel more comfortable healing in my childhood bed, but my sister's family was staying with us as they moved houses, and so was my brother—along with, mortifyingly, his best friend, who was working for my dad. This guy was incredibly attractive, funny, and kind, which deepened my self-consciousness, especially when he saw me in my post-surgery compression garments (tan spandex shorts that hugged

my thighs and stomach tightly while my wounds healed). Before my operation, I'd imagined that I would soon feel sexy and desirable; now the very thought of a guy wanting me seemed ridiculous. I stayed in my room as much as possible and cried myself to sleep. On the rare occasions when I would venture out and interact with my family, I pretended everything was fine. I was supposed to be old enough to make this choice for myself, and I tried to prove that by showing no signs of regret.

After my body had healed a bit, my mom took me shopping for new clothes. I don't remember her saying I looked beautiful or thin, but she *was* proud that I could fit into a smaller-size shirt. I didn't tell her that I thought my body looked weird—that although my arms, legs, and stomach fit into reduced sizes, they didn't seem to fit *me*, and that I was more embarrassed about my body than ever. I reluctantly bought a short pleated skirt from Old Navy, which I never wore once. Instead of the tank tops I had fantasized about, I wore long-sleeved shirts that covered my new stretch marks.

I started college that fall. At parties, other people talked about making out and having sex, but I couldn't imagine anyone wanting to kiss me, let alone have sex with me. But I laughed along with everyone and tried to fit in, partly by drinking heavily. I felt like being thinner gave me license to eat everything that had been "off-limits" when I was fat, and I went totally overboard. Inevitably, I gained weight. As I watched the number on the scale go up, that old childhood fear came back: *What if I keep getting bigger?* I told myself that if I ever reached a certain specific weight, I would kill myself. *I can't stand living in this body*, I thought, *and if it gets any worse, I won't.* I never reached that number, so I don't know if I would have acted on this urge, but it felt very real to me at the time.

My college major was acting—kind of ironic, given how looks-focused that field is. During my second year, I got a note from a professor following a practice

audition. It said I looked like I was not "in" my body. Of course, I interpreted this as a criticism of my weight. I talked to another instructor, one I trusted, about it. To him, the note seemed like it was about the way I was carrying my body, not its size. I probably looked insecure during my audition, he said. Being comfortable in my body didn't mean losing weight, according to him—it meant not apologizing for my physical presence. I was legitimately baffled by this. How could I be comfortable in—even, as he suggested, *proud of*—an overweight body? What would it look like to be OK with my body the way it was? What did it mean to be "in" one's body?

He urged me to stop being so mean to my body and instead to try to care for it and, by extension, myself. This was seriously a revolutionary notion to me, and I was a little bit scared to think about it, but also excited to take it on. I decided to try making peace with my body. The first step was to catch myself whenever I started an internal stream of negative commentary about my shape, my weight, my personality, my value. The second was to let go of long-held resentments, the most pressing being the ones I had about my mom.

My decision to have liposuction was based, in part, on a hope that it would make my mother like me. I thought she hated me, that she thought I was ugly, and that she was disappointed that I didn't turn out the way she wanted me to. I wanted to talk to her about all this, so I agreed to accompany her on a weekend yoga retreat. Doesn't that sound relaxing? "Yoga retreat"? It did to me too. But once we got there, she was her old self, criticizing every little thing I did. I stayed silent and tried to just get to the end of the trip without exploding, but on the last night, as she drove me home, it started to rain, and she went on a tear: "Why are you wearing sandals?" she asked. "Didn't you know it was going to rain? You should be wearing socks and shoes."

That's all it took. Years of resentment and anger and hurt welled up in me, and I finally let them out. "Can't you see how miserable I am?" I shouted. "You did this to me! This is your fault!"

Then something miraculous happened: My mother apologized. "Everything I did was wrong," she said. "I should never have told you to lose weight. You were fine as you were, and I'm sorry." I wish I could say that her apology brought me some relief, but unless she could go back in time and deal with her destructive feelings around bodies and weight before she cursed me with them, there wasn't really anything she could do to make up for what she did to me. Maybe this sounds pessimistic, but it's actually freed me a lot: I no longer expect my mother to make me feel better or to mend our past. I accept the imperfect bond we have now, and I've come to understand that loving and respecting myself is *my* choice—not hers.

Since then, I've gotten very good at taking care of myself. I go to therapy and take medication for depression, which I was diagnosed with a long time ago but didn't truly deal with for years, because obviously being thin was SO MUCH MORE IMPORTANT than feeling emotionally OK. Not being depressed anymore has been invaluable in letting me recognize parts of myself I actually feel proud of: I'm a caring friend and sister, a responsible employee, and a loving girlfriend. Amazingly, some of the things I love about myself are physical: I have a really pretty smile, and my butt looks good in a pair of jeans. I happily wear the sleeveless shirts I once dreaded, which show off a tattoo I love on my upper arm. Shopping is still not the most fun thing in the world, but it's not traumatic anymore, either—I make an effort not to berate myself when I can't fit into something that's too small for me, and I usually find stuff that makes me feel OK about how I look. When I get home and show my boyfriend a new outfit, he tells me that I'm sexy, and *I believe him*. I get this validation from myself, too—when I look at recent pictures of myself, I think,

Wow, she's super cute. I exercise to feel good, not to lose weight; it helps me remember that my body's got more important things to do than maintain some unrealistic physical ideal. This is what progress looks like for me.

I'm not saying my body image is perfect these days. I'll always find this part of my life difficult to some degree. But the moment I begin to feel self-hatred about my weight, I talk about it with someone I love—it's a lot easier to come to terms with these things when you can be open about them with others. During one such conversation, a friend told me something about her relationship with her own body that's always stuck with me. She said that she'd realized that she had a choice: She could be thin or she could be sane, but with the body and the brain she has, she can't be both. That's true for me, too.

Sometimes, the fact that I have to choose between them really pisses me off. But that's OK. I don't beat myself up anymore for not always being able to extend the militant body-positivity I have toward others to myself. I forgive myself for not being "perfect." I can even allow myself to have the occasional shitty afternoon and not let it consume me, because I know acceptance is something I can, and will, continue working on forever.

Being honest with myself about my experiences—including the negative ones, like my surgery—has made them far less powerful, shameful, and scary. I'm learning to say that, yes, I had liposuction, and even though the aftermath was incredibly hard, I actually don't regret it anymore. The way my body was affected by it tells a story of emotional pain and damage, but that story ends in survival and perpetual growth. My stretch marks and scars remind me that, even if I've been through some serious shit, I am strong and beautiful. Sometimes, it just takes a lot of reflection (and therapy, and pissed-off afternoons) to finally feel OK in your body—no matter what that looks like for you. ❀

HOW TO LOOK LIKE AN UNTOUCHABLE EMPRESS

Steel yourself against the world with this regal makeup tutorial.
By Indigo. Playlist by Dylan.

This tutorial was inspired by the 2006 film *Curse of the Golden Flower*. Even though the story is set centuries ago in an imaginary Chinese dynasty, the movie's opulent visuals, generous use of green and gold, and, on the character of the Empress (played by Gong Li), gorgeous, intricate makeup really speak to me today.

Here's a DIY that'll help you show your own inner empress to the world!

WHAT YOU'LL NEED:

- A red eyeliner pencil. (You can also use red lip liner—just check the package to make sure it's safe to use near your eyes.)
- A gold eyeliner pencil.
- Red and gold eye shadow.
- A shimmery pearl pink or soft gold eye shadow or highlighter.
- Black eyeliner.
- Mascara.
- Red lip liner and lipstick. (Feel free to substitute another color for this look—it would also look great with a black or beige shade!)
- Blush.
- An eye shadow brush.
- A blush brush.
- Optional: eyebrow powder or an eyebrow pencil.
- Optional: orange eye shadow.
- Optional: an angled eyeliner brush.

STEP ONE

Get your face ready! Apply foundation and/or concealer as you normally would (or wouldn't). Feel free to leave your eyebrows alone, but if you want to commit 100 percent to this look, use an eyebrow razor to shave off the tails, as I did, or cover the ends of your brows with concealer.

TWO

Draw a winged line from the outer corners of your eyes up toward your temples with the red liner.

THREE

With that same eyeliner, roughly fill in the outer half of your eyelid, which is where the same color of eye shadow is going to go. This will make the color bolder. Do the same on the inner half with the gold liner. Don't worry about blending just yet!

FOUR

Sweep the red shadow from the middle of your eye up toward your temple, covering the red liner on your lid.

FIVE

Add the gold eye shadow to the inner corners of your upper-eye area.

SIX

Blend the edges between the colors with your eye shadow brush.

SEVEN

Apply a light color of your choosing, like pearl pink or a soft gold, under your brow and in the corner of your eye as a highlight. Blend it with the rest of your eye shadow using a little bit of your gold (and/or orange) shadow.

As I added more gold, I also added more red, since the shadow I used wasn't super-opaque on my skin. If at any point while you're blending, you notice one color is getting lost in the mix, just go back in and add more until you're happy!

EIGHT

With the black eyeliner, trace a medium-thick outline along your upper lash line. Don't make it *too* thick—you don't want to cover up your eye shadow!

NINE

Add a little bit of eyeliner to your waterline. (I initially forgot to do this step, which is why my makeup looks a little different here, but here's where it should go in this process!) Line your lower lash line with the red liner.

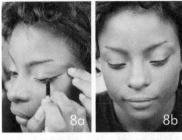

TEN

Apply mascara to your upper and lower lashes.

ELEVEN

With the brow powder or pencil (or just some black eyeliner), gently draw straight lines along the bottoms of your eyebrows, angling them up slightly at the ends. (Don't make them too angled or you'll look angry.)

TWELVE

Fill in your brows, being careful to end them in a point. Think of the finished product as a very slender triangle.

THIRTEEN

Now the easiest part of the look: the lips! Prime them with lip liner, then go over that with your lipstick of choice.

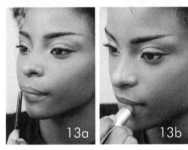

FOURTEEN

Now you're going to do a makeup trick exactly like one the Empress uses in the movie: Gently press your finger into a bit of gold shadow. Apply it to the middle of your lips and blend it subtly outward as you contemplate your plans to usurp your husband's throne…or whatever it is you're looking to conquer!

FIFTEEN

For extra drama and color, apply blush to your cheekbones. Follow the direction of your eye makeup, sweeping it upward toward your temples.

SIXTEEN

And that's your final look! Now go prepare your armies and take the world by storm, your Highness.

HIGH LIFE, LOW BUDGET

1. PARTY – BEYONCÉ (FEAT. ANDRE 3000, KANYE WEST + J. COLE)
2. ROLLIN' WITH MY HOMIES – COOLIO
3. CLUB ACTION – YO MAJESTY
4. OH – CIARA (FEAT. LUDACRIS)
5. THIS IS HOW WE DO IT – MONTELL JORDAN
6. DANCE – ESG
7. FUN – SLY & THE FAMILY STONE
8. TEENAGE GIRLS – BAD SPORTS
9. FUNSPOT – AUDACITY
10. CASE RACE – MEAN JEANS
11. LET US PLAY YOUR PARTY – THE SPITS
12. I WANNA GO HOME – HOLLY & THE ITALIANS
13. WHIPS & FURS – THE VIBRATORS
14. LOW BUDGET – THE KINKS
15. SATURDAY NIGHT BLUES – NATURAL CHILD

WHO WILL SURVIVE IN AMERICA: A KANYE ROUNDTABLE

In which we talk about everything Yeezy's taught us.
By Brodie. Illustration by Ruby A.

I'm willing to bet that you already have an opinion on Kanye West. He's maybe the most divisive celebrity around—he's called an egomaniac about as often as he is a genius, and everyone I know has different reasons for either loving or hating him. My own feelings about Kanye are EXTREMELY POSITIVE—his music is one of my failsafe tools for self-care, and I have a different track to suit every feeling ("Monster" when I need to rage out, "Clique" when I'm super excited, "Lost in the World" when I need to believe in love). Kanye is so much more than a performer—he's also a consumer of, and groundbreaking commentator on, lots of areas of modern culture. I consider his interviews academic texts that should be studied as key reference points about art, fashion, race, fame, architecture, film, technology, and music, all of which he speaks about

frequently and brilliantly. There are *so many things* Kanye cares about, and he wants the world to care with him.

That list includes himself, which, depending on your attitude, is totally awesome or really off-putting. I was recently talking about Kanye with my fellow Rookies Jenny, Julianne, and Amy Rose, and we discovered we're all on the "awesome" side of that divide. We agreed that what people take as Kanye's arrogance is really just confidence, and wished we could talk about this to the WORLD. Then we were like, duh, we *can*! So we had this Very Official Roundtable about our love of 'Ye. No matter what your feelings are about Kanye West, I hope you'll come away feeling less "Bound 2" the criticisms you might have of him! OK, sorry, that was terrible. But we learned a lot from one another, and hopefully you'll appreciate this discussion, too.

Jenny started the conversation by talking about how Kanye's rap career blew up in late 2002 after he was almost killed in a car accident. His jaw was fractured in three places, and he was forced to take time off to recover. Before that, he was known as a producer (he worked with Jay Z and Beanie Sigel, among others), but not as a rapper or a performer. He used his recuperation period to make something of his own, and the result was "Through the Wire," which he performed *literally* through the wire that was holding his injured jaw shut. The song's video starts with a title card that reads:

Last October, Grammy-nominated producer KANYE WEST was in a nearly fatal car accident. His jaw was fractured in three places. Two weeks later, he recorded this song with his mouth still wired shut…so the world could feel his pain!

That paragraph was what made Jenny a fan: "It was so ridiculous and childlike in a way, and yet so urgent and moving," she said during our discussion. "What an exquisite thing to have escaped death and then, while you're still recovering from having nearly died, wanting to make a song, and then actually recording that song, and *then* wanting everyone to experience that feeling of getting to live and make things." The song, she pointed out, "exemplifies everything we love about Kanye: his total unwillingness to peddle in false humility, his big ambitions, how he's both his own harshest critic and his biggest supporter, his SUPREME EXQUISITE TASTE, his rather large capacity to laugh at and make fun of himself (as long you're laughing with him, NOT at him), his self-awareness, and his vulnerability."

Critics love to call Kanye an egomaniac, but there's something very positive and powerful about believing in the art you've created. When Spike Jonze interviewed him for *Vice* in 2007, Kanye said, "The bottom line is…I'm a fan of really great stuff. So, you know, by the fact that I'm really great, by default I'm a fan of myself." Later in the same interview, he elaborated on that notion:

I'm not supposed to say how great [my work] is. Somebody's supposed to come in and be like, "Aw, man, that is just the craziest shit I saw in my life!" and I'm [supposed to] be like, "Oh, do you think so? For real?" That's ignorant! Actually, that's disrespectful to the person who just said it. That's me acting stupid, like I didn't know it was good. […] What my grandfather told me to say is, "You got good taste!"

"It took a while for all that to sink in, but it's really inspiring," Jenny said. "I always find a way to lessen my achievement; I fail to show other people that I'm proud of my work, even though that's why

I share it in the first place. There's something so radical and simple about taking pride in what you do."

As girls, we know how heavy the pressure is to be humble and modest about our achievements and to not take up too much space. People of color experience that same kind of pressure (and for women of color it's at least twofold). Kanye knows that people want him to act eternally grateful for being allowed entrance to the club of Black People That White People Care About (Sometimes), but he chooses instead to have confidence in his craft, to appreciate its worth, and to make sure everyone else sees it too. As Julianne puts it, a lot of the criticism lobbed at Kanye after every public interview he does "comes from people not wanting to see a black man who won't shut up, and who prominently displays his ego (which, frankly, is pretty commensurate with his talent). These are things that white men do all day long without ever having to field the vitriol that Yeezy does."

He's also unafraid to call out racism. Maybe you've seen the video from a 2005 fundraiser for victims of Hurricane Katrina. Kanye was scheduled as a speaker and given some prepared lines to read alongside the actor Mike Myers. Kanye went totally and unexpectedly off-script, making a desperate and emotional plea on behalf of the hurricane's neglected survivors, most of them people of color. He also called out the media for their unfair portrayal of the black families who lost their homes, and added, as Myers stared straight ahead like a deer in headlights, "George Bush doesn't care about black people."

"I felt so much solidarity with that moment," said Jenny. "It is so rare to see a person of color insist on speaking what is in his heart—and being heard."

Julianne agreed: "It was beautiful, and I think allowed a real psychic release for our collective feeling of helplessness and despair during that time." And Amy Rose added:

Kanye refused to soften a plain-long truth about racism which was perpetuated on an enormous

scale and *ruined people's lives*, and he was vilified and portrayed as "out of control" by certain parts of white America simply for pointing out that injustice. Like, "Look at this crazy black man pulling THA RACE CARD!" (Which, by the way, is not a real thing.) But he was *totally right*. It's so telling that people dig their heels in against Kanye most mulishly when he refuses to pretend that racism isn't REPUGNANT AND FUCKING EVERYWHERE—it was a similar deal with people's reactions to his stage invasion at the VMAs.

The "invasion" Amy Rose was referring to was, of course, the 2009 Video Music Awards on MTV, where a very drunk Kanye charged the stage during Taylor Swift's acceptance speech for best "female video," snatched the mic from her, and announced that Beyoncé's "Single Ladies (Put a Ring on It)" should have won instead.

This was undoubtedly a jerk move, but Julianne pointed out that it "was motivated by the idea that MTV was boxing out a black woman because of her race," a notion that Kanye later, albeit unwittingly, confirmed when secretly recorded audio of a rant he delivered later that night was leaked to the press. "There ain't gonna be no more motherfucking Elvises with no James Browns," he says on that recording.

After the scandal, he apologized repeatedly to Taylor for ruining her moment and implicating her in a much larger societal problem that she had no personal hand in perpetuating, but the damage to his reputation was done. He was dressed down by the tabloids, Swifties, and even President Obama, who called Kanye a "jackass." So intense was the national disapproval of Kanye that he left the country for nearly a year.

Those two moments put him squarely at the top of the world's collective shit list, but the aftermath turned out to affect his life in a hugely positive way. As he said in an interview (KDWB radio) a year after the debacle, the experience of losing so many things he'd worked so hard to get—record deals, the respect of his peers, mainstream cultural acceptance—freed him up to do his most honest work:

> Because of everything that I been through, it's got me to the point to be able to be a way more expressive artist, to deal with way more reality. You can't take anything away from me at this point. I completely lost everything, but I gained everything, 'cause I lost the fear.

There wasn't much he could do placate a public who already saw him as "crazy," so he stopped trying to temper his views in his music, about racism or anything else. The next album he made, 2013's *Yeezus*, is arguably his most powerful work yet. Inspired as much by architecture, furniture design, and industrial production techniques as it was by 1980s house music, the record feels like a protest by way of fine art. On songs like "New Slaves," "Blood on the Leaves," "Black Skinhead," and "Bound 2," Kanye directly and unapologetically tells listeners what his experiences have been as a black man in America, ripping into the racism he and so many others continue to face, no matter how much they achieve.

"I'm SO INTO THE FACT that Kanye used the super-commercial medium of 'a Kanye West record' to deliver this very smart, vicious racial theory to THE MASSES. To me, that was such an incredibly noble and populist act," Amy Rose said about this album. "When I saw him live a few months ago, he was so clearly in love with his fans and wanted us to have the TRUTH: that the world really IS a very frequently fucked-up place for people of color, and that the people who try to make you believe otherwise are the ones who are in the wrong. [That message] absolutely shines in his newest songs."

That show was part of Kanye's "Yeezus" tour, which was as artistically wide-ranging as the album it supported. The per-

formances were more like abstract theater pieces than rap concerts: The set featured a 60-foot-wide circular screen mimicking a view of the heavens, a giant mountain that turns into a volcano, an actor playing Jesus (not even kidding), dozens of classically trained dancers, and plenty of elaborate costumes. Amy Rose reported: "When I saw him, he cited the filmmaker Alejandro Jodorowsky's influence on the set, alluded to Biblical scripture and Greek drama, and performed lengthy monologues on the nature of fame, individuality, and personal freedom. I spent the whole show feeling like I had been punched in the gut in the best possible way."

Not that any of this shielded Kanye from public scrutiny—in fact, everything he does seems designed to simultaneously silence his past critics and invite new ones. At one stop on the "Yeezus" tour, an audience member was kicked out for interrupting a ballad to yell, "Take that shit off!"—"that shit" being one of the jewel-encrusted Maison Martin Margiela masks the rapper wore over his face for the first two hours of the show. Kanye stopped the show and spit back, "You can see my face on the internet every motherfucking day. I came here, I opened up a *mountain…* and you tryin' to tell me how to give you my art?"

He's been an artist for most of his life. As he told the director Steve McQueen in *Interview* back in January:

> I'm a trained fine artist. I went to art school from the time I was five years old. I was, like, a prodigy out of Chicago. I'd been in national competitions from the age of 14. […] So the joke that I've actually played on everyone is that the entire time, I've actually just been a fine artist.

His melding of aesthetic and musical innovation is what's made his work so consistently game-changing. It's clear that he's committed to perpetually seeking out new ways to communicate his creativity, which is what makes it ill-informed and, yes, bigoted, to discount him as anything

less than an artist. When people say Kanye is "ranting," they should step back and think about what it might feel like to have spent your whole life painstakingly honing a craft and to have created a body of work that draws in all of your life experiences and artistic obsessions and offered it to the world, only to be told, "You're a rapper! You can't do that!" Kanye's confidence is not cockiness for its own sake; it's a necessary weapon in his battle against his critics and his own insecurities. He needs to yell louder than the people who are telling him he's doomed to fail, or their voices will drown out his own.

This was painfully apparent after the *Jimmy Kimmel Show* "parodied" a serious, highbrow interview Kanye did with Zane Lowe on BBC Radio in 2013, in which 'Ye thoughtfully discussed his artistic inspirations and goals—by replacing the men with child actors who repeated their conversation verbatim. The skit reminded many viewers—Kanye included—of the not-so-distant past wherein African-American entertainers were cast almost exclusively as cartoonish, dim-witted punch lines for white people to laugh at and/or denigrate. I don't believe Jimmy Kimmel had vitriolic intent nor even fully understood why what he was doing was so racially fraught, but that doesn't excuse the segment, which embodied the way white men have traditionally asserted their dominance over people of color.

One of my favorite writers and pop culture commentators, Ayesha A. Siddiqi, eloquently articulated the anger and frustration so many people felt about the segment in a series of tweets at the time:

> One thing White America can't abide is a POC who takes themselves seriously. […] That's why Kanye means so much to so many people, he refuses to respect the message of "know your place." […] White artists are never lampooned for believing in themselves the way Kanye constantly is. […] We're told: creative, confident, person of color #picktwo

None of this is to say there aren't valid criticisms to be made of Yeezy's work. As both a fan of his music and a proud feminist, I'm often caught in the moral tug-of-war of trying to either justify the incredible elements of his work to overcompensate for the misogynistic ones—or avoid thinking about them altogether because Kanye has been such a positive force in my life and the world. But the sexist aspects of his work do exist, as much as I wish they didn't.

Amy Rose also falls in the "die-hard but conflicted fan" category:

My feelings about Kanye and women are, by and large, NOT GR8, but that's obviously mad complex when I think about his intense bond with his late mom, the concept of white women as status symbols, etc. While I adore him, I sometimes still feel queasy about the sexist moments in his work. To illustrate: The "Yeezus" tour was seriously the best show I've ever been to, but I was really distraught over the fact that he made his female dancers wear face-concealing masks and put them in sheer bodysuits so they appeared naked, effectively erasing them as actual people, reducing them to objectified bodies—and then USING THEM AS A THRONE. He literally *sat on them* like they were nothing more than inanimate furniture to him.

Kanye is not perfect, and, as a fan, it's important to acknowledge that. If Kimmel had questioned Kanye's repeated use of the term *bitches* on *Yeezus* after 'Ye had openly questioned the usage of that word just a year earlier, I could've been on board with his lampooning. But putting his very valid points in the mouth of a child with a sippy cup…*not so much.*

When it comes to Kanye's social politics, it's helpful to consider the culture in which he exists as an artist and person. Jenny brought up how intensely conflict-ing it can be for someone like Kanye to navigate the media as the hero of the story he's telling:

Kanye came from a middle-class background and went to art school, and I actually kind of think his relative class/economic privilege adds to people thinking he's arrogant. It's like people wanna see black and brown kids from low-income neighborhoods overcome hardship to show determination and pride. They don't wanna see it from a black nerd with a good education who doesn't have a heart-wrenching story of poverty. Without that crucial element of pity, black ambition becomes "excessive," "crazy," and "delusional."

"That's why white-savior movies like *The Blind Side* win Oscars," said Julianne. "And the only nominations for movies about people of color are things like *Slumdog Millionaire*, which uphold this narrative of poor, sad, helpless POCt on the UPLIFTING COME-UP (often via whitefolx). White people benefit from reinforcing their class privilege, in culture and IRL." We as a culture can't create a pity-based narrative about a man who releases an album called *Yeezus* that includes a track called "I Am a God," so what can we do with him? We ask him, "Who do you think you are to call yourself that?" and tell him he has no right to such confidence. Kanye addressed this idea in the interview with Lowe:

Would it have been better if I had a song that said, "I am a n***a?" Or if I had a song that said, "I am a gangster?" Or if I had a song that said, "I am a pimp?" All those colors and patinas fit better on a person like me, right? But to say you are a god, especially when you got shipped over to the country that you're in, and your last name is a slave owner's—how could you say that? How could you have that mentality?

Kanye speaks up for himself because he knows he's worthy of inclusion among the ranks of musical artists. But there's still one creative medium he's barred from, despite working tirelessly at it for almost the entirety of his public music career: fashion. No matter how loud he knocks, the high-fashion community refuses to open the door and let him in; his aspiration to design clothing is perhaps the most laughed-at element of his endlessly ridiculed public persona. As he told Lowe:

I am so frustrated. I've got so much I want to give. I've got ideas on color palettes, ideas on silhouettes, and I've got a million people telling me why I can't do it, that I'm not a real designer. I'm not a real rapper either. I'm not a real musician either.

Kanye is clearly not afraid to bring high art to populist products like music videos and album artwork; fashion is just another way to put his specific, genius stamp on accessible art. But, as he said in a Sirius Radio interview, Sway in the Morning, 2013, this is seen as distasteful, and even shameful, coming from a rapper:

[When you're] trying to learn about clothing, you got the whole hood calling you a f** for even liking clothes or being at the runway shows. […] then you got your constant public perception being brought down. […] Then you got shoes like the Nikes [that Kanye designed] selling at $80,000, and the head [of Nike] won't even get on the phone with you. […] You got every single door closed on you.

This is not a request for pity—it's a demand to be treated with the same respect as other people of his stature, regardless of his race or his main profession. In addition to his wildly successful

Nike designs, Kanye has collaborated on two collections with the French label A.P.C., designed shoes for Louis Vuitton, Bape, and Giuseppe Zanotti, and has a collaboration planned with Adidas. And that's all in addition to the two collections he showed at Paris Fashion Week in 2011 and 2012. If any other person—celebrity or not—had a résumé like that, there would be no question as to whether they "deserved" their own line. But the rules are different for Kanye.

"I think this is in part because he's a person whose work is of enormous cultural importance to poor people and people of color," Amy Rose said, "and he isn't afraid to openly discuss his feelings on race and class politics in America—two things the notoriously racist and wealth-motivated fashion industry might not appreciate."

Despite this disrespectful treatment, Kanye remains an impassioned fashion fan. Here's Julianne:

> One of my favorite moments this year was watching Kanye perform at Madison Square Garden, where he digressed into an angry monologue about the recently appointed creative head of Yves Saint Laurent, Hedi Slimane, and how he was still mad that "Hedi" had tried to ban him from seeing the shows of "Phoebe" [Philo, of Céline] and "Raf" [Simons, of Dior] at Paris Fashion Week. Just as I was thinking, *Like 350 people in this 20,000-person arena even know what the hell he's talking about!*, my friend, who was in a different row, texted me, "What is he talking about?" But Kanye just wants everyone to be on his level, and that level is excellence.

At the end of their interview, after Kanye had spent AN HOUR bringing every question around to fashion, Lowe asked him why he'd want to spend (read: waste) his time pursuing clothing design, when he could be doing things that people would perceive as more "important."

Without any hesitation, Kanye responded: "You can't tell me what dreams to have." That made me cry the first time I heard it, because it felt like the summation of all his life's work: Everything he's ever done, he's achieved in spite of people telling him there was something better or different or more "right" for him, and this is exactly what makes him the brilliant, innovative, and globally adored artist he is today.

That particular interview is also great because Kanye dedicated himself not only to advocating for and defending himself and his dreams, but also to professing a similarly deep respect and understanding for his listeners, reiterating what he's been saying for years—that his work and career is really not all about him, but about all of us:

> Go listen to all my music. It's the codes of self-esteem. It's the codes of who you are. If you're a Kanye West fan, you're not a fan of me, you're a fan of yourself. You will believe in yourself. I'm just the espresso. I'm just the shot in the morning to get you going, to make you believe you can overcome the situation that you're dealing with all the time.
> [...]
> I've always felt I can do anything. That's the main thing people are controlled by: thoughts, the perceptions of themselves. They're slowed down by the perception of themselves. If you're taught you can't do anything, you won't do anything. I was taught I could do everything, and I'm *Kanye West* at age 36. So just watch the next 10 years.

Kanye inspires creativity and reminds us that we have something important to say, no matter how we choose to say it. And when I say "us," I'm including Kanye himself. He needs that reminder to continue speaking his truth to power, even if the consequences might include being excluded from some music industry events or Fashion Weeks. His work gives voice to people without a platform, people too

scared or quiet to speak for themselves. As Amy Rose remembered:

> When I saw him perform, the number one message he had for the audience was to trust our convictions, and it came across as genuine and heartfelt, not self-help-y—I have a very low tolerance for "motivational" speeches. After a 15-minute monologue about disregarding anyone who tries to shut you down, he finished by saying, "The truth is inside you, and it always has been." He was crying, and so was I—that bond between Kanye and the audience was like nothing I have ever felt, for real, because his belief in himself and in all of us was so palpable.

That's the root of this conversation, really: It's not just about *Kanye West, the person*, and it's not just about the music or the clothes or the album art. It's about pushing yourself to think harder—to *be better*—and to give your creations to the world and hope they follow that example and do the same. As Amy Rose said, this is the truth at the heart of Kanye's message. I'm so glad he's never stopped challenging expectations in pursuit of his dreams, because his dogged insistence on seeing his artistic vision through has given the rest of us a new creative standard to aspire to, an ideal about which we can all say with certainty, "Yeezy taught me." ☺

THE GILDED AGE

Sequins and solitude.
By Petra.
Styling by L...

Thanks to India for modeling, and to Mary Katrantzou and Vans for lending us clothes and shoes.

Violet, Blue,
Violet, Dame,
Violet, Sweet,
Violet Yellow,
Virginia Creeper,
Virgin's Bower,
Volkmannia,

W Wallnut,
Wall-Flower,
Water Lily,
Water Melon,
Wax Plant,
Weigela,
Wheat Stalk,
Whin, ... Anger.
White Jasmine, ... Amiability.

Z Zephyr Flower, ... Expectation.
Zinnia, ... Thoughts of absent friends.

~ FINIS ~

Design by Sonja. Watercolor by Brooke Nechvatel.

APRIL 2014: LOST AND FOUND

Happy April, Rookies!

This month's theme is LOST AND FOUND: "me time," self-reflection, creativity. As Rookie staffer Rose sez, "Solitude can be a revolutionary act." And while I sometimes feel that we humans are all deeply connected, I more often agree with what Morrissey sed to Amy Rose when she interviewed him last year: that we are solitary creatures who LIVE AND DIE ALONE. I know it sounds awful, but except on particularly bad days, I don't really find this bleak or depressing. I think it's freeing to realize that you have your own consciousness and can choose whatever you want to include in your world. That you are your own best friend, and can even be your own role model.

Where it starts to get tricky is if you ever feel like your own enemy. You know how people have trouble with breakups because every little thing they see reminds them of their ex? I have often felt that way about myself, where I've been so UTTERLY SICK OF ME that even being in my own room is mortifying because it's like ALL ME, EVERYWHERE. And I can't turn to any of my usual favorite movies or books or any other safety-blanket tools because I've, like, copyrighted them as "central to my identity" or whatever. I can't talk to my friends because they're like, "Welp, I can't *make* you like yourself, but, you know…you're not *that* bad," and I'm like, "BUT YOU ONLY HAVE TO SEE ME DURING OUR LUNCH PERIOD—I HAVE TO LIVE WITH ME ALL THE TIME." I haven't known this feeling for a long time (whaddup @ getting older). I think it happens at the apex of puberty and is heightened when you fully realize for the first time that you have to spend every day of your life with yourself. Your mannerisms, your habits, your face, your ugly laugh. Every hour. Of every day.

I stopped feeling like such a burden on myself by letting go of my aspirations to be (and disappointment when I wasn't) as miraculously confident as Beyoncé or Madonna. Instead, I turned to comedians who have a sense of humor about their own issues, and who use these subjects to access greater human truths and connect with people. See: Tig Notaro's standup act about her mother dying, breaking up with her girlfriend, and being diagnosed with cancer, which is *also* a meditation on using comedy to deal with life's biggest sads. I also started reading writers who choose to look outward and discuss the world, but also use their revelations about art and relationships to access deeper parts of *themselves* in a constructive, interesting way. See: Chris Kraus turning art criticism into a rumination on attraction, feminism, and her experiences with both.

All of this led me to do a lot of my own writing, some to share with people and some to keep just for me. After a day of observing others, returning to myself and marking my perspective on everything and everyone I'd seen, like a dog peeing on a fire hydrant, felt like keeping a terrific secret. I began to understand that even when you write about the world, you are writing about yourself, and that I could either get bashful and worry about seeming like a narcissist, or I could go with it in the hopes of learning more about who I am and how I might come to hate that person less. Somewhere in my blackened heart, I contained multitudes. I'd have to learn to love some and try to change others, but could no longer shut them down altogether with knee-jerk self-loathing.

Not everything I've written was good, but what was important was giving myself the space to let my own complexities unfold, instead of just accepting my "I SUCK" impulses as fact the moment they kick in. Well-written or not, these thoughts were *mine*, and "mine" slowly stopped feeling watermarked with innate horribleness. Having to be alone—for a walk to school or for the rest of my life—no longer filled me with dread and fear; it became an opportunity to experience the world in a different way, like rewatching a mind-blowing movie to try to actually *understand* it. Eventually, I *loved* being in my room alone, surrounded by everything that formed who I am, and I gained the Beyoncé/Madonna-levels of confidence that I feel today. (*In an infomercial voice:* "Thanks, solitude!")

So, this month of Rookie is not necessarily about being all "I DON'T NEED YOU!" as much as it is about the tension between being yourself and being part of the world. (It might be best read from a lighthouse, gazing out at the sea.) Rookie reader Bethany Lamont was the first to urge us to do a kind of melancholy seaside theme, and she summarized most beautifully what it's like to make peace with being alone: "Water does not have to drown you or to trap you; it can lead you to someplace better. The ocean kinda feels like a labored metaphor for the future: cruel, expansive, and unknowable. But it's also awesome in a terrifying sort of way."

love, Tavi

HOW TO BE ALONE

Your favorite person to hang out with could be you.
By Krista. Playlist by Eleanor.

I love being alone. I am *obsessed* with being alone. It's kind of my favorite way to spend my time. I mean, I love hanging out with my friends and my girlfriend, but prolonged interaction can be exhausting, and I need my solo time to recharge after socializing.

I know that many of you can't relate to this—for lots of people, interaction is energizing, not energy-depleting. If you are one of those people, that's great! But at some point, maybe even right this second, you may find yourself completely on your own, and when it happens, I want you to *enjoy* it.

Over the years, I have happily and voluntarily spent *vast* amounts of time by myself, and by now I am an expert on the subject—a true artiste when it comes to solitary pursuits. Being alone is no big deal! It is part of the human experience! It can actually be really helpful, and even enhance the time you spend with other humans. You can not only get through it, but truly like it!

The first step to being happy alone is to realize that you're a cool person to hang out with, and that the things you like to do are fun because they're fun for *you*. (And really, who else's opinion counts when you're alone?)

Getting comfortable with your own company is partly an exercise in figuring out what *you* actually *want* to do when no one is asking you to compromise, whether that means sleeping in, watching movies, going on long bike rides in new neighborhoods, or building elaborate machines that fry up breakfast for you. If it makes you happy, it's an acceptable thing to do when you're alone. The end.

The next step in learning how to be alone is to practice. You don't learn all the words to Beyoncé's "Countdown" well enough to lip-synch to it the first or second time you hear it; most people who are new to hanging out by themselves aren't instantly masters of that, either. Start

small, by taking a long nature walk by yourself (sans iPod!) or going to a coffee shop without any friends (bring a book or a magazine). Then build up to bigger things, like eating at a restaurant (again, reading material is crucial) or a concert without your pals.

The good news about practicing being alone is that there are ENDLESS activities that can be accomplished in the company of one's own baddest self. Here are some I'd particularly recommend:

• Watching every single movie a director you like has ever made—or reading every book a favorite author has written—in chronological order.

• Repeatedly watching a single cult classic movie, like *Mean Girls*, *Labyrinth*, *The Craft*, or *Clueless*, until you can flawlessly (and impressively) recite lines from memory.

• Getting sucked into a show (or several) that people reference all the time—like *Strangers With Candy*, *Bob's Burgers*, *Twin Peaks*, *The Simpsons*, or *Arrested Development*—but that you've never seen.

• Going to a movie alone. It is so freeing to watch a film and have the space to think your own thoughts about it instead of repeatedly glancing at a friend's face to see what *they* think.

• Rereading a book with a character you have a crush on (for me, it's Brett in *The Sun Also Rises*) and then spending an alone day emulating her/him. Wear an outfit you think this person would wear, and try doing some of the things they would do, whether that means

laughing airily in a store at something the cashier says, arching an eyebrow at someone instead of answering them, or calling everyone "darling" in a breathy voice. You get the idea.

• Deciding on a new karaoke jam and practicing it to perfection, complete with dance moves, so you'll have it ready to pull out and astonish people with on a moment's notice.

• Sitting alone in a café to watch people and eavesdrop on their conversations.

• Going to an art museum and noticing the art you're drawn to, as well as the art that puts you off, and thinking about why. (Visiting a museum alone is the best way to do it, IMHO, because then you don't have to get dragged through exhibits someone else is excited about; you're free to head straight to the Impressionist paintings or modern photography or sculpture gardens immediately, no compromises or pathways through medieval sword scabbards required.)

If you are committed to the practice of being alone, you can actually run through this list pretty quickly. So what's next? It's time to acquire and maintain an obsessive hobby. Ohhhhh yes. There are so many obsessive hobbies to choose from! Journaling. Blogging or collaging. Photography, sewing, painting, pen-pal-ing, yarn-bombing, or collecting incredibly specific things like vintage cookbooks with luridly colored, gross-looking pictures of weird food. Whatever your obsessive hobby is, make it your private thing you only do with you. I shall now disclose some of the hobbies I engage in only when I'm with me, myself, and I, including:

- Photographing my two pet bunnies with props and costumes.

- Thrifting for said props and costumes.

- Collecting terrible lesbian erotica books from the '70s and '80s.

- Going to Sephora with Luca Turin and Tania Sanchez's book *Perfumes: The A–Z Guide* and smelling all the perfumes they either love or hate.

- Perfecting my pedicure art. (My greatest *feet* [hardee har har] has been a tiny emoji on each toe.)

- Watching *Hoarders* and then going on a decluttering bender in my apartment.

- Sending postcards to my mom.

- Walking through my neighborhood and looking for a baby robin that's fallen out of its nest but still needs love and wants to be my pet, trained robin. (I've never been successful, but I will keep trying until the day I die.)

- Searching for delightful tiny objects such as puffy rainbow stickers and plastic charms from vending machines to include in care packages for friends.

- Watching YouTube makeup tutorials for extreme looks and trying to copy them.

- Writing poetry in a particular coffee shop I go to only when I'm by myself.

The list goes on. If you haven't found your own hobby yet, there are just so many waiting to be obsessed over, all on your own time.

Sometimes, when you're really stressed out, the best way to use your alone time is by practicing Extreme Self-Care. Extreme Self-Care is when you dedicate a chunk of time to pampering and fussing over yourself. It's like a solo spa night, but dramatically amplified. It can be done after something traumatic, like a breakup or a horrible day; when you're feeling blue; or just because you think you're great and want to spend some more time with you. On my ESC nights, I turn off my phone and hide my computer, and then I run myself the most lavish, bubbly bubble bath possible. While the tub is running, I pour an icy drink into a fancy glass (it must be a fancy glass) and then apply this bright-green face mask I have that's supposed to tighten pores but actually doesn't do anything except get me into character for Extreme Self-Care. When the bath is ready, I light some candles around it, put on a record (usually something high on drama, like the opera *Carmen*) and turn the volume *way* up. Then I get in the tub, where I soak for ages and do full-body exfoliation with scrubby gloves, all

while the opera wails in the background. When I get out of the bathtub, I zip myself into my beautiful fleecy Forever Lazy pajamas (they have a zippered butt and crotch so you can go to the bathroom *without ever having to take them off*), pad into the kitchen, and make an enormous toasty sandwich before retreating to my bed to watch whatever mindless reality show captures my fancy that night (I just discovered *My Cat From Hell*).

The point here is lavishness and drama, darlings. Extreme Self-Care is all about making yourself feel *immediately* bet-ter in a *big* way, and taking gleeful pleasure in something that you, and only you, want to do. *Revel* in your alone time. Spoil yourself with how much you love you.

The thing about being alone is that it doesn't have to include feeling *lonely*. Doing active, productive, fun, and/or indulgent stuff by yourself can actually stave off loneliness. Getting to know yourself when you're by yourself will also help you identify those moments when you *do* feel isolated and sad, and need to reach out to other people for help and companionship—which is another act of Extreme Self-Care.

I know it can feel like *now* will never end, but it is entirely possible that you won't have this much time to yourself again for a long time. When you're alone, think about it as a non-permanent, yet still important, part of your life that is shaping who you are as a person. And even in the shorter term—almost nothing is more satisfying than realizing you had an amazing day, all by yourself. ✎

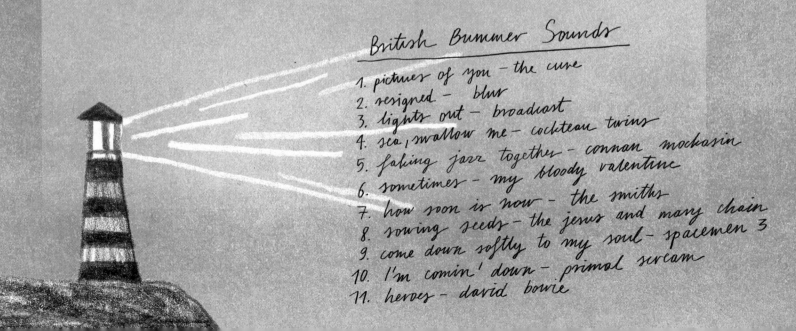

British Bummer Sounds

1. pictures of you – the cure
2. resigned – blur
3. lights out – broadcast
4. sea, swallow me – cocteau twins
5. faking jazz together – connan mockasin
6. sometimes – my bloody valentine
7. how soon is now – the smiths
8. sowing seeds – the jesus and mary chain
9. come down softly to my soul – spacemen 3
10. I'm comin' down – primal scream
11. heroes – david bowie

ALL RIGHT HIDING

Pencil in some quality time with yourself. By Shriya
Thanks to Fatema for modeling.

I NEEDED TO SEE A REFLECTION OF MYSELF:
AN INTERVIEW WITH ALISON BECHDEL

One of our favorite cartoonists sheds some light on storytelling, movie watching, and Harriet the Spy.
By Brodie

Alison Bechdel is a cartoonist, author, and, it must be said, total hero. Over the course of her career, she's dedicated herself to asking the wider culture for more dynamic representations of women in books, comics, and film, and to providing them herself. In 1987 she started publishing her landmark comic strip *Dykes to Watch Out For*, which ran in newpapers nationwide for nearly 20 years—chances are, you've heard of the "Bechdel Test," which gauges the visibility and realism of female characters in movies and is based on a *DTWOF* strip she wrote more than 30 years ago. In the past decade, Bechdel has also written two graphic memoirs about her relationships with her parents: *Fun Home*, published in 2006, and *Are You My Mother?* (2012).

She said during a talk she gave in Melbourne last month, "Telling the truth has always been a compulsion to me." You can tell when you look at her work, whether she's telling the truth about her queer friends' lives in the 1980s and '90s or about the family secrets that dominated her childhood. She graciously spoke to us about how, when she realized she couldn't find honest representations of herself and people like her in the media, she decided to create them herself.

BRODIE What inspired you to become a cartoonist?

ALISON BECHDEL We're all cartoonists at the beginning. Like, all children draw. But most people stop telling stories with pictures [eventually]. So for me, it's not really why I became a cartoonist; it's why did I not ever stop?

Did you tell people, when you were very young, that you wanted to become a professional cartoonist?

Yeah, I did, until I was 13 or 14 and people started discouraging me by saying, "Oh, you know, there aren't very many openings for cartoonists. There are the comic strips in the newspapers, and none of those people ever die, so you won't be likely to get a job."

And it's like, "Why don't you study business? Just in case!"

Or dentistry.

You went to Oberlin College—what did you study there?

I majored in art, but I was thinking I would go into graphic design or book design—something practical like that.

Is there something now, that, looking back, you wish you'd studied or learned more about earlier in your life?

Huh. [*Super-long pause*] No. Stuff has worked out pretty well for me in terms of knowing what I need to know, when I need to know it.

What were you doing, life-wise, when you started drawing *Dykes to Watch Out For*?

I was just out of college, and I had given up on the idea of being a cartoonist. I started drawing [*DTWOF*] just for fun. I wasn't thinking about it as any kind of serious, professional effort; I was drawing cartoons about lesbians for me and my friends because I didn't see images of people like us out in the world, and I felt like I needed to see a reflection of myself.

How did it turn into a published comic strip?

I was showing it to my friends; at the time I was also volunteering at a feminist newspaper. Someone said, "Why don't you put some of these in the newspaper?" So I did, and then I got a wider readership. It was still just for fun; I wasn't getting paid for it. But once I got it in the newspaper, I had to keep doing the strip every month, and that was really great practice. Finally, after two years of doing that, I started submitting the cartoons to other newspapers and charging money for it and I started to syndicate myself.

Did you ever have someone that you asked for advice before you worked it all out?

Not at the very beginning. I've always been kind of a loner; I always think I have to figure everything out on my own. That's something I *would* tell someone starting out: Ask people for advice.

I don't know if I'm a great person to give advice to young people on how to get started, because things have changed so much! Like, there aren't print newspapers the way there used to be when I was in my 20s; it's a very different landscape. It's much more internet-based now, and there are many more opportunities I know nothing about. But the principles of getting your work out there and not being afraid to give it away in the beginning—all of that is still true.

Fun Home **brought your work to a wider audience. What was that first bit of mainstream success like, after you'd spent years working on a niche comic strip?**

It took a while for what that meant to sink in, and I'm *still* adjusting to it. I'm used to being the underdog, you know? When I was doing *Dykes to Watch Out For*, I was the outsider, fighting for inclusion. And then, one day, they just opened the door and…included me! And it was disorienting, like, *Oh! Now what?*

It's been amazing, and one especially great thing about it, for me, has been that my *Dykes to Watch Out For* comics are taken seriously now in a way that they weren't when I was doing them. That makes me really happy.

I've heard that you're kind of shy. How do you reconcile that with telling really personal stories in your books?

For some reason, I have this exhibitionistic streak, even though I'm a pretty shy person. My autobiographical work is the way I connect with other people. I don't necessarily do it personally, but through my work, I'm willing to make myself vulnerable.

Sometimes, when I'm writing personal pieces for Rookie, I have to overcome a nagging voice in my head that's saying, *Oh, who'd want to read about me?* Which is something I think a lot of writers, especially female ones, have to come to terms with—saying, "My story matters, and it's as important as anyone else's." Did you have to get over that voice in order to tell your stories?

Yes. I have to get over that every morning when I get out of bed! It's tough, but part of how I manage that problem is, I always try to write about something else in addition to myself. My book about my father was also a book about different writers that my father loved; the book about my mother was also a book about psychoanalysis and how therapy helps us. Personally, if I'm reading someone's memoir, I'm not interested in just the story of their life. Even if it's the most riveting story imaginable, I also want something larger in that story.

When you're working on a book, what does your day look like?

I try really hard to get up and be at my desk as soon as I can every day. Even though I'm a cartoonist, I'm not always drawing; I do a lot of thinking and writing before I put my drawings down, and I write best in the morning. So, an ideal day for me is to write in the morning, like, from eight until one, and then to convert [that work] to drawing. I can draw fine later in the day, and even at night, but my writing brain doesn't stay sharp.

I've read that you work straight into [the image-editing program] Adobe Illustrator. Did you have to take a course to learn how to use that kind of software?

I haven't taken a course, because I feel like I would be overwhelmed by all the millions of possibilities, so I very carefully just learn the stuff that I think will help me. In fact, earlier, when you asked if there was anything I wish I had learned earlier in my career, I was gonna say, "All of this computer stuff!" But Illustrator and Photoshop didn't exist then.

You've said you loved the book *Harriet the Spy* when you were a kid. Why did you appreciate that story so much?

I was just fascinated by Harriet's *notebook*—her impulse to write, her adventures. She was literally spying on people, going up in that dumbwaiter, observing life, and then writing it down. It just seemed like the whole point of life, you know? Here was a kid who wrote about something real.

I think, as a young lesbian, I was also picking up on this heroine as a lesbian character. But, you know, she was a child—there's no way to really say that Harriet is a lesbian. As I got older, I was curious about [the book's author] Louise Fitzhugh, and I eventually found out that, yes, [Fitzhugh] was gay. It was something about [Harriet]…she was not interested in boys, she was not interested in dresses, she had zero interest in the things the girls in the other books I was reading were interested in. I think that's what I was picking up on. Harriet was all about her work.

Over the years, the Bechdel Test, which is based on one of your comics, has become the standard for measuring how women are represented in film. [The "test" measures gender equality in movies according to three criteria: (1) Whether there are at least two women in it, (2) whether those women ever talk to each other, and (3) if their conversation is ever about something other than a man.] I'm wondering if that's a lot of pressure.

It's been confusing to me, because it wasn't like I sat down and said, "Here! I now decree that this is the Bechdel Test!" It somehow just evolved through this network of feminist film students. But, yeah, I feel really proud—what a great legacy! It does feel connected to my work, [which] has been all about creating women characters who are fully human, three-dimensional protagonists. So I like that.

My friend who introduced me to your work told me how affecting it was for him to see your character in *Fun Home*, who, as a college student, sought out gay literature wherever she (you!) could find it. He said it reflected his coming-out experience of trying to find *any* character experiencing something even slightly similar to what he was going through. Do you ever hear from people that one of your works has been *that* text—the book they've searched for that actually relates to their lives?

People have told me that, and it's *so* amazing. You know, I could just die now and feel like I've done something useful. It's funny—when I think back about that chapter, about my own searches—I was reading really depressing things like *The Well of Loneliness* [the 1928 novel by Radclyffe Hall]. It makes me happy to think that I've provided updated alternatives to some of that stuff. It's a huge honor, and a deep delight.

Finally, what have some of the highlights of your career been?

Huh! Gosh…I guess one amazing thing was when *Time* magazine named *Fun Home* their number one book of the year. That was pretty huge—not just "graphic book," but *book*, of the year. That's the pinnacle of my career to date. ඞ

OUR WORLD ALONE

An epistolary meditation on Lorde, Flannery O'Connor, the grotesque, and the ache of being a teenager.
By Tova Benjamin

4/28/2014

Dear Allen,

It's been almost a year since we first met in the corner of that theater in New York City. We had both bought the day-of student tickets and I had a crush on you the moment you sat down next to me. After the play we wandered around the city and pretended we were only excited about the play, and not each other. It had just rained. We sat in Central Park. You asked to see me again, but I was flying home to Chicago the next morning. When I got home, I called you. You answered. We talked. Then, I began writing you emails. I wrote this one back in December, right after your 20th birthday, when you had already forgotten about me.

I found it again recently, just as I'm at the cusp of so many things. In a few weeks I'll turn 20, too. Soon I'll be transferring schools, leaving the city I grew up in, my friends, and everything I know. I'm scared to be at the edge again, and finding this old letter reminded me that there are all kinds of edges to be at.

Now I write to a different boy. His name is Paul. I might have forgotten about you, if not for the emails still saved on my hard drive.

For now,
Tova

12/17/13

Dear Allen,

We still haven't addressed the fact that I send you emails at strange hours—2, 3 AM—without really knowing you. But you still haven't responded to any of them, so I don't bother asking you about it. I just keep sending them. My friends say you probably think I'm crazy. Last night I read *I Love Dick* again, just to feel better about myself, these messages, and your silence. I came across this line: "But loving you'd become a full-time job and I wasn't ready to be unemployed."

I underlined it because it was just your 20th birthday, and for the entire day I was struck with the significance of that. The day felt important, like the birthday of someone I've known intimately. It made me wonder about my own age. About still having "teen" slapped onto the end of my number.

There was another passage from *I Love Dick* that I underlined:

> I feel so teenage. When you're living so intensely in your head you actually believe when something happens you've imagined, that you've caused it. [...] When you're living so intensely in your head there isn't any difference between what you imagine and what actually takes place. Therefore, you're both omnipotent and powerless. [...] [Teenagers are] so far in [their heads] that there's no difference between the insides of their heads and the world.

I've never really strongly identified as a "teen" nor thought about belonging to that particular species until this year, just as I'm almost done being one. I bought Lorde's CD when it came out a few months ago, and I've been listening to it on repeat since. On the way to school, on the way to work, on the way home, while driving in the rain, on my way to a Halloween party with all my friends singing along in the backseat. Lorde and her CD accentuated this teenage identity I've let myself adopt lately, before I let it go forever.

For a while, I didn't bother trying to understand why I like her so much, why it aches to listen to her music, why it haunts me until I turn it on and chase the ghosts away. But lately I've been reading a lot of Flannery O'Connor, the Southern writer whose short stories are filled with complicated characters and gruesome endings, and I'm beginning to understand a bit more.

In Flannery O'Connor's writing, I saw everything I was familiar with but didn't have words for. I became obsessed with how she approaches religion in her stories. I knew she was describing the Deep South, where a stranger might randomly call you a Yankee, but she could have been describing the Hasidic community I grew up in and left. Her characters are self-righteous, complicated, naïve, and so terribly well-meaning. She describes a world filled with well-worn traditions that seem odd to everybody except the people raised with them. She wrote in my language, the language of the grotesque.

When people hear *grotesque* they think of gross, weird, disfigured, ugly, and comically distorted. But *grotesque* can also mean fascinating, fantastical, strange, magical, unusual, eccentric, just plain odd. It's also a way to describe the aspects of life that repulse us, humor us, and make us uneasy all at once. The grotesque takes on forms we are familiar with but distorts them until they start to contradict themselves. O'Connor's short stories speak of things we are familiar with—death, religion, farms—but present them in a way that twists our assumptions and plays with our expectations.

I think this idea of the grotesque accurately describes the world of a teenager, which simultaneously involves itself with the outside world and keeps its distance from it. *When you're living so intensely in your head there isn't any difference between what you imagine and what actually takes place.* This could also be said about the places we can't escape from that also feel like home. I feel this way about my old community. The community that raised me is a large part of my identity and defines me in so many ways. At the same time, I remain completely contradictory to my community. I don't look like them anymore, think like they do, or keep the traditions.

Most days, the world feels overlarge as it teems around me, and I struggle to keep steady and feel relevant within it. I stumble, and feel entirely unbalanced and worthless. On those days I feel powerless, and I am driven by a need to make the world feel bearable and navigable. When we're young children, most of us have people we can trust to tighten our world up so it's nice and small and cozy. But then we get older, and by the time we're teenagers we've realized that *religious* doesn't always mean "good," and that our parents are right about many things, but not everything. Because more things are suddenly possible, the world, as we see it, gets bigger. I remember the first time I saw my parents cry, and how it eventually stopped surprising me to see them cry, to realize they don't know all the answers. And the world got wider. I remember when I went to the psychiatric unit for the first time and realized I wasn't the only one who constantly felt like dying, and that I couldn't always trust authority figures to be looking out for my best interests. It was important that my world grow, but with each of its growth spurts came a feeling of powerlessness, and a consequent urge to grab on to things and draw them near and tighten my world again. When I've drawn my world in to a comfortable size, I feel omnipotent again.

All of this is possibly the reason why teenage romances feel so intense and monumental, because they become the home bases in an otherwise insecure world. I dated my first boyfriend when I was 17, and when we broke up I felt like I was let loose into a big, open world. I was glad to be alone in my own head, but there was something frightening about losing that security. For a long time, his positive opinion of me kept me anchored in a world that shifted unexpectedly. He loved me intensely, completely, and overwhelmingly. It felt special and singular, and it provided me with a cozy and safe world within the bigger world I had learned to mistrust.

The narrator in Flannery O'Connor's short stories seems at once omnipotent and powerless. She critiques each of her characters and almost mercilessly destroys most of them at the end. But throughout the stories there is a feeling that the narrator is no better than the characters she condemns. In writing these letters to you I feel powerful. Here, between these lines, I can create a world where you care about what I have to say. Here, I have created a space for myself within the huge world where I feel as though I have no say. Maybe this is why I keep falling in love with boys who won't answer my letters, because it's a chance to create a world that's small, one that I can steer.

The best way to approach these worlds—the small teenage worlds we create to make life bearable, the Hasidic bubble of Orthodox Jews in West Rogers Park, the farm in the Deep South—is through the language, the art, and the music that engage with them while contradicting them. Through identifying the contradictions and being fascinated and delighted and sickened by them all at once. Through facing them, confronting them, and fusing them, which Flannery O'Connor does in her writing, and Lorde does in her music.

I love Lorde because she participates in the big, outside world, but creates her own small world inside it. This is why her music aches. Why it haunts. Why it feels so right. She is a pop singer whose music and persona contradict how we expect pop to look and sound. She is a teenager who relishes being young but refuses to be patronized. She is a girl who contradicts our conventional ideas about femininity. She sings about being bored with the everyday but also celebrates the beauty of those mundane moments—the driving through tree-streets that are intimate and tight over highways that are fast and long. Listening to her music, you get the feeling that she is participating in these worlds of youth, suburbia, and love, while observing them from afar. She sings about climbing under underpasses and drinking with teens with shiny mouths, then admits that she isn't one of them. Her songs sneak their way into that private place inside me that worries it won't ever truly belong to any world. That private place I think most of us have.

I love Lorde because her lyrics sound like the letters I write but never send. They also sound like the letters I write and then send when I shouldn't. Like this one. Like the six or seven other letters I sent you, filled with the grotesque, contradictory thoughts I'm tired of trying to hide. I love hearing these thoughts play. I love hearing her voice tell me of teenagers whose heads catch on fire; the feeling matches my own bored evenings, sitting in my friend's bathroom, letting her cut my hair because I don't want to feel pretty anymore.

I also love how much Lorde references the body. She gets how odd bodies are, and how nuanced. I like that a song about fear and growing up is called "Ribs." When I listen to it, I feel the ebb and flow of a chest breathing in and out, of a world growing big and small as a teenager grows vulnerable and fearless. It shrinks my world even as it enlarges it.

When I read *I Love Dick* last night to feel less alone, I thought about how glad I am that Lorde is a pop artist. I think connecting with other people, whether it's over music or food or favorite toilet paper brands, is another way to reclaim our worlds when they feel intimidatingly large. She seems to me to be someone who would never want to be inaccessible.

I wonder how you feel about being 20. I wonder if your world gets large and scary and if it breathes threateningly beneath your ribs. Mine does all the time. The more I write to you, the more I like you, and I begin to get better at excusing you.

I hope you'll understand about me not wanting to quit this loving you and missing you and not wanting to change the CD in my car. I hope you'll forgive me for writing so many letters. I hope you'll understand how writing to you shrinks my world too, how knowing you're out there makes me feel less alone, but also hyperaware of my own loneliness. I wish you weren't in another state so that I could see you, but you're also the last person I'd like to see, and I'm embracing these dualities. I will keep dragging out these grotesque parts of life because they're as compelling as they are repulsive, and it's incredibly satisfying to confront them all.

Love,
Tova ✉

A DETAILED ACCOUNT OF AN OBSESSION WITH / PERSONAL EXPERIENCE OF DEATH AND LIFE AND STUFF

by Esme B., 2014

TO MAKE A REALLY LONG STORY STILL VERY LONG BUT A LITTLE SHORTER: SINCE BEFORE I CAN REMEMBER, I'VE HAD AN OVERWHELMING PREOCCUPATION WITH **DEATH**

WHEN I WAS A KID, I'D LIE AWAKE AT NIGHT TRYING TO GET MY HEAD AROUND IT.

BOTH OF MY PARENTS ARE ATHEISTS, SO THE SUBJECT WAS NEVER REALLY SUGAR-COATED IN OUR HOUSEHOLD.

SO YOU MEAN AFTER WE DIE THERE'S JUST NOTHING?!!

≡YAWN≡

'FRAID SO, HONEY.

BUT WHAT ABOUT HEAVEN?!

HEAVEN IS AN IDEA, INVENTED BY PEOPLE WHO ARE AFRAID TO DIE. THERE'S NO SUCH PLACE. NOW GO BACK TO BED, WOULDJA? YOU GOT SCHOOL TOMORRA.

03:15

IT ALSO PROBABLY DOESN'T HELP THAT I COME FROM A FAMILY OF NOTORIOUSLY GLOOMY PEOPLE:

6FT

COUSIN VIGGO
UNCLE PETE
COUSIN KAYE
AUNT CHLÖ
GRANDMA LENORE
GRANDPA ERIK
MY BRO MISTY
MY DAD STOFFER

MEET THE BLEGVADS: MY DEAR LITTLE GANG OF MISERABLE GIANTS.

SO I'VE SPENT A LOT OF TIME BUGGIN' OUT ABOUT STUFF LIKE THE APOCALYPSE...

AND ILLNESS...

I THINK I FEEL SOMETHING

AND VIOLENT DISASTERS

I ATTENDED MY FIRST FUNERAL AT THE AGE OF 8, AND MY FIRST GRANDPARENT DIED WHEN I WAS 13 – BUT DESPITE THIS (AND MY CONSTANT RUMINATIONS ON THE SUBJECT) I NEVER REALLY "GOT" THE REALITY OF MORTALITY UNTIL MY GRANDPA ERIK DIED THE OTHER DAY.

WHEN I WAS A KID I LIKED ERIK OK AS A GRANDFATHER, BUT AS I GOT OLDER WE CAME TO BE VERY GOOD FRIENDS. AFTER MY GRANDMA DIED HE STARTED DOING A LOT LESS, BUT WE HUNG OUT A LOT MORE. I STARTED STOPPING BY HIS HOUSE AFTER SCHOOL TO EAT ICE CREAM AND BITCH ABOUT BOYS.

HE TAUGHT ME TO LOVE SARDINES ON TOAST, JAZZ + CLASSICAL MUSIC, THE SIMPSONS, PIPE TOBACCO, THE TOUR DE FRANCE AND, MOST IMPORTANTLY, DRAWING (HE WAS THE DOPEST ILLUSTRATOR.) IN COLLEGE, I'D HAVE DINNER WITH HIM EVERY FRIDAY, AND ONCE HE GOT A WHEELCHAIR, I'D TAKE HIM OUT TO THE PUB IN THE AFTERNOONS.

... AND THEN HE JUST NEVER CALLED! WADDAYA THINK THAT **MEANS**?!

IT ALL MEANS THE SAME THING: **MEN** ARE **SCUM**. I **KNOW**, 'CAUSE I'M **ONE OF 'EM**. **NONE** OF US CAN BE TRUSTED, AND WE'RE **ALL** **ALWAYS** UP TO **NO GOOD**.

YOU SHOULD **QUIT SMOKING**. IT BOTHERS YOUR MOTHER, AND IT'S **BAD FOR YOU**.

SO SHOULD **YOU**. PIPES ARE WAY WORSE FOR YOU THAN CIGS, Y'KNOW.

YES, BUT I'M **OLD**, AND MY LIFE IS SO **BORING** AND **GLOOMY**. ALL MY FRIENDS ARE **DEAD**, AND I HAVE **NOTHING** TO **DO** ALL DAY... EXCEPT SMOKE THIS **PIPE**.

IN THE LAST YEAR OR SO OF HIS LIFE, ERIK'S HEART STARTED GETTING WEIRD, HE STOPPED DRAWING ALTOGETHER, AND HE BECAME A LOT MORE FRAGILE THAN BEFORE—BUT IT DIDN'T REALLY BOTHER ME. HE STILL GREETED ME WITH THE SAME CHEERFUL YELP OF "HALLO, ESMÈ!!!", HIS EYES STILL TWINKLED, AND HIS WIT STAYED SHARP. HE SPENT A LOT MORE TIME IN BED, BUT THAT SUITED ME FINE—THE SUMMER BEFORE I MOVED TO NEW YORK, I'D RIDE A BIKE TO HIS HOUSE ALMOST EVERY DAY, TO WAKE HIM UP AND HAVE A CHAT. MANY OF OUR CONVERSATIONS FROM THIS TIME WERE, OF COURSE, ABOUT DEATH, WHICH HE WAS ALWAYS HAPPY TO TALK ABOUT.

BUT AREN'T YOU **SCARED TO DIE**?!! I'M **TERRIFIED**!! I THINK ABOUT IT **INCESSANTLY**!!!

WELL, **NO**, BECAUSE THERE ISN'T REALLY ANYTHING TO BE SCARED **OF**... WE **ALL** HAVE TO DIE, YOU KNOW. IT'S JUST A PITY WHEN IT HAPPENS TO OTHER PEOPLE, AND THEN WE HAVE TO LIVE ON, MISSING THEM.... BUT YOU WON'T BE SCARED OF IT FOREVER. IT'S PROBABLY JUST YOUR **AGE**.

MOSTLY I'M SCARED OF **YOU** DYING. YOU'RE SO **OLD** ALL OF A SUDDEN. IT'S GONNA **BLOW**.

OH, YOU'LL **MANAGE**. BUT WHILE WE'RE **ON** THE **SUBJECT**, I LOVE YOU VERY MUCH AND I'M GLAD WE GOT TO KNOW EACH OTHER SO WELL. I'M VERY PROUD THAT YOU'VE DECIDED TO BECOME AN ARTIST, YOU'VE BEEN AN EXCELLENT GRANDCHILD AND I COULDN'T HAVE ASKED FOR BETTER—SO WHEN IT **SNEAKS UP** ON US, KNOW THAT I'LL BE DYING **HAPPY**, YES?! NOW, STOP YOUR **BELLYACHING**, AND GO FETCH YOUR OLD GRANDPA A **CUP OF TEA**, HHMMM?

THE NIGHT BEFORE I MOVED TO NYC, I WAS LIKE:

I'LL BE BACK IN A YEAR. PLEASE TRY AND STAY ALIVE UNTIL I GET BACK, OK?!

I FULLY INTEND TO BE EXACTLY WHERE YOU LEFT ME... BUT LET'S JUST SEE HOW IT GOES.

FOR THE FIRST FOUR MONTHS, I SENT POSTCARDS AND CALLED WHENEVER I COULD. EVERYTHING SEEMED COOL UNTIL CHRISTMAS, WHEN I SUDDENLY GOT A TERRIBLE FEELING THAT SOMETHING WAS UP. A WEEK OR TWO BEFORE HE DIED, I BOUGHT A PHONECARD TO TALK TO HIM ONE LAST TIME.

DOMINION OF CANADA

UNITED STATES

MEXICO

OH, HALLO, ESMÈ! WHAT'S WRONG? ARE YOU CRYING??

≡SOB≡ YEAH!! OH GRANDPA, I JUST HAVE A WEIRD FEELING THAT SOMETHING'S WRONG WITH YOU! ARE YOU GONNA DIE?!?

WELL, YES, AS I TOLD YOU, I SUPPOSE I WILL ONE DAY?

BUT I MEAN SOON! LIKE NOW! ≡SNORT≡ I DUNNO, I CAN JUST FEEL IT COMING!!!

WELL, I'M TERRIBLY SORRY, DARLING, BUT THERE'S NOT REALLY MUCH I CAN DO ABOUT IT, IS THERE? TRY NOT TO WORRY, OK??

EUROPE, ETC.

AFRICA↓

TWO DAYS LATER HE WAS TAKEN TO THE HOSPITAL WITH AN INFECTION, AND BECAME VIRTUALLY INCOHERENT. MY MOM SENT ME DAILY EMAIL UPDATES, AND I ASKED MY BOSS IF SHE THOUGHT I SHOULD RUSH OFF HOME. WHAT SHE SAID REALLY STUCK IN MY MIND:

I DUNNO, LOVE... I MEAN, I DON'T WANT YOU TO LEAVE, BUT YOU MUST, IF YOU FEEL LIKE YOU SHOULD— MISSING THIS ISN'T THE KIND OF THING YOU WANT TO REGRET FOR THE REST OF YOUR LIFE, Y'KNOW??!

IT WAS SMART ADVICE, BUT I DIDN'T LISTEN! THIS WAS DURING THE POLAR VORTEX, AND A LAST-MINUTE FLIGHT WOULD HAVE BEEN SO EXPENSIVE - IT FELT LIKE THE UNIVERSE WAS TELLING ME TO STAY PUT.

WHAT'S MORE, EVERYONE BACK HOME WAS EXPECTING HIM TO RECOVER AND BE HOME FOR AT LEAST A FEW MORE WEEKS. SO I LISTENED TO THEM INSTEAD OF MY GUT-AND, WITHIN A WEEK, I FOUND OUT HE'D KICKED IT FROM SOMEONE'S FACEBOOK STATUS AT 7AM.

...HUH?!

HE HAD DIED, AND I HADN'T BEEN THERE, AND THAT WAS THAT.

IN THE WEEKS FOLLOWING ERIK'S DEATH, I WAS BASICALLY A MESS. I DREADED GOING HOME — I WAS FEELING VERY SELFISH AND INTROVERTED ABOUT THE WHOLE THING, AS IF I WERE THE ONLY ONE SUFFERING, AND NONE OF MY FAMILY COULD POSSIBLY UNDERSTAND WHAT I WAS GOING THROUGH. ONE MINUTE I'D BE TOTALLY FINE, AND THEN THE SMALLEST THING WOULD SUDDENLY CAUSE ME TO LOSE MY SHIT.

...AND THEN WE'LL HAVE TO START THINKING ABOUT THE KITCHEN STUFF...

MY MOM

THE KITCHEN STUFF? THE KITCHEN STUFF?! WADDAYA MEAN, THE KITCHEN STUFF? WHERE DO YOU SUGGEST WE EVEN BEGIN WITH THE KITCHEN STUFF ?!?!?!?!!!?!?! WHAT DOES THAT EVEN MEAN ?!!?

BUT EVENTUALLY — AFTER A FEW MORE HYSTERICAL FREAK-OUTS — I SUCKED IT UP AND GOT ON A PLANE TO ENGLAND. ERIK HATED FLYING TOO, SO I INVOKED HIS SPIRIT FOR COMPANY.

OH, YOU'LL BE FINE — TO DIE RIGHT NOW WOULD SIMPLY BE TOO IRONIC, EVEN FOR YOU. JUST DON'T LOOK DOWN.

WHEN I LANDED IN LONDON, STOFFER WAS THERE TO MEET ME DRESSED FROM HEAD TO TOE IN HIS FATHER'S CYCLING TWEEDS.

WHAT THE —

THEY'RE ERIK'S PLUS-FOURS! I'VE BEEN WEARING THEM FOR A FEW WEEKS, I DON'T REALLY KNOW WHY... I THOUGHT THEY'D MAKE YOU LAUGH.

I GUESS EVERYONE MOURNS IN THEIR OWN WAY

EVEN THOUGH I WAS GLAD TO BE HOME, WITHIN THE HOUR I COULD FEEL MYSELF REVERTING FROM A MATURE (LOL) ADULT INTO THE FURIOUS TEENAGER WHO HAD ONCE LIVED HERE. I FIGURED I SHOULD DITCH THE JOINT FOR A LITTLE BIT...

IT WAS NICE TO SEE MY PARENTS AGAIN AFTER SO LONG — BUT ABSOLUTELY NOTHING HAD CHANGED.

OH SWEETIE, YOUR SKIN!! WHAT ARE YOU EATING OUT THERE?!!

HEY, ES, Y'GOT 'NY DOPE? I HAVEN'T SMOKED POT SINCE YOU GUYS FLEW THE COOP.

OH STOFFER, IS THAT ALL YOU EVER THINK ABOUT?! SHE JUST GOT OFF A PLANE, FOR GOD'S SAKE.

COULDN'T LEND ME A TENNER, COULDJA? PAY YA BACK TUESDAY!

HAVE YOU BEEN READING THE ARTICLES I SENT YOU ON 'MINDFULNESS'?! AND YOU'RE MAKING YOUR BED EVERY DAY IN NEW YORK, RIGHT?!?

NOW, TELL US EVERY SINGLE THING THAT'S HAPPENED TO YOU SINCE WE LAST SAW YOU. GO!!!!

E.B CIRCA 2005

(THIS IS A MIRROR BTW)

FLAT-IRONED HAIR

OVER-PLUCKED BROWS

ABSOLUTELY NO PATIENCE

WAY TOO MUCH INNER-EYE LINER

PUSH-UP BRA

JUICY COUTURE VELOUR HOODIE (YUP!)

UH, YOU GUYS? I THINK IMA TAKE A WALK AND MEET MISTY OFF THE TRAIN FROM SCHOOL...

KAYE AND I ALSO SPENT AN AFTERNOON GOING THROUGH THE ATTIC, WHICH WAS MOSTLY FULL OF PHOTOS, ART PROJECTS, AND JUNK FROM MY CHILDHOOD. IT GOT ME THINKING ABOUT INHERITANCE:

METAPHYSICAL INHERITANCE (TASTES, HABITS, BEHAVIORS) →

DOOM 'N' GLOOM

SARDINES ON TOAST

A STEADY RIGHT HAND

PHYSICAL INHERITANCE (FAMILY TRAITS) →

BIG NOSES

FREAKISH HEIGHT (+ BIG FEET)

EYEBAGS

MATERIAL INHERITANCE (A SELECTION) ↘

ERIK'S PJs + DRESSING GOWN

MANY SOCKS

VARIOUS DECORATED ENVELOPES, POSTCARDS AND LOVE LETTERS

ORIGINAL MAURICE SENDAK DRAWING THAT I CAN'T BELIEVE THE OTHERS LET ME MAKE OFF WITH

Pears Soap

Pears Soap

TONS OF ART MATERIALS INC. THE DOPE WATERCOLORS WITH WHICH I PAINTED THIS COMIC + HALF-FULL SKETCHBOOKS

BIG OLE WOODEN PEARS SOAP BOX OF "ERIK'S SOUVENIRS" INC. LOTS OF PHOTOS AND TEENSY TREASURES (E.G. ACORN PIPE)

neither / both

Deciding to change my "outer" gender to match my inner one was one of the scariest things I've ever done, and then I did it all over again.
By Tyler. Playlist by Brittany.

Two nights ago, I went to my friend's weekly one-woman karaoke night at a local gay bar. I had just accompanied her on Nicki Minaj's "Fly," and I got offstage feeling really good about my performance. As I was walking back to my table, a man approached me and said, "You're amazing!" He looked like he was in his 20s and a few drinks deep, and although he wasn't my type, that kind of attention is always flattering. I was probably blushing. Then, still smiling, he asked me, "What's your gender?"

Taken a bit aback by his sudden forwardness, I struggled for a few moments to formulate an appropriate response. What I came up with: "Ummm…hmm. Uhhhhh…"

"Yeah, that's cool!" the guy said, upbeat as ever. "I just wanted to know what gender you identify as."

About 15 seconds passed before I managed to say, "Umm…uhhhh…androgynous, I guess?"

After this incredibly satisfying exchange, we went back to our respective tables and never spoke again. *I need to get better at answering that question*, I thought. But, see, it's complicated.

If that man had asked me the same question last year, I wouldn't have skipped a beat before proclaiming, "I'm a guy." I thought I had it all figured out. I had made a conscious choice to be a man, despite having been born with what's thought of as "female" equipment. I was so sure, in fact, that I was a guy that I underwent a lengthy transitioning process, involving hormone shots and close monitoring by a therapist, to get my outside appearance in line with my inner self—who was a man, no question.

But the big problem with our insides is that they're always changing. As I approached my two-year mark on testosterone, I began feeling less sure of the choice I was making. I started to feel stifled by my chosen gender identity, buried under the trappings of manhood. My outside had ceased matching my insides, and that didn't feel good at all. What had been a source of freedom—getting to choose what gender to present myself as—started to feel like a trap.

It's terrifying to decide to stop taking testosterone after two years of regular injections. Even scarier, for me at least, was the prospect of facing ridicule from my friends and from strangers on the internet when they learned that I was going back on this decision that I had been so passionately sure of just a few years ago. I was afraid that people would latch on to this idea that my transition was a "mistake" and use it to discount the validity of other people's transitions. I feared the street harassment that comes with looking at all "feminine." I feared that I would never look more feminine, that I would always be perceived as "a man." But most of all, I feared the unknown: Where was I headed? What exactly did I want to look like, or "be"? What if I was making a huge mistake?

However, I knew that a way bigger mistake would have been to try to stifle the inner voice that was telling me I wasn't happy and that I needed things to change—again. After I took my final testosterone shot in June 2013, I felt a mixture of excitement, embarrassment, and confusion. How much would my appearance change, and how rapidly? What would people think when they saw me on the street? I was truly alone on this journey—no one I knew had experienced anything like it—so I took one baby step at a time in whatever direction felt right for me.

The first one was shaving my legs, something I hadn't done in four years. Or, rather, shaving *one* of my legs, which seemed to express how I was feeling at that point: *I'm in between, and I don't care what you think about how I look.* The next step was buying an outfit that made me feel good: a comic-book-print bandeau under a white tank top, black cutoff shorts, and black platform sneakers with hot pink satin laces. I was nervous about wearing the outfit in public, but my desire to look cute trumped my nerves. Wearing things that made me feel attractive gave me a little confidence boost, which was all I needed to focus less on what others thought of me and more on my own happiness.

One thing that made me happy was spending time with a great friend that I grew up with. She has always loved and supported me, and she was a perfect sounding board for whatever I was going through at a given moment. She'd check in with me almost daily, asking, "How are you doing? What effects are you experiencing from the hormone shift? What pronouns are you feeling right now?" She felt like a safe person with whom to experiment with presentation and pronouns. And there were a lot of experiments: One day I'd want to be referred to as *she*; the next, I preferred *they*—as in "I just saw Tyler; they came over and we watched a movie"—which is where I am right now, I think. Sometimes I wanted to wear a strapless dress with face stubble, sometimes a hoodie and red lipstick. Even though everything about me was in flux, I knew my support system was stable. I am so lucky to have this friend in my life; she allowed me to actually enjoy this process of discovering who I was and what I wanted.

I've been off hormones for 10 months now, and I still don't know how to articulate my gender identity in a word or two. That might seem super uncomfortable, and it does make for some awkward moments in bars, but mostly it is actually a pretty freeing feeling. The way I think of myself changes from moment to moment, and instead of fighting it, I just go with it. I'm learning to exist without analyzing every aspect of myself or trying to force myself to feel, live, or look any certain way. I love looking in the mirror and watching my features contradict one another.

Sometimes I feel like my gender is an optical illusion: Light me from one angle, and you'll see a pretty girl; from another, I look like a pretty boy. I am neither, and I am both. Many people will never understand how I feel, but what matters to me is that *I* understand *myself*, even if I can't find myself in words. The possibilities seem endless. ★

busy being free

1. i blame myself – sky ferreira
2. all falls down – kanye west feat. syleena johnson
3. gypsy – fleetwood mac
4. mona lisas and mad hatters – elton john
5. cactus tree – joni mitchell
6. the only living boy in new york

   – simon & garfunkel

7. me and bobby mcgee – janis joplin
8. lucky – britney spears
9. head full of doubt / road full of promise – the avett brothers
10. all apologies – nirvana

NOT ABOUT LOVE

Or: Why I don't care where the "cool boys" are hanging out tonight (or any night).
By Gabby. Photo by Allyssa.

Ever since I started writing for Rookie, I've had this fantasy that one day I'd write a piece about how it's worth it to wait for love, using myself as an example. An excerpt from my imaginary essay:

So, in conclusion, if you ever doubt that it gets better, just look how I turned out! All those years of being chronically underwhelmed by the boys in my town and wondering if there was something fatally wrong with me because I just couldn't relate to the romantic woes chronicled in Taylor Swift songs didn't matter. It took me a while to find my really hot yet nonthreatening boyfriend with a heart of gold, but who cares, because hey look at this pic of us looking fun yet elegant while sharing a plate of nachos!

But it's been two years since I started writing for Rookie, I am now 20 years old, and this mythical boyfriend has still yet to materialize. The lyrics of "We Are Never Ever Getting Back Together" are still a huge mystery to me because I don't know

what it's like to resent a boy I used to love because I've never been in love. My crushes have been brief and never developed into anything meaningful. I've never even kissed anyone, not even in a casual way. I still have yet to "bloom" (ew) and, honestly, I don't even care.

Or, at least not very much. I'll admit I've found myself browsing a Yahoo! Answers page entitled "20 and never been kissed. Am I a loser?" at 2 AM more than once. I don't like telling people this, because I don't want them to jump to conclusions. Late bloomers don't really have the coolest reputation (even though, believe it or not, we are EVERYWHERE—in your schools, your neighborhood parks, your local supermarket!). I'm afraid people will think I'm naïve or uptight or judgmental. Sometimes I get backhanded compliments, e.g., "Whoa, that's so weird, you're not even ugly!" Which I guess means I have a bad personality? Which I don't really want to think about—like, what if I think I'm totally cool talking to some boy, but if I saw video footage of me interacting with him I'd realize I'm actually a huge monster.

So I do care a little, but only when I think about what other people might say about me. Most of the time, I think I'm really awesome. I don't generally experience FOMO or envy people who have romantic or sexual partners. I used to think that there was a list of experiences you needed to check off before qualifying as a *real* person. The first thing on the list was kissing, and until I had done at least that I would be banned from Grown 'n' Sexyville USA (population: cool people who have it all figured out). I'm not a prude (I hate that word—it makes me sound like an elderly person crowing about America's wayward youth); I truly admire people who are

totally confident about experiencing physical things just to find out what they're like. Of course, I feel weird sometimes when people around me are talking about sex and I don't want to call attention to my virginal ways, so I nervously tug at my collar and just kinda nod along, like, "Oh yeah, TOTALLY been there!" But when I finally kiss someone, I want to feel completely compelled and excited to do so, and that has just incidentally not happened yet.

Back in high school, when I'd moan about being "alone forever" (a very silly but very valid thing to feel at the age of 15), a lot of well-meaning adults, like my parents or teachers I was tight with, tried to reassure me by saying things like "Teenage boys have terrible taste!" and "Boys are going to love you in college, just wait!" and (my favorite) "Boys are just intimidated by your beauty!" All of these "helpful" remarks just made me mad—why should I have to make myself less powerful and/or wait around looking "pretty" until some dude with "terrible taste" finally notices me?

Sometimes love and sex do sound like some really rad TV show that everyone is live-tweeting about and I can't watch because I don't have cable. I'm psyched to find out what all the fuss is about one day, when I get the chance to watch it. Right now, though, I'm busy and happy with what I'm doing, so I don't really want to put my life on pause just to accommodate the pursuit of meeting boys. I don't want to invest hours in scrolling through dating websites or start picking my activities based on what boys will be present where. I can't count the number of times I'll ask a friend to go somewhere with me and she's like, "Will there be any cool boys there?" I don't know! I don't care! Can't we just do what *we* want to do, and if "cool boys"

happen to be present, that's like a bonus item you get when you order something off an infomercial? Like, it's delightful when it incidentally happens, but I'm not going to *not* order a Perfect Brownie pan for just $19.95 + $7.95 for postage and handling just because no one's throwing in a free oven mitt.

I don't hate the idea of love, I just hate everything you're supposed to do to find it: all the weird guesswork and annoying logistics, the posturing and the texting and the watering down of your personality so as not to scare anyone off. I love my friends, and I get that some of this behavior is caused by nervousness, but I just don't want that to happen to me. I like being happy and busy. Those also happen to be two qualities I find very attractive in other people. If and when I meet a happy, busy dude at school or at a concert or a party or wherever "cool boys" happen to be when they're not hanging out in dating apps, and I feel compelled to kiss him and he wants to kiss me

too, I'll know I've found something special. But until then, I'm gonna keep working on being the most boss bitch I can be regardless of whether I've had a dude's tongue in my mouth.

Occasionally my friends will be like, "Maybe your standards are too high?" To which I say *so what*—I don't think my standards are high, they're just the right standards for me. Making out with someone I'm not totally into sounds horrible to me! And anyway, it's not like I don't have love in my life—I have great, love-filled relationships with my friends and my family. Why are those relationships treated as somehow

less important to the project of being a happy, fulfilled adult than romantic love?

Of course, the question "What if I DIE ALONE?" sometimes creeps into my brain. But then I just roll my eyes at myself, because, first of all, *everyone* dies alone, and second, why is that a bad thing? I find it freeing to consider that I'm the only person I'll always have in this life. I've loved spending the past 20 years getting to know myself, doing whatever I like, beholden to no one. I don't actually think I'll *never* fall in love—in fact, I'm pretty psyched for that to happen at some point. But if I get to spend a bunch more time alone, I'll consider it a gift. I'm a pretty dope person to hang out with. ℝ

COLORING BOOK

A sartorial homage to Henri Matisse. By Eleanor and María Inés. Styling by Verity Pemberton. Thanks to Effie and Rachel for modeling, to Kate for assisting, and to the Tate Modern for their invaluable help.

NOTHING REALLY MATTERS

Embrace your insignificance!
By Stephanie. Playlist by Anaheed.

The hiking thing started by accident. I had one really close friend in Seattle when I moved here back in July, a girl I've known since high school. We were stoked to see each other as soon as I arrived, so she invited me and my husband, Scott, to go on a hike with her family the day after we moved into our new apartment. I was a little bit wary. I remember texting her, "Only have crappy sneakers, that OK?" She replied that she just wore Converse and the hike was easy enough that her two young children were coming along.

Now, I am not a nature girl by any stretch of the imagination. As a kid, I had to be dragged on my family's yearly camping trips, the entirety of which I spent complaining. I don't like being cold or getting wet. I have trouble sleeping in any bed besides my own, let alone in a sleeping bag on the floor of some tent. I'm afraid of spiders. And let's not even talk about the bathroom situation. I have a tiny bladder, and stumbling out into the woods in the middle of the night to find a grody outhouse is basically my worst nightmare.

When I decided to move to Seattle, nature was a big selling point—even from my house, you can see the Cascade Mountains and Mount Rainier, and there are trees everywhere, including the big Douglas firs that Agent Cooper is so fascinated by on *Twin Peaks*. But to me that stuff was like a pretty picture frame around a city that had everything I *really* like: tons of great vegan food; cool music, theater, and art; and (especially) a vibrant literary scene.

I also moved to Seattle to escape. I had lived in or near Chicago for most of my life, and I'd spent about a decade trying to make a life there as a writer. I'd had lots of ups and downs along the way, but those fluctuations had, in my last four years in the city, begun to plateau at a level I was unsatisfied with. I had published two novels but was unable to generate any interest from publishers in the next two, and I was

earning my living from bartending instead of writing. Not the worst situation in the world—at least I had a job—but far from my dream of being a recognizable name as an author.

I knew moving to a new city wouldn't magically make all of that go away, but emotionally, I needed to shake things up. I felt restless, unsatisfied, and insignificant, and it was turning me into a walking pity party. There was a lot about my career that I couldn't control—like publishers wanting to buy my books—but I couldn't let those things control my happiness. So I chose to move to a new state and try new things: Maybe I could get a job at a nonprofit or a university—something that would occupy my mind so I wouldn't obsess about writing all the time. And after five years of writing during the day and bartending at night, I looked forward to working normal hours so I could spend my evenings and weekends hanging out with Scott and the new friends I hoped to make in Seattle.

So when my friend invited us on a hike, I thought, *Hey, that's a new thing! Why not?* The next morning, I put on my crappy sneakers and followed her and her two young children into the mountains outside Seattle for an easy one-mile walk. A born-and-raised city girl, I took deep lungfuls of the fresh, sweet-smelling air—it felt as good as downing a bottle of icecold water on a hot day. Though we'd parked by the highway, we couldn't hear it or see it, thanks to the ginormous trees that formed a magical soundproof barrier between us and the traffic. There was so much to see: mossy rocks, purple flowers peeking out from behind tall trees. The best part was discovering where the trail led: a little pond covered with lily pads. My friend had to stop her kids from running through the trees to jump into it, and I totally empathized with their impulse. The whole experience was pretty magical.

Sunday hikes quickly became a tradition for Scott and me. It was a relatively cheap way to spend time together—and since I didn't have a job for my first two months here, cheap was important. We were also trying to make friends in our new city. Talking to new people has always been hard for me; I found, however, that people in Seattle *love* to talk about hiking! The subject made for easy conversation with the other people in our building and folks I met at parties. Plus, there was just something about picking fresh berries in Discovery Park, climbing to the top of Rattlesnake Ledge to gaze out at the Snoqualmie River Valley, or taking in a magnificent waterfall view at Wallace Falls that was deeply satisfying in a way that striving to get published never was.

One Sunday seven months after our first hike, Scott and I decided to head west to Olympic National Park. It was just a four-hour drive from Seattle, but when we got there, it felt like we'd been transported to a completely different world: It was scarcely populated, and the traffic noise, sirens, jackhammers, and shouting that I'm used to hearing in the city had been replaced by the sounds of wind and rain, the rushing of the river, and the occasional bird call.

But my favorite things there were the trees. Within the park's boundaries is the Hoh Rain Forest, which contains tons of old-growth trees, many of which have been there for literally hundreds of years. Awe-inspiringly huge and covered with moss, they looked otherworldly, noble, and just *wise*, somehow. Like they'd seen everything.

We stopped to study an almost comically massive tree labeled "giant spruce," and suddenly, a bald eagle flew by just above our heads. I had never seen a bald eagle IRL, but I knew they were pretty common in Seattle (I guess they're attracted by the old trees and the salmon—thanks, Wikipedia!). It flew by too fast for me to take a picture, which bummed me out for a second because I wanted proof that it had really happened. But then I realized that I'd been there, I'd seen something that most people don't see often if at all, and that was what mattered. My photographs couldn't show how that moment made me feel any better than they could do justice to the giant spruce, whose sheer massiveness none of my pictures could capture.

We ended up hiking seven miles that day, our longest hike to date, but I was too wrapped up in observing everything and thinking about that eagle and all those centuries-old trees to notice. Those trees were alive long before I was, and they will still be here after I'm dead. That bald eagle doesn't even know I exist, and here I am still writing about it. I was suddenly struck with an overwhelming sense of my own insignificance.

I had felt insignificant before, of course: in Chicago, where I felt unnoticed in a sea of other writers; and in grade school and high school, where I had some amazing friends, but often felt like the least important person in the group, like I was there only because one person liked me, and no one else would miss me if I vanished. I felt professionally and socially insignificant, and that made me sad, bitter, and frustrated. But this feeling in the forest was different: I felt insignificant in a *good* way. Because, sure, those trees don't care about me, but you know who else they don't care about? Beyoncé. President Obama. Mark Zuckerberg. Oprah. The Dalai Lama. The Pope. A bald eagle has never heard of any of those people and doesn't give a shit about a single one. A giant spruce can live for 700 years; our short, tiny lives mean nothing to it. It may sound strange, but no thought I've ever had has been as liberating as this one.

I've spent an inordinate amount of time in my life worrying about how I'll be remembered in the end (of high school, of college, of a certain period of life, or my whole life) instead of focusing on what *I'll* remember. A therapist I was seeing for a while asked me constantly if I was "living in the present," because I wasn't. I was always worrying about either the past or what the future held. That day, staring at that ancient tree, I wondered why I was making my problems so *huge*, when, compared with the life of this tree, my *entire existence* (let alone my writing career!), is just a blip, an insignificant nothing.

I don't mean that in a nihilistic way, like "we are all insignificant so we shouldn't bother doing anything." I kind of mean the opposite: If your life is just a teeny tiny blip on the radar, the only meaning it has is what you give it, and the only person it needs to mean anything to is *you*. For me, that means not stressing out too much about any one project or about being "known" in any way, and focusing instead on enjoying my time on the planet as fully as possible each and every day.

So, if you are feeling insignificant *in a bad way*, or just plain burned out from stressing about the relative success or importance of what you're up to, I encourage you to find ways to revel in what a *huge thing* we're part of. Though I love going into nature to do this, you don't necessarily have to. I've conjured these feelings by looking out a window on a plane or a long drive or even on the train ride from the Bronx to Manhattan or Manhattan to Coney Island. I've also felt them in history museums and on my couch while watching the new *Cosmos* hosted by Neil deGrasse Tyson.

In the very first episode of that show, Neil explains how, if the history of the universe were compressed into a calendar year, humans would appear in only the last hour of the last day. *All* of our recorded history would take place in the last 14 seconds of December 31. I mean, *whoa*. If that's true—and Neil deGrasse Tyson said it was, so it is—it's beyond silly for me to stress out and compare my own work, career, or life with anyone else's. It would do me, and all of us, good to learn to step back and experience everything that's out there, and relish this tiny blip of time we have existing as part of this huge, wonderful world. I'm doing that more and more these days, and I'm happier than I ever knew was even possible. ☺

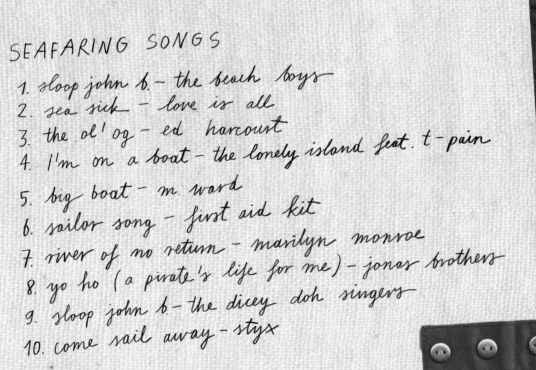

SEAFARING SONGS

1. sloop john b. - the beach boys
2. sea sick - love is all
3. the ol' og - ed harcourt
4. I'm on a boat - the lonely island feat. t-pain
5. big boat - m. ward
6. sailor song - first aid kit
7. river of no return - marilyn monroe
8. yo ho (a pirate's life for me) - jonas brothers
9. sloop john b - the dicey doh singers
10. come sail away - styx

Dear Rookies,

This month's theme is Together, but this letter is about a breakup. I have weighed the tackiness of writing about this kind of thing on the internet, and concluded that what I have to say about it is not that much more personal than the other stuff I've been sharing online for what is now a third of my life: the relationships I have to my favorite books/movies/bands, my ever-evolving beliefs, my most precious memories. I'm also motivated by the hope that drives most of what we humans do—that by putting this stuff out into the world, I will feel connected to another earthling for a handful of minutes (and I don't just mean through wifi, hyuk hyuk), which is ultimately what Together is about, and which becomes a much more urgent need once you no longer have someone to spoil you with kisses.

GOOD THING ABOUT BREAKUPS #1:

The urgency of the aforementioned need for connection causes you to discover love and beauty in places you might not have otherwise, what with the easy happiness provided by a healthy relationship. (Not that there is ANYTHING to be romanticized about an *un*healthy relationship. I mean that sometimes when shit in your life is going really well in traditional ways, you forget to stop and smell the roses [-scented perfume, Glow by J.Lo].)

Real Live Diary-Entry Proof:

Before the breakup, when everything was going effortlessly well, I was talking with Allyssa and Shriya, and they told me about the way the sky looked on a bus ride home recently, and how it was so beautiful that it made them both cry. I had so much trouble relating to that. I knew that I would have related at one point, but that piece of my heart was hibernating—the one that used to so determinedly seek out such small golden secrets as, like, an act of rebellion against sadness (sadness of my own, but also some gray idea of it as a looming sky presence, killing us all slowly with TV dinners and the like).

That is one thing I have valued dearly about being a teenager: hating everything so much that love becomes a means of survival. Not romantic love, but general life-love. This has come back to me since the breakup, despite the expectation of girls and women going through heartache to lash out at any forms of romantic love that surround them in their time of mourning, to yell at strangers seen kissing in public and throw Nilla wafers at the TV when a commercial for a dating website comes on. Granted, there was nothing bitter about my own separation—we're both moving at the end of the summer and just decided to rip off the Band-Aid instead of drowning in anxiousness about how to enjoy our remaining time together—but I have found little truth to this cliché.

GOOD THING ABOUT BREAKUPS #2:

Going through heartache makes you genuinely happy to encounter love *somewhere* on this godforsaken planet, whether or not it is one you are directly experiencing.

Real Live Diary-Entry Proof:

Rivkah pulled me onto the first car of the subway and stood me at the front window, where we watched the oncoming tracks disappear beneath our feet. At one point a little boy got on with his dad and his brother and watched with us. Sitting to our left was a middle-aged couple, the woman taking forever to get a steady photo of the man but smiling the whole time, just beaming at him, and he was shy-looking, but the opposite of annoyed, more like psyched that they were so happy to be with each other. It didn't make me sad, because it did not have to be a breakup thing; it was a human/life thing.

See also: that time I walked down the street into a gust of wind and it felt, legit, like a hug.

See also: the other day when a guy asked a girl to prom in French class, and it didn't feel like a personal attack on my current emotional state; it felt like, yay, more positivity in the world: General Love: 1. General Bad Stuff: 0.

It takes a bit of effort to feel this hippie-dippy confidence that the world and I are generally on the same team, but…

GOOD THING ABOUT BREAKUPS #3:

They offer access to heartbreak, one of the most universal experiences ever, one that ultimately makes you feel more like an alive human who is part of something and less like a bitter ghost who hates everything.

Real Live Letter-I-Once-Wrote-Claire Proof:

The world is a lot bigger than Oak Park, our high school, or the stupid people currently in your life. I'm not talking about the art world or the community you'll find at college. I'm talking about the entire planet Earth, I'm talking about the movie you told me about that made you cry, where it just showed a bunch of clips of life in different forms, babies crying and insects mating and stuff. That's the world that you're a part of.

Lots of people like to express concern that by staying connected through phones and other robots invented by our generation's greatest minds (Jimmy Neutron and T.J. Henderson), we young'uns are missing out on the human Together described above. I'm not one to indulge pointless arguments about the inter-

Design by Sonja. Title lettering by Lisa Maione. Painting by Brooke Nechvatel.

net, but I will say that, as somebody who has spent a good chunk of her time on earth documenting and sharing it for the WWW to see, I don't feel robbed of privacy or purity, because once I got out of middle school and over myself, I stopped seeing the idea of other people in general as innately gross/bad. The sociologist Richard Sennett, who wrote *The Fall of Public Man*, said in an interview with the CBC, "We take it for granted that when we are really present, when we're really alive, really there for someone else, we're going to be hidden from a crowd rather than in the midst of it." I read this in *Let's Talk About Love* by Carl Wilson, who then summarizes the rest of the interview:

> He traces this viewpoint to the second half of the 19th century, when the public cultures that had been evolving in cosmopolitan cities went into retreat, due to elite paranoia about crowds (mobs) and the rise of bourgeois family life and psychology. Exteriors became suspect; the interior, inwardness, became the wellspring of truth. And that's the onramp en route to the gated community.

So while I am an avid journaler and all-around fan of solitude, I don't think there has to be anything particularly vile about the fact that the internet has often been, and will more often be, the onramp en route to a feeling of Together. I get that something feels less sincere about sharing stuff on a site with "likes" and "reblogs" than on a typewriter, or in the sand, or using tiny twigs like a Wes Anderson credits sequence, but there was a time when even novels were conceived of as tacky and dangerous to society. And now everyone wants to save the printed word! If you have nothing to lose and nothing to prove, and don't think being in public is necessarily a performance, then the way I and many people reading this have grown up—typing out our feelings to friends we've never met, sharing life's minutiae when it seems to have some value—does not seem intrinsically dirty, or like some kind of loss, or less truthful than the way our parents did it.

There are, of course, armpits of the internet that should never be crossed—I have Comment Block installed for a reason. But I love the internet's excitement when an artist we love drops a new album the way I love a power pop ballad. Sometimes this desire to be part of a whole is FOMO, sometimes it's the disturbing dopamine rush from seeing new Instagram notifications, but often it's just the itch to learn from and share with other people, and what could be more pure, human, and/or earnest than that?

The filmmaker Jonas Mekas said in an interview in 2000:

> When I see a film and I like it, I want to share my enthusiasm for it with others. There is so little in this modern commercial world that is really and truly exciting […] that it's very important for me that those little fragments of beauty, of Paradise, are brought to the attention of friends and strangers.

The Lester Bangs character in *Almost Famous* said:

> The only true currency in this bankrupt world is what you share with someone else when you're uncool.

Accounting for this currency makes me feel as wealthy as the *Wolf of Wall Street* guy. We all feel a little uncool, we have all known pain, and this commonality serves as the basis of so many kinds of Together that my heart feels more ready for it than ever.

Real Live Diary-Entry Proof:

I read Liz Armstrong's [2012] Rookie article "Breaking in a Broken Heart" in the car this morning and started crying when she said, "You are loved." It was extremely special to get to read Rookie to feel better. I have a much greater understanding now of… I guess what we can mean to people and how incredible this connection is and how crucial it is that these spaces exist, not, like, to Journalism and Media, but just in making people feel better.

I've always felt a little too inside it or maybe a little too happy, more recently, to get how much some people relate to it and hold it close on an emotional, not just intellectual, level. But now I understand the immense comfort of knowing that something like this exists, that people care, that we're all feeling everything. I'm crying! I love what I do so much, and I love everyone I get to work with and for. This is really good fuel now for finishing the Yearbook work I've been too sad to tackle. It's no longer just "I want to make something that'll blow people's minds," but more: I want to make something beautiful, safe and scary in all the right ways, loving and there for people. It's not just about killing it 24/7 and Coming For Yr Job and being, like, empowering and kickass, or about wanting people to find that they are strong in simply a Robyn/CEO way, but letting people be strong human beings who can fully know and love themselves enough to extend that feeling to the world and populate our earth with good friendships, meaningful art, and stuff to make us all laugh.

I have had this mission since the beginning, but it's been easy as of late to feel like more of a "career woman" than like an often-lonely high-schooler. But when I finished Liz's article, I just didn't care, from a job standpoint, if that piece (or any other) got enough "traction" or whatever, because it helped me so much, and if it can do that for just one other person, that's enough for me. There are so many different kinds of love, and I can't believe my luck in feeling this kind so strongly.

This month's theme is Together. This letter started with a breakup, and it ends with a new beginning. As with writing about my relationship, I have weighed the tackiness of including a diary entry so blatantly self-serving and Rookie-complimenting, but as I turn 18 and graduate from high school into a series of unknowns, one thing is very clear: Rookie has a life of its own, comprising and nurtured by so many voices outside of mine. Thank you for that. I can't say it enough.

love, tavi

still lives

Shots from a movie in María Fernanda's head.
By María Fernanda

Thanks to Alonso, Celeste, Cheryl, Fera, Jordon, Leo, and Zaid for their help.

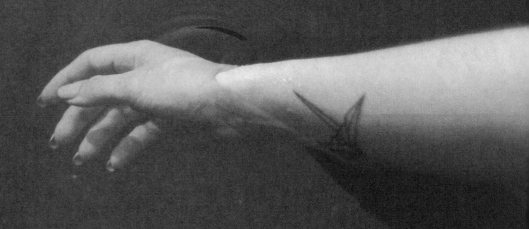

It really isn't you, it's life; and it's not them either, it's life.

It's lonely at the top.

- I want to go to Japan. We should go together.
-Okay.

-It's okay to be imperfect enough to need someone.
That's the idea behind all relationships.

-There is a whale that has been swimming alone since 1992.
-I don't want to be alone.

(comfortable silence)

Star CRossings

A scene report and interview with the cast and writer of The Fault in Our Stars.
By Hazel. Illustration by Kendra.

By now, you may have heard of John Green's YA novel *The Fault in Our Stars*. You may also have heard that a big-deal movie based on the book is coming out on June 6. Both are about Hazel Grace Lancaster, a 16-year-old who likes hefty books and *America's Next Top Model* in equal measure. Hazel has cancer and attends a regular support group for teenagers with the disease. That's where she meets Augustus Waters, a terribly handsome cancer survivor. Then the two of them do that thing that teens in novels are wont to do: fall in L-U-V.

I've never been to a movie set or a press "junket" or whatever, so at the event, I'm as intimidated as any other enormous fan of Green's books would be. Every time I introduce myself to a producer, another writer covering the event, or really ANYBODY, they say, "Oh, Hazel! How fitting."

The press group I'm part of is taken to the church where one of the book's first scenes is being filmed. It's the one where Hazel and Augustus first meet at the support group, which is held in a cross-shaped house of worship that Hazel calls the "Literal Heart of Jesus." Augustus, the cutest boy in the room, flirts by aggressively staring Hazel down, and Hazel stares right back in defiance. "Finally, I decided […] to stare back," she says in the book. "After a while, the boy smiled, and then finally his blue eyes glanced away. When he looked back at me, I flicked my eyebrows up to say, 'I win.'" I knew right then that I was obsessed with her.

You can't help loving Hazel and Augustus as a pair. Unlike the couples in many other teen-romance books, Hazel and Augustus aren't hyper-glamorized, plus they're hilarious. I won't say much regarding the end of this book, but I will tell you that it made me open-mouth sob uncontrollably, and I rarely cry over books.

In high school, I had seen John Green's name in my Tumblr feed, where girls fawned over the wisdom in his highly quotable vlogs (created with his brother, Hank) and his previous YA novels, *Looking for Alaska* and *Paper Towns*. After reading *TFIOS* two summers ago, I've counted myself as one of those adoring fans, so you can imagine my excitement when, in September, I got to fly to Pittsburgh to watch part of the movie being shot. Even better: I got to talk to some of the cast members, like Shailene Woodley, who plays Hazel, and Ansel Elgort, aka Augustus Waters—plus John Green himself! Here's my account of that extremely rad day.

In the movie, the rest of the support group isn't played by actors, but by real-life teens battling cancer. Part of what makes *TFIOS* so affecting is its unflinching depiction of terminal illness, which is all around us—in all likelihood, every person you and I know has been impacted by it in some way. It's a part of everyone's life, but thinking about it still makes a lot of people really uncomfortable. When *TFIOS* came out in 2012, there was some controversy over whether the subject matter was "appropriate" for teenagers (the *Daily Mail* called it "sick-lit") and whether giving the main character a fatal disease was too emotionally manipulative. I don't think it ever occurred to these critics that teenagers, like all humans, truly do suffer. Also, reducing the plot to a "cancer story" is deeply offensive. *TFIOS* is, first and foremost, a love story about two snarky teenagers who *also* happen to face an illness that affects millions of young people just like them.

John Green drew inspiration for the novel from having worked at a children's hospital for six months when he was 22 years old. He says that most stories about childhood cancer portray "people living with cancer as mere tragedies, or merely brave," something he wanted to avoid. "There's something about characterizing someone that's merely brave that dehumanizes them," he says. "People say, 'Oh, I could never live with that.' Well, of course you could. And you would, if you had to."

I'm happy to report that John Green online = John Green in person, lest you thought he was catfishing all his beloved fans with fake wit. He's the exact embodiment of his enthusiastic tweets, his wisecracking vlogs, and his completely accessible overall web presence. The first question I blurt out after shaking his hand is the most self-centered one possible (yes, it's about my name, ugh). He tells me that he chose the name Hazel because the character was

"in between worlds"—youth and adulthood, life and death—and the color hazel is between brown and green. I can feel a dorky grin spread across my face.

Hazel says in the novel, "There will come a time when there are no human beings remaining to remember that anyone ever existed or that our species ever did anything. […] And if the inevitability of human oblivion worries you, I encourage you to ignore it." Augustus (Gus for short), meanwhile, wants to make the biggest mark he can while he's still alive. When I meet Shailene Woodley in the church basement, I ask if she sympathizes with Hazel's worldview. "It's funny," she says, "because I [would have] related more to Gus when I was that age. I was like, 'Oh there's so much to do, there's so much to change! I want to be remembered and help the environment!'"

Describing her character, Shailene says, "She doesn't think she's special in any way, shape, or form, and that's kind of what makes her special. I'm inspired by her ability to recognize the faults in the world and to see the wrong in them, but not feel like it's her job to correct them. Those are important lessons for all of us to learn."

John Green says working with terminally ill children made him really angry, because he felt they had been denied access to a good life. He dealt with those feelings by writing *TFIOS*, and eventually came to believe that "the universe doesn't care very much about individuals, but that doesn't prevent you from having a good life. It wasn't impossible for those kids to have a good life just because they died so young. I realized it's possible to have a good life *and* a short life."

My favorite thing about *The Fault in Our Stars* is the way Augustus and Hazel sarcastically bicker and joke with each other, like when Augustus makes fun of what Hazel asks for when a wish-granting organization comes calling: "You *did not* use your one dying wish to go to Disney World with your parents," he admonishes her. John Green's characters don't talk the way people my age actually talk—instead, Green says, his teens talk like real ones "want to think they talk." Fair enough: If Romeo and Juliet can talk to each other in poetic verse, Augustus and Hazel can convey their love as dramatically as they want. "I'm interested in using text to reflect emotional reality," Green says. "Now, we don't speak to each other in sonnets [laughs], but that's a very effective tool for capturing the idea of love that was destined and fated to be."

What he really hates is when people say real teenagers aren't as smart as Hazel and Gus. "[That] tends to be something adults say. I don't think adults give teenagers enough credit as intellectually engaged people. The way teens approach big, important, interesting questions is more interesting than how adults do it, because [teenagers] tend to ask them without fear or embarrassment. They're willing to ask why suffering exists, or 'What's the meaning of life?' Adults ask those questions under 72 layers of irony for fear of appearing unsophisticated."

The second scene we get to see is the one where the couple leaves a group counseling session. Augustus asks Hazel if she wants to see a movie, then puts a cigarette to his lips. When Hazel becomes furious, he explains that it's only a metaphor: "You put the thing that kills you right between your teeth, but you never give it the power to kill you." In each take, Shailene and Ansel do something a little different. After one, Shailene looks at Green and asks if the scene is "up to your 'cute' standards?" Green smiles and replies with a thumbs-up: "Yes, extra cute."

Although Green knew he was writing a sad story, it didn't fully hit him how emotionally demanding the plot was until he began watching the movie being made. "I tried to make the book as funny as possible, but it *is* about dying when you're young. I don't know why anyone would read a sad story. It seems horrible. But this is not a sad story. This is a love story, really."

A lot of people ask him what happens after the book ends, but he says he can't answer those questions because he just doesn't know: "When you start giving people answers to things outside the text, it gives the author a power I don't want to have. I want *you* to have it. I want *you* to be making those choices."

Of course, for those clamoring for more *TFIOS*, there's always the movie. Shooting it has proved grueling, especially for Ansel, who recounts one particularly devastating scene in which Augustus becomes intensely ill while driving and calls Hazel to come get him: "I was acting like a four-year-old. It's the toughest thing I've done as an actor." Nat Wolff, who plays Augustus's blind friend Isaac, also had a hard scene, in which he had to smash a wall of trophies in anger: "I had to smash a couple of certain points, but in the heat of the moment, I smashed all the wrong spots. Good times."

One particularly memorable moment on set came when, after a long, tiring day of shooting, Green heard piano music coming from the church sanctuary at 4:15 AM. "I heard this sad and sweet, seemingly improvised song, and I went in and saw Nat and Ansel playing together," he recalls. "When you've been up all night, and you're so tired, to have this moment of seeing them connect so deeply was really extraordinary."

For Shailene, *The Fault in Our Stars* has been a transformative experience. She says the book taught her to live in the present and to be aware of what's happening around her, rather than worry about the future or feel guilty about the past. "The thing about John Green, and this book," she says, "is that these aren't new ideas—it's just a way of articulating these thoughts we have in our hearts, in words that make sense. People are going to see it and be affected." ☆

freewheeling

A bicycle trip through the Outback.   By Kim

Last fall, I took a bike trip through rural Australia. Over two weeks, we covered nearly 200 miles, watching the landscape change as we followed the path of a long, wide, winding river. By day we collected firewood and bathed in the river. At night we cooked by campfire. We crossed at least seven state borders and got at least eight flat tires. I didn't cry even once.

Big thanks to Nat Howells for taking three rolls of film and being able to adjust camera settings whilst riding a bike.

Some of us grew up with two parents. Some of us had one, or three, or four. Some of us were raised by grandparents or aunts or uncles or siblings. We all know that family can take infinite forms, but what happens to kids when their biological family is incapable of taking care of them (at least according to the state government)? In the U.S., in many cases, those kids end up in the foster system, where a valiant army of social workers, case officers, lawyers, law guardians, judges, and foster parents do their best to provide safe, healthy temporary homes for them. But the foster system, like any family, is far from perfect. Having spent time in foster care makes it much less likely that you will get a high school diploma or a job, and much more likely that you will serve prison time or become homeless.

It takes incredible strength to survive and flourish when the odds are stacked against you. Here are four amazing girls who defied those grim statistics. **Tamar, Cristina, Mitsuka,** and **Kiana** all spent their teenage years in the foster system; they also share an astonishing capacity for forgiveness, breathtaking resilience, and an irrepressible ambition to define their own lives, rather than let them be defined by what's been done to them.

Do Right by Me

Four amazing girls, raised in foster care, who beat the odds.
Interviews by Rose. Photography by Sandy.

TAMAR, 19

I have always had a smart mouth. And I never took no shit from nobody. I'd always talk back to teachers. One day I got into a fight in religion class. Some kids were teasing me and I said, "If you don't stop, I'm gonna stab you." My teacher told me I was gonna get suspended. I knew I went too far.

After I got suspended, my mom gave me the silent treatment and then a beating. Things were already strained at home. My father has bad dementia and was in a nursing home. My grandmother came to live with us—she is blind. I cooked, I cleaned, I made sure the aprons were pressed. I was 9 or 10, in fifth grade, and there was a lot on my plate.

Finally, I reached my wit's end. I couldn't deal with it anymore. I tried to kill myself. I just didn't want to be around anyone. I just didn't care.

There was this guidance counselor who had gained my trust. I went to her in the morning before school and told her what [pills] I had taken. I can't describe the scared look in her eyes. I didn't get how serious the situation was [before that]. The police came and got my mom and she told them I was just craving attention.

That guidance counselor visited me in the hospital more times than my mom did. You don't know how it messes with your head when you are in a psych unit and your mom doesn't even bring you the necessities you need. It really just makes you appreciate certain things so much more.

It's ironic: Family court is supposed to bring families together, but it tore ours apart. In court, my mom said that I was making everything up. Some things in life you cannot fake. You cannot fake blood test results. You cannot fake rape kits. It either happens or it doesn't.

I had an order of protection against me, so I couldn't live in that house anymore, and I was still underage. In foster care I have a roof over my head, a place to sleep, a place to take a shower, and foster siblings to take care of.

At the end of the day, friends won't be there for you. As much as family messes with you, family will forever be there with you. *With* you but not necessarily *for* you. As many troubles as I might have with you, I'm depending on you to do right by me. Because you're my mother.

I have to try to move on. She made a mistake, but I have to move on. I have to prepare to be by myself.

CRISTINA, 24

When I was little, Mom used to leave us alone, sometimes for two or three days, sometimes for weeks at a time. I got used to it. One night when she wasn't there, the cops came and got [me and my siblings] dressed and took us to the Administration for Child Services [ACS] building. I felt bad for my siblings. My brother was two and my sister was five. It was worse for them because they needed Mom. I needed her too, but I was already 10. I found out later that when my mom was arrested, she told the cops that we were home alone. So she snitched on herself.

They placed us at a stranger's house. I was a well-behaved kid, but my siblings weren't. The lady we were placed with was a cop, so she'd pull out her handcuffs and threaten us. It was terrible.

My mom got clean and we went home. But she eventually got back into drugs, and it got to the point again where she'd disappear

for a week. I was fine, but my siblings were young. It's hard to see kids go through that. Especially when you're also a kid.

I started missing school to watch them. One day I had had enough. I said to her, "I'm not gonna watch them anymore. You say you're gonna come back, and then you don't come back for days or weeks. It's too much." She said, "You don't want to take care of them, so leave." I was telling her, "No, no," and she physically took me out of the apartment. I left and never came back. It was four in the morning, and I was just walking around and sitting in the park. I saw a girl I knew and she said, "Come with me, you can stay in my house." So it became like that. I just went from house to house to house. I didn't see my siblings anymore. I know that they eventually got taken by ACS. At that time I wasn't thinking about them. I regret that now.

I knew girls who did the stupidest things for cash or clothes. I never did that. The easiest thing for me was to watch kids or wash clothes [for money]. Eventually,

I returned to the foster care system so I could get my work permit.

Sometimes at people's houses, bad things would happen. It messed me up. I don't want to be dramatic, but you never forget, no matter how strong you are. But I just keep moving forward. I'm very emotionless, stiff. Very nonchalant. Not showing [emotion] helps me to not feel it. I just put a block on it, and that's it. When you get hurt too many times or everything is negative in your life all the time, you have to find a way around that, or you're going down.

The twist of the story is that my mom is doing good, and now she needs help. She's been clean for years, and she's trying to make up for what she did. I feel like I have a family now, because now when I come home, my mom treats me like I'm a little kid. I guess she feels like she has to make up for it. I'm not going to say I'm over it, but I forgave her a long time ago. Now my siblings are the ones who will never let her forget what happened.

MITSUKA, 20

I was born in Haiti. I left my mother there in 2007 to live with my father in the U.S. I didn't really know him before he brought me here. My stepmother and I didn't get along, and my father wasn't looking out for me, so I came to New York to stay with my uncle. But then I wasn't getting along with my uncle's wife. If she asked me to do something and I didn't do it, she would start beating me. So my uncle asked me to leave, even though I had nowhere else to go. I was 15, 16, and they didn't care about kicking me out in the middle of the night and making me sleep on the street. I didn't get money from my family or anything like that. No one was helping me. I was all alone.

I ended up moving in with my boyfriend, who was 19, when I was 17. My father called the police and they called my boyfriend and started to threaten him that I had to go back [to Haiti]. I went to my uncle's house, and he called the cops and told them I was crazy and a liar. The

cops took me to Kings County Hospital to examine me, but I wasn't crazy. When they looked for my uncle to take me home, he was gone. It's like he wanted to leave me there for good. So they called ACS. ACS came and they took me that same night. I was there for a night, and after that they placed me in a home.

They placed me with an American woman and her Haitian husband. I was thinking that we're gonna have a good relationship because he's from Haiti too, but he was really strict. He told the caseworker he don't want me there. At that time I was in ninth grade, age 17. They moved me to another home, with a woman from Trinidad. She didn't feed me, and there was barely food in the house. She didn't give me any money— she was supposed to give me $80 a month plus about $300 every three months for a clothing allowance. I knew the foster agency paid her that money, but when I discussed it with my caseworker, nothing changed.

When I found out I was pregnant, I told my boyfriend. He said something about an abortion, but I didn't want that,

so we just stopped talking. I moved to an alternative maternity shelter where I finished ninth grade. I liked it there. I made a couple of friends. It was peaceful. All I wanted was to relax and not think about all the family problems and bad things and moving from home to home.

I gave birth to my son, Ricky, in 2010, when I was 17. I was supposed to go back to the high school, but because I didn't have anyone to watch Ricky, I missed a lot of days. Eventually I had to drop out of high school.

I was discharged from foster care six months ago, and I got this apartment. I had taken a home-health-aide class and the class for the GED, and I was doing good for myself. I got a job and I started to save money. I'm trying to get my GED and see if I can get a better job.

I have been through so much, and I don't want my son to go through the same thing. I never want to be separated from Ricky. I want him to know his mother loves him and cares for him. I don't want him to feel how I felt.

KIANA, 20

My first time I went into foster care, I was 13. My [birth] parents used to beat me a lot. I went to school after my dad had beaten me and I had welts all over my body. The teacher saw it and she called it in.

They took me to the ACS building on First Avenue. I didn't want to be there, I wanted to be at home with my friends, so I kept leaving, and they kept coming to get me. They didn't have a placement for me, so I stayed [in the ACS building]. That's when I caught my first charge as a juvenile. We were in class, and I was acting up. A security guy came and asked me to get my books and he said something to me and I said something back, and the next thing I know I was beating him.

I went to Spofford [Juvenile Detention Center]. I was there for two weeks. I hated it. So depressing. Then I went to Crossroads, where you await your trial. It was like real jail. You couldn't wear regular clothes—you had to wear a jumper. My mom visited me like twice the whole year I was there.

From there I went to a detention center in Brentwood, in Long Island, which was all right. I was there for two years. I found out that I didn't go home as soon as I was supposed to because my mother didn't want to come get me. I was like, *What does she think this is, a babysitting service?* Yes, I did the crime, but I just feel like if she was being more of a mother, I wouldn't have to be in the ACS building in the first place.

When they released me, she didn't even come get me. When I got home, we started fighting again, even fist-to-fist fighting. One time she let her friend hit me. I'm like, "You gonna let a man put his hands on me? What type of mother is you?" But that wasn't the first time she let a man put his hands on me.

You ever read the story of *A Child Called It*? About a child who was beat mercilessly? A lot of things that he went through, I went through. My mom never understood what she did wrong. She always blamed me. She could never take responsibility for what she did.

When I was 16, I found out that I was pregnant. I had too much pride at the time

to tell my baby's father I needed help. I didn't know what to do, so I went to the [ACS] office and I said, "The father's not gonna support me and this baby." They drove me to some place in the Bronx, a maternity group home. I gave birth to my son three months early. No one in my family came to visit while I was in the hospital. Not my mother, not my grandmother, not my baby's father.

I applied for housing when I was 17. My son was special-needs, so it was only three months before they offered me this apartment. I haven't talked to my mom in a year. I haven't met a more dysfunctional family. My sister is 12, and it's like a sequel. Whatever I went through, she's going through. I want to get her out of that house.

Sometimes I love my mom, even now, after everything. I think about the mother she could have been, and the moments that we had that were good. But the stuff she do, to this day I can't understand. It just don't register in my head. Because now I am a mom, and I couldn't imagine doing that to my son. I don't want my son to struggle like I did. I refuse.

you can be free:
an interview with janet mock

In which we talk about her feminist icons, how teenagers are way cooler than the media thinks, and why she identifies with Tracy Flick.

By Julianne. Illustration by Kendra.
Playlist by Anaheed.

Pardon the hyperbole, but Janet Mock may be the best person ever. I felt this way after reading her 2013 book, *Redefining Realness: My Path to Womanhood, Identity, Love & So Much More*, a beautiful, powerful memoir that follows Janet from her early days in Hawaii, where she grew up as a transgender girl, to her current position as a high-profile (and still young!) writer and activist who inspires people everywhere to live exactly as they want to live.

She decided to come out as trans in a 2011 essay in *Marie Claire* magazine; since then, she has worked hard to increase the visibility of transgender people, including starting the hashtag #girlslikeus, which encourages trans people to share their stories on Twitter.

My feelings about her greatness only intensified when I actually got to talk to her on the phone last month. You know how sometimes you're talking to someone and they're just so *on it* that their voice crackles with electricity? That's how Janet was.

JULIANNE So much of *Redefining Realness* is your very specific memories from your childhood, some of which are so wrenching! How did you remember all of that, and how were you able to get it all out in your writing?

JANET MOCK I started by writing journal entries. I made a commitment to myself to write 500 to 1,000 words every morning—to just catalog every memory, even if it was just a fragment, on paper. Once I really got into that space and got disciplined, I was able to reimagine what happened and to mine the feelings and the details of that time period. That's why there are a lot of

pop culture references, because I watched so much TV! I would try to remember certain things by asking myself, *What song lyrics was I trying to memorize? What type of dance moves was I trying to learn?*

But then you have to remember the pain, too, and that was the hardest part—the wrenching part, as you say—having to revisit that, not as an adult, but going back and feeling it again as a child who didn't have much agency over their body and how it felt to go through those traumatic events. So I just had to be very kind to myself as a writer, but also kind to those who had wronged me. I had to be kind about the mistakes people made and how they contributed to my pain.

As a fellow writer, I have found when you're accessing those painful things, there is an instinct to lie to yourself, in order to protect yourself. How did you avoid that?

There are certain moments in the book where I call myself out for wanting to soften things or exclude things, and that was part of being transparent. I was committed to being transparent not just through the stories I chose to tell, but throughout my writing process. I talk about my mother's suicide attempt, and about not wanting to [write about it] because I didn't want to see her that way. Also, some of the details of the sex work I went through as a teenage girl—sometimes I wanted to erase those from the record of my life. But being honest about that actually helped me. It relieved me from my silence and shame, and hopefully it can help other people feel that sense of relief about something that may be heavy

that they've been holding on to for a long time.

Was wanting to find that relief one of the reasons you started writing the book?

Yeah. At first I wasn't writing with the intention of making a memoir—I just did it 'cause I wanted to have a record for myself. It was a selfish project—there was no sense of intersectionality or social-justice jargon or anything like that. It was just about me, this girl, and her story and her pain. I was trying to get it as raw as possible on the page so that I'd know that it was real.

But when I stepped forward publicly in *Marie Claire*, I was like, *Wow, there's a powerful story here that I think I'm supposed to tell.* I don't mean that in a boastful way—there just aren't many books by young marginalized women like myself who did what I did, the way I did it.

Since that *Marie Claire* piece came out, social-justice ideas and words like *intersectionality* have become way more widespread, especially for young people, partly because of Tumblr. Have you seen a shift?

Ooh, Tumblr's powerful, yes. Those words are very powerful tools for describing this oppression, and it's great that some people have access to them. But most people don't. For me, it was super important to not use those terms in the book, because they exclude a lot of people who don't have educational access, or who may not be engaged in social-justice stuff but who want to be enlightened about things and have their political conscious-

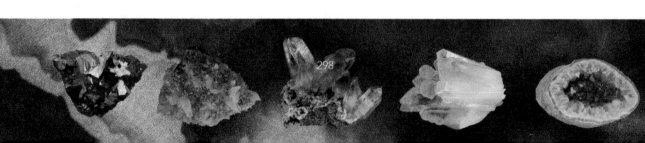

nesses raised a bit. I wanted to write the book for everyone—including that girl who I was in seventh grade who didn't even know the term *transgender*. I wanted to give her a book so she could also feel like she was in the know, without being talked down to or made to feel like she has to aspire to something "higher" when she already has all the knowledge she needs to define her own experience. It's not for me to define it for her. So I wanted to use words and language that she understands.

Your book has done a lot to help trans people be recognized in the larger culture. Did anything help you feel recognized that way? There aren't that many books out there like your book.

My reflection of myself has always been a composite of many images and people that I have met along the way. I talk a lot about Beyoncé and Clair Huxtable and Toni Morrison, and I talk about the trans women who were in my life as a teenager, and the women around me when I was growing up: my father's sisters, my grandmother, and my mother. I saw all of these women as mirrors, and made them into my own little mirrored mosaic.

But regarding the whole genre of "trans books"—I guess they would call them "transition stories" or "transition books": So many of them do not have the intersection of youth, and that's pretty important, because young people oftentimes don't have much body agency in our culture. Like, your parents can literally pick you up and take you somewhere and put you wherever they want and tell you what clothes you can wear and what clothes they're willing to buy you. All of these things are what makes finding yourself and expressing yourself and your own authenticity difficult. That's one of the things I notice when I speak to young people, that sense of struggling with their lack of agency. I just tell them that, yes, you do have agency, despite your parents. Live your life on Twitter, put up some selfies! Reblog some things! Self-representation is so important.

In terms of trans women, I'm happy that there are more of us visible in mainstream media. Platforms like Tumblr and YouTube allow people to create images that they don't see in the mainstream media—and to also talk back to mainstream media when they fuck up. Rookie is a testament to that!

Thank you, we're trying! You've talked about how reading the work of several female authors of color—like Zora Neale Hurston, Maya Angelou, and Toni Morrison—helped you get to a place where you could "just be." As you were reading them, did you feel like you were being seen?

I think the first one I was exposed to was Maya Angelou, in probably eighth or ninth grade English class, when we read *I Know Why the Caged Bird Sings*. Being the only black student in class, I was like, *Oh god, we have to read this?* I knew everybody was gonna look at me and think this was my experience. But then I read it, and I was like, *Oh my god, this* is *my experience!* It was powerful to read—specifically the parts where she talks about sexual abuse as a child. That was something that I had never told anyone I had gone through, so seeing that someone had written it down in a book that we were reading in class, I was like, *Oh my god—this exists in the world?*

So that was one of those things where I was like, *I need to go to the library and read more books.* Because I also didn't have access to books, unless it was in school. (I always talk about my youth struggle of never being able to order anything from the Scholastic catalog that was passed around in class, and always yearning for those books to be delivered to me the following week!) [Reading *I Know Why the Caged Bird Sings*] prompted me to get a library card and just sit among those stacks and read books by women who looked like my self-image. That was important to me, because [those women] lived the life that I saw myself living one day, as a black woman. In my own reality, that didn't exist for me yet. I was

this trans girl who wasn't out, who wasn't revealing herself to the world or even to herself. It was so helpful to be able to look into those books and be like, *Wow, this is what life could be like for me.*

But the top one would be Zora Neale Hurston's *Their Eyes Were Watching God*. For me, that book was everything. The idea of this woman on a quest to find herself and to find the right kind of love and fulfillment and identity and not being smashed into her community's fantasies of her—that gave me so much agency. It pushed me to dream of greater possibilities for myself. It just blasted my mind open! You can be free!

What were you like as a teenager?

By the time I turned 13, I had met my best friend, Wendi. When you have a pivotal bestie, you kind of become the same person, but you also complement each other. Wendi was so unabashedly unapologetic about who she was that no matter what I did— even when I started transitioning—I could never seem as "out there" as her. I was always slightly in her shadow, which gave me safety. From 12 years old all the way until we were 18, we were like close close close tight. So when you ask me what I was like, I can't talk about my teenage self without talking about Wendi, because we're so linked.

But I was very internal, if that makes sense. I think I was a deeper thinker than my best friend was. I enjoyed the library. I enjoyed quiet space, because I didn't have that at home. But I also wanted attention, right? I was always kind of seen as a natural leader—people listened to me, and what I said mattered.

I loved school, and I was someone that people would ask for style advice. I always seemed like I was with it. I wasn't a popular girl, but people liked me. I wasn't ever going to be the prettiest girl in school, because I was a girl that wasn't even supposed to exist. But I hung out with the popular girls, and they were my friends, so that gave me access points. It was almost like I was tolerated because I had these cool friends. So I always felt like I was internal, but I bet a lot of people from high

school would remember me. I felt invisible, but I knew I wasn't—I was *so* visible.

I think that once you're out of high school, you start to understand that the way people see you does not necessarily line up with how you see yourself.

Mm-hmm. I had this sense of like…*oh my god, I was such a victim*. But then I realized that I'd internalized what people think trans people go through in high school. Like, it was tough, but high school was tough for a lot of people! I'm sure that my multiple lay- ers of identities that I inhabit made it more difficult [for me], but I still enjoyed high school. I wanted to go every day.

It wasn't my peers who gave me problems—it was mostly teachers who didn't understand how I could thrive, how I could be so liked, how I could be in marching band and debate club, how I could be captain of the volleyball team and be elected a student leader and become a peer mediator. They didn't understand how a trans girl could do all those things, so it's almost like they didn't want it to be true.

When I was in the eighth grade, me and Wendi started a petition to get the intermediate school to allow us to wear makeup. [*Laughs*] I didn't include this in my book because it's something I forgot, but other people remembered us going around with a clipboard and some notebook paper and getting people to sign a petition so that we could wear makeup. In my memory [Wendi and I] just walked into school wearing makeup. I don't remember ever getting in trouble for it. I was *that* student, though, that's who I was. When I watch *Election*, I'm like, *Oh, I was soooo Reese Witherspoon!*

Related, the times I've seen you speaking on TV, you seem to have so much grace and poise. Where do you learn those things?

In the mirror!

Do you think [poise is] something you can learn, or do you just naturally embody it?

[*Laughs*] I feel like because I've had to juggle so much, there's not much that bothers me. There are a lot of high-pressure things that are stressful—especially live TV appearances! They're *so* stressful, no matter what. Even if it's a "safe" environment with a host you really like, it's still super stressful. What grounds me in this idea of having "good composure" or being eloquent or graceful is over-preparedness. Over-preparing puts me at ease and allows me to be present. I can control how I act, how I react, how my face looks, how I sit, and what comes out of my mouth, which allows me to appear as though I'm totally at ease. It all comes from just growing up, juggling a lot at home, family dynamics, my own struggles with identity—wanting to be great, you know? Daring for greatness. Juggling all of these things was the boot camp. But preparedness is what grounds me. Knowing your environments so you can expect them, and even knowing the failings of your culture. Like, if you're going into a racist, capitalist, sexist corporate environment, and you know what it is and its failings, then you can know how to operate around it. You kinda seem like #unbothered.

What do you do when you are suffering, and how do you help your friends when they are suffering?

The space of suffering, I struggle with, because I'm part of a community that's so steeped in trauma. A lot of people talk about trans women of color and the violence that we deal with. But when we're together, we don't talk about that. Because the world will remind us of that. We know that when we walk in the world, we are under attack. We understand that. And so when we get together, we wanna talk about Beyoncé and have a couple cocktails, you know? Hang out and just *be*. Just be *happy*. Being happy together builds our sisterhood, but it also builds our resolve. It's just like, *This is revolutionary for us to be in this world and its suffering and to deal with suffering, but be fucking happy, too*. We don't need to sit in it all the time, because we exist in it.

Do you keep inspirational Post-it notes around your workspace?

Well, I do have one that my boyfriend, Aaron…he was listening to an audiobook about the *I Love Lucy* show—it's random, but he loves inside-Hollywood stories. The head writer who helped create that juggernaut of a television show said that the two things that matter in Hollywood are ownership and perception. So I have a Post-it note that says OWNERSHIP + PERCEPTION.

The work that I do, it really informs me. I want to own the content I make—I don't want to just be a subject on someone else's show. I want to be leading those conversations. Perception is the idea of definition—I can create the image of myself that I allow others to see. And I can maintain my boundaries in a public world.

Also, I have a sticker on my planner that says IT'S YOUR TURN TO CHANGE THE WORLD.

Speaking of, I read that you work with Youngist, a platform for young people to do citizen journalism and have an amplified voice in mainstream media. What do you do there?

I mostly just give editorial advice, but I think it's so important for any silenced group of people, like young people, to have their own platforms. Everyone loves to talk *about* millennials—I guess that's you guys!—but it's important to give them power to have their own voice. Everyone always asks me, "What advice would you give young people?" and I'm always like, young people know *exactly* what they wanna do! If they want advice from me, that young person will come to me, you know? They know their experiences. They know what they're going through. They know who they are. My job is not to talk down to them, or to give them some aspirational message. It's just to let them know that they have all the power to determine their own lives, to define them, and to declare them.

Youngist takes the political and pop culture news and really gives [millennials'] take on it, instead of older people always being like, "The millennials are taking selfies! They're so absorbed with themselves!" It's like, uh, no, look on YouTube, look at what they're doing.

It's nice to hear you say that—those selfie articles are so make-fun-of-able.

It's always like some 50-year-old cisgender white hetero man talking about young girls and what they're doing. It's like, this is so *pervy*, first of all! [*Laughs*] It's these people who think all young people are the same. No, they're not! It's really simplistic and reductive, and I think young people can just, like, grab their computers and blow shit up. 👄

Bombastic Anthems

1. We Are Young - fun. (feat. Janelle Monáe)
2. More Than A Feeling - Boston
3. Surrender - Cheap Trick
4. Empire State Of Mind - Jay-Z (feat. Alicia Keys)
5. Tiny Dancer - Elton John
6. Don't Stop Believin' - Journey
7. Die Young - Ke$ha
8. Hold On - Wilson Phillips
9. Born to Run - Bruce Springsteen
10. We Are the Champions - Queen
11. We Can't Stop - Miley Cyrus
12. Good Riddance (Time of Your Life) - Green Day

Rookie Regulars

Design by Tavi. Title lettering and illustrations by Caitlin. H.

Just Wondering

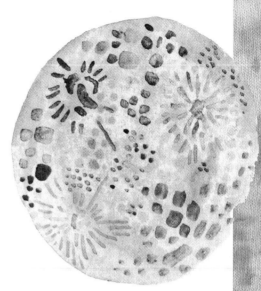

All your burning questions, answered by regular people.
By the Rookie staff. Illustration by Kendra.

I'm 19 and I've never been in a relationship, or even on a date. I'm not shy, and I can have a normal talk with a guy I like, but somehow, right when I am starting to think something might happen between us, it turns out they consider me "just a friend." What am I doing wrong? My friends have told me I should pretend to be more "girly" and "simple-minded."
—Mariana, Mexico

You sound like you're armed with a couple of great tools for dating: You're proactive and outgoing, which is already two steps ahead of where I was at 19—I could barely even talk normally with people I thought were SEXAY. And you've got the gift of self-possession, which will help you in all your romantic endeavors to come. Yeah!

I'm not sure from your letter whether the "just friends" part of your flirting attempts happens before or after you've actually taken the step of asking your crushee out. You say it's around when you start to think something "might happen" between the two of you, which makes me think you might be waiting for *him* to make the first move. If that's the case, it's time to take matters into your own hands! It sounds like you're comfortable being upfront with crushable dudes, so next time you see a special guy, be as clear as possible about your intentions, to avoid any just-friends-style confusion: "You are super. Do you want to go on a date with me?" That should take all the ambiguity out of the situation!

If you keep actually asking guys out and being turned down, that's a different kettle of fish. I know it can be supreme-ly discouraging, but again, can I say how great it is that you know what you want and how to go after it? This means that you'll be ready to PRESS PLAY when a dreamy guy comes along who likes you back. Keep in mind that rejection from this or that person (or people) doesn't mean there's anything wrong with you! There are so many reasons why someone might not respond to a romantic overture: They might be in a bad place in another area of their life, they might like someone else, they may not be interested in romance at all, or maybe they're getting ready to make a big life change that makes starting a relationship inconvenient. And, of course, they just might not like you *that way*. That hurts, I know, but it sounds like you've been able to move on from rejection in the past, so chalk it up to experience and move on. Behind every "successful" wooing are countless rejections, so take every "no" as a step toward a "yes" with someone else.

Based on the assumption that you are interested in an equal, awesome, loving relationship (and not an exhausting, de-bilitating one based on falsehoods), I don't agree with your friends' advice to pretend to be something you're not, especially if that includes the term *simple-minded*. Also, I plain can't see the benefit in going out with someone who would *want* their partner to be dumb—like, *urgh*! If you're a smart, curious individual who likes experiencing new things and/or discuss-ing ideas, being with someone who's not into that stuff would just be pure fun-killer.

As far as the "girly" thing goes, I wasn't aware that ALL DUDES IN THE WORLD like women to act super "femi-nine"…and that's because it just ain't true. It's *everyone's* prerogative to act as "mascu-line" or "feminine" as they like, and there are guys who are attracted to girls any-where along that spectrum. Sure, some guys seem to date only traditionally girly girls, but plenty more have tastes that in-clude girls who don't embody those traits. Anyway, you can't read minds to figure out the "right" way to act with any par-ticular guy. That's not to say you can't be a bit more flirtatious or dress up more when you're around someone you're crushing on—do that for sure! But when you're romantically involved with a guy, ideally it's because he likes you for who you are and who you want to be—not because you conform or aspire to a made-up ideal that you're guessing they might like. Putting on a false front is emotionally taxing and unsustainable in the long run. It's an un-fair way to treat yourself, and it's unfair to the other person, too—no one likes to be lied to (which is kinda what you'd be doing if you pretended to be something you aren't).

You opened by telling us that you're 19 and have never been on a date. DON'T WORRY. THAT IS TOTALLY FINE AND NORMAL. I know you're excited to step to it and experience the wonderful world of romance and sexxx for yourself, and that's great! But don't feel like you're weird or even unusual. Dating and love are a matter of timing in addition to com-patibility and attraction and all that stuff.

But if you're keen to kick-start your dating life, it's not a bad idea to start with your friends: Tell them you're interested in spending time with dudes *romantically* (*oooh*), and ask if they know anyone they can invite on your next group hang. If you start by thinking about what *you* want in a guy, and let other people know what that is—rather than obsessing over what some hypothetical guy might want in you—your romantic journey may start sooner than you think. Good luck! —Estelle

I have depression. It's severe enough that I never really know how I feel—about anything—other than depressed. I didn't think this was fair to my boyfriend, so I broke up with him. I know I love him platonically, but I can't count on any other feelings. Meanwhile, he's very affectionate and puts 100 percent of himself into relationships, and that made me feel even worse than I already did. We tried just being friends, but it didn't work, so now it seems like we might be getting back together, and I don't know if I can do this. How can I be fair to him without feeling like an awful person? Is it worse to date someone that you know deserves better treatment, or to leave them no choice?—Katie, 18, Scotland

This guy sounds wonderful, but I think you're focusing on the wrong things here. Although your depression may seem sad and pitiful, it's actually a very tough beast that will try to distract you from tackling it by any means necessary while it has its claws in you, and you have to learn to put it in its place. At the moment, it seems like you're more invested in your relationship than you are in building your coping skills, and that needs to change before you (and, by extension, the people you're romantically involved with) can be happy.

Your instincts seem to be telling you that this is not a good time for you to date, and I think you should respect those feelings, but rather than end your romantic relationship because you want to protect other people from you, do it because you need to prioritize *your own mental health*. Do you see the difference there? You're not selfish, and you're not a monster who hurts people indiscriminately—you're a

girl fighting depression, which is a very real and destructive psychological disorder, and right now you need to devote *all* of your energy to doing that, because you deserve to be well.

You also deserve understanding from the people who care about you. My suggestion is that you sit this gentleman down and tell him clearly that you have to dedicate yourself to caring for your own brain right now, and that it's too hard for you to do that while also trying to be someone's girlfriend. Let him know what you need from him as a friend, be it a shoulder to cry on, an occasional afternoon at the pizza place when you're feeling lonely, or respect for your boundaries while you take steps to manage your depression. Or all of the above! Then ask if he's willing to provide you with that kind of support, *without* the romantic elements of your relationship, at least for the time being. If he's not, let him know you'll be in touch when you're feeling a bit stronger.

When you have severe depression, you can be so flooded with sad and bad feelings that you become numb to them after a while. It takes effort to drain the flood and return to the regular tides of emotion. Right now, you need to concentrate on that battle without beating yourself up about a relationship. This is not just OK—it is *necessary* for your happiness. I know you have that fight inside you, or else you wouldn't have written. You seem to have an enormous heart, and I think it'll serve you greatly on your path to well-being. —Emily

I've become pretty disenchanted with relationships, but I really like the physical aspects of dating. Is it OK to just hook up with people until I feel more confident about who I am and whom I'm looking to spend the rest of my life with?—Lily E., Decatur, Alabama

The *rest of your life*, girl, damn! That sounds like a lot of years that you'll be spending with this potential future boat o' dreams. I imagine that it will take a *while* to find somebody worthy of so much of your time. I also imagine that you will sometimes feel the great urge to attach

your mouth/body to the mouths/bodies of others during this waiting period. (I imagine this because it's exactly what you wrote. Pretty perceptive of me, I know. Bring me your hardest advice questions and I'm pretty much guaranteed to spew out all manner of beautiful insights like this.)

Before we get into the ostensible matter at hand (and mouth/body) here, allow me to address the *real* Just Wondering that you hid in this question all coy, like, "This is the idea I really want someone to talk to me about, the soulmate thing, but I've been let down before, so I'm gonna couch it in this lascivious 'n' devil-may-care sex query, lest people think I am a herb who wants to feel a thing."

Look, dude. I absolutely believe in true love. It's the thing I believe in maybe above all other things in life—you can find it in friendships, in artwork, in sunny pockets of the afternoon where you just feel lucky to be hanging out in the world, and, of course, in romantic partners. I wonder if I could ever spend my whole life with someone, if they were dope enough. Probably. I also think I could, and will, spend stretches of my time on earth with other long-term partners, exploring, you know, the "physical aspects of dating" (YOW). It's OK to believe in, like, the thing Plato wrote about in the *Symposium*, where the playwright Aristophanes talks about how we're all half-people casting about for the missing double that will complete the erector set of our selves— it's the theory that everyone has a missing partner who fits them perfectly, in all places, like wearing a flawless bodycon dress but better, since it's UNDYING, WHOLE, ENDLESSLY ROMANTIC LOVE. That's like at least 12 flawless bodycon dresses, in terms of feeling good, probably.

Of course, it's fine to not believe in a one and only. And you don't have to pretend—and I'm not saying you're doing this here, but others reading it might be, and I did it myself, once upon a time— that you do believe if you don't. In my pre-18 years, I used "not having met the right person" as an excuse for wanting to put my mouth/body to extensive, diverse work because I didn't want people to think I was a skank (no such animal, by the way): "I just haven't found THE ONE! That's why I have to make out with this incredible-looking bohunk/Betty whose chest I'm already groping! *Sigh!*" Just kiss (or whatever) him/her/them, darling-thing. You don't have to explain a thing to anybody. It's five thousand percent fine.

I guess this brings us to the body encasing the heart of your question: **Yes.** Make out with whomever you like. Just make sure you're doing it because you want to, not because you feel like you're supposed to or like you're rotting away for not being with someone you actually adore instead of whatever rando is around to make you feel like you're "normal" for being Young Person Having Kiss Experience! High School Party!

Since you mentioned building confidence, I'm gonna mention it too (those incredible advice-giving instincts kicking in again, I know, PayPal me a high five or something): The phrase "until I feel more confident about who I am" seems to me to be an expression of almost terrifyingly on-point acumen in re: understanding that you need room, as a young person, to grow and shred at will, and that sometimes that process involves experimental games of TONSIL HOCK-AY. If this is what you meant, I should be PayPaling *you*, because that's amazing, and: **Yes.** BUT. If you meant "until I hook up with enough people that I feel ready to settle down without some sense of missing out on a broader spectrum of bods and babes"…HA, just kidding, that's also totally fine! Do it up. Wait, wait, though: On a serious note, if you're saying that you need to hook up with people IN ORDER to be confident that you are an attractive, rad person, that's where I cock my head a little. You don't. You already are. I know you know that—I'm just making sure. (And if you don't know it, GET TO KNOWING IT, SERIOUSLY.)

Anyway, I love you a lot, and I'm wrapping up, but finally, it doesn't sound like you're all that "disenchanted with relationships" from where I'm typing this to you (empty bathtub—long story).

Based on the last part of your question—that "rest of my life" business—it sounds like you believe in true love just as fervently and ferociously as I do. You will find amazing people everywhere, if you make yourself available to them—people who will hang for the short term (HOOKIN' UP, HOOKER!!! WOO) and the long term (Aristophanes, if you want). Do whatever you feel is right, and OF COURSE it's OK so long as you're safe and respectful of yourself and other people. I'm sorry if someone hurt you, or something. Fuck that person, for real, and you can tell them I said it. Now go have a great time. Yes! —Amy Rose

I haven't had Facebook for two years. I found it too tiring to maintain another persona, and I was constantly comparing myself with others when I was on it. A lot of people act like it's weird that I don't have it, though—some are even hostile about it. One friend told me that employers are less likely to hire you if you don't have a Facebook account. Should I just suck it up and re-register? I'm kind of nervous that if I do, people will look at my history and see that I haven't been doing much for the past two years. —Claire, 18, Sydney

I am saluting you for being both decisive and mysterious. I didn't have Facebook for years, and I never felt bad about it for a second—it always felt like a part-time job to keep up with people in what felt like a superficial way, and I was not willing to welcome ol' man Zuckerberg as my new information overlord, so I peaced right the hell out.

I can understand feeling pressured to rejoin—people can be relentless about things *they* think are good for you. But remember that you quit for a valid reason: You were tired of maintaining a persona and comparing yourself with others. If staying away from Facebook makes you feel happier and better about how you interact with the world, it is 100 percent the way to go.

Do you use other social media? The next time someone gives you lip about not being on FB, just say, "Duh, I'm on Twitter, where everyone fabulous hangs out and I can send a message to Chan-ning Tatum if I want to." If you don't use *any* social media, that's even better—they'll be scrambling to figure you out, and you'll keep 'em guessing about how you spend your time, which is really none of their business in the first place. Just by not having FB, you're halfway to mastering the sort of aloofness people struggle their whole lives to adopt! If people won't let up on the pressure, remind them that it's very rude to get up in your face like that.

Here is something I can promise you: No employer cares whether or not you have Facebook, unless you are applying for a job as a social-media person (or a job *at Facebook*), and there are privacy laws in most countries that prevent employers from accessing your private online information, anyway. Most potential employers just want to know that you're not a liability or a weirdo, and there are a bunch of other ways to find that out. Don't get Facebook just to get a job! (Would you even want a job that requires it?)

Right now I have a fake Facebook for work (with a fake name, all fake bio information, using an email associated only with my Facebook account)—you can always go that route if you need to. But trust me: You're not missing out on anything by not being on there. And what you're gaining in time and mysteriousness is invaluable. —Danielle

I'm ending a pregnancy and could use some moral support. Is there such a thing as life after having an abortion? While I have very little doubt that I'm doing the right thing (for everyone), I still feel really confused. —M., 17, Chicago

I'm not going to talk to you about the medical risks or political/religious implications that come with having an abortion, because that information is available to you on a website called Google that you may have heard of. Here, we're not going to focus on *what your abortion means for the world*, because the answer to that would simply be "only what it means to *you*," and so that's what we'll be thinking about today.

I can tell you with an ironclad certainty that there is a life after abortion, M. I know because I'm living one right now, and so are a ton of other people all around both of us: Every year, 1.3 million American women make the choice that we did. *You are not alone*, and making this choice doesn't make you evil, selfish, or deviant. You have the right to decide what happens to your life and to make informed choices about your future (and how your actions might impact the futures of others), and I want you to keep remembering that as you go through this process.

Having an abortion is emotionally complicated, and often very difficult, for lots of reasons. It's natural to feel sad and/or conflicted about it, even when your circumstances are such that choosing otherwise would disadvantage everyone affected (although I'm not saying you're fucking yourself over if you decide to have a baby as a teenager—everyone's choices and situations are their own). There are some people out there who believe that going through with an abortion is bad or immoral no matter why you're doing it (and if you, the person reading this, are one of those people, that's fine, too, just as long as you're not hassling others for their actions or mindsets if they disagree with you). But you have to trust yourself to know what's best for you, because you do.

Not only is there life after an abortion, but that life is usually the reason someone chooses to get one in the first place. When I got pregnant at 19, I tried to rationalize carrying a child to term in many different ways. But when I was done agonizing, I knew that having a baby with nearly nonexistent financial security would mean that the life that would follow that decision would be incredibly hard for that potential kid—not to mention for my family, my boyfriend, *his* family, and me. I also thought about putting my non-baby up for adoption, then considered how I've always wanted to become a foster parent because there are already more than 400,000 children in need of permanent homes in the United States *alone*. I wasn't acting heartlessly by making the choice to have an abortion. Had I

carried that pregnancy to term, I would have been trying to make myself feel better in the short term, based on someone else's idea of what would be the "right" thing to do, and meanwhile I'd be giving yet another kid a hugely disadvantaged start in life. Part of what makes it so hard to have an abortion is the fear that doing so makes you a terrible person. That's obviously not true in any way, but even if it's what some people believe, would you rather potentially look bad in the eyes of a bunch of people who would judge another person for making a painful and complex decision, or make an irreversible choice by having a baby you don't want just to appease them? Seriously.

But that hypothetical child's life isn't the only, or even the main, reason you might choose to have an abortion. What I want you to be thinking about is *your* life. Although there are people in this world who don't want you to believe this (see above in re: judgy judgers), it is completely OK to get an abortion to *preserve your own happiness*. You have the right to avoid permanently committing yourself to a future you don't want. You do not have to pay the disproportionate penance of having an actual child for accidentally becoming pregnant (and if bringing life into the world feels like a punishment, you probably should not be having a baby anyway!). It's not self-centered to make the choice you know will be right for you in the long run; it's actually the most ethical thing you can do here. When I weighed this decision as a teenager, I knew I had to think about not only my figurative baby's quality of life, but my own. The two are basically inextricable anyway, honestly.

So, I had an abortion. I sobbed for weeks, but I also stayed in college and avoided creating a lifelong bond with an unstable person whom I didn't love (and who also wasn't ready to care for a child) and/or destitution. Most of all, I remembered that I was giving myself the care I needed to be happy, instead of creating more unhappiness in the world by having a baby I was incapable of raising. I know that one day I'll be in a position to raise a child, whether I choose to do that

through pregnancy, fostering, or adoption—*if* I want to, and *only* if I'm ready to fully support that kid, emotionally and financially.

The main bit of advice I would give you is to allow yourself every single feeling you might be having right now, without judging yourself. When I went through this, what helped me most to keep my footing in the aftermath was to let myself feel heartbroken, and guilty, and not guilty, and angry, and *all of it*. These feelings don't have to make sense or support some "position" about how you feel politically. They're going to be intense, and you have to meet them head-on so you can work through them. Write in a diary. Talk to people you trust and who love you—or don't, if you can't handle it. I was very private about my abortion when it happened—I probably told three people, and that small circle of intimacy was right for me because I knew that some of the people in my life might not understand, and I didn't want to open myself up to their scrutiny. If you're feeling psychologically fragile, as I was, be discerning about whom you tell—but *do* confide, if you can, both in yourself by being honest about every single one of your feelings about this, and in people you trust and who love you. It helps immensely. And if you find that you're still feeling shaken about this whole thing in a few months, find a therapist.

Eventually, time will pass, and you willl stop thinking about it constantly, and you'll come back to yourself and your life. Like every experience you have as a person, your abortion will be a part of you forever, but also like any other single thing you go through, it won't define who you are on the whole. Consider what you think when another person ends a pregnancy: Do you think that women who make that call should feel shame or regret? My guess is that you don't, so extend that courtesy to yourself, too. I absolutely believe you know what's right for you, and I deeply respect that you are advocating for yourself and making an informed choice. I'm certain your life after abortion will be a fulfilling, successful, and happy one. Good luck, my love. —Amy Rose ☽

Dear Diary

The secret public journals of five teenage girls.

Britney

June 12, 2013

On the subway on Friday, a disheveled man who looked like he hadn't slept indoors in a while turned to me and said, "It is my job to find the one that I love." Then he told me how many push-ups and pull-ups he does daily, using the train's metal poles to demonstrate. I managed a polite smile, in accordance with one of New York's many subway etiquette guidelines (along with "let people off before you get on" and "if you see something, say something"). But it was hard to smile, because his words struck a nerve with me.

I have made it my mission to be loved, and it is slowly tearing me apart. Yes, my family loves me, and so do the friends that I constantly count on. But I want the type of love that does not fit into any boxes—one that's not strictly romantic, platonic, or familial. It is warm, and thinking about it makes me imagine running through the woods without ever having to stop, free of worries. It is the type of love that would hold you back from doing anything horrible.

My elementary school teachers used to teach us to take a moment while we were reading a novel to reflect on the story. Now I do this with my life. I ask myself, *Am I happy?* At first, I answer, *Yeah, of course—I just hung out with so-and-so.* But after a few moments have passed, I realize how temporary that joy was and that I have been lying to myself about my own emotions.

I don't want to feel as though my life will be validated only if I get that kind of unconditional love from another person. I want to be able to wade through this seemingly endless river of confusion without holding someone's hand.

June 26

I. Graduation

It rains on graduation day; my English teacher calls it "sympathetic weather." I convince myself that this is not the end, but the beginning, of my very own coming-of-age novel/movie. My friends and I are the Holden Caulfields, Cher Horowitzes, and Veronica Sawyers of the world. We are each trying to discover our unique selves.

We will officially leave middle school behind in just a few hours. The air is thick and hot with our simultaneous breathing as we crowd together under the awning of Brooklyn College (our own school's auditorium isn't big enough to hold the 400+ graduates and their families). We were supposed to be inside ages ago, but the heavy doors are still shut. "LET US IN!" my friends and I scream to no one, throwing our umbrellas at the building. Soon almost everyone around us has joined in. The doors finally open. We crowd in, yelling, much to the dismay of the teachers waiting inside.

Thirty minutes later we are all lining up to go onstage and receive our diplomas. One of my best friends, Sydney, is starting to hyperventilate. "I can't do this," she whispers. I grab her hand and lead her away from the loud chatter and laughter of our classmates.

"It's fine, OK?" I say, though I'm not sure I believe it myself. "I know exactly how you feel."

"It's just that I fit in so well with you guys," she says. "Next year, I'll have no one." It's all sinking in—we won't be together next year; we'll all be scattered across the city in different high schools.

I feel my eyes begin to well up even though I promised myself that under no circumstances would I cry. I was afraid that if I became emotional, I wouldn't be able to stop. Sydney is speaking the truth, and I can't help agreeing with her.

"What am I going to do next year?" I say. "You guys let me be immature one minute, serious the next. You don't think I'm weird. I've never felt this way before about any of my friends, and now…"

I've always wanted amazing friends like these, and now I have to leave them behind.

It feels like graduation is not actually happening—how can we be graduating already? Throughout the ceremony, I laugh at funny memories that spring to mind. I come close to crying again. I hug my friends, my teachers, my mother—but nothing feels real. If someone were to pinch me, I would wake up. When my name is called, I clutch my diploma with sweaty palms.

II. Prom

Prom is at an Italian restaurant a couple of blocks from school. I am 45 minutes late. When I walk in, everyone else is already there, sitting with their friends. I can tell it's going to be bad. I stand there awkwardly and pull at my dress while I try to casually scan the room, only to lock eyes with my former crush. If this were a romantic comedy, he would walk up to me and smile and ask if I wanted to join him. But this is real life—my life—so I end up running in the other direction to find my friends' table. He sees me, but hopefully he just thinks I'm trying to find my friends.

After that, everything goes downhill.

My prom date is even later than I am. He disappears as soon as he arrives. He reappears later, while I'm dancing with my friends.

"Guess what?" he says, grinning.

"Wha—" I begin.

"I'm dumping you!" he says before

running off. I watch him put his arm around a girl I've never seen before; he leans in and says something to her, and they both erupt in laughter.

"Oh my gosh!" says a friend, letting out a shocked laugh. I muster a tiny, crooked smile as I struggle not to cry or go over and punch him in the face. I feel like someone has punched *me* in the stomach—not because I liked him, but because I have once again become the loner watching other people be happy.

My best friend reaches out and pulls me into the dancing masses, but I can't bring myself to dance—it feels too stupid now, especially since everyone else is using "dancing" as an excuse to grind against one another. "I have to go," I yell over the music. I run to the back of the room and sit with Sydney.

"This is so dumb," I say, grabbing a handful of ice from the bowl in the middle of the table and popping it into my mouth.

"Agreed," she says. She gives me one of the earbuds sticking out of her iPod. We sit and listen to Flobots' "Handlebars" while everyone around us runs around, dances, and hops from table to table to visit their friends.

Someone throws butter on the dance floor, and everyone is forced to sit down for three minutes while it gets cleaned up and our assistant principal yells at us about this "butter incident." This is one of the few good parts of the evening; the situation itself is hilarious and, for once, no one is grinding.

I spend most of the rest of the night being forced to listen to people recount how so-and-so kissed them, and how exciting it was to make out.

At the very end, things pick up. My favorite songs are playing and I'm dancing with a small group of my friends. *This* is how I want to remember middle school—I want to remember the happy parts, the ones that made me want to stay, and the ones that made me feel lucky for the experience. I think of all the laughter we've shared, all of the jokes we've told one another, how the fun we created shaped this experience for me. I want to remember the beautiful times.

May 28, 2014

One of the best feelings in the world is finding out that someone that you have really, really liked for months feels the same way about you. One of my best friends and I are going out now, and even though it has only been a few days, I don't think I've ever been happier. Her being in my life is literally the best thing that has ever happened to me, and I just want to hang out with her and give her mix CDs and crumple up all of the poems that I wrote during worse times. My life has become euphoric because of her existence in a space formerly occupied by final essays and exams and half-made plans for summer. I feel like I'm growing up, and, oddly enough, it isn't terrifying.

There is so much I want to say about all of this that I don't know how to take the time to express any of it eloquently—I just write everything that comes to mind. But I'm content at the moment just sharing everything. ♦

Katherine

July 24, 2013

Sunday night I was hanging out at home with my brother, and naturally our conversation turned to the Kardashians. We had determined which Kardashian each member of our family is most like and were beginning to refine those comparisons when my mom walked into the kitchen.

Davis told her who was who, then he began to list everyone's secondary Kardashian personality, like: "Mom is the Scott Disick of Kris Jenners. Katherine's the Kim Kardashian of Kourtney Kardashians. I'm like…what am I? Just Khloé?" And I was like, "Yeah LOL." Later I said he was the Kylie Jenner of Lamar Odoms of Khloé Kardasians, but mostly he's just a more self-aware Khloé and is sore because he would rather be Kourtney because she's our favorite. Mom was agitated because we told her she was Kris, and she remembered that we once told her that we hate Kris. But she can't deny that she and Kris are twins, down to the fact that they both love any house decoration that has a rooster on it. Dad may have some Bruce Jenner or Lamar Odom in his equation, but he mostly transcends comparison.

I think I'm the only one who didn't complain about their Kardashian analogue. In fact, I am OVER THE MOON about mine. Sometimes Kim and Khloé just don't catch on to what is going on around them, but Kourtney *always* knows what's up. She's the smartest Kardashian sister, and she knows that. Also, she does this thing where she'll be trying to help someone and she'll ask, "What is this doing for you?" And sometimes when her sisters are tormenting her she will call them "you sick freaks," which proves how alike we are, because that's how I react to my brother when he's being annoying, and I'm always doubtful that anything I do is actually beneficial to anyone.

Netflix Instant provides a single word in its "This show is" section for *Keeping Up With the Kardashians*: *scandalous*. This makes no sense. OK, there was a sex tape, but is that really, truly "scandalous"? It's definitely a scandal in that many media outlets reported on it, but it's not actually shocking, it's just something people habitually call a "scandal." (And anyway, only the first episode of the first season really deals with the aftermath of Kim's tape.) Is it just that the Kardashians' money, their tendency to rock clubwear in the daytime, and their frequent mentions of genitalia (usually via the euphemisms *saussige* and *vajeen*) give them an aura of "scandal"? They're a tight family that's concerned mostly with supporting one another and making loads of money—what could be tamer than that?

January 1, 2014

I just sent an email to my advisor asking for the code I need to register for a January class. Most students take the month off, but the university is still officially open, and you can elect to go back early to make up some credits or work on an individual project. I want to go back early to avoid being home, even if it means I have to take a random course and read Ayn Rand or some other torture.

Being home has been nice in a lot of ways. I got to hang out with my brother and our baby cousin (the only acceptable baby in the world). I've gone to the movies, driven my car around, taken advantage of

having food around 24/7, and watched a lot of TV. But I need to leave. Here's why:

1. My mom is treating me like a child/idiot. I went out to dinner with her one of the first nights I was here, and when we were done eating and I started to ask the waitress for a box for the rest of my food, my mom cut me off and asked for one on my behalf. Then she smiled at me and said, super condescendingly, "I know that's hard for you." O. M. G. Like, I know she's trying to be sensitive to the fact that I hate being in public, but I haven't had significant difficulty talking to restaurant staff since like 2008. Yes, sometimes I panic and want help doing stuff like that, but I usually ask for it when I need it. Plus, if she truly cared about my fear of interacting with strangers, she would have ordered for me at the beginning of the meal, right?

There's an episode of *Sex and the City* where Carrie brings Miranda bagels to be "a good friend," but she forgets the cream cheese. Miranda calls her out on this, because it's evident that Carrie just wanted to come over to talk about her own recent breakup, or else she would have remembered the cream cheese. My mom wanted to be helpful, but it seems like she *really* just wanted to demonstrate that she "understands" me, without actually doing the work of understanding me.

2. The way my mom is treating me reminds me of how angry she'd get whenever I wanted to stay home from Sunday school or social gatherings. She used to talk about how sin and doubt were signs of the devil's influence.

I remember all of the things my family and friends took it upon themselves to diagnose me with: anxiety, depression, Asperger's, ADD. It made me feel defective, like I was born spoiled the way food can be spoiled in the making. I imagined a black tumor rapidly growing inside me, representing whatever made me feel afraid of and distant from others.

I used to picture myself at the bottom of a series of dark, labyrinthine subterranean tunnels that glowed red and

emitted red flames. I imagined that God had left me there, and that the only ways out were to be morally pure and to socialize, or to reject God and his "plan" for me outright, whereupon I could find happiness in this life but would be condemned to spend my afterlife in hell, which terrified me. I thought that I might one day write about all of this, and that the second option would make for better writing.

I think I came up with the labyrinth in fourth grade. My friend and I got into a series of books called Daughters of the Moon. It was about teenage girls who had magic powers because they were secretly goddesses. We copied the moon-shaped necklaces they wore with yarn and tinfoil, called each other Serena and Vanessa after two of the main characters, and pretended to be them at recess. When we wrote down the names of these books for a class reading competition, our teacher was alarmed. When she learned that they included witchcraft and—worse—sex, she contacted our parents.

I remember crying as my mom yelled at me that night. I remember not knowing what about those books she was so afraid of but figuring it out later. At the end of our talk, she held up the second book, *Into Cold Fire*, and asked me what color it was. The cover was red. "Do you know what that is?" she asked. I didn't answer. "It's the color of the Devil. This girl"—she pointed to the girl on the cover, who happened to be Serena, the character I pretended to be—"is the devil."

This incident is really, really, really funny to me now because it's really, really, reallllllyyy funny, but it was horrifying to me then because it confirmed all of my fears about myself: that I was unfit for society and also morally bad, condemned to hell. It also set the template for how I would think about sex once I found out what it was: as a dark ritual that your soul would be punished for engaging in. It's taken years for me to release my self-image from the grip of these ideas. They made me so miserable for so long.

I know that I have some social anxiety and a disposition that favors observation over participation, but I also have the ability to work through my anxieties and

confidence so that it's possible for me to be with other people, because there is no tumorous mass of evil within me. Being home makes me remember how I used to feel. Being at school means I can continue progressing.

3. The mundane here is worse than the mundane there. Saturday night at dinner, my mom recounted a *hilarious* story that a woman from my grandmother's nursing home had told her at the home's Christmas party. The woman listed everything she'd made for Christmas breakfast the year before. She'd made a bunch of really good food, but when she sat down to eat, she realized she'd forgotten to make eggs. My mom repeated the "zinger" (SHE FORGOT TO MAKE THE EGGS) and laughed, and my dad laughed his fake laugh.

At school, there is much that is mundane and plenty of false laughter, but I would rather listen to an infinite number of people talking about studying than hear this kind of story again. If I'm going to be frustrated and bored in any capacity, I would rather do it there, where there are people I like and where even the boring things at least have a point.

January 22
"Can you give me a kiss, Brisen?"

My baby cousin obliged, leaning forward and surprising me with a huge wet kiss on the mouth. A few days later I had a fever. I reassumed the habits of my younger self, the one who spent summers and breaks alone in my room like a sickly shut-in, although I was perfectly healthy. Now that I was genuinely ill, I was afraid people wouldn't believe me, but I didn't have the energy to perform my sickness as proof. I felt dizzy and weak. I had to remind myself that I'm not always like this. I am not what my parents (and I) think I am.

My grandmother and I recently took a road trip together to Florida. On our second day of driving, we stopped at a Texaco station. I stepped out of the car to stretch and was paralyzed by the hot humidity, the first real warmth I'd felt since September. A heron appeared in front of me like a fig-

ure from a dream, as if he had summoned his own existence in the flash of an eye. He looked dirty and cheap. In the gas-station-snack world he would be those barbecued pork rinds that are actually Styrofoam peanuts with powder on them. I was staring at him when my grandmother, not for the first time, said, "I want to teach you how to live dangerously."

"Please do," I said, but I wasn't sure what she had in mind. Did she think I should be going out more? For the past few days I had accompanied her to everything she asked me to, and I always had fun. I asked her to do stuff with me, too, and I made sure I talked about the kinds of things I do at school. I felt like it was clear that I'm decently active, but I guess not?

She repeated her exhortation Sunday morning at brunch. I told her I didn't know what more I could be doing. Did it have to do with parties and alcohol? I invited her to visit me at Smith next year—she could hang out with me and my friends and see how we are. (This is the best fantasy life I've ever created.) She could "live dangerously" with us, I said, insinuating that there are stories I just can't tell her, the way she has stories of nights out that she won't go into detail about, even when I ask. There are definitely things I won't tell Mimi, but they're not the kinds of stories she's looking for.

"I've been the wild card in certain groups," I said.

"I just want to see you live more dangerously!" she said again, but, in her typical fashion, refused to go into detail.

Maybe she meant dating? I just turned 20, and I have never dated anyone. I have neither kissed nor been kissed. I have expressed interest in no one (and vice versa). I have flirted with *very* few people (and vice versa). I feel mutual attraction with very few people. I've had potentially delusional inklings that some of my friends' parents have been attracted to my energy, and sometimes that feeling, real or imagined, was mutual. Having a boyfriend would help my case, but that's not something that's currently available to me. I wasn't about to try to pick someone up on a weeklong trip to Florida with my

grandmother—that would probably be *too* dangerous for her.

Should I have told her about my crushes? I hate talking about that stuff. It makes me feel like some large part of me is being ripped out of my body. "I have a crush on every boy," I falsely moaned to my friends at sleepovers in middle school and early high school, to make them laugh and to get them to stop asking me about crushes. So I can't tell Mimi about my crushes. Crushes are a safe space, a private space, and there's something about them that makes me melancholy.

Should I have told her how once, in a darkened pizza parlor in Arizona, sated with pizza and drunk on the feeling of deep bonding that one can feel only after a week of camping, doing construction work, talking about God around campfires, and not showering, a boy turned to me when no one was looking, caught me wiping tomato sauce off my face, and said, "God, you're so pretty. Like…gorgeous?" When I didn't respond immediately, his expression dimmed and he said, "Did you know that?" And then I *continued to not respond. I did not move or change my expression or make a noise.* I just sat there and stared at him for a minute, then I stood up, walked slowly to the bathroom, and bent over the toilet to vomit. I didn't end up puking, but I stayed in there for a long time, sure that I would.

I didn't tell her this story, because although it might convey the kind of devil-may-care attitude she seems to be looking for, it would also show her that I am incapable of interacting with people, and therefore incapable of actually "living dangerously."

My parents would probably agree with her. They think I'm a shut-in. And I am sometimes, but not always, not even most of the time, and on the whole it is not as pitiable and boring as they suggest, nor as tragic and final as I sometimes feel it is. It's so many different things at different times.

This diary doesn't help my case with my parents. But I determine what I write about here, so it's my fault, really. This is the persona I so often choose to show the world. I hold it up and turn it this way and that in front of my peers like I'm on QVC show-

ing off a gaudy ring. Depending on how the light catches it, it can look elegant, tragic, funny, inconsequential, pitiful, embarrassing, brilliant, dignified, dull. When I look at it in the privacy of my room, I can see how much of it is me and how much is a lie.

I think I live pretty dangerously now. I accept every invitation to hang out. I get out of my dorm room as much as possible. And since I read Charlotte Brontë's novel *Villette*, I've been trying to avoid ending up like the main character, Lucy Snowe, a woman who finds herself stuck in isolating circumstances and habits.

God, Lucy Snowe! Has looking in a mirror ever made me feel as much like I would vomit everything in my body—all the food, viscera, bones, and deeper layers of skin, until I am paper-flaked to pieces—as this book did? Lucy's story aligned with my reality in many ways, which scared me enough to convince me that I should change the way I live and how I experience, consider, and choose isolation. Lucy takes pride in being emotionally removed from things as they are happening, but she is uncomfortable being alone. I am trying to lessen the distance between myself and things that are happening around me. Lucy dresses in dark, plain clothing and suppresses her personality; I want to dress more distinctly and to be more social in general. Lucy tries to avoid interacting with people who are mean or thoughtless or who strongly disagree with her philosophies about life. I would like to be more open to getting to know all kinds of people, instead of giving up immediately when something doesn't instantly click.

Mimi wants me to experience more danger, but I've always felt it everywhere. I've faced danger and acted despite it many times. I've tried out for plays and dance shows in high school. I go out a lot even though it's often, if not emotionally grueling, at least incredibly distracting.

There have been times when I've lived less dangerously, and those have had their own rewards. Every day I've spent hiding has been as rich with drama as every day I have tried to connect with someone.

There was the drama of the dark and necromantic world I lived in when I was younger. The moral confusion and the fire-

filled labyrinth I imagined as its metaphor.

The drama at the start of each new friendship, and at the end. My friendship with Chloe, my first friend at my new school, and still the one I am with most often. The drama of our difficulties, and the way friendship morphs into new good shapes and new bad shapes.

The drama of starting to have a close relationship with my brother. Of helping each other out.

The drama of deciding whether or not everything you feel is based on something you've imagined. Having my first crush at Smith in my French class and being unable to feel even the despairing kind of hope I generally use to torture myself, because that kind of hope hinges on possibility, and I thought she had a boyfriend. Feeling instead a different kind of hope that is a fevered knowledge of impossibility.

Discovering later that what she had was an ex-girlfriend, recently anointed. Getting lunch and overhearing her friend ask her how she felt about the breakup. Hearing her respond that she felt bad, but wouldn't after this weekend. Feeling unsure if she looked at me when she said it or if her friend grinned slightly and knowingly when she noticed me watching them. Being unable to read her body language because her movements were too slight to be certain. Experiencing a sublime feeling akin to being taken over by a fever when she tapped my ankle three times under the table when we were studying together later that day, because I think the second and third tap *maybe* lingered. Changing my position to check. Being unable to concentrate all afternoon and for days after, feeling feverish while reanalyzing our interactions and wishing I had risked embarrassment and said something, lived more dangerously. Beating myself up for everything I had said around her, and for everything I hadn't said. For missing chances to ask her the questions I wanted to ask. For missing the opportunity to have any connection with this person. Later, I recited to myself: "I made you up inside my head."*

I think I made you up inside my head. There are so many experiences that I might have only imagined. So many aspects of my friendship with Chloe, so many looks from people, so much of many things. There's a madness that comes with being often isolated and struggling to connect with others while also being incredibly naïve and exceptionally inexperienced.

I remember a scene from the French movie *Fat Girl* where, in sight of her sister and the dude her sister is flirting with, Anaïs swims back and forth between a pole holding up the diving platform at a pool and the pool's ladder. As she reaches each one, she holds it and talks to it and kisses it like it's her lover. What she tells these inanimate suitors is intelligent but naïve: "Women aren't like bars of soap, you know. They don't wear away. On the contrary, each lover brings them more, and you get all the benefit." Then: "You make me sick. How can you disgust me and attract me so much?"

When I go to bed, I feel myself expand into the surrounding darkness and feel myself walking, moving, touching surfaces as I move about with people I love. Talking to them and using my hands to touch the words we've spoken.

I'm in Florida with Mimi, and I realize how much I love her. A great side effect of getting older has been being able to talk to her and having her share more with me. I have my brother. I have my dad. I have school and people I like there.

I feel fine. I'm not bitter or overly tragic or any of the other things my family says I am after reading these entries. I'm just in limbo, swimming back and forth between my own two poles. I have, if not an early life lived dangerously, one in which I have keenly felt everything. In fact, I have had hundreds of real experiences. I'll have more. ♦

Ruby B.

June 5, 2013

I've had a crush on Sophia* since the first day of school. A crush that is platonic, but burning. It is much more than a wish-I-was-your-friend crush. It's an obsession. It's looking at pictures of her and memorizing her face, and trying to follow her to her classes so I can watch her hair sway behind her. She is perfect. Until last Friday, she did not know I existed.

Sophia is a senior this year. Friday was her last day of school, excluding exams. I had been spending two months vowing to say hi to her before she left for college and I'd never see her again, but I didn't have the courage. Every time I tried to approach her I felt my heart race and couldn't get any closer.

Then on Friday I was in study hall in the school cafeteria, sitting at a table with some acquaintances, just listening to music and minding my own business, when Sophia and her pack swooped through the door and sat down two tables away. She had her hair up in a bun and was wearing shorts and a tank top. She looked like a goddess. My brain stopped. I ran out of the room.

Fifteen minutes later I had gathered myself and was ready to re-enter. Just as I was about to walk through the door, Sophia walked through the other way. I experienced her passing in slow motion, free strands of hair framing her face and blowing backwards. I thought about how this was the last time I would ever see her. I felt my legs propel me forward and suddenly I was right in front of her, looking at her face.

What came out of my mouth was completely involuntary. I was so stunned by this sudden, unprecedented proximity and eye contact that I asked if I could hug her. She said yes and I wrapped my arms around her and didn't squeeze because she is delicate and I was afraid I would break her. Then I did something else unexpected: I gave a very loud and passionate speech confessing my feelings about/for her. I don't remember the words of it. It had something about "infinite beauty." Then I ran away.

She chased me. I thought I was about to get beat up. But she caught up and told me to give her another hug. "You're too cute," she said. I said something along the

---

* From Sylvia Plath's poem "Mad Girl's Love Song."

* Name has been changed.

lines of "uvhbsjkndckbs." I walked straight into a wall. Then I waited for her to leave.

My friend Sam was in the hallway. I couldn't hear over the sound of my heart. I yelled to him and he came over. I felt like I was in a dream. I could barely get the words out for my euphoria: "I hugged Sophia."

November 6

"Good thing your father brought all your stuff. You're not going to be able to wear what you've got on now." The nurse rummages through the giant plastic bag whose large blue print reads:

PATIENT BELONGINGS
RUBY BOOK: ADOLESCENT
INPATIENT UNIT

"Take off your pants," she says. "They've got stringy things—what are they, Tripp pants? Hardly practical." I don't respond as I take them off. She throws a pair of gray sweatpants at me. "Lots of pockets, though. That's nice."

I pull on the sweatpants and hand over my shoelaces, hair elastics, and hat.

"Oh, we changed some policies," she says. "You can't bring pillows, blankets, stuffed animals, makeup, or hats." I watch as a couple of orderlies gather my things and carry them away.

"I can't have my pillow?"

"No."

"Can I wear my hat, just for right now?"

"You can wear hats in your room. I'll give it back later." In a few hours, I will learn this was a lie.

That evening I sit in an uncomfortable chair in a circle of other uncomfortable chairs filled with members of the Adolescent Inpatient Unit. No one's shoes have laces in them.

"What's your name?" says a girl around my age, maybe a little bit older.

"Ruby."

"Really? That's sort of a weird name for a white girl. Why are you here?"

"I don't really feel comf—"

"Just forget it," she says, interrupting me. "I bet you're just 'stressed about school' or something, like every other fake bitch

who comes here. You know there's no Starbucks, right?"

"Actually, if you'd—"

"Whatever. You just don't know what it's like here, in an actual psychiatric hospital. It's not as easy as you think."

"This isn't my first time," I snap bitterly, "and I didn't come here on vacation. I don't want to be here, but I probably need to be. If you don't believe me, leave me alone." I fold my arms and glare into space.

"What's on your arm?" she says, speaking softly now. "That looks…really… really bad."

I pull down my sleeve as quickly as I can and turn to walk as far away from her as possible, which is about 30 feet.

I told myself I'd never let it get this bad. I told myself I'd tell my therapist everything. I told myself I'd never let myself get so out of control that I'd end up here again.

I scream.

March 12, 2014
> *But now that I'm older*
> *My heart's colder*

I'm in this weird place where Arcade Fire knows me better than anybody. Even though I'm 16, just a few months ago I would carefully arrange all my stuffed animals on my bed so as not to hurt any of their feelings. I still think of them by their names and have a sense of their distinct personalities.

When I walked home the other night, I pretended I was from a different planet, or a different time. I was full of fake wonder.

Real wonder is no longer part of my life. I'm not a child anymore. In a way, this is something I've always wanted, but now that I know I'm grown up, it's sad. It happened too fast. I'm old and bitter.

At 16 I understand death better than I hoped I ever would. I understand grief and pain more than I wish I did. I did months ago, too, but only now has the last bit of innocence managed to escape. The world looks almost completely dark.

> *Our bodies get bigger,*
> *but our hearts get torn up.*

I've gained weight and don't have the body of a child anymore. I was skinny and boyish-looking less than a year ago.

My heart is darker now. For years it's been hardening and now it's finished.

April 2

When I was around 10, I wrote in my diary that I'd never weigh more than my mom. She was skinny and narrow-shouldered and short, with bony elbows and prominent cheekbones. She ate gluten-free and exercised a lot and would often complain about her weight or her looks, and I would reassure her that she looked great.

I settled on a number, and I made a promise to myself, in writing, that my weight would never surpass it. But I was just a kid in middle school when I made that promise. I hadn't hit puberty yet and I didn't know that one day I'd grow tall and broad-shouldered and thick.

Between the ages of 12 and 13 I had bulimia, but I hid it so well that nobody knew. After a year of throwing up, I realized it wasn't making me any skinnier, so I stopped. Then we moved to the States and food was everywhere, and I started gaining weight.

Candy was really what did it, and the CVS right around the corner that supplied it to me. My friend Owen and I would go and buy tons of candy and eat it day after day, and it wasn't long before I hit my self-imposed maximum weight.

On and off, I stopped eating. I exercised compulsively even though I didn't really know how to exercise. My "workout" consisted of stuff we did in gym class: jumping jacks, running up and down the stairs. I counted calories obsessively. I self-harmed when I thought I'd eaten too much.

I was diagnosed with EDNOS: "eating disorder not otherwise specified." I thought that was what they called you when you weren't skinny enough to be anorexic. I kept binging and starving and not talking to anyone about it. I wasn't throwing up anymore, and I wasn't losing weight. In fact, I kept getting bigger and bigger, until I couldn't fit into my mom's jeans anymore. I was heavy, bloated like a corpse, and covered in scars.

I hated my body for betraying me. Punishment was the only form of control that I felt I had over it.

I've never opened up about this as much as I am right now.

This week I had a psychotic or spiritual experience, I'm not sure which. I became unstuck from time, and I was a little child, and I was with my mother, and I was a chubby baby and she loved me anyway. And then I was old and unattractive, married to Peter, and we were still very much in love. That all lasted years, but in reality I was gone only 15 minutes.

When I came back to the present, I realized that my life and my existence were even bigger than the seemingly huge numbers that I had let define me. I realized that the people who love me do so without taking my body into consideration.

I understand now that my parents didn't raise a body, and a body is not what Peter fell in love with. My body is a spaceship that my mind travels the universe in. My body is an avatar.

These epiphanies came all at once, and they did what no amount of therapy or hospitalization or pills could ever do. They made me truly accept myself, all at once, just like that. ♦

Marah*

April 16, 2014

My name isn't really Marah, but that is the name I've chosen to write under here. I can't use my real name, because it might put me in danger. Let me explain.

The city I live in was once magnificent. In spring, it bloomed. We used to wake up to the sound of birds chirping and the scent of flowers. Spring is here again. But what kind of spring is this? We now wake up to the sound of falling bombs.

Every day, we open our eyes to our bleak reality in Syria: to the mortar shells that bring fear, death, disease, and destruction. For the past three years, civil war has

---

* Marah is a pen name created to protect this contributor's identity. Marah's diaries were produced in collaboration with Syria Deeply (syriadeeply.org), a digital news outlet covering the Syrian crisis. They were translated from the Arabic by Mais Istanbelli.

robbed us of our loved ones, destroyed our special places, hurt our close friends. Take, for example, my neighbor's daughter: At just seven years old, she has lost the ability to speak after a rocket landed close to our street.

The change happened in spring 2011. I was 15. Some young Syrians were peacefully protesting the government, asking for more political rights. The government responded with brutal force and attacked its own citizens. Since then, things have gotten worse and worse. More than 140,000 people have been killed in the civil war.

Today, my city's once-friendly face has been replaced by the suffering of its residents. Among the many things I wish I hadn't seen: a young boy who has been exposed to chemical weapons but has no access to medical treatment, an old man who feels powerless after losing his legs to a bomb, a young man who wears black sunglasses to hide his severely scarred face from children who might be frightened by the sight, a young woman who is blind because doctors lacked the proper medical equipment to extract the shrapnel from her eyes.

The bombings have turned my city into a ghost town of decrepit buildings and charred trees. Even our animals weren't spared. You often see a limping dog, a dead cat, a bird mourning its destroyed nest.

During the hardest times, when bombs fell from the sky, we dreamed of bread. We rationed our food intake to one meal a day. You never get used to sleeping on an empty stomach.

I remember vividly the day someone smuggled some cattle feed, or fodder, into our city. We milled the feed (mainly a combination of grass, hay, and straw) to make dough. It didn't take long to get used to the bad taste and weird texture of our new "bread." It brought us a semblance of happiness when eaten with the olives, juice, or yogurt we might have on hand.

Our collective will to eat inspired us to get creative with the fodder. We cooked it like it was rice or wheat. We became so accustomed to eating cattle feed that we almost forgot what chicken, meat, and fruit even looked like.

One of the hardest days was when we heard that a car carrying fruit and candy had entered the city. At first, we were beyond thrilled, but our happiness was fleeting. The exorbitant prices for the items on display meant no one could actually afford them.

That day, I saw a young boy with holes in his shoes squeeze his mother's hand as they passed by the fruit car. He begged her for an apple. Holding back tears, she promised to make him "fodder cake" when they got home. Who would believe that the availability of fruit could be worse than never even seeing it? Is it not a child's right to have an apple, a banana, or a small piece of candy?

We have been stripped of our rights, starting with food. We try to entertain ourselves to forget our hunger, but we no longer have electricity, which makes it difficult. I feel like I'm living in the Stone Age. We wash our laundry by hand and burn wood to keep warm. In this new world, everything we know is gone. We miss the things we took for granted, like TVs and laptops.

The children are supposed to stay indoors at night, but we get bored. My mother keeps my little brother busy by making him break firewood. The skin on his small hands has become thick and callused. He executes his chore angrily, with an air of rebellion. He lives with a prevailing sense of deprivation. His feelings, like mine, have changed without our knowledge or will.

I can feel myself forming a grudge against people who live in other cities. I wonder, *Why did this happen to us? What fault have we committed to live this bitter reality? Why were our childhoods stolen?*

April 30

Since my father's death, it's just my mother and my siblings and me. We try to move forward, but it's hard. We feel weak, somehow lacking. Maybe it's because we have lost our loved ones, or because life around us has changed drastically, leaving us with new burdens to carry.

I miss my mother, even though she is right here with me. Life's hardships have turned her into a machine whose

only purpose is work. In the morning, she sends us off to school before heading to the market. When she gets home, she starts preparing a fire to make us dinner. This routine takes up her whole day. She no longer asks me about my day or my studies. She forgets to say good morning or goodnight. Her life is burdened with new responsibilities that keep her away from me.

I yearn for her love and tenderness, but she forgets that my need for her warmth is greater than my need for food or books. Perhaps my father's death left her numb, or maybe her responsibilities as the sole provider of our household are now so great that she has decided to bury her emotions altogether.

Two years ago, she used to play with us. She was the one who taught me how to play badminton, cards, and chess. Once she was our playful guide and our companion; her spirit was vivacious, her laughter contagious. Now she is unable to teach us anything other than patience and steadfastness. On her one day off, she tries to spend time with us, but underneath the happy façade she puts on for us, I can feel the terrible pain and sadness she keeps hidden inside. Her first wrinkles have appeared below her eyes.

I often slip into her bed at night. She puts her arm around me and rests her palm on my cheek, and I feel her warmth seeping into my veins and reaching my yearning heart.

Sometimes, I feel for her. I see her withering away as she tirelessly works to support us. Other times, I resent her for neglecting us emotionally. But she is the only one I have left. I am drowning, helplessly trying to hold on to her. When you look at her, you see a body without a soul. I miss her warmth and her gentleness, her sincere laughter, and the sparkle in her eyes.

Words can't express the feelings I have when a neighbor or a friend talks to her about getting remarried. I lie, telling her it's her right to remarry, but my mind and my heart can't accept what my tongue says. She quickly reassures me that she will never let her children down by remarrying, as long as she's alive.

May 7

In my city, guys and girls have undergone a radical change. Since the start of the uprisings, everything has changed: their opinions, their aspirations, the way they talk, their expressions, and even the way they look.

We used to have great conversations. We loved music from the West as well as local stuff, and we would race to listen to the newest albums. We loved movies of all kinds, in all languages, especially comedies. We were interested in fashion and design. We were attracted to anything new. We lived a wonderful life. We made adolescent mistakes.

Now we have turned into old women and men. All we can talk about is food, electricity, water, firewood. There is no cellphone coverage and no television. We are deprived of our teenage pastimes.

Shopping used to be one of my favorite things to do. I loved going window-shopping with my friends after school and getting excited about a bright-colored purse or a shiny pair of shoes. Now we display that same level of excitement over rare treats like a piece of fruit. Can you believe it? We never expected this to happen.

We used to see the boys around school, carrying flowers and wrapped presents for their beloveds, wearing their nicest clothes. Their eyes were filled with love, happiness, hope. Now, the streets around the school are empty, and all the guys are out fighting on the front lines. When we happen to see them, their hair is shaggy and their shoes are dirty. Now they carry rifles instead of roses. If you look at their faces, all you see is worry and frustration.

Everything has turned upside down. Everyone is depressed. Sometimes we laugh and cry at the same time. How did this happen to us?

I feel sorry for myself and for all my fellow Syrian youth. I hope that our situation changes soon, so that our souls and dreams might reawaken. I'm afraid we will regret living through our teenage years without the normal teenage rites of passage. This is not how youth is meant to be lived. Will this war damage us for the rest of our lives? How will we make up for what we've lost? ♦

Naomi

January 22, 2014

Seconds after turning my light out, I thought about the pancakes me and my flatmates might make the next morning. Then I thought about the weed tea that a friend had mentioned in passing earlier. Then I thought about writing this. Then about his fingernails, because I had made a point in my head to write about his fingernails. For some reason, when we talked, our first serious sober discussion, I studied his fingernails. Very short and small, just a part of his hand, not a stand-alone feature. Stubby, for the strings of guitars and basses. I ran my fingertips over and around them. It was somewhere to look.

Our hands touched often during the two hours we spent holed up in my bedroom, an arcane sort of physical contact very unlike sex. I wanted to kiss him, even though I knew with all certainty that I couldn't, and that was the worst. I wanted to kiss him, but the longer the discussion went on, the less I wanted to kiss him, and that felt even worse than the worst. The worst is knowing you can't, but worse than the worst is realising you might not even *want* to. Or recognising that, as he pointed out, it would be better not to—that it would be "WRONG." That drove me mad.

When I was young, I assumed that love was the simplest thing. I was brought up to regard Jesus's love as the pinnacle, something to aspire to. The love of not just the Jesus you see painted in that nauseatingly soft light, but also the Jesus who knocked over tables in a temple out of pure seething anger. In amongst the feelings of love that make me float like a cloud, lord knows I've felt that sort of fury, too. I threw my ex's mug out of the flat window just to see it shatter. That feeling has validity. But love felt more important. Love overrode everything. Nothing else mattered—not the complications, not the illness, not the sadness. I knew that Jesus forgave before there was even anything to forgive, so I did that too.

Some part of me still believes that the Bible is right and the world

is wrong. It is a simplified idea of love that really only belongs in a child's lullaby. Maybe that echo of belief is the only thing that soothes me into not giving up on basic human interaction. But the world is fucking complicated. No, not the world—the world pretty much runs like clockwork: rain falling, poles spinning, plants growing. It's the people that are complicated.

Jesus cried and Jesus laughed and Jesus starved. I've cried to the point of puffy eyes, laughed within the same hour, and eaten absolute crap (not comparable to starving but near enough) within the last day. But Jesus didn't have to survive a boy who remains stubbornly in close proximity for most of his waking and sleeping life. Maybe that means it's not important.

I'm beginning to think my feelings are wrong. I am worried that if people knew about my feelings—if they knew how much I feel about one single person, that I still want more, that I am writing this much about it—they would think less of me.

I feel like my whole fucking life is founded in love, so what does anyone expect me to do? I can't help that I grew up in a cross-section of worlds: one religious, which taught me that love is the most important thing; and then this society, which teaches me that love is where I find my worth. I am figuring out the most complicated facet of human existence; I should be allowed to cry and wallow and walk around in a daze.

I saw a small baby on the London Overground the other day. It looked tiny and peaceful, asleep without a thought, completely unaware of the cruelty of the world. I thought about how that little existence was a rare patch of uncomplicated space.

I turned off my light again and tried to think about pancakes. I tried not to hear the footsteps passing my door. I tried not to know who they belonged to.

March 5

I hardly journal anymore—I've been turning to letters instead. So on Friday I emailed my mum and dad:

Hey, folks, Mama and Papa, etc. etc.,

I've had a weird day, one of those days where it's easier to have minimal outside-world contact—but I've been OK. DON'T WORRY, OK? I've been reading a lot of stuff today, and I read through Dad's emails and found one that he sent just after I got to university. It made me emotional, because when I came to uni, I wanted to be like everyone else—I made a conscious decision to tell as few people as possible about my history/mental health, etc. And that's why it's hard on days like today. Even with the people I have trusted enough to tell, Erica especially, it's really hard to vocalise it, because they've never experienced those dark days with me. But you two have. So I wish I had you to pat me on the back and tell me I am doing well. Because I *am* doing well: I am in London, and I go to lectures and galleries on my own. But in my desire to be "normal" and to treat myself no differently than I would anyone else, I rarely acknowledge the fact that I have achieved so much.

Dad's email reminded me how strong I am. I don't tell myself that enough. I tell myself I SHOULD be doing this, I SHOULD be doing that, that life should be a breeze.

Uni has taught me that life is hardly a breeze for anyone. This makes me feel somewhat better, but worse at the same time. I am not "special"—other people get sad and have loads of shit to deal with too. But then I think that I should be better at dealing with *my* shit.

The past is always sort of there. I carry it around with me, and it makes me feel distant from some people. The memories are the worst. I cried a bit this evening, and it was sort of a happy cry because I realised I am here despite how shit last summer was. It was SHIT. And I have to find ways to deal with the fact that it was shit. I have to accept that it was shit. I have to accept that there has been a lot of shit in the past. And being in the past doesn't mean it has gone away.

But other people only see what I am now. This is a complete catch-22, because that is how I *want* to be seen—it is more who I really am—but there are reasons why I feel or act the way I do sometimes.

In fact, all of my past is the whole reason I am who I am NOW. I can't separate the two. How can I get them to be friends with each other?

I have been trying to remind myself that my anxiety is not my fault. It is an illness that I actually take medication to control, and I still can't control it 100 percent of the time. I live with it every single day, I am reminded of it every single day—it is part of my life. I am OK with that. But it is *not* the same as "just being sad." It is not just an emotion that other people experience regularly. They might get a taste of it every now and again, but to put myself on the same playing field with everyone else does me a disservice. I need to remember that. I need to give myself a break.

There is more I wanted to write, but I am tired. My main point was actually going to be to thank you both for being there through all of that. Making a fresh start and having new friends is such a pleasure, but they don't know me like you do. They just don't know. And that is incredibly frustrating sometimes.

So this makes me miss you and also reminds me how much I love you and how much you have done for me.

Lots of love, Naomi

April 23

I am staring at a blank page, something I've done every Sunday for two and a half years. I am more fulfilled as a person than I have ever been, but somehow that makes it harder to write. When I started writing my weekly diaries for Rookie, I was still haunted by the depression I'd had the summer before. I had just turned 16 and it hadn't been very sweet.

I thought you were meant to know much more at the age of 16 than I did. I had felt the same way about turning 15, 14, 13, etc. Every 24th April I knew less, had less, than I thought I should. By 16, I thought I should have life pretty much figured out; the fact that I didn't, I believed, meant I would never be successful or content. Instead I was spending all my time at home, unhappy and tired.

Rookie, this brand-new baby of a creation, was the light at the end of that summer tunnel. I read Tavi's call for submissions as an opportunity to be involved in something special for once, instead of just watching from the sidelines. When I think of that moment, I see a blank grey slate with a few flowers beginning to grow. I got to write about my slow crawl out of agoraphobia, my building back up from the dirt of my life, my numerous "firsts" after being so sheltered for so long, my falling a bit apart again, and finally my move to a new city, full of new firsts. Today, I can say I've never been more proud of myself.

I think I needed to leave home for a while to learn to actually look after myself. I had to remove myself from the damaging cycles that were so easy to get caught up in while sitting stagnant in the same house I'd lived in for 13 years. I couldn't have become an adult if I had stayed home, having Mum to make my doctors' appointments, buy my food, pick up my prescriptions.

Those prescriptions—my antidepressant, my birth control pill—are the main reason I have to remember to make my own appointments at my new health centre in London. I always forget till the last minute and stress at the thought of ringing the centre at 8:45 in the morning to see if there have been any cancellations. But I always manage to do it. Then I walk to the pharmacy, brandishing that green slip of paper as if to say, "I am not ashamed of people knowing that I have my own type of malady; I am treating it, and I am treating it by myself." There is no one to hold my hand.

If I do ever need someone to hold my hand, it's usually Erica. When I arrived a few days late to student halls, she opened the door of her flat and said, "Things have been happening!" We went to her bedroom straightaway and that was that. Instant friendship. And that was really when my life began. My favourite activity is still flopping down on her bed, where it's OK to be quiet.

My most precious possession is my Oyster card, for the train. It is mine, it has my name on it, and it makes going anywhere in London so simple. I like to keep the things that could flare up my agoraphobia as simple as possible. I have gone back and forth between Birming-ham and London more times than I can remember, but every journey is different. Though I am beginning to memorize the order of particular landmarks by the tracks—power stations, bridges, wind turbines, fields of yellow, and caravan parks—my feelings are not as reliable. Every time I come back home something new has happened: People who are new become old, but old people become something new. Trust shifts; I have different things to talk about, different things to laugh about. All the way back and forth on the train, I am constantly weighing what to love and what to hate. What is right and what is wrong. But answers are not what I am looking for.

My happiness is much more invested in people now that I don't spend all my time alone. I don't trust falling in love, but I trust friendship way more than I ever thought I could. I still feel a shadow of my agoraphobic past from time to time, and I still remember acutely what it feels like to be paralyzed by anxiety.

Sometimes I can move on from those thoughts easily; sometimes my face tenses when I remember my worst moments. But then I go outside for fresh air, or tell Erica, or get on the next train to see St. Paul's or Tower Bridge or the National Gallery. I'll buy flowers and put them on my windowsill, or rearrange my bedroom and feel renewed.

Or we'll go out, like we do, and I'll dance with lovers and strangers and bestow kisses on those I have no romantic feeling for, but want to protect from the bottom of my heart. I want to protect them from themselves, because I know how much harm one person can do to their own skin and bones. If only I could reach out more to other people and teach them what I know. But I also know that a person can only ever help themselves.

I've always been a person that has worth, though for a long time I allowed myself to be convinced otherwise. But I am going to be 20 years old tomorrow, and the optimistic me will not let bad things define me anymore. I've had years of experience being tormented—I think that's enough to be going on with. I am not the same person I was. I've grown and grown.

Life is more fun now. Life is happier without hatred—of oneself or of people and their actions. It's good to realise that they are just living their lives too.

I don't know whether any of this says anything, or enough of what I have to say. Whenever someone related to any of my diaries, it gave me a rush. It felt good to be reminded that what I feel is real, and that other people feel the same. That is perhaps the best thing about living in a community like this one.

Turning 20 means I won't be writing these diaries for Rookie anymore. I remember one of things I wrote to Tavi the first time was that I had "a lot to say." I have too much to say. I hope it has been enough. ♥

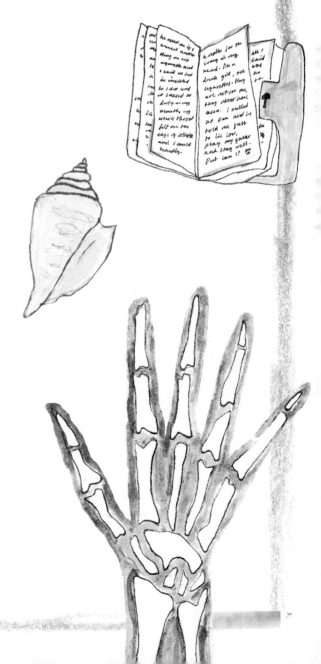

Caitlin

What were they
like when they were
my age?

Am I doing enough
to be who I want
to be?

Am I good enough?

Who am I ?

Just. Stop. thinking.

(I can't)

it's
been
too
long

paranoia

does
anyone
care

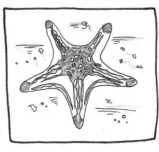

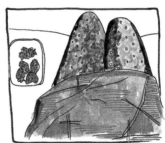

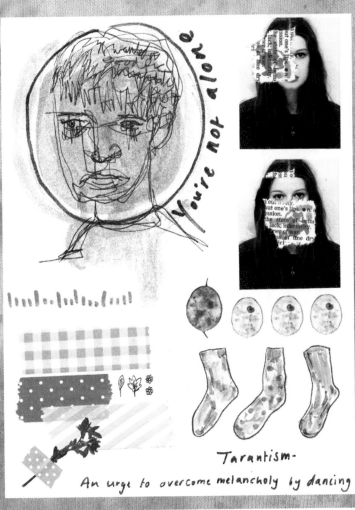

You're not alone

Tarantism-

An urge to overcome melancholy by dancing

Jordana Bevan
Submarine

15

Suzy
Bishop

Moonrise
kingdom

12

Enid Coleslaw
Ghost World

It is sad to
grow up and
leave fictional
characters
behind...

16

15

Charlotte flax
Mermaids

Juno

16 17 15 13 14

15

Diane
Trainspotting

The Lisbon Sisters The Virgin Suicides

RELYING ON THE SMALL DETAILS

men with
Precise
hair
cuts

book
dedications

Strangers
coming and
going at rail stations

Public
transport
fabric
designs

the
changing
Colours
of stirred
drinks

the ghosts of
Wet leaves left
on pavements

the
fragility
of toilet
paper
(really)

those who take
care of tiny
things

i saw a
man who
had strapped
apple juice
onto his
bike, with
multiple ropes

dressing
all in black

Extra-Special

NO-PIXEL

Yearbook

THREE

EXCLU-
SIVES

How to Be a Boss

The baddest boss of all preps us for world domination.
By Grimes. Illustration by María Inés.

Something I didn't realize when I started making music was that any entrepreneurial endeavor involves hiring people, creating a company, and becoming a businessperson. So, while you may know me as a musician, in practice I am also a boss. I'm the CEO of two companies, Grimes Creative Corp. and Fairy Tour Corp., and I just started Roco-Prime Productions with my brother. This is simultaneously very cool and very stressful. I'm definitely not the best or most experienced boss. I'm also a young, female boss, which can present a very particular set of practical and emotional challenges. Here, I've compiled a list of things that have been useful to me while I've been figuring out how to be in charge, in the hope that some of them might help any of you who are doing what I'm doing (aka learning as you go).

• You will never hear more people tell you that you're wrong than when you're succeeding. After my album *Visions* came out, I spent a really long time freaking out because people were telling me that in order to take "the next step" in my career, I would have to become a much better "musician," that I'd need a backing band, etc. I now realize that (a) none of those people have music careers, and (b) I wasted a lot of time trying to do things I was told were "important for every professional musician" to do, without realizing that as a fan, I am far more interested in things that I've never seen before. The point is, listening to haters is pointless. People are judgmental about everything—often because they feel threatened. Ignore them. I think this applies to any business or creative thing, because tomorrow's world will not look like today's. Doing something different is probably

better than doing the same things that other people do.

• Jump rope. It is the most efficient way to get cardiovascular exercise in any kind of weather, without going to a gym. Exercise is very important if you're dealing with depression or anger issues—and any job in the entertainment industry will cause both.

• Stop working when you're tired—but don't get lazy. I sometimes boomerang between working for 22 hours in a row, and then collapsing and realizing that I don't have to adhere to a fixed schedule and watching every episode of *The Sopranos*. I would not recommend this system. Schedules are amazing: eight hours of work, eight hours of sleep. The other eight hours are fair game. (I have not mastered this one, but when I can get it going I'm a lot more productive.)

• Hold on to your work. Once upon a time, Elvis Presley wanted to record a cover of Dolly Parton's song "I Will Always Love You," but on the condition that she sign over half of the publishing royalties—money the songwriter gets whenever someone plays or performs their song in public—to him. Dolly said no, and many years later Whitney Houston sang "I Will Always Love You" in a movie, and it became probably one of the most memorable (and lucrative) songs of all time. So it's very important to maintain ownership of your intellectual property. Copyright everything. DO NOT FORGET TO DO THIS. There are so many ways you can get screwed if you don't copyright your work. Conversely, treat your collaborators with respect and give credit where it is due.

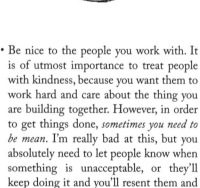

• Be nice to the people you work with. It is of utmost importance to treat people with kindness, because you want them to work hard and care about the thing you are building together. However, in order to get things done, *sometimes you need to be mean*. I'm really bad at this, but you absolutely need to let people know when something is unacceptable, or they'll keep doing it and you'll resent them and it creates bad vibes.

• Read/watch biographies of people you admire. I've learned more from this one practice than from anything else, really. Also, if you're around someone who does what you want to do, ask them questions and watch them work.

• Bette Midler once said, "I firmly believe that with the right footwear, one can rule the world." I used to try to wear heels, and it was a disaster. Now I always prioritize comfortable shoes. Also, avoid wearing white: Busy people don't have time to change clothes very often, and white gets dirty fast (unless you are Olivia Pope). Just find one or two things that look cool that you can also sleep in.

• Avoid dating someone who does the same job as you. If you do end up doing that, make sure they don't resent your success and that you don't resent theirs.

• Try to date someone who is good at cooking. It will save time.

• If you are tired and you need to be peppy, drinking a bit of straight hot sauce really works.

• Keep a pen and paper on your bedside table. Good ideas often come as you're falling asleep, and you won't remember them in the morning.

• Just because someone has more qualifications than you doesn't mean they're better than you. We live in the age of technology, so you can google anything you don't know how to do. The only thing you *can't* google is how to be creative and unique. Your thoughts have more value than a degree or a parent in the same field or whatever. I always think about my grandfather, who became an engineer with only a seventh grade education. It's a very cliché thing to say, but nearly anything is possible if you set your mind to it.

• Really, the most important thing is eliminating self-doubt. This is basically impossible for me, but I've found that if I *act* like a boss, I can convince myself that I *am* a boss when I need to be one. I copy things that I've seen politicians and actors do; I make eye contact with people; I try to keep my shoulders back and my head high; I gesticulate wildly and sometimes take long pauses (silence can be very intimidating). I try to act like I'm powerful, onstage and off. I am often treated with disrespect, but I respond as respectfully as I can, because it makes trolls look stupid when you don't stumble. As time has gone by, I've noticed that the crappy people have been phasing out and I'm surrounded more and more by people I trust, and with whom I share mutual respect—which, by the way, breeds real confidence. ☆

Ten Tips for Better Songwriting

*The genius behind a handful of Rihanna, Beyoncé, Katy Perry,
and her own singles teaches us how to craft victim-to-victory jams.*

By Sia

1. Let the song write YOU!

2. Try squiddlydoodling freely over the chords. Use your intuition.

3. The winning melody is more often than not the very first thing you sing.

4. Trust in it.

5. Try to have at least three or four chords in a song. Two-chord songs can get monotonous.

6. People tend to like songs about victory! I call them victim-to-victory jams.

7. You can make more things rhyme by singing them than you might think. I rhymed *chandelier* with *exist*.

8. You don't have to go in having something to say. If you get out of your own way and clear your mind, the universe will send something your way—something that will help someone, some- where, in some way when they hear it.

9. If you want to write clever songs, more power to you. If you want to make money, keep it simple. If you're going for the dollaz, you have to write things that everyday people can relate to. (Even if you're not in it for the dollaz, it's nice for your listener to be able to identify with whatever you're crooning about.)

10. Only do it if you absolutely love it. Otherwise, find the thing you love, and do that. 🐷

Sister Crush:
Dakota & Elle Fanning

A hard-hitting account of this adoring friendship.
By Tavi. Illustration by María Inés.

Friend Crush is a recurring feature on Rookie in which we interview two best friends, individually, about each other. For *Yearbook Three*, we decided to get all familial and talk to two of our favorite sisters, Dakota and Elle Fanning, and it turns out they'd wanna be friends even if they weren't related anyway! These two are whip-smart and charming as all hell, so much so that they bring out the wordy old grandma in me. And they've been in some of my favorite movies. Dakota: *The Runaways*, *The Motel Life*, *Very Good Girls*, and goddamn *Coraline*, to name a few. Elle: *Somewhere*, *Ginger & Rosa*, *Super 8*, and the new *Maleficent*. They also voiced the sisters in *Totoro* together as toddlers, so, you know, AHHH. Behold: two giggly conversations about stealing clothes, pulling pranks, and their shared wish to play enemies onscreen.

TAVI What's your favorite thing you've stolen from Dakota's closet?

ELLE FANNING [*Laughs*] Wow, I've stolen so much from my sister's closet! You feel so cool in your older sister's clothes. They're always just a notch better than your own. Now I'm so much taller than her that I can't steal her clothes anymore, which really sucks. But when I was little, I remember this one specific outfit: I put on this little hat she had, and these little brown penny loafers, and this little navy sailor dress. I wore it out one day when Dakota was in New York, and the paparazzi got a picture of me in the whole outfit. It was terrible! She called me, like, "I see you on the internet—you're in all my clothes! You gotta take them off your

body right now!" I was like, *Great, thanks, paparazzi—you totally ruined that.*

So busted! Have you guys played any really good pranks on each other?

I get into pranking more than she does. She's kind of above that. I did this one prank basically every April Fool's Day when I was really young, but it never worked. I'd get ketchup and sparkly purple eye shadow and put them all over my body—the ketchup was fake blood and the eye shadow was supposed to be bruises. But it was obviously sparkly—it didn't look anything like a bruise. Then I'd be like, "Oh my gosh, I'm scared!" in this whole dramatic performance. My parents would go along with it, but my sister would be like, "Oh, Elle. It's just eye shadow. You do this every year."

Is there anything you used to find annoying about her that you've come to appreciate?

Maybe her loyalty. You know how when you're a little sister, you wanna know everything, and you're always badgering everyone, like, "What happened? What happened?" Dakota knew when I was too young to hear about something—even things she maybe talked about with my mom—and would always brush me off. That annoyed me so much. But now I appreciate it. When I tell her my secrets, she really keeps them.

When you started acting, did Dakota act as a mentor at all?

I obviously started acting because of her, because I saw her doing it and she looked like she was having so much fun, so I was like, "Ooh, I wanna try it too." It's funny—sometimes I'm like, "Would I be acting if my sister hadn't started before me?" Maybe I would've found a way, but I also owe it to her.

Do you guys ever talk about your roles or acting processes?

We don't really talk about movies or anything. We keep [our acting work] really separate. But we both know how movie sets work, so it's nice to come home and talk about the crew, the catering, stuff like that. You know, "How's the food on set?" That type of thing. But I never read her scripts, and she never reads mine. And then when I go to one of her movies, I can really sit back as just a normal audience member, without knowing what's gonna happen to her character or whatever. That's exciting.

When you watch her in a movie, are you able to see her as the character, or are you like, "Hi, Dakota"?

You are like, "Oh, that's my sister," but she's also so otherworldly good that even I find myself seeing her as another person. It's the strangest thing. One movie that really impacted me was *Now Is Good*. She had cancer in that film, and that affected me so bad. I was at this screening, and I cried and cried uncontrollably, and I kept crying afterwards. It was really embarrassing how much I was crying. Everyone was like, "Oh, that's probably because you just saw your sister have cancer."

It's like watching your own worst nightmare.

Exactly. It was so strange. I love that movie, but I don't think I could put myself through that again.

You two are so often referred to as a duo, and it is amazing that so much talent can come from one family, but how do you maintain your sense of individuality? Has it been challenging to carve out your own path, as a younger sister?

Yeah, definitely, when I was little. I started out playing my sister at a younger age in flashback scenes in her movies. So when people recognized me at all, they would say, "Oh, are you Dakota Fanning?" And I would have to say, "Oh, no—I'm her sister."

That finally changed when I did *Somewhere*. I was 11, and it was one of the first red carpets I'd ever walked down. I wore, like, a real designer-type thing. And then your individuality can finally be shown, and people look at you and they see that you don't *actually* look like Dakota, you know?

What would be your dream project to do with Dakota?

It would be nice to not play sisters in a movie. It would be fun to play friends, you know? Maybe I could boss her around a little bit. That would be fantastic. Maybe I could be the rebellious bad friend.

❦ ❦ ❦

TAVI **You're the older sister, so I assume you've influenced Elle a lot. But are there ways in which she's influenced you?**

DAKOTA FANNING Elle has definitely been more of the influencer. She's more of a free spirit, while I'm more restrained and quiet. She has taught me to be more open and to let myself go more, and to have more fun.

That's lovely. I have two older sisters, so I'm very familiar with the experience that siblings can have of sharing things—certain movies and TV shows and food and stuff—that are only yours. Do you and Elle share anything like that?

Yeah, god, there are so many things that only sisters will understand. We have this one thing: It's not exactly one of those things, but I would lie to her a lot when we were younger, and I would trick her into believing all kinds of crazy stuff. So we made up this saying—it was based on "pinkie promise," but we called it "pink-a-link." If one of us said "pink-a-link," you knew we were telling the truth, because we'd never go back on that. [*Laughs*]

What was the worst lie you told her?

I would do this horrible thing—oh my god. We lived in this community of townhouses, and there were these drains in the road, like sewage drains. They were, like, holes. When I'd get mad at Elle or when

I wanted to her to do something, like play something, and she didn't want to do it, I would tell her, "If you don't play this with me, I'm gonna throw you down the drain." She would freak out and scream, and I'd be like, "OK, fine, I won't do it if we just play this. If you'll just play this with me, I won't throw you down the drain." And she'd go, "OK! OK!" That was pretty damaging, thinking about it now. That's an awful thing to do to a child!

When I interviewed her, she told me that she couldn't handle watching movies where you're terminally ill or dying.

I know. I didn't watch that particular movie with her, but I did hear from someone that she was very upset by it. Which is so the opposite of me, because when I'm watching a movie where something like that is happening, it doesn't affect me at all. I was there, and I know it's not real. But she was kinda traumatized by [that].

How does it feel to watch her in movies? Do you get lost in it, or are you like, "There's my sister"?

I can really get lost in it with her. I really am a proud older sister and so happy for all of her successes, and I enjoy watching her so much. And at moments I definitely think, *Oh, that's so Elle*—just when something she does [on screen] reminds me of the way she is in real life. But I can get lost watching her and forget that she's my sister.

Is there anything that used to annoy you about her that you appreciate now?

Her being so free and wild and crazy. When we were younger, I'd be like, "Aaah, stop singing! Stop dancing! It's so embarrassing!" But when you get older, you lose those qualities, because everybody tells you that they're weird and annoying, and that everybody should be, you know, boring. That's when you realize that who you were as a child was actually so much more interesting. I think my sister has been able to keep that childlike "free-ness" that most people lose. I have definitely grown to appreciate that that's actually a cool way to be, not an embarrassing way to be.

What would your dream project be to work on with Elle?

We've had a lot of opportunities to work together to play sisters. I think that's what everyone expects us to do one day, to play sisters like we are. I think—and I think she feels the same way—it would be much more interesting to not play sisters!

Yeah, she said that too.

It might be fun to have to be mean to each other in a movie or something. We get along pretty well, so that would be playing the opposite of what our relationship is like in real life. But mostly I would like to surprise people and not be sisters!

She said she wanted to play a part where you're not sisters and where she can boss you around and be mean to you.

[*Laughs*] Yeah, great. Yeah, I'm sure she does. I fulfill the "bossy older sister" stereotype for sure, so I bet she would like to reverse that.

She told me that she has stolen from your closet. Have you ever stolen anything from her?

Oh yeah, I do it all the time! I was at my parents' house in L.A. last weekend. I was just visiting for a day or two, and I hadn't really brought any clothes with me. Elle wasn't there, so, yeah, I went into her closet and [took some stuff], and inevitably something finds its way back home with me. This is actually really sweet—this shows what a better person she is than I am: There was this jean jacket, this vintage jean jacket that was amazing and so great and I loved it. I was like, "Please, can I wear it?" She was like, "No, you can't!" And I was like, "Please, can I?" I ended up wearing it out, and then I was leaving the next day, and I was like, "Can I take the jacket?" She's like, "No, you can't take the jacket. I need it." I was like, "OK, fine." When I woke up the next morning, the jacket was sitting in my suitcase. *Oh, she's gonna let me take it!* So cute.

That's so sweet. You two!

It *was* really sweet.

We're All Just Doing What We Can:
An Interview With Shailene Woodley

The star of the new film adaptation of The Fault in Our Stars *talks to us about nature, life lessons, and feminism.*
By Hazel. Illustration by María Inés.

At 22, Shailene Woodley has already played an impressively diverse range of roles on TV and in movies. She was teen mom Amy Juergens on ABC Family's *Secret Life of the American Teenager*, a geeky wallflower named Aimee Finecky in *The Spectacular Now*, and Alexandra King, the angsty teenage daughter of a couple in crisis, in *The Descendants*. Her latest role is Hazel Grace Lancaster, the snarky, strong-willed protagonist of *The Fault in Our Stars*, based on John Green's 2012 novel of the same name. A 16-year-old cancer patient whose wide-ranging interests include reality TV, the environment, and Augustus Waters, the love of her life, Hazel is a complicated character, but Shailene manages to embody her and keep her grounded throughout the film.

I got to meet Shailene in September in Pittsburgh, in a church basement where *TFIOS* was being filmed.

HAZEL You were on *The Secret Life of the American Teenager* for seven years, playing a teen mom. Since the show went off the air last year, you've been open about how restricting that role felt to you, and about your increasing discomfort with the direction the show went in morally in its last year. Did you feel stuck in that situation?

SHAILENE The thing is, when you're on a television show, you don't really receive the script until right before you begin to shoot it. And the scenes were constantly changing. Because the show lasted for so long, it was a great lesson in terms of when you make a commitment, you have to stick to it.

Hazel and Augustus have kind of unwittingly become the public faces of teens with terminal illnesses, partially because there are so few narratives on that subject that don't try to glamorize or sentimentalize it. Was it important for you to accurately portray what it's like to be a teenager with cancer?

Hazel stands for all teenagers: teens with cancer and teens without cancer. That was one of the things I loved most about the book. There's this thing in America where if you have something, it puts a label on you. [Cancer] is just one part of Hazel. *The Fault in Our Stars* emphasizes how every teen is the same. When I met teenagers who were going through treatment, I quickly realized that what they were going through didn't define them. At the end of the day, some of them had just had their first kiss, or they just got their period. It really is a coming-of-age story at heart, just with that added emotional experience.

You've played many roles that I think could be considered feminist, but you recently said that you don't identify with feminism because, in your words, "the idea of 'raise women to power, take the men away from the power' is never going to work out, because you need balance." Does having a fleshed-out, well-written, powerful female character in a movie take away from the same kind of power in a corresponding male character?

Not at all. But I actually don't examine roles that analytically—I think that's much more of a curator's thing to notice. For me, it's about art and relating to a character's emotional roller coaster, versus trying to identify and label what a character exists as in the world and what their stereotype would be.

Out of all the characters that you've played so far, which of them would you say you relate to the most?

I would say a healthy mix of all of them, but I feel like I really relate to [*Divergent*'s] Tris. She's extremely brave and selfless, in a way that you don't see very often. I was raised by two psychologist parents, so I have a deep-rooted sense of empathy that was ingrained in me as a child, but I'm also a fighter, not a flighter. I like to approach life and meet it halfway, if not all the way.

One thing you seem to share with Hazel Lancaster is a very special appreciation for the natural world: You make your own beauty products, you eat clay. When did this passion for nature and environmentalism begin?

I was in high school, and I was on the quad on a really windy day. I looked up, and there were these beautiful pine trees that had released all these pine needles in a great flurry in the air. Then I looked down, and there was all of this trash from students who'd decided not to throw it in the trash can but just left it on the ground. The juxtaposition between the beautiful pine needles in the air and the trash on the ground really took my breath away and made me recognize at a young age that I have a choice in this world about which wolves I'm going to feed and which path I'm going to walk. It was a defining moment. I chose to start investigating different lifestyles and alternative living. I want to be the best version of myself every day—the healthiest version of myself possible, the kindest version of myself. It's also our responsibility to think not of the mark we're going to leave on the world, but about what we're leaving for our future ancestors, to help them enter the world with.

I get the sense that there's a side to Hollywood that you don't connect to—the glamour and the artifice.

I mean, as we're talking right now, I'm getting my makeup done, because we're about to go to an event tonight. But you have to make it work for you. We're the rulers of our own queendoms or kingdoms or whatever you want to call it. The woman putting the eyeliner on me happens to be my best friend. At the end of the night, we get to come home to each other's arms and really feel the tranquility and calmness of our relationship.

One of the big themes in *Divergent* is girls who help each other, rather than compete against each other. Have you ever had any issues with girl hate?

Not with girl hate so much as with… I would call it girl insecurity. Society encourages us to compare ourselves with other people. But comparing leads to despair in every situation. I remember, growing up, when I would compare myself with other women and their bodies and faces and personalities. That's when I felt most uncomfortable in my own skin and in my own life. When you realize that you can [instead] celebrate these women and their existence, it frees your soul to celebrate your own unique flavor. We're all human, and we're all just doing what we can. You might as well have fun with it. ✳

Feast on This

In the kitchen with singer/saucier Kelis.
By Julianne. Illustration by María Inés.

It's possible that Kelis is not the only chef/musician in the world, but we're pretty sure she's the greatest. Five years ago, the lifelong R&B singer enrolled at Le Cordon Bleu, a culinary academy in Paris that's so intense that she spent an entire semester focusing just on sauce! Since then, she's served delicious barbecue to her fans at SXSW, shot a special for the Cooking Channel (*Saucy & Sweet*), released an album called *Food*, developed a line of sauces (called Feast), and talked to us about what she loves about cooking for others. "You want the moments that you have in life to be great or memorable," she said. "You want music you can put on and eat food that you love and share with people you care about and laugh. I do this because this is what I was given to do, and this shit feel is good!"

She also gave us her (vegan!) recipe for brussels sprouts—and if anyone can make this unfairly maligned vegetable feel good, it's Kelis.

KELIS'S FEEL-GOOD BRUSSELS SPROUTS

What You'll Need:
3 tablespoons coconut oil
1 pound brussels sprouts, cut in half the long way
1/4 cup chopped shallots
1 tablespoon chopped garlic
A pinch of sea salt
A pinch of ground black pepper
1/2 ounce almond slivers
1/2 ounce black currants

How to Do It:
Place a pan over medium heat. When the pan is hot, put the oil in there. Wait a minute for the oil to heat up, then place the sprouts, flat side down, in the pan. Add the shallots, garlic, salt, and pepper. Cover the pan and leave it alone for a few minutes, until the flat sides are golden to dark brown. Add the almonds and currants, eat, and enjoy.

JULIANNE Was it weird to go to culinary school in 2008, at the age of 29, after not having been in school for a long time?

KELIS It was totally nerve-racking at first! I'd been out of school forever, and I was super-feeling first-week-of-school syndrome. You definitely have that "Oh my god, is everybody gonna hate me?" moment. But there was not a lot of time to dwell on, you know, "Am I gonna make friends?" [*Laughs*] I was worried that people would think I wanted special treatment, or that they assumed I was just there for some sort of marketing scheme, or whatever. But none of that was the case. It ended up being the best year of my life. We were all there for one purpose, so it was about self-triumph. I learned so much about myself and, obviously, my craft, that it was amazing. I had a ball. Also, you really appreciate school a lot more as an adult! [*Laughs*] It was just like, "God, I wish I felt like this all through it!" It was actually awesome.

Your new album has such a community feel: It samples people laughing and hanging out, you named some of the songs after the food you were eating while you were recording—and you called the whole thing *Food!* Were you addressing the idea of emotional nourishment with this album, too?

I've been doing this for a long time, and everything's gotta feel collaborative. I'm not trying to get all the glory for anything, and you want people around who are contributing, who involve themselves in this nice cooperative. Not just with music, but with everything. To the extent that I'm happy with what I've made, I feel blessed to be able to create this, and now I want to share it. Having people around you who have the same values—it's a cliché at this point and it seems overly simplified, but that's what it is. You wanna work with the people who want to work with you. My mom used to say, "Don't ever love anybody who doesn't love you back." She was talking about men, but I knew what she meant—in life. The point is, it makes sense in friendships, work relationships, and partnerships to be like, "I like you, I like what you do, what can we offer the world together? Because I think we could do something cool."

At Rookie, we are really obsessed with pizza. I have to ask: As a Cordon Bleu–trained chef, do you eat pizza? What's your favorite kind?

I love pizza! I'm a New Yorker, so it's part of our DNA! If I'm home and I have time, I will totally make pizza. But then if I'm gonna make it, I try to get fancy and try to do some overly healthy flaxseed-and-bulgur-wheat-type shenanigans. Then, of course, I pile it on with bacon and meatballs! It's all about balance! I love making pizza, I love ordering pizza, and I love the fact that everyone's always happy with pizza. Quite frankly, it's, like, bread and cheese. It's hard to ruin that. ▼

Build Your Own Throne

A lifestyle DIY.   By Tavi

The great Beyoncé Knowles-Carter once said, "I have no desire for anyone else's throne. I am very comfortable in the throne I've been building for the past 15 years." Since coming across this gospel at the beginning of 2014, BUILD YR OWN THRONE has become my everyday motto. Not because it motivates me to become a Beyoncé-style world dominatrix, but because it helps me become more of *myself*. It's something to remember when you feel competitive or jealous of others. When you are trying to do something you've never seen before and want to feel like a trailblazer instead of delusional. When you're overwhelmed by the myriad voices telling you which path to follow into adulthood. No, BYOT is not about rising to the top of anyone else's standards, winning stuff, or needing everyone to know that you're the best.

BYOT can be applied to every aspect of life: *Do I want to succumb to pressure and attend this house party, or will I be happier watching a movie in bed? BYOT!* Today, though, we will focus on building your own throne *creatively* and *professionally*, because it is a philosophy that has guided my writing, editing, Rookie-founding, and other endeavors since I was a wee lass, and I have gathered here some of the tips 'n' techniques that have helped me stay in the BYOT mindset. The practical circumstances are different for everybody, so this is more about your head- and heartspace as you approach a life of making stuff, be it a zine, a website, a sculpture, a supercomputer, a book. So sit back on your velvet seat of self-love and badassery, dismiss anything that doesn't jibe with you, and take note when something does. And if I get motivational-speech-y, GOOD: I want to spread motivation on this earth like mono at a summer camp.

1. GET UP IN THE MORNING.

In the words of Muhammad Ali, "The best way to make your dreams come true is to wake up." Some days, I wake up so excited about life and the world and all the possible things that can be created that I can't help jumping out of bed and eating something healthy and putting on an outfit that will help me plug into workzone (shoes necessary, no pajamas allowed). Some days, I can't get through an episode of a show I like because my only thought is: *YOU CAN EITHER WATCH* BREAKING BAD *OR YOU CAN BECOME AN ACTUAL SUPER-HERO.*

2. OR NOT.

On other days, I'm really fucking depressed and I don't want to get up and I don't want to do anything and I wish I could disappear. There is a very popular internet thing hopping around on them social media accounts these days that goes: "YOU HAVE AS MANY HOURS IN A DAY AS BEYONCÉ." Ugh. Not only does that reignite all my existential crises, it's just absurd. Putting aside even our vast differences in resources, I am just not Beyoncé. Everyone has a different threshold for how much work they can produce, and a different chemical makeup affecting how they feel day to day.

One of the most crucial things to remember in the midst of all this BYOT pump-up is that you will not always feel pumped up, and that is OK. Sometimes creating things will alleviate your depression and/or any emotional turmoil you might be experiencing, but sometimes the only thing you can do is just get through the day. Be nice to yourself! Watch something that'll make you laugh. Talk to someone who loves you, and believe them when they say so. If this makes you feel unproductive, here are two ways that not actively creating can still be productive:

(a) Absorbing things like a sponge. When you can't make your own work, appreciate the work of others. Read interviews with them to learn how their perspectives were formed. Consider this your "research period," a time to see how other people process life. Don't let yourself get intimidated or discouraged by the amazingness of others—it's OK that you can't write like Junot Díaz, because you can read Junot Díaz, and that is completely amazing! Seriously: How lucky are we all that we can feel a connection with other human beings through something as seemingly arbitrary as the arrangement of a few letters? You might also be all, "But if I pay that much attention to other people's work, MINE won't be original." Look, we all have to go through a phase of writing knockoff Sylvia Plath poetry. The important thing is that it'll get you where you need to be. The utter genius goddess Zadie Smith spent her teen years transcribing Agatha Christie stories word for word, then she made slight changes here and there until she got to a new idea, sort of like songwriters do with their favorite pre-existing riffs. It's too late in the history of our civilization for you to make ANYTHING completely untainted by influence, but anything you take in, you do so in the way that only *you* can. Patti Smith's memoir, *Just Kids*, is a delightful example of how she used the work of others to lose herself before finding herself. (This is all discussed in the July section of this book, too.)

(b) Actually experiencing life. It's hard to make art about your life if you've spent the past few days indoors with creative block! Hang out with people. Take a walk. Say yes to an experience that could surprise you, or stick with the seemingly mundane, which artists like Adrian Tomine and, hell, JERRY SEINFELD have proved is never as dull as it seems. *Only the fool watches Seinfeld and sees only "a show about nothing,"* as ye olde adage goes.

If your lack of motivation gets really awful, talk to a doctor—mental health does not stifle creativity or dull life's tones. It actually clears your brain of destructive thoughts and helps you think more clearly and make more stuff you are proud of. And don't buy into the rhetoric of people who fancy themselves particularly noble for *not* getting healthy as a means of *living on the edge.* Again, everyone is different. Your throne will be its dopest if it is built on the terms that work best for you.

3. MAKE SHIT CONSTANTLY.

There is a certain kind of constant creating that does not have to be so stressful or loaded or polished as everything Beyoncé puts out. This is what I call MAKING SHIT CONSTANTLY, because the point is not that you're making *incredible* work constantly, but that you give yourself space to let any and every idea pop out of you. Like with actual shit. Then, if you wish to share it with the world, you can always post it to RateMyPoop.com—it's totally generous when artists leave a trail of all their work, so we get to see where they started, and how their ideas began to take shape. (Look up Lena Dunham's college-era short movies on YouTube.) And if the idea of that archive freaks you out, you can also just flush today's shit down the toilet, opening yourself up to more new ideas tomorrow.

Even if it means just designating your most boring class as a doodling period, making shit constantly makes you feel like less and less of a stranger to the thing you want to get comfortable with. What matters is not that everything you make is amazing—it won't be, for anyone, ever—but that you begin to approach creating as an extension of your thoughts instead of as some kind of *test.* Says Miranda July:

Like, OK, let's say one day I write a thing I don't like. I guess I could say that it is "inauthentic." But that is so harsh. I could also say that it was the thing that I had to write to get to this next thing, and there is no way to get to that other one unless you write the wrong one. So it is totally authentic for being that stepping-stone.

4. LIVE WITH CONSTIPATION.

Making shit constantly is a wonderful habit, but don't be hard on yourself if you find you work at a slower pace. I admire some artists' abilities to make shit constantly, but as a reader/viewer/listener, it can get tiring to have to *see* it all. Of course, nobody *owes* me anything, but sometimes it's like, *Why would you waste our time with something you yourself don't even like, just to stay relevant?*

It's just as neat to watch someone really take their time with their work as it is to see it flow out of them like a heavy period. (No non-gross analogies in this piece, please!) Last time I spoke with Lorde/Ella, she told me she's waiting a little bit to work on another album, as anything she could write now would be too similar to *Pure Heroine.* It's inspiring to see someone who has the self-awareness to be like, "You know what? This creation isn't my best. The world doesn't need to see it. I respect my audience and I want to give them something I'm proud of, whether they end up liking it or not."

This doesn't mean that you should put something out into the world only if you believe it is perfect, because few of us think our work is *perfect,* and because perfection is a boring goal. Nor does this mean you should go through a whole identity crisis with every word you write, wondering whether or not you *deserve* to have a voice. On that note:

5. FIGHT FOR YOUR RIGHT TO DO ANY OF THIS AT ALL.

Is making art narcissistic? Who am I to think anyone should care about what I have to say?

Shouldn't I be reflecting on more-important life questions instead of making a comic about my breakfast?

Of COURSE it's narcissistic to make art, in the same way that it's narcissistic to raise your hand in school, or to think you have anything worth saying, ever. But it's also part of the human condition to contemplate how you're feeling and share it with others. In fact, doing so is necessary to your mental and emotional health, and you can't do anything that is at all un-narcissistic without having this basic amount of respect for yourself. I mean, imagine a life where you *don't* follow all the thoughts that beckon you to your own depths. You would die all in one pathetic piece, having never fully known your many layers, nor the human relationships that these vulnerabilities open us all up to.

I'm not saying we should shut ourselves off from the problems of the world, and the ways in which we may be contributing to them, just to reflect upon our own fascinating personalities. But I am thinking of the Rookie readers who've asked about this stuff online or at events, and I know that I'm not speaking to an audience of people looking for permission to navel-gaze, but people who are maybe too used to hearing that they have nothing worthy to give the world. Which makes them recoil whenever they even try to figure out what their thing is.

Let's do the stuff that gives us reason to live and let's give it our all, and maybe it *will* end up meaning something to someone else, the way I have felt completely saved at times by my own favorite artists. Wanting to make stuff, and wanting recognition for it, is not dirty or wrong or an act of selling out. Nobody benefits when you withhold passion from your work because you're worried that comics/songwriting/coding is not as worthy a pursuit as, say, medicine. It does not make you a *better person* to sprinkle your work with apologies and explanations. IN THE WORDS OF DANTE:* Say what you need to say.

---

* Dante = John Mayer.

If I sound flip, it's because I have found that I personally have no choice but to take an un-nuanced stance on this matter when I want to get stuff done. And that if I'm already trying to make something, I should just go all the way instead of holding back. And that it's exhausting, as both a creator and a consumer, when a creation is filled with disclaimers and justifications. You'll always check yourself and rein it in later, but to have an "it" at all, you may need to take a page from Wayne Koestenbaum's essay on Susan Sontag ("Reflections: Susan Sontag 1933-2004," *Artforum*): "[She] threw away security and pusillanimousness for the sake of daredevil phrases." I WANNA.

6. FIND BRAVERY IN YOUR BRAVADO.

SO: How to get to this place? To paraphrase Kanye West, you must find bravery in your bravado. It takes a lot of time and energy to question my worth every single time I'm trying to make shit constantly, so I highly recommend finding the tools you need to fill yourself with knee-jerk bravado instead (in other words, *fake it till you make it*). Anything that helps you to suck it up, trust yourself, and go H.A.M. should be easy to access at times like these: playlists, mantras, inspirational Post-its. No one is too cool to do this. And, if you really want to just fucking make something, there's no time or reason to worry about being cool.

I think much of creating can be divided into two parts: vomiting and editing. You purge what's in your brain, then shape your throw-up into something with clear meaning, kind of like a vulgar art installation. But you can't vomit clearly and honestly without momentarily convincing yourself that you have an amazing gift to share with the rest of us. This does not make you a harmful narcissist. This makes you capable of the baseline of creativity, and no matter how "aw, shucks" your own favorite artist appears, they, too, needed some bravado to get where they are today.

Might I also add that I have never, ever heard a white male friend question whether he deserves to be heard or is qualified to offer his opinion on something? My dear Rookie reader and star-crossed friend: TAKE WHAT IS YOURS. TAKE UP SPACE.

7. OPEN YOURSELF UP.

Now that you feel like a superhuman, it's time to find the strength to strip yourself down to your *barest* humanness. To explore the stuff you're most ashamed or scared of, or embarrassed by. This can be hard or sad or weird, but it can also be cathartic. Don't drown yourself in gratuitous sorrow or seek out pain and abuse. AT ALL. (It may take some trial and error to learn when you've crossed over into one of those extremes.) But know that the thing you feel most insecure about, the wound that stings the deepest, the thought you think is dirtiest—these may be direct lines to a deeply satisfying thing that you make all on your own. And whatever you create from them may be a direct line to a new perspective on this thing that is torturing you. This process will remind you of your own general strength and ability, not only as an artist, but as a person. Like in the chorus of Leonard Cohen's "Anthem," which my mom has recited to me since I was little. It basically says to forget goals of perfection, because although everything is cracked and broken, "that's how the light gets in."

Not only could opening yourself up and spilling your guts out be therapeutic for you, but someone else might relate to your guts, and then you'll both feel less alone. From *The Bell Jar*: "There is nothing like puking with somebody to make you into old friends." It's true: The shit that brings you closer to someone is rarely a fun party, but more often a tough conversation or a sad, deflated night.

This isn't the ONLY way to make something great, or something that you love. Art is also amazing as an *escape* from the horrors of everyday life. But let it be known in these pages that no matter how scary it can be to make yourself vulnera-

ble, *you're* still the one doing it, and the power is in your hands. That's why Stevie Nicks never looks like some kind of *victim* of *heartbreak*, you know? She's *choosing* to share. She writes songs about her own memories, her thoughts and feelings, using her words. These are not secrets we discovered and busted her for.

Most important, be nice to yourself throughout this process. It's self-destructive and detrimental to creativity to be too critical of yourself. Some more Miranda July for you (from *Mono.Kultur*, 2008):

> I am of course trying to make it authentic, to make it ring clear, to accurately convey a specific feeling. But the way that I go about doing this is by removing judgment, which is very hard work. Removing judgment is not the same thing as saying everything is great—in fact, nothing is great, and nothing is bad either. That is the place to begin. And then there is a rigorous process of refining, rewriting, reworking, so that that core place is not obscured, so it can shine through.

8. DO IT YOUR WAY, IN SMALL WAYS.

Let's say you feel held back not because you're worried your pursuit is an insufficient one, or because you're afraid of being vulnerable. Maybe you're just clueless as to how to actually do the thing you want to do, on a technical level.

L'internet is an invaluable resource for this stuff. The founder of Nasty Gal didn't go to college—she watched lectures on YouTube. Seriously. And now she's a gazillionaire. *I know.* There is no limit to what you can learn—on a practical level and head/heart-wise—from this glorious well of information.

But perhaps knowing what the heading on a screenplay looks like is not a huge priority for you right now 'cause the muse is in and you are bursting with inspiration. Just write your thing, man! The other stuff can come later. Or, in some cases, never. Miranda July didn't bother using quotation marks in her first book. Joni Mitchell had to invent her own guitar tunings because she'd had polio as a child and her hands couldn't form regular chords. Some more Koestenbaum for us all: "Why mask your articulations, muting their force, maintaining conventional appearances?"

And then there's this:

I write this way not merely because I enjoy being irreverent or atopical but because when AIDS hit in the early 1980s I decided not to waste my maybe very short life writing what I didn't want to write or obeying rules that in the grand scheme of things (death) didn't exist. The imminence of nothingness was the only rule I would obey.

9. BUT SOME RULES ARE ACTUALLY REALLY GREAT TO KNOW.

You'll be able to discern which ones. Like, the technicalities of where to put what numbers on a screenplay page are maybe not essential, but understanding the "rules" or structures of other movies will *help* you, not stifle you, because rules are more fun to break when you actually know what you're messing with. I feel more confident trying out a weird kind of essay format because I know that I can write a standard one with a clear through line. I feel I am more equipped to appreciate experimental writers because I have read *the classics*. Well, OK, I actually feel like I'm missing out because I've really only read a *few* of the classics, because it was high school English and no one was really checking my annotations (all vague variations on "Wow," "Oh no!" and "Haha").

Blank pages are terrifying. The zillion possibilities of everything you could make are all so intimidating. If you find a way to challenge yourself, you'll find possibilities you hadn't even realized were there. *Rules force you to be creative.*

10. SUSTAIN YOUR FLOW.

So you've found YER ZONE. How do you make sure you can access it on the regs? That you still love this thing you're building your throne out of, especially if you should be so lucky that it becomes something you make a living off of—in other words, a *job*? I sustain my passion in three ways:

(a) Staying motivated. This is all the "find bravery in your bravado" stuff that we talked about earlier. I make signs for my bedroom and my workspace. I listen to Kanye and Nicki Minaj and Lil' Kim and Madonna and Beyoncé and other confidence boosters.

(b) Staying inspired. This is all that "absorbing other people's work" that we talked about earlier. Watch, read, and listen to stuff you haven't encountered before. If it's too intimidating to think about seeking this stuff out yourself, there are one billion websites that will do it for you. Some of my favorites are Brain Pickings, It's Nice That, ROOOOKIE, and, hell, just stalk the tag for a thing that you like on Tumblr. This is the stuff that makes you want to up your game, that shows you the many different inspiring ways in which different people look at the world, and that opens your mind up to new approaches you can take with your own stuff.

(c) Staying aware. You know the part in *Elf* where Buddy says to the department store Santa, "You sit on a throne of lies"? AVOID THAT. Remember who you are doing this for—could be yourself, could be a handful of your friends that you just wanna make laugh, could be strangers that you'd like to help feel less alone. For me, in working on this magazine, staying aware means keeping up with what our readers have to say about it instead of operating from an isolated cave of my own wants and needs. It means remembering that Rookie is for you guys, not for some adult who may be reviewing it. It means thoroughly considering your criticisms instead of writing off any negative comment as hater-y. Basically, you don't want your throne to start off with a solid foundation but then become a hollow, garish, delusional tower from which the thing that once mattered to you starts to look like a tinier and tinier dot, until you just lose sight of it completely. Remember as often as possible how lucky you are that you get to do what you love (and maybe even make a living from it).

I keep a folder on my desktop for these three flow-sustaining activities. It contains the Rookie piece about Kanye (also found in this book), interviews with people who've blown my mind and made me want to be better, clips of my favorite eye-altering movie scenes, letters from Rookie readers about what Rookie means to them, etc. I highly recommend keeping such a toolbox handy, as well as private—if you start displaying it all on a public platform like Tumblr, you may start to feel like you're *curating* it for the sake of likes and reblogs. THIS IS YOUR POWER SOURCE. KEEP IT PURE.

11. OTHER PEOPLE.

Speaking of Tumblr and likes and reblogs, let's discuss *other people*.

When other people give you feedback on your work, remember, whether the feedback is negative or positive, and even if you feel like you totally bared your soul in your work, that there are plenty of degrees of separation between who you are, the thing you made, the thing this commenter saw, the way they processed it, and the way they chose to express the way they processed it. Don't internalize feedback—negative *or* positive!—as a statement on YOU AS A PERSON. It may be a statement about your work, but it's often also very much a reflection of the feedbacker.

Learn the difference between constructive criticism and plain trolling. Some trolls are bored enough to disguise their trolling as constructive criticism and to dress up their troll responses to what you do in fancy words and long paragraphs. Usually, truly constructive criticism will reveal itself in time—if you find, days later, that a positive comment has stuck with you, maybe that feedbacker tapped into one of your strengths, and now you have a kind of safety skill to toy with if you get lost in a creation later. If a negative comment has stuck, walk yourself through why that might be, and you'll find that you either do need to improve that aspect of your work, or that you are unnecessarily insecure about it and a troll just found your weak spot. This is when it's good to get out of your head and talk to people whose opinions you have reason to trust. Or get off the internet. Or make something new.

One last thing about trolls: I am a fan of deleting and blocking. I don't think it shows weakness; it just protects you from having to spend another moment of your life thinking about that person. It might feel undemocratic and un-internet-y to silence someone, but you don't owe anyone your attention, and you are in no way obligated to engage with people who have nothing of substance to offer. You do not owe it to anyone to be their weird internet stranger that they project their own shit onto. Preserve your bubble and block all chumps.

12. *OTHER* OTHER PEOPLE.

Not feedbackers, but other artists. *Jealousy. Envy. Competition.* Comparing your work or success with others' is a waste of time, because ultimately there's no better or worse; there's just different. *Every* comparison is apples and oranges, because everyone is so different, and even if you and someone else are working in the same medium, you're still individuals with different histories, life educations, approaches, and outputs. But it takes a really good, *mature* day to be able to tell yourself that and believe it, so in times of hysterical jealousy, refer to the below strategies:

(a) If you think another person is truly better than you, learn from them. Make your urge to absorb what they know bigger and more tangible than your feeling of envy by writing down the specific thing they do that you wish you knew how to. It is selfish in a wonderful, necessary way to look at someone who makes you want to seethe with jealousy and decide instead to benefit as much as you can from knowing what makes their work strong.

(b) If you think you are truly better than another person, *still* step up your game, in order to set yourself so far from them (or anyone else) that any further competition is nonsensical. RuPaul once said that what finally motivated him to get his shit together and try harder to put himself out there was watching the group Deee-Lite getting popular, 'cause Ru was like, *If people only knew how great I am!*

Don't let those Band-Aids be your only way of combatting envy, though. This is *your throne*, and even if someone else is getting more recognition or seems to have found more of their own voice, the last thing you want is a throne that is a sad imitation of anyone else's. Says Etgar Keret, in *Rookie Yearbook Two*:

> If you try to write like Nabokov, there will always be at least one person (whose name is Nabokov) who'll do it better than you. But when it comes to writing the way you do, you'll always be the world champion at being yourself.

13. LIVE FIRST; CHOOSE YOUR IDENTITY LATER.

Speaking of being yourself: A friend once overheard Tilda Swinton giving an interview at a restaurant where the journalist said something like, "When you go back to where you're from, do you act different from how you are in Hollywood?" Tilda replied simply: "I'm basically from another planet, and on that planet, we don't think about things like this; we just live."

It's tempting to assume an *artistic identity*, like it'll get you into the Zone to go, "I AM A WRITER, I AM HEMINGWAY, I AM DICKINSON."

But avoid that for as long as possible. It's limiting to put all your eggs in one basket and then model yourself after a vague stereotype of that basket. Don't define yourself by the *kind* of work you do, but by THE WORK YOU DO. That way, it'll be easier to avoid feeling competitive with or jealous of other people working in any given medium, to make the thing you *want* to make instead of the thing you think you're *supposed* to make, and to get over impostor syndrome, because all you're trying to be is yourself, after all, and how can you be an impostor at that? Plus, where do these ridiculous notions of what makes you a Real Writer come from? Do you have to be a bad husband who lives by the sea? Or a skinny white lady in New York City with a bottomless shoe closet? George Saunders did his early writing on the bus, riding to and from his day job writing technical reports for an environmental-engineering company. That's nowhere near the romantic ideal of a writer's circumstances, but it makes no difference when you're reading his wonderful stories.

Your domain is not one medium, your domain is *you*, and *you* can be expressed in so many different ways. Try 'em all, withholding any self-criticism, because the point is not so much to make a million perfect things as it is to exercise different parts of your brain and let this medium change the way you approach that medium, etc. You might be worried that trying a new thing will subtract from the energy you have for your other thing, but as someone who tries many, many things (and is able to reconcile it all thanks to role models like Miranda July, Carrie Brownstein, David Byrne, Kanye, and Susan Sontag), I promise you that the opposite is true. If anything, all your different pursuits will inform and feed one another in a wonderful way. Maya Angelou: "You can't use up creativity. The more you use, the more you have." So USE AWAY, ROOKIES. I expect to see so many thrones populating this here earth ASAP. ♛

Anatomy of a Song

In which Lorde talks about writing the tunes on Pure Heroine, *and shows us some false starts and early drafts.*
By Lorde. Illustration by María Inés.

Full disclosure: This is the first time I have ever done this. Usually, the finished song is all I'll let anyone see. These early drafts and fits and starts of things that eventually became songs have sat unopened in the bowels of my laptop since I wrote them, so you can understand why I might be a little nervous sharing them. Even while I'm writing this, the spaces between my fingers are starting to get sweaty. GO EASY ON ME, ROOKIES.

"STILL SANE"

"Still Sane" came about toward the end of the album-writing process, after we'd been in the studio for 10–12 hours a day, five days a week, for about four months. I hadn't been feeling great mentally—I'd been putting all this pressure on myself to write "Royals 2.0," and I think it may have been school holidays, so in some small, petulant way I felt like I was missing out on the things my friends were doing.

I kept thinking back to my birthday earlier that year, and how I had woken up in the morning and almost immediately started writing songs about death (haha) and about the feeling of time moving, and that period when you can get away with stuff because of being a child coming to an end. I knew it was just a phase and that I would be fine, but everything I had felt on this topic seemed very bright-colored (kind of mottled reds and oranges), and I wanted to get every facet of it down.

The tone of the song is contradictory pretty much straightaway: The first line, "Today is my birthday and I'm riding high," sets the next one, "Hair is dripping, hiding that I'm terrified," up for a fall, which shows you how confused and excited and scared I was about getting older and moving into a career that made me leave a lot of being ~young~ behind.

My favorite part of the song is the chorus, this fast chunk of defiant thoughts that's like the positive side of my brain jumping in and saying, "You got this": "Riding around on the bikes, we're still sane / I won't be her tripping over onstage / Hey, it's all cool." But then immediately this worried, foreboding voice is offering: "I still like hotels, but I think that'll change." We put a really deep version of my voice under this part; it makes me think of having this huge jaw, open wide, with every thought and feel tumbling out.

We had been listening a lot to a band called JJ, who make this soft, dreamy electro that steals and reimagines lyrics from people like T.I. Structurally, their music is very free—their melodies go somewhere new with every line, and things like line length are really all over the place. After making an album full of very beat-driven music, it felt cathartic for me to get to create something so lacking in pop structure. When the beat does come in, it's submissive, slinking away into the back corners of the song. We panned the hi-hats so you hear them from all over the place—I kept seeing them as small black birds in the sunset-colored landscape, scattered like the contents of my brain.

The "all work and no play" part, where that line repeats and alternates with lines that allude to how I really feel, returns to that contradictory pattern: One second I'm happy to be working hard and keeping ahead ("All work and no play keeps me on the new shit"); but the next I'm just plain lonesome ("Lonely on the new shit, yeah")—very successful, but lonely (which is a recurring source of freakout for me).

The song ends on the more positive reaction to hard work—I wanted to leave the listener (and myself) with the assurance that in spite of the mixed emotions

and colors coming out in this song, it was a phase, and I knew I would be OK.

A couple of earlier drafts of this idea (very rudimentary and flitting from idea to idea). The first one is from my 16th birthday.

new thing new thing new thing

Insert Table Chart Text Shape Media Comment

Today is my birthday and I'm riding high
Wet hair hiding that I'm terrified
But it's the summer and the words are hot
Everything I say is falling right back into everything I'm not
In the swing of things
But what I really mean is
i don't know if i'm swinging yet

and I love hotels
and is that gonna change
they take me through the dark
then they let me go home

ALL WORK AND NO PLAY

I can feel us giving up

If only bad people live to see their likeness all milky in stone
What's gonna happen with me?
On the weekend I was in another country
what's gonna happen with me?

birthdays

Insert Table Chart Text Shape Media Comment

It's my birthday
I am sixteen
I am thinking of all the things I've not done
It's my birthday
I'm a failure
Don't tell me that I'm still young

"BUZZCUT SEASON"

This is one of the first songs I wrote for *Pure Heroine*. It's from December 2012. I was listening to a remix of Rihanna's "Stay" by Them Jeans on the ferry and the train on my way to the studio that morning, and I was feeling super inspired. My manager came to the studio that day (we let him in about once a month) and [my co-writer/ producer] Joel and I played him this song called "Headgame" that we had written a few days earlier. It was the first song we had written since the *Love Club* EP, and it had this really grating vocal loop in the background and was just generally not a good song. My manager told us as much, which was what we needed to hear, but it seemed really harsh at the time, and we spent the next few hours in a complete funk. Nothing was clicking or working, so I did this thing I sometimes do when things aren't working, which is to leave Joel alone to mess around with his keyboard while I go sit in a little storeroom down the corridor, which for some reason has about 10 thrift-store paintings of mountains on the walls. A change of scenery usually helps me figure out what I'm doing, and there's nothing in the world that urges you to *try* like a bunch of snowy mountains. So I started playing around with a lyric that began: "I remember when your head caught flame." Almost straightaway, I felt this prickling in the backs of my hands, and I could kind of see the whole song in front of me. I ran back to the studio and we stayed there till one or two in the morning writing it, and my parents shouted at both of us. It was worth it.

Buzzed heads are a very potent image to me—all of my guy friends would use clippers on one another frequently and impulsively every summer, when it was too hot for hair. There's something so tough but so vulnerable about the fuzzy, pale-skinned head of a friend being shorn clean.

> *And I'll never go home again*
> *(Place the call, feel it start)*
> *Favorite friend*
> *(And nothing's wrong but nothing's true)*
> *I live in a hologram with you*

That chorus actually took us several hours of tossing different options back and forth before it got anywhere. Melodically, I think it's my second-favorite chorus that I've written—the head-toss-y, impulsive first line is the kind of thing you say as a kid and instantly regret, and its melody is

climbing but sad. This was one of those songs where I didn't really know what it was about until after we'd written it, and then it helped me see something clearly. I was writing about a friendship that was lovely but stifling, one I'd been trying to tell myself was OK, but it just wasn't working. We had spent a lot of time doing summer things—being by a pool, going to parties in warm dark air—and those things were all I could picture while I was writing it. I remember closing my eyes and seeing on the backs of my lids how water looks with light on it, all dappled and shimmery. I was inside this hologram, which was sweet and good, but not real or lasting. "Nothing's wrong when nothing's true" still tastes sad when I sing it.

Earlier drafts of this idea had all the imagery, but something about how I wrote it that day made me realize that it wasn't the contented story I had thought it was. The line "All the girls with heads inside a dream" was talking about me, I think.

explosions on the television
jump from the roof into the pool
the hottest months were good to us
my mattress on the grass
peach juice dripping down your limbs
bitten thumbs and smallest hymns

now it's the longest day all year
your fingers braiding my hair
make those jokes but i cant laugh i know all this will never last
we don't have to do anything but this

Coca-Cola with the sweet burnt taste
I don't like it
Turning over in the bright hot rays
I think I like you
Shutting your eyes to the song that plays
We've got forever to live
Calling everyone who knows this place
Tell them to start it

"TEAM"

This is the song I am most proud of. When I hear it I get a little happy crinkle in the corners of my eyes.

After we wrote "Still Sane," Joel called my manager, who called me and said I should take a few days off—Joel knew I would never do it if *he* suggested it. So I lay around and celebrated not having to take a boat-train-bus combo twice a day, and I got some perspective on what we'd written for the album. It was good and I was proud of it, even though it didn't have a "Royals 2.0." But it still needed… something—one more big, happy, triumphant blowout to round out the spectrum of feels.

So while I was relaxing, I was grooving to "Pyramids" by Frank Ocean. What I think Frank does really well in this song is to vault between two atmospheres: He's stirring up Cleopatra and her nobles having this epic banquet, but he knows this song is a 21st-century party jam as well. I liked the idea of celebrating with a group of my friends, isolated from everyone else, and saw parallels between a Grecian or Tudor or Egyptian throwdown and the kind of thing we do on Saturday nights. So I started writing this:

Call all the ladies out
They're in their finery
A hundred jewels on throats
A hundred jewels between teeth
now bring my boys in
their skin in craters like the moon
the moon we love like a brother
while he glows through the room
We'll shatter all the cups
red beneath our feet
we're feasting on the ruins
of the things we dreamed
we live in cities that
you'll never see onscreen
we live in cities that
you'll never see onscreen
and everyone competing
for a love they won't receive
cause what this palace wants
is a sweet release

The great final thought I wanted to write into the album was this idea that I would basically try as hard as I possibly could to use my voice for good. I wanted to let my friends in high school, and their friends from other schools, and their friends too, know that as long as people would listen, I'd try to say what they needed me to say. It sounds pretentious, but if teenagers don't like my music, I probably wouldn't make it. I kept spinning this quote around:

we're on each others' team /
we're on each others' team /
i'm batting for you every time i breathe

But that didn't feel right. I had that line about living in these tiny pockets far from the world of the movies I watched, but I couldn't quite lock it all together.

When we went back to the studio, Joel had come up with the opening melody before the beat comes in, and I quickly wrote a lyric that had that parallel-times thing I was looking for. The song came relatively quickly after that, I think, but there are two moments that stick out to me.

We were recording the second verse, the lyrics of which are:

so all the cups got broke
shards beneath our feet
but it wasn't my fault

The first half of this verse has three lines. But in the studio, I was trying to make this work:

so all the cups got broke
shards beneath our feet
but it wasn't my fault
the chandelier's envy runs deep

I kept singing it like that in the vocal booth, trying to squeeze in all those words while keeping it a light bit of wordplay, but it just tanked.

Finally, Joel said, "Why don't you take out that [last] line?" which sounded like the worst idea ever—three lines

in the half-verse instead of four?! But then I thought about it for a while, and we recorded it that way, and it totally worked! It freed up that line and kept the feel jaunty enough for a listener to feel slightly out of step without knowing why. Now, every time I hear those lines, I smile, thinking about how the tiniest irregular thing can freshen up a clogged verse. Sometimes you just gotta cut off a finger.

The other thing I remember really clearly from writing "Team" is one of those things about songwriting that keep you chasing the wide-open impossible—something that reminds you, when it seems like it's never going to work, to have faith. The rest of the song was more or less written, and we'd hit on this magical set of chords for the chorus, but I hadn't quite written its lyrics. I told Joel to loop those chords, and we must have listened to them over and over a hundred times. He kept asking me to show him what I was writing, but I refused. I wrote and rewrote,

writing your golden, all-summarizing, everything-makes-sense-now essay paragraph, except you only get a few words [in the case of "Team," 36] with which to do so). Eventually, I told him to loop those chords again. I stood up from the couch and sang him the whole chorus as it is in the song—my best chorus yet, this hot-pink, perfect melody that I'll probably never get close to again.

> We live in cities
> You'll never see onscreen
> Not very pretty
> But we sure know how to run
>   things
> Living in ruins
> Of a palace within my dreams
> And you know, we're on each
>   other's team

The way the words sit when you know they're right is the best feeling in the world. ✎

CROSS your Heart

By Anna Shechtman. Illustration by Monica Ramos.

Anna Shechtman started constructing crossword puzzles for her school paper when she was 14 and published her first one in the *New York Times* at 19. She is a rad human all around, and we're honored that she made this puzzle just for us! Answers on page 350.

ACROSS

1 "Way cool!"
7 Editor-in-chief of 71 across
11 They start movies and music
14 In working order
15 No. on a bank statement
16 *Apocalypse Now* setting, informally
17 Pop star Swift
18 Genetic strands
19 Spanish gold
20 Possible cause of a novice's success
23 Fergie's 2007 hit "Big Girls Don't ___"
25 "There's ___ in team"
26 Dance performed by Michelle Obama and Jimmy Fallon, with "the"
27 Verdi opera adapted by Elton John for Broadway
29 Meas. in a recipe
31 Actor ___ Michael Murray
32 New owner's first residence, maybe
37 Tour in a pumpkin patch, perhaps
38 Cough drop
43 Unpolished or unprofessional performance
45 Recurring feature in 71 across, starring Jon Hamm or Judd Apatow, among others
49 Designer Derek
50 2009 Beyoncé power ballad
51 C-sharp equivalents
54 Pen point
56 Some printers
57 Group attending orientation in the fall
61 Dr. Seuss's *If I ___ a Zoo*
62 Sitarist Shankar who inspired the Beatles
63 "Relax, soldier!"
66 "Ich bin ___ Berliner"
67 ___ *Brockovich*
68 Painter of *The Turkish Bath*
69 Actors Westwick and Harris
70 Pub. like Salon, Slate, or 71 across
71 Online magazine with an annual yearbook… or a synonym for the beginnings of the answers to 20, 32, 43, and 57 across

DOWN

1 Word of contradiction
2 Smart ___ whip
3 How a diary is written
4 Ready, willing, and ___
5 Work your butt off
6 Sans-___ (kind of typeface)
7 Taint, as a reputation
8 Bad marks in high school?
9 Subject of essays by Lena Dunham, Mir-anda July, and Sarah Silverman in 71 across, slangily
10 John Lennon's 1971 "___ Hard"
11 ___ *Said*, 2013 film featuring 7 across
12 Oldest girl in the Brady bunch
13 Like ham and salmon, often
21 Fake
22 Filmmaker Jean-___ Godard
23 Gift inside a card from a grandparent, maybe
24 British singer-songwriter ___ Ora
28 Opposite of "Dep." on a flight board
30 Diatribe
33 Spanish aunt
34 Beat-thumping club genre
35 Soft: French
36 Old Testament book before Neh.
39 Indifferent sigh
40 Where to find two of a kind?
41 Big ___ (7-Eleven drink)
42 Cupid's Greek counterpart
44 Hot activity in a bed?
45 Like HBO shows and some YouTube videos
46 '90s show *Are You ___ of the Dark?*
47 Beck of TV and Close of film, e.g.
48 Some grad school degrees: Abbr.
52 Number of times 71 across posts each weekday
53 Smug sleaziness
55 *Gossip Girl* role for Leighton Meester
58 Sneaker brand
59 "___ extra cost!"
60 ___ lily (Utah's state flower)
64 Number after cinque
65 Suffix with legal or journal

The Buttbrynth

A work of friend-and-fam- iction by our favorite tween.
By Tina Belcher. Illustration by María Inés. Playlist by Anaheed.

Tina, the eldest daughter on Bob's Burgers, has long been a Rookie hero. We admire her tween swagger, her obsession with butts, and her pure, lustful heart. Those three qualities combine magically in her erotic friend fiction, which we learned about in season two of the show and haven't stopped thinking about since. We begged Tina for a peek inside her top-secret notebooks, and she graced us with this, a tale of adventure, intrigue…and butts.

Tina and Jimmy Jr. are in the multi-purpose room at school rehearsing for the eighth grade play, The Buttbrynth. *Tina paces the floor.*

"For I have come from very far and I have struggled with many things that were a struggle," Tina says. "I have fought my way here through the Buttbrynth to the Butt-castle, and now I stand before you to claim back what is rightfully mine, Mr. Goblin King Man. You…you…damn, I can't remember the rest of the line." Tina picks up her script and starts to flip through it. She looks

over at Jimmy Jr., who is dancing furiously nearby. "Jimmy Jr., are you even paying attention? The play is tomorrow night! We have to practice!"

"Relax, Tina, no one's gonna care about the play when they see how loose this caboose is."

Tina yells, "Jimmy Jr., stop dancing! OK, dance a little more. No, stop! Can't you take one thing seriously?"

"You're right, Tina." Jimmy starts to shake his moneymaker even more.

Tina seethes. "Oh Jimmy Jr., I…I… I love your butt but I wish someone would take it far away from me!"

A figure appears in a puff of smoke. Tina gasps. "David Bowelie?" She looks at her script. "From *Buttbrynth*?"

"Yes," says the figure, "I am David Bowelie, but it's Mr. Goblin King Man to you. I'm here to take Jimmy Jr.'s butt. See you later." David Bowelie vanishes in another puff of smoke, which smells oddly of fart.

Tina exclaims, "Whoa, that was pretty crazy."

Jimmy Jr. grabs his hindquarters. "Oh no! Tina! My butt! It's gone!" He turns around to reveal a buttless backside.

Tina screams! "I can't help but feel slightly responsible," she laments.

Jimmy Jr. scowls at Tina. "*Slightly* responsible?"

"OK, Jimmy Jr., I'll get your butt back. But…um…how do I do it?" All of a sudden, a giant labyrinth appears before Tina and Jimmy Jr. "Oh," Tina says. "That's probably how."

Tina and Jimmy Jr. enter the labyrinth. A small figure approaches them. It's a deformed rabbit the size of a tiny human who looks strangely like Tina's sister, Louise.

"I am Louerb, the Keeper of the Maze," the figure says. "Who dares to pass must solve this riddle: What's round and kinda near the ground and is a one-way ticket to Brown Town?"

Tina thinks a moment. "A butt."

Louerb frowns. "Dammit, I think my riddle might be too easy. You shall pass. What happened to that guy's butt?"

Tina says, "Mr. Goblin King Man stole it. And it might be my fault. I mean, it *is* my fault. But Jimmy Jr.'s kinda sensitive about it, so maybe don't bring it up? And oh, hey, can you tell us how to get through this thing?"

Louerb says, "It's really just a straight shot."

"Really?"

"Yeah. Don't go left. Don't go right. Go straight."

Tina looks again at the labyrinth, and sure enough, there's a straight path right through. "Oh. Thanks."

"Happy to help!"

As Tina and Jimmy Jr. continue down the tunnel, Jimmy Jr. spots a bit of cooked chicken and grabs it. "I'm hungry from butt-loss," he says.

"Hey," shouts a plump troll with a bowl cut who looks oddly like Tina's brother Gene, "that's my chicken! Who dares steal the drumstick of Gern, the Troll of the Straight Part of the Labyrinth!?!"

"Sorry," Tina says. "We didn't know it was your drumstick. Hi, I'm Tina."

"Hi, I'm Gern. Wait! I already said that! Now I have embarrassed myself, and in front of the chicken!"

"OK." Tina starts to inch forward. "Well, we're just gonna go now."

"Not so fast!" Gern says. "None passes this way without first defeating me in the ultimate challenge: a burrito-eating contest! Here's your burrito! On three."

Tina starts to count: "One. Two. Oh, you finished yours."

"Yes. But now I'm in, like, a really good mood. So you shall pass."

"Wow, thanks. Nice meeting you, Gern," Tina says, and she and Jimmy proceed down the path.

"Don't I know it!" Gern calls after them, as he heads off in search of more food.

Tina and Jimmy Jr. approach two doors. One is peculiarly in the shape of Tina's mother, Linda, and the other is in the shape of Tina's father, Bob.

"Hello," says one of the doors. "I am Lindargh."

"And I am Boob," says the other door.

"One of us leads to Mr. Goblin King Man's castle," Lindargh chirps.

"And one of us leads to the dungeon," Boob says.

"And we're not gonna tell you which one," sings Lindargh, "'cause we're married and we love each oooooootheeeeerrr!"

"Aw," Tina says, "that's a weird reason not to tell us, but still, married doors? That's so sweet."

"Yeah, I know," Lindargh says. "Gimme a kiss, Boob."

"I can't, Lindargh."

"Come on, Boob, gimme a kiss."

"It's very difficult. Because we're doors."

Tina grabs Jimmy Jr.'s hand and takes a step forward. "OK, well, this is a tough choice, because for some crazy reason I love both of you so much, but we're gonna go with Lindargh—ahhhh!!!"

As Tina and Jimmy Jr. step through the door, they fall down a long, slimy, never-ending slide. "Ahhhhhhhhhhhhhh omph!"

Tina and Jimmy Jr. land in a great hall. "A butt would have helped that landing," Jimmy Jr. says as he rubs his non-bottom. Tina glances around. Her eyes lock with none other than David Bowelie, Mr. Goblin King Man.

"Looking for this?" David Bowelie says, holding up Jimmy Jr.'s butt.

"My badonkadonk!" Jimmy Jr. cries. Suddenly, Tina and Jimmy Jr. notice dozens of other people around them, dancing to strange but captivating music that is similar to, but not exactly like, Boyz 4 Now.

"You'll never get this butt back! Ha ha ha ha ha!" cackles David Bowelie. All the other people in the great hall start to dance as if against their will. "Dance, everyone! Dance until all of your butts fall off! I'm going to have so many butts after this!"

Tina's rump starts to move. "No! No!

I won't! I won't dance until my butt falls off! Oh, if I could only remember the line that breaks this spell!"

Jimmy Jr. says, "Tina, you're a really good dancer."

Tina says, "I know, Jimmy Jr. But I have to concentrate. What is that line?"

"You'll never remember it, Tina. Script lines are very hard to memorize! You're doomed!" David Bowelie cries.

Tina shouts, "You're not gonna win, Mr. Goblin King Man! For I have fought my way here through the Buttbrynth to the Butt-castle, and now I stand before you to claim back what is rightfully mine. And you…you…"

David Bowelie interrupts her: "Don't say it! Don't say it!"

Tina says, "You have no power over this…power butt!" David Bowelie screams, and all of a sudden…

Tina and Jimmy Jr. are back where they started, at school. "We're back! We made it back!" Tina exclaims. "Jimmy, is it…?"

"It's there," Jimmy Jr. says, holding on to what the good lord gave him.

"You know," Tina says as she reaches for Jimmy Jr.'s butt, "I better just check to make sure. Still checking. Still checking. Still checking." 🕸

HANGING OUT with The BELCHERS

1. BAD GIRLS - St. VINCENT

2. WHEN YOU WERE MINE - CASIOTONE FOR THE PAINFULLY ALONE

3. WALKING THE COW - FIREHOSE

4. THE HARRY TRUMAN SONG - LINDA BELCHER

5. BIRDHOUSE IN YOUR SOUL - THEY MIGHT BE GIANTS

6. THANKSGIVING SONG - THE NATIONAL

7. I AM A GIRLFRIEND - NOBUNNY

8. ROBOTBOY - ROBYN

9. BURGER AND FRIES - ALLEGRA

10. IF YOU WERE HERE - THOMPSON TWINS

11. TAFFY BUTT - CYNDI LAUPER

12. IT'S TOUGH TO HAVE A CRUSH WHEN THE BOY DOESN'T FEEL THE SAME WAY YOU DO - OK GO

Keep Yourself Creative:
An Interview With Haim

On starting their band, their love of Kate Bush, and the surprisingly awesome nature of Segway tours.
By Hazel. Illustration by María Inés.

It's hard not to love Haim. The trio of supremely talented musical sisters—lead vocalist Danielle, bass player Este, and multi-instrumentalist Alana—make folk-meets-pop music that has drawn comparisons to Fleetwood Mac and other '70s rock groups while sounding definitively modern. I was only passingly familiar with their music when I saw them play last summer, but by the end of their set (which included Este recounting a story about giving a boy her phone number only to have him scoff at its Valley area code), I was a true fan through and through. They're every bit as charismatic when they're talking as when they're singing: I think it's fair to say that anyone who meets them, sees them play, or just listens to their album, *Days Are Gone*, wants to be their best friend. I am no exception, so I was excited to get to talk to Este and Alana recently while they were on tour.

HAZEL Why don't we start out by finding out a little bit about when and why the three of you decided to start the band…

ESTE We've been in different bands our whole lives. We would play at school functions and, like, our parents' office parties. So we never did it for money or anything. It was always for charity. My dad was really, really adamant about that. But it was only when Danielle had graduated from high school that we all started toying with the idea of us coming together and learning songs. We'd never really tried that. We liked it so much that eventually we made it a regular thing. When we had amassed five or six songs, the obvious next step was to play a show for our friends. We had so much fun doing that show that we decided to play more shows. And we all kind of decided that we wanted to make music—it's what we wanted to do for the rest of our lives, and we wanted to be able to do it together.

How do your individual tastes and personalities influence each other as a group?

ALANA I think we try to one-up each other with musical discoveries all the time. That's kind of what makes being in the band so fun. As much as we're sisters, we're also individuals. So all three of us get excited to share with each other all these little discoveries.

ESTE A couple years ago, we all simultaneously discovered Kate Bush. I'd heard "Running Up That Hill"—it was a song that you heard in a club, or you heard a cover of it. It was a really great song. But I never felt the need to explore [Bush's music] until I was at UCLA, taking a Bulgarian-music class. My professor put on this Kate Bush song that had Bulgarian folksingers doing backup vocals, and he explained how that really brought her music and the kinds of harmonies she was doing into a different realm. I just remember sitting in class getting really emotional and really, like, goose-pimply. It was really, really intense. I had an intense emotional connection to the song. Of course, I went home and started getting really obsessed with it and had to learn everything about it. I really, really get deep when it comes to anything I'm into.

It's funny, because literally that same week, Danielle came to me and was like, "Have you heard this record *Hounds of Love*?" I was like, "Are you fucking kidding me?" And then Alana got really into it. We started looking at different ways of utilizing harmony and vocals and drums and [thinking differently about] how we want things to sound. That was kind of a jumping-off point for us. After that it was, you know, a free-for-all.

Sometimes critics, when they talk about Haim, focus on the men [James Ford and Ariel Rechtshaid] who helped produce most of your debut album, last year's *Days Are Gone*, which seems like they're trying to degrade your status as musicians.

ESTE I think people forget (or don't really know) that we have a very heavy hand in the production as well. We have a very heavy hand in *everything* involving our music. Every last little detail, it comes from us. The good thing about the producers that we work with is that they're willing to let us have a voice and an opinion.

ALANA I don't think that there was much of that kind of response when the record came out. I was actually completely happy with what people were saying, because they really did give us a lot of credit. I feel like a lot of people, when they listen to us, know that we had a lot of say in what we were doing. And it was really gratifying to work with people who were awesome and who knew that the only way you can work with us is if you are completely open to collaboration. Ariel and James were super open to collaboration. And that's why, when I listen to the record, it seems like us. It doesn't seem like anyone else.

You guys are on tour a lot. What do you like to do in your downtime, if you have any?

ESTE A lot of stuff we like to do is explore the city that we're in. We love traveling and seeing new places and exploring. We've been known to take many a Segway tour of cities.

On a Segway?

ESTE Yeah. Segway machine. Helmets and all. It's actually a really fun way to get, like, Cliff's Notes of any city. You're on a fucking Segway, which is so much fun, first of all. And hilarious, at the same time. We have entire iPhone photo albums dedicated to Segway tours that we go on.

Would you ever consider buying your own personal Segway?

ESTE Maybe when I make, like, Jay Z money, I would consider it. As of right now, I'm more concerned with, I don't know, can I get my shoes fixed? Because they're broken—the heels are broken. Can I fix them on tour?

Do you have any particularly memorable moments from touring?

ESTE The things that stick out are the moments where you're at like Brixton Academy in London, which was pretty amazing and really, really special for us. Playing *Saturday Night Live* was pretty incredible for us as well—a crazy, surreal moment for us.

ALANA I think it's being able to go to all of these places I'd never dreamed of going to, like Finland and Norway, and playing shows there. Having people sing our lyrics back to me in Finland is just surreal.

You have this amazing fan base, largely made up of women around your own ages. And a lot of them seem really obsessed with you—there's even fan fiction about you online! I'm sure meeting fans who are super into you guys was exciting at first, but has it gotten old?

ESTE No! Have you ever watched the Tenacious D show [*Tenacious D: The Greatest Band on Earth*] on HBO?

No.

ESTE Well, I was really into Tenacious D when I was in high school. That show was on then, and there was this episode where they meet their biggest fan, and Jack Black becomes obsessed with him. That's basically how I feel when it comes to meeting people at shows. I become friends with a lot of them. The cool thing about the people who come to our shows—especially the women—is that it's been a wide array, from six-year-olds to 50-year-olds. The most gratifying thing to me is hearing from the women who say they've become really involved in music and now they want to *play* music and *write* music. They're really grabbing the bull by the horns. That's the best part for me.

ALANA I just like meeting other girls. There's something about being able to talk to other women about music—all over the world, we hear the same thing, which is women being passionate about music. And about film and writing and being creative. That's really inspiring.

ESTE All the bands and musicians I was a fan of growing up had a very close relationship with the people who went to their shows and listened to their music. I always was a bigger fan of people like that than people who sort of kept their fans at arm's length. I just never understood why they felt the need to do that, because obviously it's a relationship. Without the music, the fans wouldn't have something to be a fan of, and vice versa—you can't really have one without the other. So why wouldn't you have a relationship with the people who enjoy your music? I don't know. I just really enjoy talking to the people who come to our shows. Men come to our shows too, but it's obviously a different relationship with the women. I find that most empowering.

Your number one piece of advice for young girls looking to start a band?

ESTE Write everything down. Don't *ever* stop writing. It's really important to keep yourself creative. Whatever talent you have, stay creative and always try and make something, whether it be something physical or something musical—I just think keeping your brain as creative as possible is really important. Because the second you let it go, it starts down a slippery slope. It's a muscle that you have to flex all the time.

ALANA That's the first step: getting excited about the creative process. And really exploring what you want to say. That's kind of what music is all about: having a message and having something to say. ✏️

Someone Who Makes You Fear Less:
An Interview With the Geniuses Behind *Broad City*

Abbi Jacobson and Ilana Glazer share their secrets to lasting friendship and creative collaboration.
By Tavi. Illustration by María Inés.

Who was I before *Broad City* (B.B.C.)? This Comedy Central treasure, produced by Amy Poehler, sprang from a web series created by and starring BFFs Ilana Glazer and Abbi Jacobson, and has become a crucial component of my personal canon of stuff I return to when I don't feel like myself. Each episode takes us on a different adventure with the duo as they take NYC by storm—a premise that would be clichéd and boring if the show at all resembled every other thing on TV. (When we first saw it, my friends and I were all like, *Wait, does the whole world have our sense of humor now?*) Besides being hilarious/energizing/the perfect mix of goofy and clever/perfect for multiple rewatches, the first season of *Broad City* also shows Abbi and Ilana continually finding themselves in each other, making it one of my favorite odes to female friendship ever. Here, these two babes discuss their friendship, how it inspires their work, and the advantages of the Nicki Minaj lifestyle.

TAVI How did you guys meet?

ABBI JACOBSON We were both taking classes at the Upright Citizens Brigade [in New York City], and while you're taking classes you form these teams to perform at other little theaters around the city. We met when we were on the same improv team.

What were your first impressions of each other, and were they accurate?

ABBI Yeah, we…[*She's interrupted by loud background noises: street traffic, then music*] I'm sorry, guys—I'm going into Bloomingdale's. It's not gonna be this loud the whole time. I really apologize.

ILANA GLAZER I'm getting a pedicure right now.

ABBI We have a thing tomorrow, Tavi, and we're both like freaking out about it.

Oh, no!

ABBI Whatever, it's a good thing. They're blasting music in here. So we met on this indie improv team—this was like 2007. And it was the first practice that we were both there for. I really thought that Ilana was maybe Alia Shawkat from *Arrested Development*. I was like, *Oh, the show's over, and it's totally feasible that she would move to New York and do improv.*

ILANA You didn't tell me that you thought I was her, did you?

ABBI No! I didn't want you to think that I was like, "Ooh, a celeb!"

Ilana, what did you first think of Abbi?

ILANA My first impression was that she was, like, a boss bitch. And smart. And cool. And I was right.

When did you realize you weren't just friends but also collaborators and brain-twins?

ILANA We had both been making shows with other people, but [at some point] I looked at Abbi and I'm like, "Why don't we just fuckin' work together? We seem to have the same values, you know?" Web series were becoming a [big] vehicle at that time, and so we were like, "What about a web series?"

Comedy, improv, all of that, is the hardest thing I can imagine doing. You're really putting yourself out there—and on the internet, too, making a web series. Did you have to build up a thick skin to deal with getting comments and notes on stuff you were making together?

ABBI Definitely. But there's a difference between beneficial criticisms and people commenting on YouTube videos. I think we're pretty lucky in terms of our comments—a lot of them are positive, which is amazing. But there are people who are just trolls, who just get off on that. Anyone who does that, I won't even give them my energy. It's a waste of my time.

ILANA It's true. There's constructive criticism, and then there's, like, misogyny and racism. It's easy to brush someone off when they're like…Oh my god, can you hear that? The pedicure chair is vibrating my body.

ABBI Wait, what color did you go with?

ILANA Matte lavender.
Ooh.

ABBI Cool.

ILANA Yeah, spring, baby. Spring has sprung, baby! So, yeah, sometimes criticism is helpful. Also, a really cool thing is that we've always had quality fans over quantity. And these quality fans have built a bubble around us, and they have been really deep and honest in defending the show.

ABBI I read all the reviews. I even read what people write about [*Broad City*] on Tumblr. It's sad that I do that, in a way, but I want to know what people are thinking about the show.

Do you guys have any tips on collaborating with a friend?

ILANA Meeting in the middle is good. Meeting in the middle is where the voice comes from, at least for us. Be direct. Push yourself to be as honest as possible. If you trust the person and there's an unconditional love there, go for it. We met seven years ago and have been doing this project for five. Over that time our friendship has grown, but there has always been an unconditional love there. We felt comfortable being real and honest early on.

ABBI Also, we each have our own individual voice. I think when you're collaborating with someone else, you have to have already established your own really strong voice, or your own contribution, what you bring to the table. Ilana and I take our own voices into our own projects, and when we come to *Broad City*, we create a voice together. We have time away from each other so we'll have stuff to write about that we didn't experience together.

ILANA It's like dating. You want to maintain your sense of individual identity, which feeds the partnership.

Do you have periods when you might not feel especially inspired or productive, and if so, how do you deal with those?

ABBI I have this thing that I do where I make lists of everything: Every place I've ever lived. Every teacher I've had. Every job I've ever had. Every vacation I've ever gone on. Those are just a little reminder that I have a lot more stories that I haven't even touched yet, you know? I think that's where people get lost, is they stop writing from their own personal experiences.

ILANA I really like that method, too. I've done that with things. But usually…you know how when you forget something, it comes back later, when you're not thinking about it anymore? That's kinda how I think about it. I just do something else: take walks or call someone and have a good conversation.

I feel like a lot of the time—and this is in no way a critique of women—when there's a comedy about women and sex is involved, it starts to feel like the comedy becomes just an excuse to get them to do, like, a raunchy thing. But the characters on *Broad City* discuss sex really casually, and their sex lives inform the plot really effortlessly, not in a "raunchy lady comedy" way, you know? How do you walk the line between showing that part of these characters' lives and… I'm not even sure what to call it, but you know the kind of thing when the joke is basically "a woman is being sexy"?

ABBI Like shock value?

Basically.

ABBI I don't know if it's something we ever really think too deeply about. I just don't think that what we think is funny is about that, usually. That's never the story.

ILANA There is one conscious thing we did, which is that you never really see guys go down on girls in anything, because that's "weird" or whatever, but we have [shown that].

On the show, Ilana's love for Abbi sometimes veers into, like, shameless lust. There are a number of portrayals of female friendship on TV where they toy with that dynamic—like, one girl will start to develop feelings for her friend and that's a conflict, or there will be a "lesbian episode" or something. But that feeling is so out in the open and seems so natural between your characters. I'm curious about where that idea came from.

ILANA I feel like my character wants to fuck all her friends, you know? That's part of it. I think it also comes from my affection for people. When I really love someone, I happen to be effusive. I guess this used to be a "joke" between me and Abbi. We express affection differently, and to her it was always like, "Oh my god, all right, I get it."

This is making me emotional about friendship.

ABBI That's cool. I like that.

On that subject, actually, what are your favorite TV or movie depictions of female friendship?

ILANA A big one for me is *I Love Lucy*. I used to have all the seasons on VHS. At first, [Lucille Ball and Vivian Vance, who played BFFs] didn't like each other. They actually became friends during the show. Abbi, I know what you're gonna say.

ABBI I was really into *Roseanne* as a kid. I loved that show.

ILANA It was huge!

ABBI It's not just the friendship between Roseanne and Jackie; it's one of the only sitcoms of [the '90s] that not only is hilarious and still holds up, but that's really complex. The characters are so *real*.

ILANA I get emotional talking about that fucking show. It changed television.

ABBI It did. It also was…[*To Bloomingdale's staff*] Are you closing? [*Back to us*] No dress for Abbi! It was based on Roseanne's life, and you could tell. It felt very raw, even when I watched it as a kid.

ILANA Another TV show that showed truly middle-class people was *Good Times*. They way they straddled comedy and…it wasn't drama, but they showed how real life can be dramatic—that was fucking phenomenal. Also, the characters just looked like normal people.

ABBI As a teenager, I really loved *Romy & Michele's High School Reunion*. It seems like that is a really great friendship.

I'm just realizing that when I asked about Ilana's affection for Abbi, I asked about it in the context of "Where did you get that idea for the show?" and you answered as if I'd asked where that came from in you as a person. So, to what extent are the show and the characters based on your real experiences?

ABBI It's hard to quantify, I guess. We don't want to invent shit—you want to try to capture shit. The degree to which we exaggerate anything is always the conversation where we meet in the middle. But we always try to base it on reality, whether it's our experiences or our writers' experiences or our friends' experiences or our writers' friends' experiences.

ILANA And with the characters themselves, we say that they're us before we started doing *Broad City*.

ABBI Once Ilana and I found *Broad City*, we had this goal and this drive; but before that, we'd spent a while treading water and figuring ourselves out in the comedy world. That's the parallel to whatever these two [characters] are trying to figure out in their lives.

Your characters request '90s music everywhere they go. What '90s music are they actually hoping to hear?

ILANA Oh, man. I don't know if this is late '80s, but the first thing that came to mind is "I Got a Man."

ABBI Yeah! [*Singing*] "What's your man got to do with me?" And, you know, some Naughty by Nature. A Tribe Called Quest.

ILANA La Bouche. *Jock Jams*.

ABBI Some Jazzy Jeff.

ILANA En Vogue. Missy Elliott and Timbaland. Maybe some early Destiny's Child. Tupac and Biggie.

Nice. Thank you. Now I know. Abbi, is your Oprah tattoo real? And how rooted in reality is your character's love for her?

ABBI The tattoo is not real, but it was really fun to have that as a tramp stamp for a couple of days. My love for Oprah, however, is very real. I used to come home from school every day and watch *Oprah* with my mom. I really do love Oprah.

ILANA Who doesn't? It's, like, positivity, you know?

ABBI Talk about a boss bitch, you know? She's like the baddest bitch.

Can you talk about your love for Nicki Minaj?

ABBI When I started listening to Nicki, I was really inspired by her bravado. This was maybe 2008 or 2009, and she was all over this Lil Wayne mixtape called *Wayne's World 4*. It really changed my thoughts—straight-up influenced me as an artist.

A few Rookie readers wanted me to ask you how you got so confident. Should I tell them to get into Oprah and listen to Nicki? Is there anything else that helps?

ILANA We are highly fortunate enough to have parents who provide much moral support. But I think it was our partnership with each other that made us confident. To go back to your question about how to collaborate: Find someone who makes you fear less.

That's beautiful.

ABBI I also think right now is a really good time where there isn't so much pressure to conform anymore. There might even be more pressure to do the opposite. But I think it's cool to be however you are, so that should be confidence-boosting.

ILANA Like Tumblr, man. Just the other day I learned about SJWs—Social Justice

Warriors—on Tumblr. They are these people who are like warriors for queerdom and uniqueness. I think they're the ones we're thinking about when we're like, "What are people going to think about X or Y in the future?" They are straight-up kids who are the fucking future. Tumblr rules.

ABBI Tavi, are you still in high school?

I graduate in like a month.

ABBI Wow, that's awesome.

ILANA As such an industrious young person, how does it feel to be in high school still?

I don't know. I'm really glad that I've always had both, because it would be really weird to be working all the time at a high school age. But at this point, I'm very ready to graduate.

ILANA Are you gonna go to college?

I am hoping to. I'm taking a gap year first, but I'm worried that I won't want to go after that.

ILANA It wouldn't be the worst thing if you didn't go.

No! Don't tell me that!

ILANA Why?

Because, like, I know in my head that I should go.

ILANA I look back on college as a vacation. It was the first time I was really sort of chilling learning. It is such a privilege. But either way, it's all good.

Talking to you guys has been a lifelong dream. Lifelong, because my life truly started when I began watching your show.

ILANA Oh my god. Unbelievable. It's an honor, dude.

I hope you find a dress, Abbi.

ABBI Thanks! I think I'm throwing in the towel. ✒

By Monica Ramos

Rookie

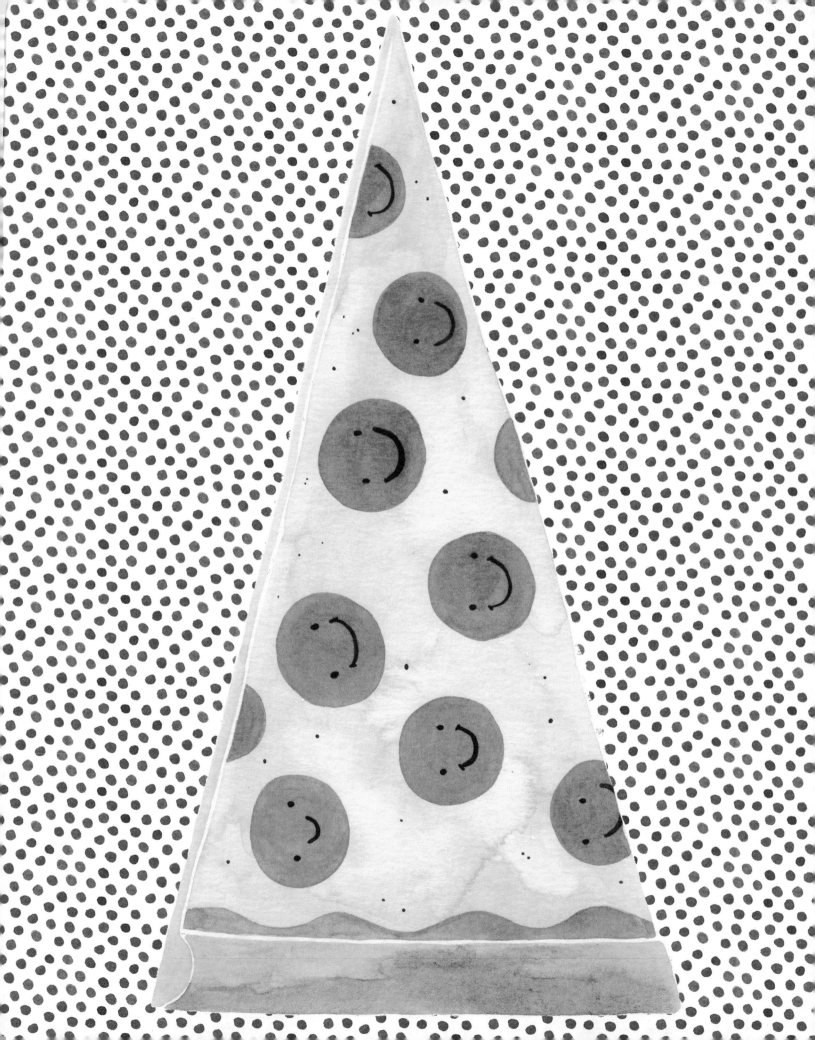

TO:
FROM:

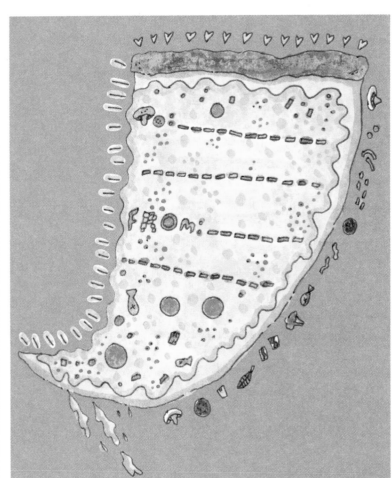

FROM:

TO: _____

FROM: _____

TO:
FROM:

By Kendra

Say GOODBYE

Have a good summer!
♡Rookie

THE BEST OF
ROOKIE
IN PRINT!

COLLECT ALL THREE BOOKS
FEATURING:

★LORDE ★KELIS★
★SKY FERREIRA★
★EMMA WATSON★
★CLARESSA SHIELDS★
★SHAILENE WOODLEY★
★AMANDLA STENBERG★
★NEIL DEGRASSE TYSON★
★ZOOEY DESCHANEL★
★DAVID SEDARIS★
★MINDY KALING★
★LENA DUNHAM★
★MORRISSEY★
★GRIMES★

AND MORE!

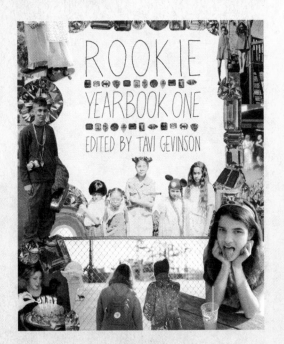

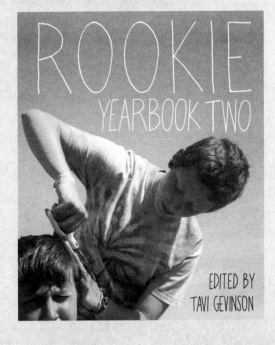

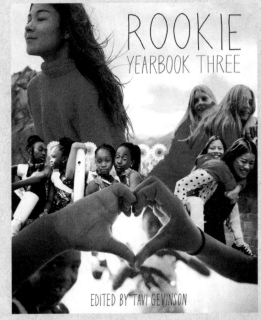

Design by Sonia. Photos by María Fernanda and Olivia.